# Security with Noisy Data

Pim Tuyls • Boris Škorić • Tom Kevenaar
Editors

# Security with Noisy Data

On Private Biometrics, Secure Key Storage
and Anti-Counterfeiting

 Springer

Pim Tuyls, PhD
Boris Škorić, PhD
Tom Kevenaar, PhD

Philips Research
High Tech Campus,
5656 AE, Eindhoven,
The Netherlands

British Library Cataloguing in Publication Data
A catalogue record for this book is available from the British Library

ISBN 978-1-84996-693-1          e-ISBN 978-1-84628-984-2

Printed on acid-free paper.

9 8 7 6 5 4 3 2 1

Springer Science+Business Media
springer.com

# Foreword

The digital revolution has enabled us to reliably store and process vast quantities of information and to communicate these data at high speed over the globe and even in space. This development has major implications for our private and professional lives as we participate in a growing number of on-line interactions. For many of these interactions, some form of security is required: We may want to protect the confidentiality and authenticity of our data or we may want to securely identify ourselves or protect our privacy, depending on the circumstances. An important side effect of the digital revolution is that copying bits or information has essentially no cost, but owners of the information want to enforce their rights by restricting its use. Similarly, searching and mining data is now feasible at a scale beyond imagination; although this development can lead to spectacular discoveries that expand our scientific knowledge, it may also undermine our legitimate right to privacy.

In the past three decades, the science of cryptology has developed a set of powerful tools to protect digital data in storage and transit, to create secure interactions, to enforce digital rights, and to protect our privacy. More generally, one can say that cryptology allows us to create complex digital interactions in which the legitimate rights of all the parties are protected. In this short time span, cryptology has developed from a tool for kings, generals, and diplomats to an ubiquitous toolbox that has spread to the devices and wallets of every citizen. Today, only the basic cryptographic buildings blocks have been implemented at a massive scale, but one can anticipate that more advanced techniques will be widely deployed in the next decade. Cryptology is built on discrete mathematics; in some sense, one can say that the digital revolution has also opened up the possibility for low-cost, flexible, and efficient protection of the digital environment.

The success of this digital revolution sometimes makes us forget an important point: The world is analog. The first area where this comes to the surface is the interaction between people and their devices: Even if a small chip the size of our thumbnail can store several gigabytes, we do have problems memorizing an eight-character password. The long-term solution may be digital memory implants; these implants will probably not be like the current RFID (Radio Frequency IDentification) implants already used in some discotheques (with very interesting privacy implications), but they may be integrated circuits with a direct connection to our brains. While we are waiting for this science fiction technology, we may make the process of identifying ourselves more convenient and reliable by using biometric features such as our fingerprints or iris patterns. Unfortunately, the measurement equipment to acquire these data is inherently noisy and, thus, a biometric matching operation is only approximate. On the other hand, we would like to apply the same nice trick developed for passwords, where we check a password $P$ by applying a one-way function $f$ to it, and verify $f(P)$ against a stored value: In this way, we do not need to store the sensitive password. The common wisdom was that digital cryptology and noisy data were not compatible and such a privacy friendly approach to biometrics was elusive. However, in the past decade, new cryptographic techniques have been developed that allow to exactly achieve this goal. These techniques also allow to derive a unique secret key from the entropy of biometric data.

From biometrics for identifying people it is only a small step to similar techniques for the identification of electronic devices, for example, based on small fluctuations in their current consumption or electromagnetic radiation pattern. One can even deliberately create complex devices that have a very high entropy and that are difficult to clone, so-called Physical Unclonable Functions or PUFs. In this way, cryptography may bring back the concept of "original" in a digital world in which today it is easy to clone bits, and tomorrow it may be very easy to clone macroscopic structures or even groups of atoms.

The analog world interacts also in different ways with the digital world. In a celebrated series of papers, cryptologists have developed a way to agree on a secret key by exploiting the properties of a noisy communication channel; later on, this work was extended to multiparty computation with noisy channels. Due to some practical limitations, it is not very likely that such a technology will be deployed for mass communications, but it is a beautiful result that helps us understand the theoretical foundations of the field.

Changing the abstraction level from the digital to the analog world has also had a more destructive aspect: In the past decade, the cryptology community has discovered that side channels—that is, physical emanations from cryptographic devices (such as power, electromagnetic radiation, sound)—combined with signal processing can result in devastating attacks on cryptographic algorithms in spite of the strong security guarantees in the digital world. This has resulted in a large research effort both in academia and industry to make systems more robust against these attacks. From a theoretical point of view, this has resulted in a move from black-box models to gray-box models such as those considered in physically observable cryptography.

The adaption of cryptology to noisy data has not happened as an overnight revolution. Since 1999, a limited number of papers has been published that have built the foundations of the area. Although this research area has not attracted many followers in academia, it was picked up quickly by industrial labs such as Philips Research, which understood the potential for applications. They have developed some of the ideas for specific technologies while performing more research along the way.

This book introduces the principles of key establishment and multiparty computation over noisy channels. A detailed overview is presented of the building blocks of cryptography for noisy data. Subsequently, it is explained how these techniques can be applied to privacy-enhancing biometrics and PUFs, followed by specific applications such as anti-counterfeiting and key storage.

It is a great pleasure for me to write the Foreword to the very first book on cryptography with noisy data. I appreciate the effort of the authors who have succeeded in describing the foundations of this new and exciting research area in a clear and accessible way. I hope that the reader will be stimulated to further contribute to development of this area as a scientific and engineering discipline and to bring this area to an increasing number of applications.

Bart Preneel
Leuven, Belgium
April 2007

# Acknowledgments

The editors would like to thank the following persons for reviewing chapters of this book: Lejla Batina, Berk Gökberk, Jorge Guajardo, Stefan Katzenbeisser, Sandeep Kumar, Klaus Kursawe, Gregory Neven, Bart Preneel, Berry Schoenmakers, Evgeny Verbitskiy, and Frans Willems.

# Contents

## Part II Applications of Security with Noisy Data

# Contributors

**Lejla Batina**
Katholieke Universiteit Leuven
Kasteelpark Arenberg 10
B-3001, Leuven, Belgium
Lejla.Batina@esat.kuleuven.be

**Ruud Bolle**
IBM T.J. Watson Research Center
P.O. Box 704
Yorktown Heights, NY 10598,
USA
bolle@us.ibm.com

**Xavier Boyen**
Voltage Inc.
1070 Arastradero Road
Palo Alto, CA, USA
xb@boyen.org

**Sharat Chikkerur**
Department Electrical Engineering
and Computer Science
Massachusetts Institute
of Technology
Cambridge, MA 02140,
USA
sharat@mit.edu

**Dwaine Clarke**
Computer Science and Artificial
Intelligence Laboratory
Massachusetts Institute
of Technology
Cambridge, MA 02139, USA
declarke@mit.edu

**Jonathan Connell**
IBM T.J. Watson Research Center
P.O. Box 704
Yorktown Heights, NY 10598, USA
jconnell@us.ibm.com

**Srinivas Devadas**
Computer Science and Artificial
Intelligence Laboratory
Massachusetts Institute
of Technology
Cambridge, MA, 02139, USA
devadas@mit.edu

**Marten van Dijk**
Computer Science and Artificial
Intelligence Laboratory
Massachusetts Institute
of Technology
Cambridge, MA, 02139, USA
marten@mit.edu

**Yevgeniy Dodis**
New York University
251 Mercer Street
New York, NY 10012, USA
dodis@cs.nyu.edu

**Blaise Gassend**
Computer Science and Artificial
Intelligence Laboratory
Massachusetts Institute
of Technology
Cambridge, MA, 02139, USA
gassend@alum.mit.edu

**Jan van Geloven**
NXP Research
High Tech Campus
5656 AE, Eindhoven
The Netherlands
jan.van.geloven@nxp.com

**Jorge Guajardo**
Philips Research
High Tech Campus
5656 AE, Eindhoven
The Netherlands
jorge.guajardo@philips.com

**Tanya Ignatenko**
Department of Electrical Engineering
Technical University Eindhoven
P.O. Box 513
5600 MB, Eindhoven
The Netherlands
t.ignatenko@tue.nl

**Ari Juels**
RSA Laboratories
174 Middlesex Turnpike
Bedford, MA 01730, USA
ajuels@rsa.com

**Tim Kerins**
Philips Research
High Tech Campus
5656 AE, Eindhoven
The Netherlands
tim.kerins@philips.com

**Tom Kevenaar**
Philips Research
High Tech Campus
5656 AE, Eindhoven
The Netherlands
tom.kevenaar@philips.com

**Jean-Paul Linnartz**
Philips Research
High Tech Campus
5656 AE, Eindhoven
The Netherlands
j.p.linnartz@philips.com

**Ueli Maurer**
Department of Computer Science
ETH Zürich
CH-8092 Zürich, Switzerland
maurer@inf.ethz.ch

**Wil Ophey**
Philips Research
High Tech Campus
5656 AE, Eindhoven
The Netherlands
wil.ophey@philips.com

**Bart Preneel**
Katholieke Universiteit Leuven
Kasteelpark Arenberg 10
B-3001, Leuven, Belgium
bart.preneel@esat.kuleuven.be

**Nalini Ratha**
IBM T.J. Watson Research Center
P.O. Box 704
Yorktown Heights, NY 10598, USA
ratha@us.ibm.com

**Renato Renner**
Institute for Theoretical Physics
ETH Zurich
CH-8092 Zurich
Switzerland
renner@phys.ethz.ch

**Leonid Reyzin**
Boston University
Department of Computer Science
111 Cummington St. Boston
MA 02215, USA
reyzin@cs.bu.edu

**Amit Sahai**
Department of Computer Science
UCLA
Los Angeles, CA 90095, USA
sahai@cs.ucla.edu

**Berry Schoenmakers**
Department of Mathematics
and Computer Science
Technical University Eindhoven
P.O. Box 513
5600 MB, Eindhoven
The Netherlands
berry@win.tue.nl

**Geert-Jan Schrijen**
Philips Research
High Tech Campus
5656 AE, Eindhoven
The Netherlands
geert.jan.schrijen@philips.com

**Boris Škorić**
Philips Research
High Tech Campus
5656 AE, Eindhoven
The Netherlands
boris.skoric@philips.com

**Adam Smith**
Pennsylvania State University
342 IST Building
University Park, PA 16802, USA
asmith@cse.psu.edu

**Pim Tuyls**
Philips Research
High Tech Campus
5656 AE, Eindhoven
The Netherlands
pim.tuyls@philips.com

**Nynke Verhaegh**
NXP Research
High Tech Campus
5656 AE, Eindhoven
The Netherlands
nynke.verhaegh@nxp.com

**Brent Waters**
SRI International
333 Ravenswood Avenue
Menlo Park, CA 94025-3493, USA
bwaters@csl.sri.com

**Frans Willems**
Department of Electrical Engineering
Technical University Eindhoven
P.O. Box 513
5600 MB, Eindhoven
The Netherlands
f.m.j.willems@tue.nl

**Stefan Wolf**
Department of Computer Science
ETH Zürich
CH-8092 Zürich, Switzerland
wolf@inf.ethz.ch

**Rob Wolters**
NXP Research
High Tech Campus
5656 AE, Eindhoven
The Netherlands
rob.wolters@philips.com

**Jürg Wullschleger**
Department of Computer Science
ETH Zürich
CH-8092 Zürich, Switzerland
wjuerg@inf.ethz.ch

# 1

# Introduction

Tom Kevenaar, Boris Škorić, and Pim Tuyls

## 1.1 An Introduction to Security with Noisy Data

Over the past decades a large range of security primitives has been developed
to protect digital information. These primitives have solved many traditional
security problems and achieved a high level of sophistication. Their security
properties are well understood. An intrinsic property, vital for secure operation, is that they are extremely sensitive to small variations in their input.

On the other hand, in several important security applications, noisy inputs
cannot be avoided. This has motivated research on new primitives that allow
for security using noisy data on one of their inputs. It has turned out that this
research brings about new developments not only in the field of cryptography
but also in various application areas such as privacy protection of biometrics,
anti-counterfeiting, and brand protection.

This book discusses recent theoretical as well as application-oriented
developments in the field of combining noisy data with cryptography. In order
to sketch the setting of the book in more detail and clarify the relevance of
the topic, we start by explaining the different parts of the title of this book
and then show how they are related.

### 1.1.1 Information Security

Until the early 1970s, the most important area of information security con-
sisted of government and military applications. Where several governmental
departments exchange or store digital data, it is important to protect certain classified information from attackers. Likewise, the military wants to
prevent sensitive information from falling into enemy hands or weapon systems from being activated by non-authorized individuals. With the advent of
the internet and the extensive storage and transmission of digital information
made possible by developments in computer technology, digital information
starts to play an increasingly important role in the industry and even in
the life of private individuals. Just like governments, the industry wants to

protect its assets and prevent sensitive information from becoming available to competitors, even when data are transmitted over public communication channels like telephone lines or the internet. For private individuals, on the other hand, it is important that their privacy and assets are protected from governments, the industry, and other individuals.

In today's world, there are many examples of devices and procedures used to protect information. The most well-known examples are Personal Identification Number (PIN) codes and passwords, often combined with smartcards and tokens that are used to control access to services, systems, and information (bank terminals, computer systems, audio and video content, etc.). Subscriber Identity Module (SIM) cards used in mobile phones contain secret identification information that grants access to mobile phone networks and protects the telecom provider from illegal use of the network. Secure web pages use a Secure Socket Layer (SSL) to prevent eavesdropping on information exchanged between two terminals. Clearly, this short list of examples is far from complete but illustrates the fact that continuously, and sometimes unknown to the user, security protocols are used to protect information.

All of these methods use primitives and protocols from the field of *cryptography*, which is the traditional branch of science that systematically investigates and develops tools for protecting information and establishing secure interactions. In order to address the basic security needs such as secrecy (privacy) and authenticity, encryption and authentication schemes have been developed. Encryption provides confidentiality of information; that is, it defines who can read a message. Authentication verifies the identity of the sender as well as the integrity of a message. In both encryption and authentication schemes, it is assumed that all of the details of the used algorithms are public. The security of the schemes depends only on the secrecy of a key that is owned by at least one of the legitimate, honest parties. As long as the key remains secret (unknown to an attacker), these schemes provide a very high level of protection. This assumption of the secrecy of the key constitutes to the so-called *black-box* model. Within this model, the security of the various encryption and authentication schemes is well understood and various methods have been developed that allow for an efficient implementation.

Encryption and authentication schemes suffice for assuring the security of information stored or exchanged by different parties. For several reasons, however, they do not provide complete information security in our modern society. The first reason has to do with the fact that the cryptographic keys first have to be generated, after which they are distributed to the various parties. *Secure key generation and distribution* is a highly non-trivial and fundamental matter in cryptography. Basically, the problem comes down to the following very simple question: How can the legitimate parties obtain or generate a secret key without sharing any secret information beforehand, if they only have access to a public communication channel that is eavesdropped on by an attacker? Traditional algorithms—in particular key exchange schemes based on public key cryptography—only offer a solution under the condition that the attacker has limited computing power and under the assumption that certain classes of mathematical problems are "difficult."

Second, it is important to look more in depth at the fundamental assumption of the black-box model, which assumes that keys are safely stored. This assumption was reasonable in the early days of information security when computers were situated in locked and protected offices. Consequently, the keys stored on their harddisks could hardly be attacked in a physical way. Nowadays, however, many secret keys are stored in devices (mobile phones, bank tokens, smartcards, etc.) that often operate in hostile environments. It has been shown on several occasions that the keys stored in those devices are very vulnerable to physical attacks. Hence, the black-box model does not provide an adequate description of real life and therefore cannot guarantee full security in today's society.

Third, it is becoming increasingly important to be able to authenticate physical objects and individuals. Individuals can be authenticated based on something they know (e.g., a PIN code or password) or on something they own (e.g., a smartcard). In order to perform authentication based on something more closely linked to an individual, physiological characteristics (e.g., the structure of a fingerprint, a face, an iris) can be used. This is commonly known as *biometrics*. Similarly, physical objects can be authenticated based on their physical properties. This form of authentication requires a link between the physical world and (traditional) cryptographic primitives. The interface to the physical world is established by measuring physical properties. These measurements are inherently noisy due to a variety of causes, such as temperature and humidity variations, small repositioning errors, thermal noise in the measurement system, and slight damage of the measured object. In order to authenticate persons or objects, reference information has to be created and stored for later use. In the case of biometrics, this reference information is personal and therefore carries sensitive information about the individual from whom it is captured. Naive use and implementation of biometric systems might therefore lead to a severe privacy problem. Likewise, in the case of physical objects, it is often important that the stored reference information does not leak information about secret properties of the object. The problem of using secret noisy data for security purposes is inadequately covered by traditional cryptographic primitives.

### 1.1.2 Noisy Data

It is not our goal to investigate in detail the sources of the noise. In contrast, in this book on *security with noisy data* we study how the presence of noise has an impact on information security and how it can be dealt with and possibly used to generate an advantage over traditional approaches. The three most important applications where noisy data are relevant for cryptographic purposes are described below.

## Private Biometrics

Before an individual can use a biometric system, biometric reference information must be stored. Later, during authentication, a live measurement is compared with the stored reference data, and if they are sufficiently close to each other, authentication is successful. From an information security perspective, storing biometric reference information in an unprotected manner will lead to security and privacy risks. Therefore, it is important to protect the biometric information—for example, by using cryptographic primitives. In this book, the approach to protecting the privacy of biometric information is to use biometric measurement data as the secret authentication information in traditional cryptographic authentication protocols. This secret biometric information is not stored but derived anew from a biometric measurement every time the protocol is initiated. Furthermore, in many authentication protocols (e.g., those based on asymmetric cryptography), the public reference information required for the protocol does not reveal information about the secret authentication information. Hence, this approach protects the privacy of biometric information. Although it will be shown that this method has several advantages over simply encrypting the biometric reference information, it also presents the problem of combining noisy biometric measurement data with traditional cryptographic authentication protocols. This book gives several solutions for transforming a biometric measurement into a robust (noiseless) binary string that can be combined with cryptographic primitives.

## Secure Key Generation

In the classical cryptographic setting, as introduced by Shannon, it was assumed that the attacker can, without any error, eavesdrop on messages (or cipher texts) exchanged between the legitimate parties. Although this early model covers many real-life situations, more general situations exist. In a first scenario, it is assumed that the attacker can only obtain a noisy observation of the communicated messages. This situation appears naturally when the legitimate parties exchange quantum messages with each other.[1] In another scenario [196], the legitimate parties and the attacker all receive data from a source (e.g., a satellite), each through a different noisy channel outside, of their control. The goal of the legitimate parties is to generate a secret key from the received data while making only use of public (but authenticated) communication channels and without sharing any secret in advance. It turns out that the legitimate parties can amplify the ignorance of the attacker on their data to such an extent that they are able to agree on a secure key by exchanging only public information.

---

[1] We mention here explicitly that Quantum Cryptography is not the subject of this book. We note, however, that many of the techniques mentioned in this book are applicable to classical post-processing used in quantum key exchange.

**Physical Unclonable Functions**

Physical Unclonable Functions (PUFs) are physical objects that are inherently unclonable. The unclonability property stems from the fact that they contain many random components. PUFs map *challenges* to *responses*. A challenge is a stimulus that is applied to the PUF and a response is the reaction of the PUF obtained through measurements. Consequently, the responses are subject to noise and are slightly different each time they are captured. The term *function* originates from the idea that the response of the object can be interpreted as the result of evaluating a (parametrized) function with the stimulus being the argument. By embedding PUFs into devices, the devices become unclonable. This makes them very useful for anti-counterfeiting applications. The challenge-response behavior of a PUF changes drastically when it is damaged—for instance, by an attacker. Together with their unclonability property, this makes PUFs very interesting as a means for secure key storage. Instead of storing keys in digital form in the memory of a device, a key can be extracted from a PUF embedded in the device. Only when the key is required (e.g., for an authentication protocol), it is extracted from the PUF and deleted immediately when it is no longer needed. In this way, the key is only present in the device for a minimal amount of time and hence less vulnerable to physical attacks.

## 1.2 An Introduction to Biometrics

As mentioned earlier, an important application area that requires a combination of cryptography and noisy data is *biometrics*, which is concerned with recognizing individuals by physiological or behavioral characteristics, or *modalities*. Recent technical and social developments have led to a widespread use of biometric systems. In the following subsections, an overview is given of the most important trends in the application of biometrics, the privacy implications for individuals, and the technical consequences of combining noisy biometrics with cryptography.

### 1.2.1 History and Early Use

Although present-day biometric systems use modern technology such as computers and high-tech electronic sensors, all of these systems are based on principles dating back several thousands of years. Early use of biometrics can be traced back as far as Egyptian times when certain sets of physiological properties were used to distinguish traders [288]. Likewise, Chinese merchants in the 14th century are known to have used hand palm prints and footprints on paper using ink to distinguish young children from one another [122, p. 38].

In the 19th century, biometric methods became more formalized and were increasingly used to *solve crime*. Alphonse Bertillion (1853-1914), at a French

Prefecture of Police, developed a system of head and body measurements to identify previously convicted criminals who tended to use aliases in an attempt to escape heavier sentences for being a recidivist (e.g., [122, 240]). Around the same time, a Scottish doctor named Henry Faulds (1843-1930) became involved in archaeological digs in Japan where he noticed pieces of pottery with a fingerprint identifying its creator. He started studying modern fingerprints and in 1880 published an article in *Nature* magazine on the forensic use of fingerprints [104]. Although Scotland Yard initially declined Faulds' offer to use his approach, a little later, through the efforts of Sir Francis Galton [120] and Sir William Herschel [145], fingerprints became popular for forensic use. However, the system was hampered by the fact that there was no simple way to sort fingerprints to allow quick identification of a suspect. Edward Henry (1850-1931), an Inspector-General of Police in Bengal, together with co-workers Azizul Haque and Hemchandra Bose, developed a system to assign fingerprints to different classes to allow for quicker identification [144]. This approach, known as the *Henry classification system*, has served as a basis for many fingerprint identification systems now in use by criminal justice organizations all over the world.

### 1.2.2 Current Modalities and Applications

In contemporary biometric systems, fingerprints are still the most important modality. From the image of a fingerprint, the (two-dimensional) locations of so-called minutiae are determined. A minutia is defined as a ridge ending or ridge bifurcation. Most fingers have about 30 minutiae [186] and a *set of minutia locations* is considered to be unique for an individual. In the last three decades, other biometric modalities have been gaining momentum.

The face of an individual has long been the modality of choice for a wide range of identity papers such as passports, identity cards, security badges, etc. Where in these applications traditionally the comparison or *matching* of the live individual against the picture was done by the human eye, automated systems for face recognition are increasingly used. In these automated systems, faces can be characterized by a variety of features ranging from positions of landmark points (such as the tip of the nose, corners of the eyebrows) to the local texture (or frequency content) of several small patches in the face. In order to increase robustness and recognition performance, face recognition systems are being developed that use special cameras to generate a three-dimensional representation of a face [40]. In most cases, the features extracted from the face have a natural ordering and therefore can be collected in a *high-dimensional feature vector*.

A third modality is the iris, which is characterized by the texture of its pigmented ligaments. An iris is usually represented as a *binary string* of approximately 2000 bits [78] and is currently considered to be the best practical modality in terms of recognition performance. Other important modalities include hand geometry, handwritten signatures, and retina blood vessel patterns. A possible future biometric modality could be DNA, for example in the form of so-called Short Tandem Repeats (STRs), as often used in forensics [48]. This would lead to a modality with a recognition error probability in the order of $10^{-12}$ for unrelated individuals [48, pp. 94-95], but at the moment this is not yet a practical modality because low-cost sensors that can quickly analyze DNA are not yet available. Furthermore, it is to be expected that the use of DNA as a biometric modality will only be acceptable if the privacy of the DNA information is guaranteed.

The increase in the use of biometrics in the past decades can be attributed to technical as well as social developments. First, there is an increasing need for individuals to be authenticated due to an explosive growth in electronic information and services, mainly on the internet. The range of internet services is very wide and includes banking, electronic newspaper subscriptions, tax filings, internet shopping, web mail, ticket sales, and gaming. The owners of such services have to protect their business from illegal access by non-paying individuals or other forms of abuse. Protection is usually implemented using PIN codes or passwords, possibly in combination with smartcards and hardware tokens. These traditional authentication methods have the drawback that they are not tightly linked to an individual: Clearly, it is possible to tell someone your PIN code or to borrow a smartcard. In such situations, adding a biometric as a means for authentication will lead to better security. The use of biometrics in such applications is made possible by the development of low-cost sensors and computers, and by the improvements of biometric recognition algorithms.

A second and probably the most important reason behind the increasing use of biometrics is the perceived threat of terrorism. Many countries see biometrics as one of the methods to mitigate this threat. For example, under the US VISIT program [84], for all visitors to the United States holding non-immigrant visas the fingerprints of both index fingers are scanned and a digital photograph of the face is taken. Most European countries are currently issuing passports containing a smartcard holding a digital photograph [102]. In the future, this photograph can be augmented with a digital image of a fingerprint or iris. In Asian countries as well biometrics are increasingly used in identity cards (e.g., [295]).

### 1.2.3 Privacy Considerations

Observing the biometric playing field, it can be seen that biometric techniques and applications are extending from the *forensic* area, where they are used to *solve crime*, to the *civil* area with the purpose to *prevent crime*. This means that biometric systems will become omnipresent, and, as a result, biometric information of an individual will be stored in a large number of locations, usually not under the control of its rightful owner. Ubiquitous storage of biometric information leads to a number *privacy risks* such as identity theft. These threats are discussed in more detail in Chapters 10 and 11. Furthermore, it is important to note that privacy concerns of the general public will probably hamper the acceptance of biometric systems.

In principle, there are two ways of protecting the privacy of biometric information. The first one is a *procedural approach* where rules, regulations, and legislation determine who has access to certain information. In contrast, in Chapters 10 and 11 *technological approaches* are discussed based on combining traditional biometric techniques with recent developments in the field of cryptography and noisy data. These *template protection techniques* should guarantee the privacy of biometric information even in the presence of malicious individuals, and, in that sense, they are preferable over procedural approaches. However, combining biometrics with (noisy) cryptography has severe consequences for the methods and approaches that are traditionally used to process biometric measurements. An overview of these consequences is given in the following section.

### 1.2.4 An Overview of Biometric Research Areas

In order to appreciate the technical consequences of combining noisy biometrics with cryptography, it is important to give a high-level abstraction of the field of biometric research, which, in essence, can be split into two areas. The first area is that of *biometric sensors*, or the biometric-specific hardware that is required to set up a biometric system. For instance, one can think of camera systems that are capable of generating a three-dimensional image of a face, sensors that look under the skin to generate an image of the blood vessels, fingerprint scanners based on laser technology, and so forth.

The second area, which is more important in the context of this book, is concerned with the *recognition algorithms* that are used in a biometric system. Recognition algorithms require biometric modalities that are sufficiently discriminating between individuals (i.e., have a large between-person variation), at the same time, different measurements of this modality of the same individual should have a small variation (i.e., a small within-person variation). The within-person variation or *noise* is caused by the biometric measurement system and by a varying interaction of a biometric with the sensor, where the latter usually introduces non-linear, non-additive noise. The research on recognition algorithms in the past decades has focused on dealing with the noise in biometric measurements such that it becomes possible to distinguish or recognize individuals with sufficient accuracy. This *recognition accuracy* is the *most important performance indicator* of traditional biometric systems. It is expressed in terms of the False Accept Rate (FAR) and the False Reject Rate (FRR). The FAR is the probability that the biometric system will incorrectly accept an unauthorized user. Likewise, the FRR is the probability that an authorized user is rejected. Therefore, the lower the FAR and FRR values, the better the (recognition) performance of the biometric system.

In order to arrive at the best recognition performance, a variety of (digital) signal processing steps is performed on a biometric measurement, such as linear and non-linear filtering to remove noise from an image, further filtering to facilitate extraction of a set of distinguishing features, (non)-linear dimensionality reduction techniques to limit the number of features while improving the signal-to-noise ratio, and so forth.

Although these signal processing techniques are often specific for and tailored to a certain modality, the final representation of a biometric (i.e., the *biometric template*) takes only a limited number of forms. First, there is the (unordered) *set* of *real-valued elements* such as naturally occurs, for instance, in describing a fingerprint using minutiae locations. Second, many biometric modalities can be represented as high-dimensional *real-valued feature vectors*.

The ultimate purpose of a biometric system is to compare or *match* two biometric templates and to decide if they originate from the same individual. Over the years, many dedicated algorithms have appeared to match two (noisy) minutia sets [186]. Matching two high-dimensional feature vectors is usually formulated as a *statistical classification problem* leading to high-dimensional and curved decision surfaces (or *classifiers*) separating the feature vectors of one individual from those of other individuals based on estimates of (continuous) probability distributions [115]. In practical situations, there is usually insufficient knowledge about these distributions, and methods have been developed that only require a limited amount of information about the probability distributions but still produce good classifiers [47, 282].

### 1.2.5 Combining Noisy Biometrics and Cryptography

The previous subsection illustrates that biometric systems use highly advanced and dedicated processing and matching techniques on *continuous* feature sets in order to arrive at an optimal recognition performance. As mentioned earlier, the techniques described in Part I of this book in principle allow protecting the privacy of biometric information. However, although not always explicitly stated, these methods assume *discrete* data representations such as discrete sets and binary strings. These methods can handle noise on the input as long as some simple discrete distance measure (such as set difference and Hamming distance) is not exceeded. When a privacy-protected biometric system is built using these techniques, not only should the privacy of the biometric information be protected, also the recognition performance should be comparable to that of traditional biometric systems. Therefore, one of the major challenges of privacy protection of biometric information using cryptography according to the methods in Part I of this book is to *represent biometric templates as discrete data* while still obtaining a good recognition performance.

## 1.3 An Introduction to Physical Unclonable Functions

The principles of biometrics as described in the previous section are applicable not only to the human body but also to physical objects in general. Many objects have features that are unique and difficult to clone and can therefore be used for identification of objects and for extracting binary strings in a similar way as for biometrics. A common setting in which these physical objects are used is to apply a stimulus and measure the response. The response of the object can be interpreted as the result of evaluating a (parametrized) function with the stimulus being the argument. The unique features of the object can be considered to be the function parameters. Because of the similarity with mathematical functions, these unique unclonable objects are often referred to as Physical Unclonable Functions, but terminology like Physical Random Functions or Physical One-Way Functions is used as well. Because of the cryptographic setting in which PUFs are used, stimulus and response are usually called a Challenge Response Pair (CRP).

This abstract description will be made more concrete in the following sections, where we give an overview of possible implementations and applications of PUFs.

### 1.3.1 History and Concepts of PUFs

In the history of cryptography there are many examples in which physical objects are used in the encryption and decryption process. For instance, in the 5th century BC, the Spartans used a device called the *scytale*, a cylinder of a certain radius. This *scytale* was owned by both sender and receiver. When encoding a message, the sender wrapped a narrow strip of cloth around the cylinder and wrote a message across it parallel to the axis of the cylinder. He then sent the unwound cloth to the receiver. Anyone intercepting the cloth would see a random-looking sequence of letters. When obtaining the cloth, the receiver wound the cloth onto his own cylinder, thus decrypting the message.

Another example is the *Cardan grille* from the 16th century—a rectangle with a number of randomly placed holes in it. In order to encrypt a secret message, the sender wrote his message onto paper through the holes, and the remaining blank space on the paper was filled in to form an inconspicuous fake message. The receiver owned the same grill and by putting it on top of the received message, he decrypted the message.

A more recent example is the Enigma cipher machine, an electro-mechanical device resembling a typewriter. It contained a number of mechanical rotors connected to electrical switches, a keyboard, and an array containing all of the letters of the alphabet, which could light up individually. The sender typed his message on the keyboard and the machine showed the encrypted message by lighting up certain letters on the device. Likewise, the receiver typed the encrypted message on his keyboard and obtained the decrypted message from the letters lighting up on his device. The Enigma is considered as an important step toward modern cryptography and it was used extensively during World War II.

Clearly, this list of examples is not intended to be complete, but it illustrates that PUFs are not the first physical objects to be used in a cryptographic setting. However, it is important to note that the physical objects in these examples are fundamentally different from PUFs in the sense that they have *no unclonable features*. They are merely (electro-)mechanical implementations of a mathematical algorithm, much like current-day computers running software implementing RSA or AES algorithms. This stands in sharp contrast to the work on PUFs described in this book, as one of the important properties of PUFs is that they are unclonable.

An important step in the reasoning about unclonability was made by Wiesner in the late 1960s. He proposed an anti-counterfeiting method [24,290] that makes use of the no-cloning theorem of quantum physics, which states that it is impossible to duplicate an unknown quantum state with a high probability of success. By equipping an item (e.g., a banknote) with a quantum system in a state known only to the issuer, it is ensured that counterfeiters cannot clone the item, but the issuer is still able to verify its authenticity. This method is extremely secure, but, unfortunately, it is not very practical because quantum states are very difficult to maintain over long time spans. Therefore, it is not to be expected that low-cost consumer devices in the near future will contain quantum systems for security purposes. Consequently, in this book we concentrate on PUFs based on classical physics.

In 1991, Simmons [253] proposed an anti-counterfeiting concept that was very different from the ideas at the time. Traditionally, authenticity marks that were embedded into items to protect them against counterfeiting were all identical and difficult to forge. As Simmons noted, the requirement that all marks have to be equal fundamentally contradicts the requirement that they have to be hard to forge. In contrast, one should use unique, irreproducible physical features instead. This approach was made possible by the use of digital signatures.

In 2001, Pappu [221] introduced the concept of a PUF or Physical One-Way Function (POWF). He proposed to use a PUF in a challenge-response setting and defined a PUF as a physical object with the following properties:

1. The object can be subjected to a large number of different challenges that yield an unpredictable response.
2. The object is very hard to clone physically.
3. Mathematical modeling of the challenge-response physics is very difficult.
4. It is hard to characterize the physical structure of the object.

Property 1 ensures that there is enough randomness such that responses cannot be predicted. Property 2 refers to *physical* unclonability, whereas property 3 represents *mathematical* unclonability. The latter prevents an attacker from using a model to mimic the behavior of a PUF that is not physically present. Finally, property 4 hinders an attacker in gathering the data necessary to make a clone. It can be considered an integral part of properties 2 and 3, but it is listed separately for clarity.

In order to satisfy all of these requirements, the object constituting a PUF needs to be highly complex. For property 2, the production process must be fundamentally uncontrollable. Furthermore, for properties 1 and 3, the responses need to be sensitive to small changes in the object's structure and in the input. For property 4, the object needs to be "opaque", (i.e., hard to scrutinize). In spite of the strict definition of the properties of a PUF, in practice the term PUF is used also if not all properties are satisfied.

### 1.3.2 Practical Realisations of PUFs

The kind of overall complex behavior described in the previous section is typically observed in manufacturing and measuring a large number of very small structures. Below, we list a number of PUF realizations and PUF-like structures. This list is not exhaustive, but it illustrates the broad range of possible physical implementations.

In [226], a tamper-evident Integrated Circuit (IC) was described with a unique identifier or key based on an "active coating." The IC is covered with a layer that contains a random mixture of conductors and insulators. Sensors inside the chip probe the coating and convert the measurement into a binary string. If the IC detects a change of the binary string, it will take appropriate countermeasures. This basic concept was further developed by Tuyls et al. (e.g., [274]), who coined the term *coating PUF* and showed explicitly how a key can be derived from measurements of the coating and how to use the result for secure key storage. In this book, coating PUFs are discussed in Chapters 12, 15, and 16.

In 2001, Pappu et al. [221, 222] proposed to use three-dimensional optical structures consisting of a transparent medium containing many randomly positioned scatterers. When probed with a laser, the reflected or transmitted light is the result of multiple coherent scattering and forms a random-looking pattern of bright and dark areas known as *speckle*. In this book, optical PUFs are discussed in Chapters 12, 13, 15, and 16.

In 2002, Gassend et al. [125] introduced the *silicon PUF*, which is based on the fact that during IC manufacturing there are always small variations, even between ICs from the same wafer. While these variations do not harm the proper operation of the ICs, they can be used as a source of randomness. In silicon PUFs, the challenge is a selection of a certain path on an IC, and the response is the delay time of a signal traveling along this path. The delay time is a combined effect of all the delays in the wires and logic devices on the path.

As a last example, we mention the *SRAM PUF*, introduced in 2007 [140]. Similar to a silicon PUF, it is based on random variations during IC manufacture. When a static RAM (SRAM) is switched on, the memory cells have an undefined state. When read out, a cell yields a "0" or a "1" depending on the precise characteristics of the cell, which are subject to random manufacturing inaccuracies. Hence, a freshly switched-on SRAM can be challenged by choosing certain memory addresses, and the response is given by the returned start-up values.

Clearly, there are many more physical structures that can be used as a PUF, and an optimal choice will depend on the application. Therefore, in the next section we discuss some applications and use models.

### 1.3.3 Applications and Use Models

The specific properties of PUFs, such as uniqueness and unclonability, make them useful for a large number of security applications. In general, the presence of the correct PUF is verified by measuring the response to a challenge using a measurement device or *reader* and comparing the actual response to reference data that are stored in the verification system. The actual PUF can be used in two main settings: We distinguish between *uncontrolled* or *bare* PUFs and Controlled PUFs (CPUFs).

In the case of an uncontrolled PUF, an external reader interacts directly with the physical PUF structure. This setting is well suited for verification using trusted readers. Since a verifier knows that a trusted reader is scanning a physical object and has not been tampered with, the only relevant property of the PUF in this case is physical unclonability. Typical application examples are token authentication, anti-counterfeiting, copy protection, brand protection, and tamper evidence.

In contrast, in the case of an untrusted reader, the verifier cannot be certain if he is receiving an actual measurement result. Therefore, not only should a PUF be unclonable, it should also be infeasible to predict responses coming from a PUF. This can be achieved by choosing a PUF that contains much randomness and/or responds slowly to challenges. Application examples are remote authentication where the reader is under the control of the prover (e.g., on-line banking).

The concept of a Controlled PUF (CPUF) was introduced in 2002 by Gassend et al. [124]. As opposed to the uncontrolled PUF, in the case of a CPUF the interaction with the physical PUF is always done through a *control layer*. The PUF and the control layer are inseparably bound together and any attempt to force the components apart will damage the PUF. As a result, an attacker has no direct access to the PUF because the control layer completely shields the PUF's inputs and outputs. This extension substantially strengthens the security, since an attacker cannot probe the PUF at will and cannot interpret the responses.

By further extending the functionality of the control layer, one obtains CPUFs that enable a number of applications that are completely beyond the reach of unprotected PUFs. One of these is *secure key storage*, where the control layer derives a secret from the PUF and runs a strong authentication algorithm (e.g., a zero knowledge protocol) to prove knowledge of the secret. In this setting, a very limited number of CRPs is sufficient, and one speaks of a Physically Obfuscated Key (POK) instead of a PUF.

Incorporating even more functionality in the control layer allows for two special applications: *certified execution* and *certified measurement*. In certified execution, a user outsources a computation task to the control layer of a CPUF. The control layer performs the computation and provides proof both of the identity of the PUF and of the correct processing of the job. In certified measurement, the CPUF contains an additional integrated detector such as a microphone or video camera. All data recorded by the detector are certified by the CPUF—for example, by creating a signature using a PUF key as a private key. This allows for verifying both the integrity and the origin of the data.

Controlled PUFs and possible implementations are discussed in detail in Chapter 14.

### 1.3.4 Current Directions of PUF Research

When building practical systems based on PUFs, several requirements must be met apart from having the important intrinsic properties of the PUF. As in biometrics, during operation a PUF system measures the properties of a physical entity, which gives rise to measurement noise. Because cryptographic primitives such as hashing, signing, and encryption by definition amplify any noise in their input, dedicated measurement, signal processing, and quantization, techniques must be developed, possibly in combination with error correction, to eliminate the noise. However, this introduces a new problem because side-information (redundancy data) needs to be stored outside the PUF in insecure storage, where it potentially leaks information about the PUF responses. Many of these issues are similar to the situation in which noisy biometrics are combined with cryptography and must be taken into account when designing PUF-based security systems. An important difference between PUFs and biometrics, however, is that with PUFs, one has some freedom to *design* physical structures that carry more information than the biometric modalities.

More on the practical side, for mass deployment (e.g., in the case of anti-counterfeiting), PUFs must be inexpensive to produce and it must be possible to use them in combination with low-cost readers. Furthermore, since PUFs are based on physical systems, the security depends on the sophistication and resources of the attacker. This is similar to the situation of side-channel attacks against physical implementations of traditional cryptographic systems. These problems with "engineering attacks" must be studied thoroughly before a PUF system can be successfully deployed. However, in this book we concentrate more on the physical, information-theoretic, and cryptographic aspects of PUFs.

## 1.4 Overview of the Book

This book is split into two parts. Part I discusses security primitives that allow noisy inputs. In most cases, the descriptions assume that some noisy source is available, generating stochastic outputs according to some probability distribution. The output of these sources takes the form of discrete symbols (e.g., noisy binary strings) and noisy (discrete) sets. Part II focuses on the practical applications of the methods discussed in Part I. It introduces privacy-protected biometric systems, analyzes the theoretical and practical properties of PUFs, and discusses PUF-based systems.

Part I is organized as follows:

The focus of Chapter 2 is on unconditionally secure (i.e., unbreakable) cryptography. Basic notions from information theory are introduced to measure the security of a cryptographic key in the unconditional setting. Additionally, protocols are presented that allow one to use noisy channels in combination with public communication to generate a secure key. Finally, some bounds are given on the maximal length of the keys that can be extracted from the noisy source.

Next, in Chapter 3, the *fuzzy commitment* primitive is introduced, which is probably the first cryptographic construction that allows for privacy-preserving biometric authentication. It requires that a biometric measurement can be represented as binary strings. It presents a very intuitive approach to the main ideas.

Chapter 4 starts with an information-theoretic approach to the biometric identification problem. Next, it is motivated that reference biometric templates have to be protected for privacy reasons. The problem of privacy and noisy measurements is investigated from a communication point of view. The chapter introduces the *helper data algorithm* as a general way to extract secure keys from noisy sources and shows how that algorithm can be used for privacy-preserving biometric authentication. The chapter can be considered as the Shannon theory of secure key extraction from a noisy source.

Chapter 5 investigates the problem of unconditionally secure key extraction from noisy data in the cryptographic setting. The main primitive introduced for that purpose is the *fuzzy extractor*. A good intuition for this primitive is given and an overview of its main security properties is presented.

Chapter 6 dives into the security problems associated with fuzzy extractors. First, the situation is addressed of an active adversary tampering with the messages (e.g., the helper data) exchanged between two legitimate parties. Second, the problem of the extraction of multiple keys (and hence helper data) from the same biometric is investigated. The first issue is tackled by extending the concept of a fuzzy extractor to that of a *robust fuzzy extractor*, which has an authentication mechanism embedded. To deal with the second problem, so-called *reusable fuzzy extractors* are designed.

In all of the previous chapters, it is (implicitly) assumed that the adversary has no access to the responses from the noisy source. Although this sounds reasonable, this assumption is not necessarily true for all biometrics. Fingerprints, for instance, are left behind on glasses, tables, and so forth. That implies that they might not be suitable for the generation of secret keys. Therefore, techniques are developed to generate the public key of an identity-based public key encryption scheme from biometrics. This subject is presented in Chapter 7.

Chapter 8 presents several protocols for implementation of the basic primitives of secure multi-party computation, such as bit commitment, oblivious transfer, and so forth for the unconditionally secure setting. These new protocols use only noisy resources and correlated randomness.

In Chapters 2-6, techniques are developed that allow extracting unconditionally secure keys from noisy sources. In Chapter 9, it is shown how privacy preserving biometric authentication can be achieved under a computational assumption by using techniques inherited from Secure Multi-Party Computation (SMP).

Part II discusses practical applications of the methods discussed in Part I and is organized as follows:

In the past years, initial work has appeared on combining biometrics with cryptography. Chapter 10 gives an overview of various approaches and it also presents an early method for privacy protection that does not require discretized feature sets.

Chapter 11 describes how biometric information can be represented in the discrete domain such that it can be used as an input for the methods in Part I, making it possible to protect the privacy of biometric information. Also, some application examples of privacy-protected biometric systems are discussed.

In a second group of applications, PUFs are used as a source of randomness.

When building security systems based on PUFs, it is important to know the most important PUF properties. Chapter 12 analyzes the information content of PUFs. A general information-theoretic model of measurements is introduced and applied to *optical PUFs* and *coating PUFs*. The results indicate how many bits of key material can be extracted from a PUF and how many measurements an attacker needs to characterize a PUF.

A more hands-on approach is taken in Chapter 13. The entropy of optical PUF responses is estimated by compressing speckle patterns. The employed compression method is Context Tree Weighting (CTW), which is known to approach the entropy of the source for a broad class of sources. The theory of CTW is extended to the two-dimensional case, and estimates are given for the amount of key material that can be extracted from noisy PUF responses.

Chapter 14 discusses applications of *controlled PUFs*. CRP-based authentication protocols are described in detail, as well as the concept of Certified Execution.

Chapter 15 gives a description of experimental PUF hardware. Details are given on optical PUFs and coating PUFs. The physical structures, the manufacturing process, and the measurement techniques are discussed.

Chapter 16 deals with secure key storage. After a formal discussion of *read-proof hardware*, it is shown how this type of hardware can be realized using PUFs. Examples are given of key reconstruction algorithms for optical PUFs and coating PUFs.

Finally, Chapter 17 describes how PUFs can be used for anti-counterfeiting by associating a product with an unclonable RFID tag. Several authentication protocols are presented that are lightweight enough to be executed on an RFID tag.

# Part I

# Theory of Security with Noisy Data

# Unbreakable Keys from Random Noise

Ueli Maurer, Renato Renner, and Stefan Wolf

Virtually all presently used cryptosystems can theoretically be broken by an exhaustive key-search, and they might even be broken in practice due to novel algorithms or progress in computer engineering. In contrast, by exploiting the fact that certain communication channels are inherently noisy, one can achieve encryption provably secure against adversaries with unbounded computing power, in arguably practical settings. This chapter discusses secret key-agreement by public discussion from correlated information in a new definitional framework for information-theoretic reductions.

## 2.1 Information-Theoretic Cryptographic Security

### 2.1.1 Motivation

The security of essentially all presently used cryptosystems is not proven. It is based on at least two assumptions. The first assumption is that the adversary's computational resources, specified within some model of computation, are bounded. This type of assumption can be problematic because it may not even be clear what the right model of computation is, as demonstrated by the recent proposal of a new computational model: a quantum computer, which is believed to be strictly more powerful than classical computers.

The second assumption is that the computational problem of breaking the cryptosystem is computationally infeasible, given the assumed computational resources. Such an assumption could potentially be proven, but the state of the art in complexity theory does not seem to be even close to proving any meaningful lower bound on the hardness of a computational problem. Important computational problems on which the security of cryptographic schemes is based are integer factorization (e.g., RSA [238]) and computing discrete logarithms in certain finite cyclic groups (e.g., Diffie-Hellman [85]).

A cryptosystem for which the security could be rigorously proven based only on an assumption of the first type would be called *computationally secure*, whereas a cryptosystem secure under neither assumption (i.e., even against an adversary with unbounded computing power) is called *unconditionally secure* or *information-theoretically secure*. Such a system is even unbreakable by an exhaustive search over the key space.[1] As mentioned, no cryptosystem has been proven to be computationally secure (except, of course, those that are also information-theoretically secure.)

Many researchers have proposed cryptosystems that are unconditionally secure, with varying degrees of practicality. The most famous (but quite impractical) example is the one-time pad discussed later. There are two types of result on information-theoretic security: impossibility results and constructive results. In this chapter we first discuss the impossibility of perfectly secure message transmission and then focus on the key-agreement problem to show that information-theoretically secure key-agreement is possible in arguably practical settings if noisy information is exploited. We make use of information theory and refer to [66] for an introduction to the subject.

### 2.1.2 Information-Theoretic Security: Perfect Secrecy and Shannon's Theorem

Let us start with the classical scenario of a symmetric cryptosystem with message $M$, key $K$, and ciphertext $C$ (see Fig. 2.1). The following security definition appears to be the strongest possible for such a cryptosystem.

**Definition 2.1 [252].** *A cipher is called* perfectly secret *if the ciphertext reveals no information about the message (i.e., if* $\mathbf{I}(M;C) = 0$ *holds).*

Equivalent characterizations of this condition are that $M$ and $C$ are statistically independent or that the best strategy of an eavesdropper who wants to obtain (information about) the message from the ciphertext is to use only the a priori knowledge about $M$ and to discard $C$.

An example of a perfectly secret cipher is the *one-time pad* that was already proposed by Vernam in 1926 [284]. Here, the message is a string $M = [m_1, m_2, \ldots, m_N]$ of length $N$, and the key is a uniformly distributed

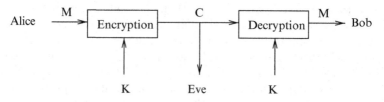

**Fig. 2.1.** A symmetric cryptosystem.

---

[1] It should be mentioned that also unconditionally security is based on an assumption, namely that our probabilistic model of Nature is (at least partially) correct.

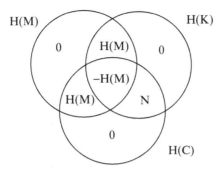

**Fig. 2.2.** Entropy diagram for one-time pad encryption.

$N$-bit string $K = [k_1, k_2, \ldots, k_N]$ that is independent of $M$. The ciphertext $C$ is computed from $M$ and $K$ by

$$C = [c_1, c_2, \ldots, c_N] = [m_1 \oplus k_1, m_2 \oplus k_2, \ldots, m_N \oplus k_N] =: M \oplus K.$$

A simple proof that the one-time pad is perfectly secret is obtained by using an entropy diagram (see Fig. 2.2) for the three random variables $M$, $K$, and $C$, as proposed in [308]. Any two of these random variables determine the third: hence, $\mathsf{H}(C|MK) = 0$, $\mathsf{H}(M|CK) = 0$, and $\mathsf{H}(K|MC) = 0$. The key $K$ is independent of the message $M$, and hence the entire entropy of $K$, namely $\mathsf{H}(K) = N$, must be concentrated in the field $\mathbf{I}(K; C|M)$, (i.e., $\mathbf{I}(K; C|M) = N$). Since $\mathsf{H}(C) \leq N$ and the field $\mathbf{I}(K; C|M)$ already contributes that much, we must have $\mathbf{I}(M; C) = 0$ (since $\mathbf{I}(M; C)$ is non-negative).

Unfortunately, the price one has to pay for perfect secrecy is that the communicating parties must share a secret key that is at least as long as the message (and can only be used once). In view of this property, the one-time pad appears to be quite impractical.

However, Shannon showed that perfect secrecy cannot be obtained in a less expensive way; that is, that the one-time pad is optimal with respect to key length. Maurer [196] proved the stronger statement that the same bound even holds in the more relevant setting where Alice and Bob can interact by (not secret) two-way communication.

**Theorem 2.1 [252].** *For every perfectly secret cryptosystem (with unique decodability), we have* $\mathsf{H}(K) \geq \mathsf{H}(M)$.

For a proof of Shannon's theorem, note first that unique decodability means $\mathsf{H}(M|CK) = 0$. The entropy diagram of the involved quantities is shown in Fig. 2.3. We have $b \geq a$ because $\mathbf{I}(C; K) \geq 0$, and

$$\mathsf{H}(K) \geq b - a + c \geq a - a + c = \mathsf{H}(M) \,,$$

which concludes the proof.

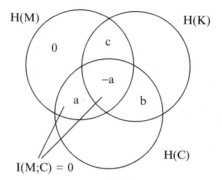

**Fig. 2.3.** The proof of Shannon's theorem.

### 2.1.3 Optimistic Results by Limiting the Adversary's Information

Unfortunately, Shannon's and Maurer's above-mentioned results imply that perfect secrecy is possible only between parties who share a secret key of length at least equal to the entropy of the message to be transmitted. Hence, every perfectly secret cipher is necessarily as impractical as the one-time pad. On the other hand, the assumption that the adversary has *perfect* access to the ciphertext is overly pessimistic and unrealistic in general, since every transmission of a signal over a physical channel is subject to noise.

Many models have been presented and analyzed in which the information that the adversary obtains is limited in some way and which offer the possibility of information-theoretically secure key agreement. If insecure channels are available, this also implies secret message transmission (using the one-time pad with the generated secret key).

The condition that the opponent's knowledge is bounded can, for instance, be based on noise in communication channels [4,73,196,303], on the fact that the adversary's memory is limited [190] or on the uncertainty principle of quantum mechanics [23,100].

### 2.1.4 The Power of Feedback

Wyner [303] showed that in the special case where a (noisy) channel $P_{Y|X}$ from Alice to Bob is available and where the adversary receives a degraded version $Z$ of $Y$ (through a channel $P_{Z|Y}$, independent of the main channel), secret-key agreement is possible in all non-trivial cases. This setting was generalized by Csiszár and Körner [73], who studied the model of a so-called *noisy broadcast channel* characterized by a probability distribution $P_{YZ|X}$, where Alice's input is $X$, whereas Bob and Eve receive $Y$ and $Z$, respectively. They introduced a quantity, called the *secrecy capacity*, measuring Alice and Bob's ability to generate a virtually secret key (asymptotically, per channel use). Their results imply that in the case of independent binary symmetric

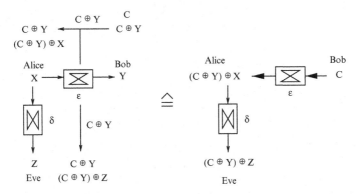

**Fig. 2.4.** Inverting the main channel.

channels, key-agreement is possible if and only if Bob's channel has a smaller error probability than Eve's.

However, the following example, given in [196], illustrates the somewhat surprising fact that by using an insecure feedback channel, secret-key agreement is possible in the above setting. We start with the situation on the left-hand side of Fig. 2.4. Without feedback, no secret-key agreement is possible. However, let us assume an *interactive* variant of this model with an additional noiseless and insecure but authentic channel. Surprisingly, the situation is now entirely different although the additional channel is accessible to Eve.

Observe first that the additional public-discussion channel allows one to invert the direction of the noisy channel between Alice and Bob by the following trick. First, Alice chooses a random bit $X$ and sends it over the noisy channel(s). This bit is received by Bob as $Y$ and by Eve as $Z$. Bob, who wants to send the message bit $C$ to Alice, computes $C \oplus Y$ and sends this over the noiseless public channel. Alice computes $(C \oplus Y) \oplus X$, whereas Eve can compute $(C \oplus Y) \oplus Z$. This perfectly corresponds to the situation where the direction of the main channel is inverted (see Fig. 2.4).

The second crucial observation is that this is exactly the binary-symmetric setting of Wyner's wire-tap channel [303], allowing secret-key agreement at a positive rate. We conclude from this example that the possibility of feedback from Bob to Alice can substantially improve the legitimate partners' situation toward a wire-tapping adversary.

Maurer [196] proposed the following interactive model of secret-key agreement by public discussion from common information (see Fig. 2.5). The parties Alice and Bob who want to establish a mutual secret key have access to realizations of random variables $X$ and $Y$, respectively, whereas the adversary knows a random variable $Z$. Let $P_{XYZ}$ be the joint distribution of the random variables. Furthermore, the legitimate partners are connected by an insecure but authentic channel (i.e., a channel that can be passively overheard

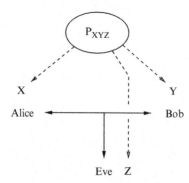

**Fig. 2.5.** Secret-key agreement by public discussion from common information.

by Eve but over which no undetected active attacks by the opponent, such as modifying or inserting messages, are possible).

This model is more general and more natural than noisy channel models since the assumption that the parties have access to correlated information appears to be realistic in many contexts. In the rest of the chapter, this model will be the basis of our considerations.

## 2.2 Smooth Rényi Entropies

Let $X$ and $Y$ be random variables with ranges $\mathcal{X}$ and $\mathcal{Y}$, distributed according to $P_{XY}$. For any event $\mathcal{E}$ with conditional probabilities $P_{\mathcal{E}|XY}(x, y)$, let[2]

$$H_{\min}(\mathcal{E}X|Y) := -\log \max_{(x,y)\in\mathcal{X}\times\mathcal{Y}} P_{\mathcal{E}X|Y}(x, y),$$

$$H_{\max}(\mathcal{E}X|Y) := \log \max_{y\in\mathcal{Y}} |\{x \in \mathcal{X} : P_{\mathcal{E}XY}(x, y) > 0\}|,$$

where $P_{\mathcal{E}X|Y}(x, y) := P_{\mathcal{E}|XY}(x, y)P_{XY}(x, y)/P_Y(y)$ (with the convention that $\frac{0}{0} = 0$). The *smooth min-entropy* and the *smooth max-entropy* are then defined by [236, 237] (see also [232] for a generalization of these entropy measures to quantum information theory)

$$H_{\min}^\varepsilon(X|Y) := \max_{\mathcal{E}:\Pr[\mathcal{E}]\geq 1-\varepsilon} H_{\min}(\mathcal{E}X|Y),$$

$$H_{\max}^\varepsilon(X|Y) := \min_{\mathcal{E}:\Pr[\mathcal{E}]\geq 1-\varepsilon} H_{\max}(\mathcal{E}X|Y),$$

where $\Pr[\mathcal{E}] := \sum_{x,y} P_{\mathcal{E}|XY}(x, y)P_{XY}(x, y)$. Smooth min- and max-entropies can be seen as generalizations of the Shannon entropy in the following sense.

---

[2] All logarithms are to base 2.

**Lemma 2.1.** *Let $P_{XY}$ be fixed and let, for any $n \in \mathbb{N}$, $(X_1, Y_1), \ldots, (X_n, Y_n)$ be a sequence of random variables distributed according to $(P_{XY})^{\times n}$. Then*

$$\lim_{\varepsilon \to 0} \lim_{n \to \infty} \frac{1}{n} \mathsf{H}^\varepsilon_{\min}(X_1 \cdots X_n | Y_1 \cdots Y_n) = \mathsf{H}(X|Y),$$

$$\lim_{\varepsilon \to 0} \lim_{n \to \infty} \frac{1}{n} \mathsf{H}^\varepsilon_{\max}(X_1 \cdots X_n | Y_1 \cdots Y_n) = \mathsf{H}(X|Y),$$

*where $\mathsf{H}(X|Y) = \mathsf{H}(P_{XY}) - \mathsf{H}(P_Y)$ is the Shannon entropy of $X$ conditioned on $Y$.*

Smooth min- and max-entropies satisfy some basic rules that are very similar to those known from Shannon theory. The following lemma is an analogue of the strong subadditivity, $\mathsf{H}(X|YZ) \le \mathsf{H}(X|Z)$.

**Lemma 2.2.** *Let $X$, $Y$, and $Z$ be random variables and let $\varepsilon \ge 0$. Then*

$$\mathsf{H}^\varepsilon_{\min}(X|YZ) \le \mathsf{H}^\varepsilon_{\min}(X|Z),$$

$$\mathsf{H}^\varepsilon_{\max}(X|YZ) \le \mathsf{H}^\varepsilon_{\max}(X|Z).$$

The following is a generalization of the chain rule $\mathsf{H}(XY|Z) = \mathsf{H}(X|YZ) + \mathsf{H}(Y|Z)$.

**Lemma 2.3.** *Let $X$, $Y$, and $Z$ be random variables and let $\varepsilon, \varepsilon', \varepsilon'' \ge 0$. Then*

$$\mathsf{H}^{\varepsilon+\varepsilon'}_{\min}(XY|Z) \ge \mathsf{H}^\varepsilon_{\min}(X|YZ) + \mathsf{H}^{\varepsilon'}_{\min}(Y|Z),$$

$$\mathsf{H}^{\varepsilon'}_{\min}(XY|Z) < \mathsf{H}^{\varepsilon+\varepsilon'+\varepsilon''}_{\min}(X|YZ) + \mathsf{H}^{\varepsilon''}_{\max}(Y|Z) + \log(1/\varepsilon),$$

$$\mathsf{H}^{\varepsilon+\varepsilon'}_{\max}(XY|Z) \le \mathsf{H}^\varepsilon_{\max}(X|YZ) + \mathsf{H}^{\varepsilon'}_{\max}(Y|Z),$$

$$\mathsf{H}^{\varepsilon'}_{\max}(XY|Z) > \mathsf{H}^{\varepsilon+\varepsilon'+\varepsilon''}_{\max}(X|YZ) + \mathsf{H}^{\varepsilon''}_{\min}(Y|Z) - \log(1/\varepsilon).$$

## 2.3 Information-Theoretic Reductions

### 2.3.1 Resources

Consider a set of *players* $\mathcal{P}$ who have access to a certain set of *resources* such as a public communication channel or a source of common randomness. Information theory (and cryptography) is concerned with the question of whether (and how) the players can use a given resource $\mathcal{R}$ (or a set of resources) in order to build the functionality of a new resource $\mathcal{S}$ (e.g., a secret communication channel).

On an abstract level, a resource is simply a *(random) system* [192] that can be accessed by each of the players in $\mathcal{P}$. For simplicity, we focus on the restricted class of resources that only take *one single* input $U_P$ from each of the players $P \in \mathcal{P}$ and output one single value $V_P$ to each of them. A resource for an $n$-player set $\mathcal{P} = \{1, \ldots, n\}$ is then fully specified by a conditional probability distribution $P_{V_1 \cdots V_n | U_1 \cdots U_n}$. (If the resource does not give an output to player $P$, $V_P$ is defined to be a constant, which we denote by $\perp$).

For the following, we restrict our considerations to situations with three players and call them *Alice*, *Bob*, and *Eve*. Accordingly, we use the letters $A$, $B$, and $E$ to denote the players' inputs and $X$, $Y$, and $Z$ for the corresponding outputs. Typically, Alice and Bob will take the role of *honest parties* (which means that they follow a specified protocol), whereas Eve is an *adversary* who might behave arbitrarily. We will use the convention that if no adversary is present, then $E := \perp$.

Let us have a look at some examples of resources, specified by a conditional probability distribution $P_{XYZ|ABE}$.

*Example 2.1.* An *authentic public ($\ell$-bit) channel taking input from Alice*, denoted $\mathsf{Auth}_\ell^{A \to B}$, is a resource $P_{XYZ|ABE}$ whose outputs $X$, $Y$, and $Z$ simply take the value of the input $A$. Formally, for any $a \in \{0,1\}^\ell$,

$$P_{XYZ|ABE}(x, y, z, a, b, e) = \begin{cases} 1 & \text{if } x = y = z = a \\ 0 & \text{otherwise.} \end{cases}$$

Similarly, one can define an *authentic public two-way channel* $\mathsf{Auth}_\ell^{A \leftrightarrow B}$.

*Example 2.2.* An *authentic secret ($\ell$-bit) channel from Alice to Bob*, denoted $\mathsf{Sec}_\ell^{A \to B}$, is a resource $P_{XYZ|ABE}$ whose output $Y$ takes the value of the input $A$, whereas the output $Z$ is constant. Formally, for any $a \in \{0,1\}^\ell$,

$$P_{XYZ|ABE}(x, y, z, a, b, e) = \begin{cases} 1 & \text{if } y = a \text{ and } x = z = \perp \\ 0 & \text{otherwise.} \end{cases}$$

*Example 2.3.* A *source of correlated randomness (with distribution $P_{XYZ}$)*, denoted $\mathsf{Source}(P_{XYZ})$, is a resource $P_{XYZ|ABE}$ whose outputs $X$, $Y$, and $Z$ are jointly distributed according to $P_{XYZ}$ (independently of the inputs). Formally,
$$P_{XYZ|ABE}(x, y, z, a, b, e) := P_{XYZ}(x, y, z) .$$

*Example 2.4.* A *common secret key (of length $\ell$)*, denoted $\mathsf{SK}_\ell$, is a source of correlated randomness $\mathsf{Source}(P_{XYZ})$, where $X = Y$ are uniformly distributed over $\{0,1\}^\ell$ and $Z$ is a constant. Formally,

$$P_{XYZ|ABE}(x, y, z, a, b, e) = \begin{cases} 2^{-\ell} & \text{if } x = y \in \{0,1\}^\ell \text{ and } z = \perp \\ 0 & \text{otherwise.} \end{cases}$$

*Example 2.5.* A *unreliable common secret key (of length $\ell$)*, denoted $\mathsf{SK}_\ell^{AB}$, is a resource $P_{XYZ|ABE}$ such that the following holds: If $E = \perp$, then the behavior of the resource is the same as for a common secret key $\mathsf{SK}_\ell$. If $E \neq \perp$, then

$X = Y = Z = \bot$. In other words, whenever Alice and Bob get a key, then this key is guaranteed to be secure (i.e., unknown to Eve). However, Eve might cause the resource to simply output $\bot$. Formally,

$$P_{XYZ|ABE}(x,y,z,a,b,e) = \begin{cases} 2^{-\ell} & \text{if } x = y \in \{0,1\}^\ell, \, z = \bot, \text{ and } e = \bot \\ 1 & \text{if } x = y = z = \bot \text{ and } e \neq \bot \\ 0 & \text{otherwise.} \end{cases}$$

*Example 2.6.* An *asymmetric secret key (of length $\ell$) with security for Alice*, denoted $\mathsf{SK}_\ell^A$, is a resource $P_{XYZ|ABE}$ such that the following holds: If $E = \bot$, then the behavior of the resource is the same as for a common secret key $\mathsf{SK}_\ell$. If $E \neq \bot$, then $Y = E$ and $X = Z = \bot$. In other words, whenever Alice gets a key, then it is also known to Bob and secret. However, Eve might cause the resource to give an arbitrary value (chosen by her) to Bob, but this will be detected by Alice. Formally,

$$P_{XYZ|ABE}(x,y,z,a,b,e) = \begin{cases} 2^{-\ell} & \text{if } x = y \in \{0,1\}^\ell, \, z = \bot, \text{ and } e = \bot \\ 1 & \text{if } y = e \text{ and } x = z = \bot \\ 0 & \text{otherwise.} \end{cases}$$

Note that a unreliable common secret key (Example 2.5) models what quantum key distribution (QKD) achieves (using an insecure quantum channel and an authentic classical channel). As long as the adversary is passive, Alice and Bob will get a secret key. On the other hand, Eve might intercept the quantum communication between Alice and Bob, but any severe attack would be detected (with high probability), in which case, no key is generated (see [232] for more details on security definitions in quantum cryptography).

### Distance Between Resources

In order to compare resources, we will need a notion of distance between two resources. For cryptographic applications, *the* natural distance measure is the *distinguishing advantage*, which is the basis of the following definition.

**Definition 2.2.** *Two resources $\mathcal{R}$ and $\mathcal{S}$ are said to be $\varepsilon$-close, denoted $\mathcal{R} \overset{\varepsilon}{\approx} \mathcal{S}$, if*

$$\Pr[\mathcal{D}(\mathcal{R}) = 0] - \Pr[\mathcal{D}(\mathcal{S}) = 0] \leq \varepsilon$$

*for any system $\mathcal{D}$ that interacts with $\mathcal{R}$ (or $\mathcal{S}$) and gives a binary output $\mathcal{D}(\mathcal{R})$ ($\mathcal{D}(\mathcal{S})$).*

This distance measure has an intuitive interpretation. If two resources $\mathcal{R}$ and $\mathcal{S}$ are $\varepsilon$-close, then they can be considered equal except with probability (at most) $\varepsilon$.

### Using Resources in Parallel

Given two resources $\mathcal{R}$ and $\mathcal{S}$, we denote by $\mathcal{R} \times \mathcal{S}$ the resource that provides both the functionality of $\mathcal{R}$ and $\mathcal{S}$ in parallel. For example, in the three-party case, $\mathsf{Auth}^{A \to B} \times \mathsf{Source}(P_{XYZ})$ describes a situation in which Alice and Bob have access to an authentic public channel (from Alice to Bob) *and* a source of correlated randomness (with distribution $P_{XYZ}$).

### 2.3.2 Programs and Protocols

Given a resource $\mathcal{R}$, a player $P$ can interact with $\mathcal{R}$ by choosing inputs $U_P$ and processing its outputs $V_P$. Technically, the way a player $P$ uses $\mathcal{R}$ can be described as a random system $\pi_P$ that starts with some input $X'_P$, then interacts with $\mathcal{R}$, and eventually generates an output $Y'_P$. In the following, we call $\pi_P$ a *program (for player $P$)*. Applying a program $\pi_P$ to a resource $\mathcal{R}$ naturally defines a new resource, which we denote by $\pi_P(\mathcal{R})$. More generally, if players $P_1, \ldots, P_k$ apply programs $\pi_{P_1}, \ldots, \pi_{P_k}$ to $\mathcal{R}$, we denote the resulting resource by $\pi_{P_1} \circ \cdots \circ \pi_{P_k}(\mathcal{R})$. Note that because all programs act on different inputs/outputs of $\mathcal{R}$, the order in which the programs are written is irrelevant.

### 2.3.3 Realizing Resources

For the following definition, we again restrict to the three-party case with two honest players (Alice and Bob) and a malicious player (Eve). A pair of programs $(\pi_A, \pi_B)$ for Alice and Bob is called a *protocol*. Moreover, we denote by $\perp_E$ the program for Eve that inputs $\perp$ to the resource and outputs $\perp$.

**Definition 2.3.** *Let $\mathcal{R}$ and $\mathcal{S}$ be resources and let $\pi = (\pi_A, \pi_B)$ be a protocol. We say that $\pi$ $\varepsilon$-realizes $\mathcal{S}$ from $\mathcal{R}$, denoted*

$$\mathcal{R} \xrightarrow{\pi}_\varepsilon \mathcal{S}$$

*if the following holds:*

- $\pi_A \circ \pi_B \circ \perp_E (\mathcal{R}) \overset{\varepsilon}{\approx} \perp_E (\mathcal{S})$.
- *There exists a program $\tau_E$ for Eve such that $\pi_A \circ \pi_B(\mathcal{R}) \overset{\varepsilon}{\approx} \tau_E(\mathcal{S})$.*

Note that the definition imposes two conditions. The first corresponds to a situation in which the adversary is passive. In this case, Alice and Bob apply their programs $\pi_A$ and $\pi_B$ to the resource $\mathcal{R}$, whereas Eve does nothing. The resulting resource should then be a good approximation of $\mathcal{S}$ where, again, Eve does nothing.

The second condition of the definition corresponds to a situation in which the adversary is active. In this case, it should be guaranteed that Eve could run some simulator[3] $\tau_E$ on $\mathcal{S}$ that would give her the same information as she would get when accessing $\mathcal{R}$.

The relation $\longrightarrow$ is transitive in the following sense.

**Lemma 2.4.** *Given two protocols $\Pi$ and $\Pi'$ such that $\mathcal{R} \xrightarrow{\Pi}_\varepsilon \mathcal{S}$ and $\mathcal{S} \xrightarrow{\Pi'}_{\varepsilon'} \mathcal{T}$, then the sequential concatenation $\Pi' \circ \Pi$ satisfies $\mathcal{R} \xrightarrow{\Pi' \circ \Pi}_{\varepsilon+\varepsilon'} \mathcal{T}$.*

In cryptography, this transitivity is also called *composability* (most notably in the frameworks for computational cryptography proposed in [51, 225]).

### 2.3.4 Examples Protocols

*Example 2.7.* A *one-time pad*, denoted OTP, is a protocol that (perfectly) realizes a secret channel using an authentic channel and a secret key (see Section 2.1.2); that is,

$$\mathsf{Auth}_\ell^{A\to B} \times \mathsf{SK}_\ell \xrightarrow{\mathsf{OTP}}_0 \mathsf{Sec}_\ell^{A\to B} . \tag{2.1}$$

The protocol $\mathsf{OTP} = (\pi_A, \pi_B)$ is defined as follows: $\pi_A$ takes as input $A'$, computes the exclusive OR (XOR) between $A'$ and the secret key, and then gives the result as input to the public communication channel. $\pi_B$ computes the XOR between the output of the public channel and the key and outputs the result.

To prove (2.1), we need to verify that the two criteria of Definition 2.3 are satisfied. For the first, it suffices to check that the resources on both sides of the identity

$$\pi_A \circ \pi_B \circ \perp_E (\mathsf{Auth}_\ell^{A\to B} \times \mathsf{SK}_\ell) = \perp_E (\mathsf{Sec}_\ell^{A\to B})$$

are equal. In fact, both of them take an $\ell$-bit input from Alice and output the value of this input to Bob, whereas Eve gets a constant.

The second criterion (for $\varepsilon = 0$) reads

$$\pi_A \circ \pi_B (\mathsf{Auth}_\ell^{A\to B} \times \mathsf{SK}_\ell) = \tau_E(\mathsf{Sec}_\ell^{A\to B}),$$

where $\tau_E$ is some appropriately chosen program. Note that Eve's output of the resource defined by the left-hand side of this equality is simply the XOR between the message and the key. This value is uniformly distributed and independent of the message. It thus suffices to define $\tau_E$ as a program that simply outputs some uniformly distributed $\ell$-bit string.

*Example 2.8.* The following protocol $\Pi$ uses a public authentic channel to transform an asymmetric secret key with security for Alice into a unreliable common secret key; that is,

$$\mathsf{SK}_\ell^A \times \mathsf{Auth}_1^{A\to B} \xrightarrow{\Pi}_0 \mathsf{SK}_\ell^{AB}.$$

---

[3] The concept of simulators in cryptographic security definitions has been introduced in [135].

Let $X$ and $Y$ be the outputs of $\mathsf{SK}_\ell^A$ on Alice's and Bob's side, respectively. The protocol $\Pi = (\pi_A, \pi_B)$ is then defined as follows: Alice's program $\pi_A$ uses the public channel to announce whether $X = \bot$ and outputs $X$. Bob's program $\pi_B$ outputs $\bot$ if $X = \bot$ and $Y$ otherwise.

*Example 2.9.* A *hashing* or *privacy amplification protocol* HA is a protocol that uses a source of correlated randomness and an authentic public channel to realize a secret key (see Section 2.4.5). Formally,[4]

$$\mathsf{Source}(P_{XYZ}) \times \mathsf{Auth}_\infty^{A \to B} \xrightarrow{\ \mathsf{HA}\ }_\varepsilon \mathsf{SK}_\ell,$$

for any distribution $P_{XYZ}$ with $X = Y$ and $\mathsf{H}_{\min}^{\varepsilon'}(X|Z) \geq \ell + 2\log(1/(\varepsilon - \varepsilon'))$. The protocol HA $= (\pi_A, \pi_B)$ is defined as follows: $\pi_A$ chooses at random a function $f$ from a two-universal (see Definition 2.9) set of functions from $X$ to a string of size $\ell$, sends a description of $f$ over the channel, and outputs $f(X)$. $\pi_B$ outputs $f(Y)$.

The proof of the above statement follows immediately from the security of privacy amplification [25, 27, 152] (see Corollary 2.3). This example will be further elaborated on in Section 2.4.5.

*Example 2.10.* An *information reconciliation protocol* IR uses a public channel to transform a source of correlated randomness $P_{XYZ}$ into another source of correlated randomness $P_{X'Y'Z'}$ such that $X' = Y'$ in such a way that the decrease of Eve's uncertainty on Alice's data is minimal (see Section 2.4.4).[5] Formally,

$$\mathsf{Source}(P_{XYZ}) \times \mathsf{Auth}_\infty^{A \to B} \xrightarrow{\ \mathsf{IR}\ }_\varepsilon P_{X'Y'Z'},$$

where $X' = Y'$ and $\mathsf{H}_{\min}^{\varepsilon' + \varepsilon''}(X'|Z') > \mathsf{H}_{\min}^{\varepsilon'}(X|Z) - \mathsf{H}_{\max}(X|Y) - \log(1/\varepsilon\varepsilon'')$ (see Corollary 2.2). In order to achieve this, Alice sends some error-correcting information $C$ to Bob that, together with his knowledge $Y$, allows him to guess Alice's value $X$. A conceptually simple way to generate $C$ is by two-universal hashing of $X$ (in practice, one typically uses error-correcting codes that have more structure in order to allow computationally efficient decoding on Bob's side).

More precisely, the protocol IR works a follows: Alice's program $\pi_A$ chooses at random a function $f$ from a two-universal set of hash functions that maps $X$ to a string of length roughly $\mathsf{H}_{\max}(X|Y) + \log(1/\varepsilon)$. A description of $f$ as well as $C = f(X)$ is then sent to Bob using the public channel. Moreover, Alice outputs $X' := X$. Bob's program $\pi_B$, upon receiving $C$, outputs some string $Y'$ that satisfies $P_{X|Y}(Y'|Y) > 0$ (i.e., has non-zero probability from his point of view) and $f(Y') = C$ (i.e., is compatible with $C$). For information reconciliation, see also Section 2.4.4.

---

[4] $\mathsf{Auth}_\infty^{A \to B}$ denotes an authentic public channel for arbitrarily long messages.

[5] A *secure sketch* as defined in [91] can be seen as a special case of an information reconciliation protocol where the *sketching* and the *recovery procedure* correspond to Alice's and Bob's programs, respectively.

### 2.3.5 Independent and Identically Distributed Resources

In information-theoretic cryptography, one often assumes that Alice and Bob can use many independent realizations of a given resource (e.g., many independently distributed pairs of correlated random values $(X, Y)$) in order to produce many independent realizations of another resource (e.g., a secret-key bit). Under this so-called *i.i.d. (independent and identically distributed) assumption*, one can study asymptotic quantities such as *key rates*.

**Definition 2.4.** *An asymptotic protocol $\Pi$ is a sequence of pairs $(\Pi_k, \tau_k)$ where, for any $k \in \mathbb{N}$, $\Pi_k$ is a protocol and $\tau_k \in \mathbb{N}$. The rate of $\Pi$ is defined by*

$$\text{rate}(\Pi) := \lim_{k \to \infty} \frac{k}{\tau_k} \ .$$

**Definition 2.5.** *We say that an asymptotic protocol $\{(\Pi_k, \tau_k)\}_{k \in \mathbb{N}}$ realizes $\mathcal{S}$ from $\mathcal{R}$, denoted*

$$\mathcal{R} \overset{\Pi_k, \tau_k}{\Longrightarrow} \mathcal{S},$$

*if there exists a zero sequence $\{\varepsilon_k\}_{k \in \mathbb{N}}$ (i.e., $\lim_{k \to \infty} \varepsilon_k = 0$) such that, for any $k \in \mathbb{N}$,*

$$\mathcal{R}^{\times \tau_k} \xrightarrow[\varepsilon_k]{\Pi_k} \mathcal{S}^{\times k}.$$

See below for examples of asymptotic protocols.

**Definition 2.6.** *Let $\Pi = \{(\Pi_k, \tau_k)\}_{k \in \mathbb{N}}$ and $\Pi' = \{(\Pi'_k, \tau'_k)\}_{k \in \mathbb{N}}$ be asymptotic protocols. The concatenation $\bar{\Pi} := \Pi' \circ \Pi$ is then defined by the protocol $\{\bar{\Pi}_k, \bar{\tau}_k\}_{k \in \mathbb{N}}$ where $\bar{\Pi}_k := \Pi'_{\tau_k} \circ \Pi_k$ and $\bar{\tau}_k := \tau'_{\tau_k}$.*

**Definition 2.7.** *Let $\mathcal{R}$ and $\mathcal{S}$ be resources. The rate of $\mathcal{R} \Longrightarrow \mathcal{S}$ is defined by*

$$\text{rate}(\mathcal{R} \Longrightarrow \mathcal{S}) := \max_{\Pi} \text{rate}(\Pi),$$

*where the maximum ranges over all protocols $\Pi$ such that $\mathcal{R} \overset{\Pi}{\Longrightarrow} \mathcal{S}$.*

It is straightforward to prove that composability also holds for this asymptotic definition:

**Lemma 2.5.** *Given two asymptotic protocols $\Pi$ and $\Pi'$ such that $\mathcal{R} \overset{\Pi}{\Longrightarrow} \mathcal{S}$ and $\mathcal{S} \overset{\Pi'}{\Longrightarrow} \mathcal{T}$; then the sequential concatenation $\pi' \circ \pi$ satisfies*

$$\mathcal{R} \overset{\Pi' \circ \Pi}{\Longrightarrow} \mathcal{T}.$$

*Moreover, $\text{rate}(\mathcal{R} \Longrightarrow \mathcal{T}) \geq \text{rate}(\mathcal{R} \Longrightarrow \mathcal{S}) \cdot \text{rate}(\mathcal{S} \Longrightarrow \mathcal{T})$.*

## 2.4 Turning Correlated Randomness into Keys

### 2.4.1 Generic One-Way Key Agreement

A generic way to generate a key from weakly correlated and only partially secure randomness is to employ an error-correction protocol and then apply privacy amplification. This process only requires communication in one direction (e.g., from Alice to Bob). This simple protocol for one-way key agreement is also used in more complex key-agreement protocols (including QKD protocols) as a last step.[6]

**Theorem 2.2.** *Let $a, b \in \mathbb{N}$ and $\varepsilon, \varepsilon', \varepsilon'' > 0$ be fixed and let $\ell := a - b - 3\log(2/\varepsilon)$. Then there exists a protocol* $\mathsf{KA} = \mathsf{KA}_{a,b}$ *(called one-way key-agreement protocol) such that*

$$\mathsf{Source}(P_{XYZ}) \times \mathsf{Auth}_\infty^{A \to B} \xrightarrow{\mathsf{KA}}_{\bar{\varepsilon}} \mathsf{SK}_\ell ,  \qquad (2.2)$$

*for any $P_{XYZ}$ such that $\mathsf{H}_{\min}^{\varepsilon'}(X|Z) \geq a$ and $\mathsf{H}_{\max}^{\varepsilon''}(X|Y) \leq b$, and $\bar{\varepsilon} \geq 2\varepsilon + \varepsilon' + \varepsilon''$. In particular, for any distribution $P_{XYZ}$ with*

$$\mathsf{H}_{\min}^{\varepsilon'}(X|Z) - \mathsf{H}_{\max}^{\varepsilon''}(X|Y) \geq \ell + 3\log(2/\varepsilon),$$

*there exists a protocol* $\mathsf{KA}$ *satisfying (2.2).*

Note that a very similar result also holds in a quantum world, where Eve's information is encoded into the state of a quantum system [232].

*Proof.* The protocol $\mathsf{KA}$ can be defined as the concatenation of the information reconciliation protocol $\mathsf{IR}$ and the hashing protocol $\mathsf{HA}$ as in Examples 2.10 and 2.9, respectively. The assertion then follows from the composition lemma (Lemma 2.4). □

### 2.4.2 Independent Repetitions

**Definition 2.8.** *The* secret-key rate *of a tripartite probability distribution $P_{XYZ}$ is defined by*

$$S(P_{XYZ}) := \mathrm{rate}(\mathsf{Source}(P_{XYZ}) \times \mathsf{Auth}_\infty^{A \leftrightarrow B} \xRightarrow{\mathsf{KA}} \mathsf{SK}_1).$$

*Similarly, the* one-way secret-key rate *is*

$$S_\to(P_{XYZ}) := \mathrm{rate}(\mathsf{Source}(P_{XYZ}) \times \mathsf{Auth}_\infty^{A \to B} \xRightarrow{\mathsf{KA}} \mathsf{SK}_1).$$

---

[6] A *fuzzy extractors* as defined in [91] can generally be seen as a one-way key-agreement protocol where the *generation* and the *reproduction* procedure correspond to Alice's and Bob's programs, respectively. The *helper string* generated by the generation procedure of a secure sketch corresponds to the message sent from Alice to Bob in a one-way key-agreement protocol.

The following lemma gives some basic properties of the secret-key rate.

**Lemma 2.6.** *Let $X$, $Y$, and $Z$ be random variables with joint distribution $P_{XYZ}$. Then the following hold:*

1. *Local operations by Alice can only decrease the rate: $S(P_{XYZ}) \geq S(P_{X'YZ})$ for any $X'$ such that $(Y, Z) \to X \to X'$ is a Markov chain.*
2. *Local operations by Bob can only decrease the rate: $S(P_{XYZ}) \geq S(P_{XY'Z})$ for any $Y'$ such that $(X, Z) \to Y \to Y'$ is a Markov chain.*
3. *Local operations by Eve can only increase the rate: $S(P_{XYZ}) \leq S(P_{XYZ'})$ for any $Z'$ such that $(X, Y) \to Z \to Z'$ is a Markov chain.*
4. *Giving information $U$ to Eve can only decrease the rate by at most the entropy of $U$: $S(P_{XYZ}) \leq S(P_{XYZU}) + H(U|Z)$ for any random variable $U$.*

The following is an immediate consequence of Theorem 2.2 and Lemma 2.1.

**Corollary 2.1.** *The one-way secret-key rate is lower bounded by*

$$S_{\to}(P_{XYZ}) \geq H(X|Z) - H(X|Y). \tag{2.3}$$

The one-way key-agreement protocol presented above is not optimal. In fact, there are distributions $P_{XYZ}$ where $H(X|Z) - H(X|Y)$ equals zero but $S(P_{XYZ})$ is still positive, as the following example illustrates.

*Example 2.11.* Let $X$ be a uniformly distributed random bit, let $Y$ be the output of a binary symmetric channel with noise $\delta$ on input $X$, and let $Z$ be the output of an erasure channel with erasure probability $\delta'$ on input $X$. Let $\delta := h^{-1}(\frac{1}{2}) \approx 0.11$ and $\delta' := \frac{1}{2}$. Then

$$H(X|Z) - H(X|Y) = 0.$$

Consider now the random variable $X'$ obtained by sending $X$ through a binary symmetric channel with noise $\mu$. Then, for any $\mu > 0$,

$$H(X'|Z) - H(X'|Y) > 0$$

and, hence, $S(P_{X'YZ}) > 0$. It thus follows from statement 1 of Lemma 2.6 that $S(P_{XYZ}) > 0$.

### 2.4.3 Advantage Distillation

There exist situations in which the expression in (2.3) is negative, but key-agreement is—somewhat surprisingly—nevertheless possible. An example is the "special satellite scenario" [196], where all involved parties have conditionally independent noisy versions of a binary signal. In this case, key-agreement has been shown possible in *all non-trivial scenarios* (i.e., even when the information the adversary obtains about this signal is arbitrarily larger than the legitimate parties).

In this case, however, *two-way communication* is necessary. A concrete example of such an *advantage-distillation protocol* is the following: Alice and Bob repeatedly compare parities of bits publicly and continue the process only in case of equal parities. Intuitively speaking, this allows them to use the authentic channel for locating positions where an error is less likely, until they finally end up in a situation where they know more about each other's pieces of information than the adversary (although the latter also learns the public communication of the protocol).

### 2.4.4 Information Reconciliation

During advantage distillation, the partners Alice and Bob compute (possibly distinct) strings $S_A$ and $S_B$, respectively, about which the adversary also has some information. At the end of the key-agreement protocol however, Alice's and Bob's strings must be equal and highly secure, both with overwhelming probability. The information reconciliation phase consists of interactive error correction and establishes the first of these two conditions.

After advantage distillation, Bob has more information about Alice's string than Eve has, and after information reconciliation, Bob should exactly know Alice's string. (A more general condition would be that after information reconciliation, Alice and Bob share a string that is equally long as $S_A$ and $S_B$.) This leads to a lower bound on the amount of error-correction information $C$ that must be exchanged; namely, Bob must know $S_A$ completely with overwhelming probability when given $S_B$ and $C$. Hence, the amount of error-correction information is at least the uncertainty of $S_A$ given $S_B$. On the other hand, the uncertainty of $S_A$ from Eve's viewpoint can as well be reduced by $\mathsf{H}(C)$ in the worst case when Eve learns $C$ (see Fig. 2.6).

Lemma 2.7 and Corollary 2.2 link information reconciliation to the conditional smooth max-entropy of Alice's information, given Bob's.

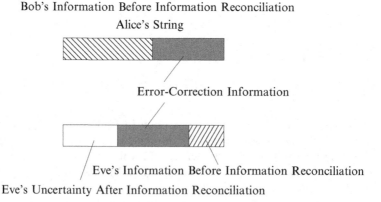

**Fig. 2.6.** The effect of information leaked during information reconciliation.

**Definition 2.9.** *A class $\mathcal{H}$ of functions $h$ mapping a set $\mathcal{A}$ to a set $\mathcal{B}$ is called two-universal if for all $x, y \in \mathcal{A}$, $x \neq y$, we have*

$$\mathrm{Prob}_{\,h \in_r \mathcal{H}}[h(x) = h(y)] = \frac{1}{|\mathcal{B}|} \; ,$$

*where $h \in_r \mathcal{H}$ stands for the fact that $h$ is chosen randomly in $\mathcal{H}$ according to the uniform distribution. In other words, a function that is chosen randomly from a two-universal class behaves like a completely random function with respect to collisions.*

An example of a two-universal class of functions, mapping $\{0,1\}^n$ to $\{0,1\}^r$, of cardinality $2^{n \cdot r}$ are the *linear* functions.

**Lemma 2.7.** *Let $X$ be a random variable on $\mathcal{X}$, let $\mathcal{E}$ be an event, and let $F$ be chosen at random (independently of $X$) from a two-universal family of hash functions from $\mathcal{X}$ to $\mathcal{U}$. Then there exists a function $d_F$ depending on $F$ such that*

$$\Pr\big[\mathcal{E} \wedge (d_F(F(X)) \neq X)\big] \leq \frac{|\mathcal{X}_\mathcal{E}|}{|\mathcal{U}|},$$

*where $\mathcal{X}_\mathcal{E} := \{x \in \mathcal{X} : P_{\mathcal{E}X}(x) > 0\}$.*

*Proof.* For any hash function $F$, define $\mathcal{D}_F(u) := \mathcal{X}_\mathcal{E} \cap F^{-1}(u)$. Moreover, let $d_F$ be any function from $\mathcal{U}$ to $\mathcal{X}$ such that $d_F(u) \in \mathcal{D}_F(u)$ if $\mathcal{D}_F(u) \neq \emptyset$.

Observe that whenever the event $\mathcal{E}$ occurs, then $X \in \mathcal{X}_\mathcal{E}$ and thus $X \in \mathcal{D}_F(F(X))$. It thus suffices to show that $\mathcal{D}_F(F(X))$ contains no other element, except with probability $|\mathcal{X}_\mathcal{E}|/|\mathcal{U}|$; that is,

$$\Pr\big[|\mathcal{D}_F(F(X))| > 1\big] \leq \frac{|\mathcal{X}_\mathcal{E}|}{|\mathcal{U}|} \; . \tag{2.4}$$

By the definition of two-universality, $\Pr\big[F(x) = F(x')\big] \leq 1/|\mathcal{U}|$, for any $x \neq x'$. Consequently, by the union bound, for any fixed $x \in \mathcal{X}$,

$$\Pr\big[\exists x' \in \mathcal{X}_\mathcal{E} : (x \neq x') \wedge (F(x) = F(x'))\big] \leq \frac{|\mathcal{X}_\mathcal{E}|}{|\mathcal{U}|} \; .$$

This implies (2.4) and thus concludes the proof.

**Corollary 2.2.** *Let $X$ and $Y$ be random variables and let $F$ be chosen at random from a two-universal family of functions from $\mathcal{X}$ to $\mathcal{U}$, where $|\mathcal{U}| = 2^\ell$. Then there exists a function $d_F$ depending on $F$ such that, for any $\varepsilon \geq 0$,*

$$\Pr\big[d_F(F(X), Y) \neq X\big] \leq 2^{-(\ell - \mathsf{H}^\varepsilon_{\max}(X|Y))} + \varepsilon.$$

*Remark 2.1.* In order to ensure that errors are corrected except with probability $\bar{\varepsilon}$, it suffices to use a hash function with output length $\ell$ such that

$$\ell \geq \mathsf{H}^\varepsilon_{\max}(X|Y) + \log\left(\frac{1}{\bar{\varepsilon} - \varepsilon}\right),$$

for some $\varepsilon < \bar{\varepsilon}$.

*Proof (of Corollary 2.2).* Let $\mathcal{E}$ be an event with $\Pr[\mathcal{E}] = 1 - \varepsilon$ such that

$$\mathsf{H}_{\max}(\mathcal{E}X|Y) = \mathsf{H}_{\max}^{\varepsilon}(X|Y). \tag{2.5}$$

Let $\mathcal{Y}$ be the range of the random variable $Y$. By Lemma 2.7, there exists a function $d_F$ from $\mathcal{U} \times \mathcal{Y}$ to $\mathcal{X}$ such that, for any $y \in \mathcal{Y}$,

$$\Pr\big[\mathcal{E} \wedge (d_F(F(X), Y) \neq X)\big|Y = y\big] \leq \frac{|\{x \in \mathcal{X} : P_{\mathcal{E}XY}(x, y) > 0\}|}{|\mathcal{U}|}$$

$$= 2^{\mathsf{H}_{\max}(\mathcal{E}X|Y) - \ell}.$$

Moreover, we have

$$\Pr\big[d_F(F(X), Y) \neq X\big] \leq \Pr\big[\mathcal{E} \wedge (d_F(F(X), Y) \neq X)\big] + (1 - \Pr[\mathcal{E}])$$

$$\leq \max_y \Pr\big[\mathcal{E} \wedge (d_F(F(X), Y) \neq X)\big|Y = y\big] + \varepsilon.$$

Combining this with the above and (2.5) concludes the proof.

### 2.4.5 Privacy Amplification

Privacy amplification is the art of shrinking a partially secure string $S$ to a highly secret string $S'$ by public discussion. Hereby, the information of the adversary about $S$ can consist of physical bits, of parities thereof, or other types of information (see Fig. 2.7).

The following questions related to privacy amplification were studied and answered in [25, 27]. What is a good technique of computing $S'$ from $S$? What is the possible length of $S'$, depending on this shrinking technique and on the adversary's (type and amount of) information about $S$?

It is quite clear that the best technique would be to compute $S'$ (of length $r$) from the $n$-bit string $S$ by applying a random function $f : \{0,1\}^n \to \{0,1\}^r$. However, Alice and Bob would have to exchange $r2^n$ bits of information to

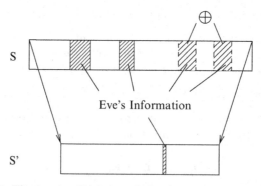

**Fig. 2.7.** Eliminating Eve's knowledge by privacy amplification.

agree on such a function. On the other hand, there exist relatively small classes of functions with "random-like" properties. Examples are so-called *universal classes* of hash functions, which turned out to be useful for privacy amplification.

We analyze the following type of privacy amplification protocols. First, Alice chooses a random function $h$ from a fixed two-universal class $\mathcal{H}$ of hash functions mapping $n$-bit strings to $r$-bit strings for some $r$ to be determined and sends (the description of) $h$ publicly to Bob (i.e., also Eve learns $h$). Then Alice and Bob both compute $S' := h(S)$.

The following is a slightly generalized version of the so-called *Leftover Hash Lemma* [25, 152].

**Lemma 2.8.** *Let $X$ be a random variable on $\mathcal{X}$, let $\mathcal{E}$ be an event, and let $F$ be chosen at random (and independently of $X$) from a two-universal family of functions from $\mathcal{X}$ to $\mathcal{U}$. Then*

$$\|P_{\mathcal{E}F(X)F} - P_{\mathcal{E}U} \times P_F\|_1 \leq \sqrt{|\mathcal{U}| \max_x P_{\mathcal{E}X}(x)} ,$$

*where $P_{\mathcal{E}U}$ is defined by $P_{\mathcal{E}U}(v) := \Pr[\mathcal{E}]/|\mathcal{U}|$, for any $u \in \mathcal{U}$.*

*Proof.* Using the Cauchy-Schwarz inequality and Jensen's inequality, we find

$$\|P_{\mathcal{E}F(X)F} - P_{\mathcal{E}U} \times P_F\|_1 = \mathbb{E}_F\big[\|P_{\mathcal{E}F(X)} - P_{\mathcal{E}U}\|_1\big]$$
$$\leq \mathbb{E}_F\big[\sqrt{|\mathcal{U}| \cdot \|P_{\mathcal{E}F(X)} - P_{\mathcal{E}U}\|_2^2}\big]$$
$$\leq \sqrt{|\mathcal{U}| \cdot \mathbb{E}_F\big[\|P_{\mathcal{E}F(X)} - P_{\mathcal{E}U}\|_2^2\big]} . \qquad (2.6)$$

The $L_2$-norm under the square root can be rewritten as

$$\|P_{\mathcal{E}F(X)} - P_{\mathcal{E}U}\|_2^2 = \|P_{F(X)\mathcal{E}}\|_2^2 - \frac{\Pr[\mathcal{E}]^2}{|\mathcal{U}|}, \qquad (2.7)$$

where

$$\|P_{\mathcal{E}F(X)}\|_2^2 = \sum_u P_{\mathcal{E}F(X)}(u)^2$$
$$= \sum_u \sum_{\substack{x \in F^{-1}(u) \\ x' \in F^{-1}(u)}} P_{\mathcal{E}X}(x) P_{\mathcal{E}X}(x')$$
$$= \sum_{x,x'} P_{\mathcal{E}X}(x) P_{\mathcal{E}X}(x') \delta_{F(x),F(x')}$$
$$\leq \sum_x P_{\mathcal{E}X}(x)^2 + \sum_{x \neq x'} P_{\mathcal{E}X}(x) P_{\mathcal{E}X}(x') \delta_{F(x),F(x')} .$$

Because $F$ is chosen from a two-universal family of functions with range $\mathcal{U}$, we have $\mathbb{E}_F[\delta_{F(x),F(x')}] \leq 1/|\mathcal{U}|$, for any $x \neq x'$. Hence,

$$\mathbb{E}_F\left[\|P_{F(X)}\|_2^2\right] = \sum_x P_{\mathcal{E}X}(x)^2 + \frac{\Pr[\mathcal{E}]^2}{|\mathcal{U}|} \leq \max_x P_{\mathcal{E}X}(x) + \frac{\Pr[\mathcal{E}]^2}{|\mathcal{U}|}\,.$$

Combining this with (2.6) and (2.7) concludes the proof.

**Corollary 2.3.** *Let $X$ and $Z$ be random variables and let $F$ be chosen at random from a two-universal family of functions from $\mathcal{X}$ to $\mathcal{U}$, where $|\mathcal{U}| = 2^\ell$. Then, for any $\varepsilon \geq 0$,*

$$\|P_{F(X)ZF} - P_U \times P_Z \times P_F\|_1 \leq 2^{-(\mathsf{H}^\varepsilon_{\min}(X|Z) - \ell)/2} + 2\varepsilon,$$

*where $P_U$ is the uniform distribution on $\mathcal{U}$.*

*Remark 2.2.* Note that the distinguishing probability between a perfect key $U$ and the function output $F(X)$ is given by half the $L_1$-distance on the left-hand side of the corollary. Hence, in order to get an $\ell$-bit key that is $\bar{\varepsilon}$-indistinguishable from a perfect key, it suffices to ensure that

$$\mathsf{H}^\varepsilon_{\min}(X|Z) \geq \ell + 2\log(1/(\bar{\varepsilon} - \varepsilon))\,,$$

for some $\varepsilon < \bar{\varepsilon}$.

*Proof (of Corollary 2.3).* Let $\mathcal{E}$ be an event with $\Pr[\mathcal{E}] = 1 - \varepsilon$ such that

$$\mathsf{H}_{\min}(\mathcal{E}X|Z) = \mathsf{H}^\varepsilon_{\min}(X|Z)\,. \tag{2.8}$$

Then, by Lemma 2.8,

$$\|P_{\mathcal{E}F(X)F|Z=z} - \Pr(\mathcal{E}|Z=z)P_U \times P_F\|_1 \leq \sqrt{|\mathcal{U}| \max_x P_{\mathcal{E}X|Z=z}(x)}\,,$$

for any value $z$ of the random variable $Z$. Moreover, by the triangle inequality for the $L_1$-norm,

$$\|P_{F(X)F|Z=z} - P_U \times P_F\|_1$$
$$\leq \|P_{\mathcal{E}F(X)F|Z=z} - \Pr(\mathcal{E}|Z=z)P_U \times P_F\|_1 + 2(1 - \Pr[\mathcal{E}|Z=z]).$$

Hence,

$$\|P_{F(X)ZF} - P_U \times P_Z \times P_F\|_1 = \mathbb{E}_Z\left[\|P_{F(X)F|Z=z} - P_U \times P_F\|_1\right]$$
$$\leq \mathbb{E}_Z\left[\sqrt{|\mathcal{U}| \max_x P_{\mathcal{E}X|Z=z}(x)} + 2(1 - \Pr[\mathcal{E}|Z=z])\right]$$
$$\leq \sqrt{|\mathcal{U}| \max_{x,z} P_{\mathcal{E}X|Z=z}(x)} + 2\varepsilon$$
$$= \sqrt{2^{\ell - \mathsf{H}_{\min}(\mathcal{E}X|Z)}} + 2\varepsilon.$$

The assertion then follows from (2.8).

### 2.4.6 Protocol Monotones and Upper Bounds

The described protocol techniques lead to *lower* bounds on the quantity of interest, the secret-key rate $S$. One is, on the other hand, interested in *upper* bounds on $S$ and, ultimately, determining $S$ precisely; the latter, however, has been successfully done in trivial cases only in the two-way-communication setting.

#### Characterization of the One-Way Key Rate

In contrast to this, the *one-way* communication scenario has been completely solved [73].

**Lemma 2.9.** *Let $X$, $Y$, and $Z$ be random variables with joint distribution $P_{XYZ}$. Then*

$$S_\rightarrow(P_{XYZ}) = \sup_{(U,V)\leftarrow X\leftarrow(Y,Z)} \mathsf{H}(U|ZV) - \mathsf{H}(U|YV) \ .$$

#### General Properties of Upper Bounds

Before we discuss concrete upper bounds on $S$, we observe that any quantity that is a so-called *monotone* (i.e., cannot be increased by any protocol and has some additional properties described in Lemma 2.10).

**Lemma 2.10.** *Let $M(X,Y|Z) = M(P_{XYZ})$ be a real-valued quantity such that the following hold:*

1. *$M$ can only decrease under local operations; that is, $M(X,Y|Z) \geq M(X',Y|Z)$ if $(Y,Z) \rightarrow X \rightarrow X'$ is a Markov chain (and likewise for $Y$).*
2. *$M$ can only decrease if public communication is used; that is, $M(XC,Y|Z) \geq M(XC,YC|ZC)$, for any random variable $C$.*
3. *$M$ is asymptotically continuous (as a function of $P_{XYZ}$).*
4. *$M$ equals 1 for a one-key bit; that is, $M(P_{SS\perp}) = 1$ if $P_{SS\perp}$ denotes the distribution of two identical and uniformly distributed bits.*

*Then $M$ is an upper bound on the key rate; that is, $S(P_{XYZ}) \leq M(P_{XYZ})$.*

### 2.4.7 Intrinsic Information, Information of Formation, and a Gap

In this section, we propose two protocol monotones. The *information of formation* measures the amount of secret-key bits necessary to generate a certain partially secret correlation between Alice and Bob. The *intrinsic information*, on the other hand, measures, intuitively speaking, the correlation that two parties share and that is unaccessible to and indestructible by an adversary. Finally, we mention a result showing that an arbitrarily large gap can separate the secrecy required for constructing the distribution from the amount of extractable secrecy.

### Information of Formation

Instead of transforming weakly correlated and partially secure data into a secure key, one could also do the opposite [233].

**Definition 2.10.** *The* information of formation *(also called* key cost*) of a tripartite probability distribution $P_{XYZ}$ is defined by*

$$\mathbf{I}_{\mathrm{form}}(P_{XYZ}) := \mathrm{rate}(\mathsf{SK}_1 \times \mathsf{Auth}_\infty^{A \to B} \overset{\mathrm{Form}}{\Longrightarrow} \mathsf{Source}(P_{XYZ}))^{-1}.$$

It is easy to verify that the information of formation satisfies the assumptions of Lemma 2.10 (i.e., $S(P_{XYZ}) \leq \mathbf{I}_{\mathrm{form}}(P_{XYZ})$). Alternatively, the same conclusion can be obtained using Lemma 2.5.

### Intrinsic Information

It is straightforward to verify that the mutual information $\mathbf{I}(X; Y)$ as well as the conditional mutual information $\mathbf{I}(X; Y|Z)$ satisfy the assumptions of Lemma 2.10; that is, they are both upper bounds on the secret-key rate. The following definition is motivated by this observation.

**Definition 2.11.** *Let $X$, $Y$, and $Z$ be random variables with joint distribution $P_{XYZ}$. The* intrinsic information *is defined by*

$$\mathbf{I}(X; Y \downarrow Z) := \inf_{Z' \leftarrow Z \leftarrow (X,Y)} \mathbf{I}(X; Y|Z') \ .$$

Again, it is straightforward to verify that $\mathbf{I}(X; Y \downarrow Z)$ satisfies the assumptions of Lemma 2.10; that is, it is an upper bound on the secret-key rate, $S(P_{XYZ}) \leq \mathsf{I}(X; Y \downarrow Z)$. On the other hand, we have $\mathsf{I}(X; Y \downarrow Z) \leq \mathbf{I}_{\mathrm{form}}(P_{XYZ})$.

### The Gap

Interestingly, it has been shown [233] that the gap between $S$ and $\mathbf{I}_{\mathrm{form}}$ can be arbitrarily large, whereas it is still unknown whether there exists a classical analogue to *bound quantum entanglement* (i.e., undistillable entanglement): a distribution satisfying $S = 0$ and $\mathbf{I}_{\mathrm{form}} \neq 0$.

**Lemma 2.11.** *For any $\delta > 0$ there exists a probability distribution such that $S(P_{XYZ}) < \delta$, whereas $\mathbf{I}_{\mathrm{form}}(P_{XYZ}) \geq 1$.*

## 2.5 Secrecy from Completely Insecure Communication

So far in this chapter, we have considered scenarios where the channel connecting Alice and Bob is authentic. In this section, we show results demonstrating that unconditionally secure key agreement can even be possible from *completely* insecure communication, i.e., a channel over which the adversary has complete control. Clearly, she can always choose to *prevent* key agreement in this case, but it should not happen that Alice or Bob believe that key agreement was successful although it was not. We consider three special scenarios in this setting: Independent repetitions, privacy amplification, and general one-way-key agreement.

### 2.5.1 Independent Repetitions: An All-or-Nothing Result

In the scenario where a random experiment $P_{XYZ}$ is independently repeated a great number of times, an all-or-nothing result has been shown: Either key-agreement is possible at the same rate as in the authentic channel scenario, or completely impossible.

The *robust secret-key rate* $S^*(X;Y||Z)$ is the rate at which a key can be generated in this scenario:

$$S^*(P_{XYZ}) := \mathsf{rate}(\mathsf{Source}(P_{XYZ}) \times \mathsf{Chan}_\infty^{A \leftrightarrow B} \xrightarrow{\ \mathsf{KA}\ } \mathsf{SK}_1) \ .$$

Here, $\mathsf{Chan}_\infty^{A \leftrightarrow B}$ stands for a completely insecure bidirectional channel.

**Theorem 2.3 [191].** *If there exists a channel $P_{\overline{X}|Z}$ such that $P_{\overline{X}Y} = P_{XY}$ holds or a channel $P_{\overline{Y}|Z}$ such that $P_{X\overline{Y}} = P_{XY}$, then $S^*(P_{XYZ}) = 0$. Otherwise, $S^*(P_{XYZ}) = S(P_{XYZ})$.*

### 2.5.2 Privacy Amplification: Authentication Is for Free

In the special case of privacy amplification, it has been shown [234] that the loss of the communication channel's authenticity does not (substantially) decrease the length of the extractable key, but the obtained key is only asymmetrically secure; that is, only one party (Alice) knows whether it is secret. (For a formal definition of such an asymmetry, see Example 2.6.)

**Theorem 2.4.** *Let $P_{XYZ}$ be a distribution where $X$ and $Y$ are identical $n$-bit strings such that $\mathsf{H}_{\min}(X|Z) \geq tn$, for some fixed $t > 0$. Then there exists a protocol $\Pi$ such that*

$$\mathsf{Source}(P_{XYZ}) \times \mathsf{Chan}_\infty^{A \leftrightarrow B} \xrightarrow{\ \Pi\ }_\varepsilon \mathsf{SK}_\ell^A ,$$

*where $\ell = (1 - o(1))tn$ and $\varepsilon$ is exponentially small in $n$.*

### 2.5.3 Robust General One-Way Key-Agreement

The result of Theorem 2.4 has been generalized in [235] to the case where Alice's and Bob's strings are not identical initially (i.e., where information reconciliation and privacy amplification have to be combined).

**Theorem 2.5.** *Let $P_{XYZ}$ be a distribution where $X$ and $Y$ are $n$-bit strings such that $H_{min}(X|Z) - H_{max}(X|Y) \geq tn$, for some fixed $t > 0$. Then there exists a protocol $\Pi$ such that*

$$\text{Source}(P_{XYZ}) \times \text{Chan}_{\infty}^{A \leftrightarrow B} \xrightarrow{\Pi}_{\varepsilon} \text{SK}_{\ell}^{A},$$

*where $\ell = (1 - o(1))tn$ and $\varepsilon$ is exponentially small in $n$.*

Roughly speaking, Theorem 2.5 states that the length of the extractable key is the difference between Eve's and Bob's uncertainties about Alice's string. Similarly, it is also possible to generate an (unreliable) common secret key.

**Theorem 2.6.** *Let $P_{XYZ}$ be a distribution where $X$ and $Y$ are $n$-bit strings such that $H_{min}(X|Z) - H_{max}(X|Y) - H_{max}(Y|X) \geq tn$, for some fixed $t > 0$. Then there exists a protocol $\Pi$ such that*

$$\text{Source}(P_{XYZ}) \times \text{Chan}_{\infty}^{A \leftrightarrow B} \xrightarrow{\Pi}_{\varepsilon} \text{SK}_{\ell}^{AB},$$

*where $\ell = (1 - o(1))tn$ and $\varepsilon$ is exponentially small in $n$.*

# 3

# Fuzzy Commitment

Ari Juels

## 3.1 Introduction

The purpose of this chapter is to introduce *fuzzy commitment*, one of the earliest and simplest constructions geared toward cryptography over noisy data. The chapter also explores applications of fuzzy commitment to two problems in data security: (1) secure management of biometrics, with a focus on iriscodes, and (2) use of knowledge-based authentication (i.e., personal questions) for password recovery.

## 3.2 A Description of Fuzzy Commitment

Traditional cryptographic systems rely on *keys*, secret bitstrings for secure management of data. For example, a symmetric-key cipher involves a secret key $x$ and two operations: encryption and decryption. The encryption operation takes as input a message $m$ as well as the key $x$ and outputs a string $c$, known as a ciphertext. The ciphertext $c$ is, in a well-constructed cipher, unintelligible to anyone without knowledge of $x$. Decryption reverses the operation of encryption: On input $c$ and $x$, it yields the original message $m$.

Ordinary ciphers rely on exact correctness of the key $x$. For example, suppose that Alice encrypts a message $m$ under a key $x$ that is derived from the password "Buddy." If Bob tries to decrypt the resulting ciphertext $c$ using the same password—but with a typo (e.g., "Budyd")—the result will likely not be $m$, or even close to $m$, but gibberish.

Human beings, of course, make mistakes. Information from physical systems—be they fingerprint recognition systems or hard drives—is also prone to error. Rigid reliance on a perfectly presented secret key $x$, therefore, can cause cryptographic systems to fail even in the course of ordinary use.

This book treats the problem of cryptographic design in the presence of noise of many different types, including bit corruptions, random permutations of substrings, and so forth. Fuzzy commitment, however, is a cryptographic primitive designed to handle the simplest form of noise: independent, random corruption of the bits of a key $x$. It works most effectively, moreover, when $x$ itself comes from a uniform probability distribution (i.e., when the bits of $x$ are mutually independent and "0" and "1" bits are equiprobable).

A cryptographic commitment scheme is a function $G : C \times X \to Y$. To commit a value $\kappa \in C$, a *witness* $x \in_R X$ is chosen (usually uniformly at random), and $y = G(\kappa, x)$ is computed. The output $y$ is sometimes called a *blob*. A blob may be thought of as a "safe" for $\kappa$. An accompanying decommitment function $G^{-1} : Y \times X \to C$ takes a blob and witness and yields the original value $\kappa$. (Some commitment schemes take $\kappa$ as an input and merely verify whether it is correct. Here, however, we consider commitment as providing a decryption capability.) A well-constructed commitment scheme has two properties. First, it is *binding*, meaning that it is infeasible to decommit $y$ under a pair $(\kappa', x')$ such that $\kappa \neq \kappa'$. Second, it is *hiding*, meaning that, given $y$ alone, it is infeasible to compute $\kappa$.

Fuzzy commitment is a kind of encryption scheme that allows for the use of approximate or "fuzzy" witnesses; that is, given a commitment $y = G(\kappa, x)$, the system allows recovery of $\kappa$ from any witness $x'$ that is close to, but not necessarily equal to, $x$. "Closeness" in fuzzy commitment is measured by Hamming distance (i.e., the number of bits in which $x$ and $x'$ differ). We denote this Hamming distance by $|x - x'|$.

An important feature of fuzzy commitment is that its security depends on the use of a random value $\kappa$; that is, $\kappa$ must be selected uniformly at random from a suitable set $C$.

The hiding property of fuzzy commitment $G$ means that a blob $y$ leaks only a small amount of information about a committed value $\kappa$. Therefore, given the right system parameters, $y$ may be revealed publicly (i.e., it need not be kept secret). Put another way, knowledge of $y$ helps recover $\kappa$ using any qualified witness $x'$, but it does not reveal enough information for someone to learn $\kappa$ itself.

Given a cryptographic system $cs$ and a secret input $x$, we can apply fuzzy commitment to derive a key from $x$ for $cs$ and at the same time render $cs$ robust to bit errors in $x$. We select a value $\kappa$ for use as the secret key in $cs$. We then make the blob $y$ available to users of $cs$. Any legitimate user with approximate knowledge of $x$ (i.e., with a valid witness $x'$) can compute the secret $\kappa$. The hiding property of fuzzy commitment, however, ensures against misuse of $cs$ by an adversary with knowledge of $y$ alone.

### 3.2.1 Fuzzy Commitment: Details

A fuzzy commitment scheme may be based on any (linear) error-correcting code. An error-correcting code comprises a *message space* $M \subseteq F^a$, a corresponding *codeword space* or *codebook* $C \subseteq F^b$, for $b \geq a$, and a bijection $\phi : M \leftrightarrow C$. Here $F$ denotes a finite set of symbols—often a small field—whereas $F^i$ denotes the full set of strings of $i$ symbols from $F$. An additional component of an error-correcting code is a *decoding function* $f : C' \to C \cup \perp$, where $C \subseteq C' \subseteq F^b$. The rôle of the function $f$ is to map an element in $C'$ to its nearest codeword in $C$; this has the effect, when successful, of eliminating noise or errors added to a codeword. We let the special output symbol $\perp$ denote a failure of the function $f$ to output a valid codeword.

In its usual application, namely the transmission of correct messages across a noisy channel, an error-correcting code is used as follows. A target message $m \in M$ is mapped into a codeword $c = \phi(m)$, a representation of $m$ containing redundancy. The codeword $c$ is transmitted across the noisy channel, yielding a codeword $c' \in C'$. The noise introduced by the channel may be viewed as the vector difference $c' - c$. The decoding function $f$ is applied in an attempt to recover the originally transmitted codeword $c$. If successful, namely if $c'$ is sufficiently close to $c$ in an appropriate underlying metric for the code, then $c = f(c')$. If the decoding procedure fails (i.e., if it does not yield any codeword), then we write $f(c') = \perp$. The *minimum distance* of the code is the smallest distance $d = |c_0 - c_1|$ between any two codewords $c_0, c_1$ in $C$, where $|v|$ denotes the number of non-zero components in $v$. Any linear code has a decoding function $f$ for which successful decoding is always possible when $|c' - c| < d/2$; often, successful decoding is possible for $|c' - c|$ somewhat greater than the minimum distance.

Fuzzy commitment adapts an error-correcting code in an unusual way. In fact, it makes no use at all of the message space $M$. We assume a witness $x \in C'$ generated uniformly at random. The secret key $\kappa$ is selected uniformly at random from the codeword space $C$. We then compute an *offset* $\delta = x - \kappa \in \mathcal{F}^n$. The blob $y$ is computed as the pair $y = (\delta, z = h(\kappa))$. Here, $h$ is a suitable one-way and collision-resistant (hash) function.

Now it is possible to decommit $y$ under a witness $x'$ that is close to $x$ (i.e., for which $|x' - x| < d/2$). In this case, we are able to apply the decoding $\kappa = f(x' - \delta)$. Figure 3.1 gives a conceptual snapshot of how recovery of $\kappa$ works in fuzzy commitment. Once $\kappa$ is recovered, its correctness may be verified by computing $z = h(\kappa)$.

## The Hiding Property

Knowledge of the offset $\delta$ alone reveals no information about $\kappa$; an attacker with access to $\delta$ knows only that $\kappa \in C$. On the other hand, the offset $\delta$ leaks a certain amount of information about $x$. Recall that $x = c + \delta$ for $c \in C$, and we assume that $x$ is generated uniformly from $C'$. Therefore, knowledge of $\delta$ reduces the space of possible values of $x$ from the full message space $M$, of size $|F|^b$, to a space of size $|F|^a$ isomorphic to $C$. This aspect of the security of fuzzy commitment is information-theoretic: An adversary with knowledge of $\delta$ can merely try to guess $x$ or $\kappa$ and will succeed with probability of only $1/|C|$. On the other hand, the value $z$ hides $\kappa$ in a computational sense: If $h$ is a one-way hash function, then an attacker cannot feasibly recover $\kappa$ for large enough $|C|$.

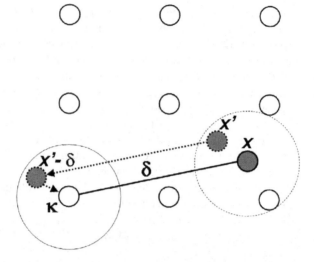

**Fig. 3.1.** A conceptual diagram of recovery of $\kappa$ in fuzzy commitment. The array of hollow circles represents a lattice $C$ of codewords, $\kappa$ being that in the lower left-hand corner. The minimal distance around $\kappa$ is diagrammed as a circle (of radius $d/2$). The offset $\delta = x - \kappa$ is indicated by the black line. A witness $x'$ is translated by $\delta$ into the region of $\kappa$ as $x' - \delta$. Provided that $|x' - x| < d/2$, the value $x' - \delta$ will lie within the minimum distance of $\kappa$. Error correction will then recover $\kappa$.

## The Binding Property

To achieve the binding property, we require that $h$ be collision-resistant, meaning that it is infeasible to compute any pair of values $(c, c')$ such that $h(c) = h(c')$. In this case, $z = h(\kappa)$ only for the correct value $\kappa$, i.e., that on which the blob $y$ was initially computed.

*Example 3.1.* As a toy example, let us consider a crude, (literally) two-bit error-correcting code. In this code, $\phi$ maps the elements of the message space $M = \{00, 01, 10, 11\}$ respectively onto the elements of the codeword space $C = \{0000000000, 0000011111, 1111100000, 1111111111\}$. Decoding follows the obvious majority rule over each of the two halves of a corrupted codeword. Thus, we can correct any noise that induces at most two errors in each half of a codeword.

Suppose that $x = 0100101101$. To create a commitment, we first select a codeword $\kappa$ uniformly at random from $C$. Suppose that we choose $0000011111$. We then compute the commitment $\delta = \kappa - x$. In this case, as for any binary error-correcting code, a natural choice of distance metric—both the "$-$" and "$+$" operators—is simply the XOR (exclusive "or"); that is, we can compute the commitment $G(x) = \delta = \kappa \oplus x = 0100110010$.

Now consider the witness $x' = \mathbf{1}000101\mathbf{10}0$. (This witness differs from $x$ in the three bits highlighted in bold type.) To decommit, we first compute

$\delta + x' = \delta \oplus x' = 1100011110$. Majority decoding on the two halves of this bitstring yields $f(\delta \oplus x') = 0000011111$, namely our original key $\kappa$.

Typically, before using $\kappa$ in a cryptographic operation, we remove its redundancy (i.e., map it to its corresponding message in $M$). In this chapter, for simplicity we will talk loosely of $\kappa$ as a cryptographic key, but in practice we mean its non-redundant representation.

### 3.2.2 Evolution of Fuzzy Commitment

The idea of cryptography in the presence of noise is a well-established one. The McEliece cryptosystem [198], developed in 1978, is a notable early example of the integration of error-correcting codes into cryptography. It relies on the hardness of a decoding problem (syndrome decoding of Goppa codes [28]) as a basis for public-key encryption. Fuzzy commitment is distinct from such work and other antecedents in its particular focus on the management of cryptographic keys benignly corrupted by noise.

While implicit in prior work, it appears that fuzzy commitment was first explicitly detailed and applied by Strait, Pearson, and Sengupta (SPS) of Lawrence Livermore National Laboratory in U.S. patent 6,038,315 (filed in 1997 and issued in 2000) [263]. Intermixed with a cryptographic apparatus aimed at Diffie-Hellman key establishment, the Strait et al. invention contains a fuzzy-commitment construction at its core. The first published exposition of a fuzzy-commitment-like construction—allowing limited error tolerance—was that of Davida, Frankel, and Matt (1998) [81]. Juels and Wattenberg (1999) [161] subsequently introduced a scheme ("fuzzy commitment"), essentially like that of SPS, enabling full use of the error-correcting capabilities of a code; they also provided basic definitions and security proofs. All three of these constructions took biometric authentication as their motivation. The research community has over the past several years produced a considerable amount of generalization, extension, and further exploration, as shown in the rich collection of work presented in this book.

## 3.3 Biometrics

Biometric authentication is the process of confirming a person's identity by means of a biological feature. Researchers have proposed biometric authentication systems for a number of body features. These include—in very rough order of actual application—voice, facial features, fingerprints, irises, hand geometry, retinas, hand vasculature, and even body odor. All biometrics have a common characteristic: They never look the same way twice. Each time a person applies her finger to a fingerprint reader, for instance, a different image results depending on the angle of presentation, the pressure of the finger, as well as actual physiological changes due to such things as chapped or chafed skin. In general, biometrics are an innately noisy authenticator.

### 3.3.1 Why Biometric Secrecy is Important

Biometric authentication systems rely in varying degrees on the secrecy or privacy of users' data. In practice, it is difficult to provide strong secrecy for the most common biometrics. People leave fingerprints on the objects they touch; they expose their faces, voices, and irises in public; they scatter images and recordings of themselves on the internet. In principle, biometric information need not be secret in order to support the process of authentication. When an immigration official checks the validity of a traveler's passport photo, she is essentially performing face recognition, a kind of biometric authentication. The official is not relying on the secrecy of the traveler's face, of course. She is relying, instead, on the authenticity of the passport photo.

Nonetheless, secrecy of biometric data can be important. Although people disperse biometric information in their wake, the *quality* of this biometric information is generally lower than that collected by a purpose-built biometric reader operating in a controlled environment. For example, the fingerprint a person leaves on a doorknob is likely to provide only a fraction of the information contained in the image created by a fingerprint reader. The fingerprint reader benefits from environmental controls on illumination and finger presentation. When a person initially registers a fingerprint in an authentication system, she may even be required to present her finger multiple times to ensure high-quality imaging.

The high-quality image registered in a biometric authentication system for later use—the equivalent of a passport photo—is known as a *template*. It is the *gap in quality* between a biometric template and a person's publicly exposed biometric data that dictates the value of biometric secrecy. To an impersonator who has access only to the fingerprints on a doorknob, much of the data in a fingerprint template will be unknown—and therefore secret. Some biometrics, in fact, are almost never exposed in the course of daily life. For example, the retina, the physiological structure at the back of the eye, is only visible with invasive scanning. Whereas retina-scanning is consequently a cumbersome biometric, people do not regularly scatter retinal images in public.

Although biometric authentication need not in principle rely on secrecy, template secrecy can help protect against biometric spoofing. For example, one research group demonstrated the ability to spoof a fingerprint reader using a "gummy" finger constituted of gelatin [189]. Such crude spoofing attempts are obvious to any observer. As biometric authentication becomes increasingly popular, however, it is also becoming increasingly automated. A number of airports around the world, for instance, offer self-service kiosks for biometric authentication, with minimal human oversight. In such situations, spoofing can be a real concern. It is of even greater concern in biometric systems for remote authentication. A biometric system that authenticates a home user to a server can assume no trustworthy human oversight at all.

Where an imposter can operate without oversight, spoofing is a risk. Ensuring template secrecy can therefore be essential.

### 3.3.2 Fuzzy Commitment for Template Secrecy

Given the need for template secrecy and the systemic problem of noise, fuzzy commitment is a ready-made tool for biometric authentication.

A conventional biometric system stores and makes explicit use of a template $x_u$ for user $u$ (e.g., a registered fingerprint). When the user tries to authenticate by presenting a fresh image $x'_u$, the system compares $x'_u$ with the stored template $x_u$. If the two are sufficiently similar—according to whatever metric the system employs—then $x'_u$ is deemed to match $x_u$, and the authentication is successful. Otherwise, the authentication fails. The weakness of this approach is that knowledge of $x_u$—that is, the basic biometric record of $u$—provides all of the information required to impersonate $u$ via spoofing.

Rather than storing the biometric template $x_u$ of user $u$ explicitly, a system might store a fuzzy commitment $y_u$. Thanks to the binding property of fuzzy commitment, $y_u$ could authenticate a biometric image $x'_u$ presented by user $u$ at the time of authentication. At the same time, if an attacker compromised the $y_u$ (e.g., if a hacker broke into a database containing $y_u$), the hiding property of fuzzy commitment would ensure the future integrity of the authentication process. Even if the attacker tried to spoof a reader, the secrecy of $x_u$ would remain a bulwark against impersonation.

### 3.3.3 Iriscodes

As a concrete example for which fuzzy commitment is particularly apt, let us consider *iriscodes*. The iris is the colored ring around the pupil of the eye (not to be confused with the retina). When we say that a person has blue eyes, for instance, we mean, more precisely, that she has blue irises. Under the impetus of Daugman [77], irises have emerged as a practical biometric authenticator. Their most attractive feature is their high level of accessible entropy. A fingerprint reader today can effectively extract at most, say, 20 bits from a fingerprint (as attested by typical industry specification of false-accept rates of at best 1 in 1,000,000). Strong cryptographic systems, by contrast, require key lengths of 80 bits or more. An iris appears to contain on the order of 249 bits of entropy [78], well beyond the length required for a strong cryptographic key. Moreover, iris cameras can often capture both eyes in a single image, in principle yielding roughly 500 bits of entropy.

The standard template format for an iris is known as an iriscode. Iriscodes have a feature particularly attractive for fuzzy commitment. The canonical measure of error between a template and an iris image is a binary Hamming distance (i.e., the number of bit differences).

An iriscode is typically 2048 bits in length. Let us suppose, however, that it may be compressed to 249 independent, random bits comprising the full extractable entropy of the iris. (This assumption is overly optimistic, as we explain further below.) That is, let us suppose that Nature endows a user $u$ at birth with a 249-bit template $x_u$ selected uniformly at random.

We can construct a fuzzy-commitment scheme as follows. We select a linear (249,80,79)-error-correcting code (via, e.g., a construction of [45]). This yields a cryptographic key $\kappa_u$ of 80 bits in length—the minimum desired for cryptographic applications—and can correct up to $\lfloor 79/2 \rfloor = 39$ errors. In other words, as long as user $u$ presents an iris image $x'_u$ with at most 39 bit errors (i.e., with a total bit error rate of just under 16%), she can successfully decommit the key $\kappa_u$. Real-world experiments [78] have recorded an average error rate of just 1.9% under good lighting conditions (although sometimes in excess of 16%).

### 3.3.4 Research Questions

Regrettably, the ability to extract the fully underlying entropy of an iriscode cannot be taken for granted. Rigorous characterization of *where* the entropy resides in an iriscode remains an open problem; that is, the individual bits of an iriscode are clearly correlated with one another, but the nature of these correlations remains to be carefully studied, despite some first steps (e.g., [142]). Successful characterization would enable the creation of a fuzzy-committment scheme offering a rigorously characterizable level of security.

Another open question is the nature of the secrecy gap described earlier. An iris camera captures a highly detailed image of the eye. How much iriscode data can an attacker in a typical setting reasonable obtain? For example, how much iriscode data is extractable from the photos that people typically post on their web pages or from the snapshot that an attacker might capture on the sly?

### 3.3.5 Biometric Applications

If and when it is possible for an ordinary user Alice to extract a cryptographically strong key from her iris (or other biometric), biometrics will be able to support a number of traditional security goals in new ways. For example, Alice's laptop can encrypt the contents of its hard drive under a key $\kappa_{Alice}$ derived from witness $x_{Alice}$ and store the resulting ciphertext $\gamma$ along with $y_{Alice}$. By presenting her iris to a camera on the laptop, generating an image $x'_{Alice}$, Alice can decrypt the ciphertext $\gamma$, restoring the contents of her hard drive. Alice could similarly protect a password keyring in $\gamma$—or cryptographic keys for authentication.

Remote authentication is another attractive possibility. Suppose that Alice registers $y_{Alice}$ with a server that also stores $\kappa_A$. When Alice wishes to authenticate herself to the server through a client machine—her own, or even a public kiosk—the server can transmit $y_{\text{Alice}}$. When Alice presents $x'_{\text{Alice}}$, she is able to decommit $\kappa_{\text{Alice}}$ and then authenticate to the server. The server need not trust the client, as even an attacker that downloads $y_{\text{Alice}}$ cannot feasibly impersonate Alice. (Of course, if Alice uses a compromised client that stores $x'_{\text{Alice}}$, then she is later vulnerable to impersonation.)

Even in a system in which it is not possible to derive a key $\kappa_{\text{Alice}}$ with the full desired cryptographic strength, $\kappa_{\text{Alice}}$ can still serve usefully as a supplementary authenticator (e.g., in conjunction with a password [142]).

### 3.3.6 "Device Biometrics"

In a loose sense, biometrics are not just for people. POWFs (physical one-way functions, also known as physical unclonable functions or PUFs), proposed by Pappu et al. [222], may be regarded as a type of device biometric. A PUF is a physical object whose responses to stimuli are unique and highly complex, resembling the output of a one-way function. Pappu et al. studied an implementation where the PUF is a piece of translucent plastic containing tiny spherical glass inclusions. When targeted with a laser beam, the PUF yields a speckle pattern. Different angles of incidence yield different, statistically independent speckle patterns. Pappu et al. proposed digital-signal processing techniques for PUFs very much like those developed by Daugman for iriscodes. Furthermore, PUF readings, like iriscodes, are subject to noise. Fuzzy commitment is therefore a natural tool to apply to PUFs. Chapters 1 and 12–15 explore applications of fuzzy cryptography to PUFs in detail.

## 3.4 Knowledge-Based Authentication

People bring noise to the world not only in what they are (i.e., their biological characteristics) but also in what they know (i.e., their presentation of facts). This source of error vexes a common type of backup authentication mechanism: knowledge-based authentication (KBA), or, more informally, "life questions." Many web sites today ask users to register answers to personal questions such as "What was the make of your first car?" "What is the name of your favorite pet?" "What is your favorite sports team?" or "What street did you grow up on?" When a user forgets her password or is otherwise required to reset it, she is asked to answer her registered questions afresh in order to authenticate herself.

Given the ambiguity of such questions and fluid nature of people's life circumstances and memories, the answers that users provide for password recovery often differ from those that they have registered. (Pets die; sports allegiances change; people move in their youth and grow up on several different streets.) For this reason, error tolerance is essential in life-question systems.

At the same time, individual life questions often have very little underlying entropy. Consider, for example, the question, "What was the make of your first car?" Before 1998 in the United States, Ford Motor Company controlled a market share of more than 25%. Thus, an attacker targeting a U.S. account and guessing the answer "Ford" could achieve high odds of success—roughly 1 in 4. Given such vulnerabilities, it is a prudent practice to secure systems by means of a list of questions, rather than just a few. (In practice today, most web sites ask only two or three.)

Finally, it is desirable, of course, for the answers to life questions to be well protected. The answers are not only sensitive personal information but increasingly support user authentication across multiple platforms. A web server can, of course, store cryptographic hashes of answers, rather than plaintext answers. Given the low underlying entropy, though, such hashes are vulnerable to dictionary attack and therefore offer little real protection. Answers may reside on a server in encrypted form, but the corresponding decryption key must be readily available to the server—and thus potentially to attackers—in order to guarantee reliable user access. Compromise of a database of answers to life questions today could have serious implications for users.

With enough underlying entropy, a *collection* of answers to life questions can support goals other than on-line authentication. As suggested in the case of iriscodes, answers to life questions might form a cryptographic key used for encryption. A user might encrypt a hard drive, for example, under the answers to a series of life questions.

These considerations argue in favor of the use of a moderately sizable list of questions. Answers should be verifiable even in the presence of noise (i.e., mistakes) but should be feasibly learnable only by the user who created them. Fuzzy commitment can support this goal. Frykholm and Juels (FJ) explore this application in [114].

## Fuzzy Commitment for KBA

Suppose that a user registers a list $A = \{a_1, a_2, \ldots, a_n\}$ of answers to $n$ life questions. These answers will have varying lengths. The user's favorite pet may be "Buddy," for instance, and her favorite sports team is the "Tampa Bay Devil Rays." It is possible, however, to hash the user's answers down to bitstrings of uniform length—each of, say, $m$ bits in length, where $m$ is large enough to capture the underlying entropy of the answers. If we concatenate these answers, we obtain a witness $x = a_1 \parallel a_2, \parallel, \ldots, \parallel a_n$ of $n$ different $m$-bit symbols.

Application of fuzzy commitment is now straightforward. Let us consider authentication as an example. At registration, the user supplies a string $x$ to a web server. This string is converted into a fuzzy commitment $y$ that the server stores in a record for the user. (The server also stores the list of life questions that the user answered, for later presentation.)

When a user authenticates, she supplies a new set of answers $A' = \{a'_1, a'_2, \ldots, a'_n\}$ to her registered questions. Concatenation induces a witness

$x'$ of the same form as $x$. The server attempts to decommit $\kappa$. Successful decommitment means successful authentication.

Although functionally similar to the use of an iriscode, there is an important technical difference here. The string $x$ consists not of bits, but of $m$-bit symbols. An incorrect answer by the user may cause corruption of a full $m$-bit symbol (i.e., a one-symbol difference between $x'$ and $x$). It is important to select an error-correcting code accordingly, most suitably with a field $F$ of cardinality $m$.

For example, we might design a system with 15 questions in which each answer is mapped to an 8-bit symbol. A (15,7,8)-Reed Solomon code over $GF[2^8]$ would then permit successful decommitment in the face of $\tau \leq 4$ incorrect answers in addition to $8 - 2\tau$ omissions (i.e., answers not provided by the user). (This parameter choice, proposed by FJ, induces a key length for $\kappa$ of only 56 bits. FJ describe techniques to boost the effective key length.)

**Remark 3.1.** In our exposition here, we tacitly assume that the answers $\{a_i\}$ are somehow converted into uniformly distributed $m$-bit symbols, inducing a uniformly distributed witness $x$. In practice, it is generally not straightfoward to find such a mapping. Indeed, without exact knowledge of the distribution of answers given by the user population, it is not possible to determine how to construct one. It is therefore necessary to assume some degree of non-uniformity in the symbols composing $x$—and in the errors induced in $x'$ as well, an issue treated at length in [114].

## 3.5 Beyond Fuzzy Commitment

Fuzzy commitment addresses applications in which the Hamming distance offers a natural bound on error. In some systems, errors are better characterized by some other metric.

For example, a KBA system might require users not to answer a series of questions, but, instead, to provide a list of personal preferences. For example, one could imagine a KBA system in which a user is asked to register a list $A = \{a_1, a_2, \ldots, a_{15}\}$ of her 15 favorite movies ("Anna Karenina," "Bonnie and Clyde," "Casablanca," etc.).

Consider what happens when this user tries to authenticate with a list $A' = \{a'_1, a'_2, \ldots, a'_{15}\}$. If $A' \neq A$, it is unclear *how to order the two lists* to ensure a correct one-to-one matching between movies. For example, we might construct a string $x = a_{\sigma(1)} \parallel a_{\sigma(2)}, \parallel, \ldots, \parallel a_{\sigma(15)}$ comprising the elements of $A$ in alphabetical order as defined by a permutation $\sigma$. How then would we construct $x'$ from $A'$? We might consider the construction $x' = a'_{\sigma'(1)} \parallel a'_{\sigma'(2)}, \parallel, \ldots, \parallel a'_{\sigma'(15)}$, where $\sigma'$ similarly defines an alphabetical ordering on elements in $A'$.

In this case, though, a single error (i.e., $|A \cap A'| \geq 1$) could induce a large Hamming distance $|x - x'|$ and cause the decommitment operation to fail.

For example, suppose that $a'_2 = a_1, a'_3 = a_2, \ldots, a'_{15} = a_{14}$, but $a'_1 \notin A$ and $a_{15} \notin A'$. ($A'$ comprises "Animal House," "Anna Karenina," "Bonnie and Clyde," "Casablanca," etc.) In this case, the answers are misaligned. In fact, $x'$ and $x$ may differ in every single position!

For this example of KBA via lists, a more suitable metric of error is set difference (i.e, $|A \cap A'|$). Viewed another way, we would like a fuzzy-commitment system that is *permutation invariant*. Juels and Sudan [159, 160] proposed a system (called a "fuzzy vault") that has this property. Subsequent work by Dodis et al., treated in Chapters 5 and 6 of this book, proposes more general and efficient constructions considers another natural metric called edit distance. Chapter 6, in particular, investigates extension into the realm of dynamic adversarial models, in which the adversary is presumed to have more power than the ability simply to compromise $y$.

Although researchers have offered some initial steps, rigorous matching of fuzzy commitment and similar constructions to real-world systems largely remains a rich, open area of research.

# A Communication-Theoretical View on Secret Extraction

Jean-Paul Linnartz, Boris Škorić, and Pim Tuyls

## 4.1 Introduction

The recent achievements in enhanced throughput, efficiency, and reliability of wireless communication systems can largely be contributed to the availability of a versatile mathematical framework for the behavior and performance of digital transmission schemes. The key foundation was Shannon's 1948 paper [251] that introduced the notion of capacity. The term *capacity* is defined as the maximum achievable rate of information exchange, where the maximization is conducted over all possible choices of transmission and detection techniques. The existence of a fundamental limit has acted as an irresistable target for ambitious engineers. However, it was only until the 1990s that the signal processing capabilities allowed a true exploitation of these insights and the throughput of practical systems closely reached the capacity limits. Another important condition was met earlier: the availability of sufficiently realistic statistical models for signals, the noise, and the channel.

The research area of biometrics is presumably less mature in this respect, but strong progress is being made into the statistical modeling of biometric measurements and of sensor imperfections. Most importantly, the notion of a distance between two biometric measurements appears to exist, where a larger distance indicates a lesser likelihood of a statistical deviation. A further refinement is that errors in measurements can be modeled with well-behaved joint probability functions.

Anticipating the further sophistication and verification of such models, this chapter proposes a framework that models the capacity and performance of such systems, initially assuming generic probabilistic models for biometric sources and sensor aberrations.

We argue that the maximum information rate of the biometric measurement channel can be related directly to the *identification capacity* of the biometric system. The statistical behavior of the biometrics as well as the variability between different (imperfect) measurements are assumed to be known in the form of a statistical model. This reveals a commonality between commucation systems and biometric systems that can covered by a variation on Shannon's theory.

In communications, reliable transfer of data can be separated from security functions such as encryption for confidentiality. The usual approach is to start with source coding to compress the input data into an efficient representation, followed by encryption. Third, redundancy is added in the form of channel coding to allow for error correction. In this regard, the biometric system is different. Biometric signals cannot be compressed, encrypted, protected by error correction, or in any other form be pre-conditioned before being offered to a sensor. Nonetheless, one needs to involve non-linear operations during the detection, for instance to prevent impersonation and leakage of confidential personal information. The second part of this chapter shows that security operations can be performed to shield important information from untrusted parties without significantly affecting the user capacity or security of the system.

## 4.2 Preliminaries

We distinguish between identification and verification. *Identification* estimates which person is present by searching for a match in a database of reference data for many persons. The decoder a priori does not know whether he sees "Peggy" or "Petra." The outcome of the identification is either the (most likely) identity of the person present, or an erasue; that is, the decoder cannot establish who the person is with reasonable accuracy.

When assessing the user capacity of an identification system, we are interested in knowing how many individuals can be identified reliably by a biometrical identification system—in particular, how this is a function of the amount of observed data and the quality of the observations.

On the other hand, *verification* attempts to establish whether the prover (i.e., the person who is undergoing the verification test) truly is Peggy, which she claims to be. The prover provides not only biometric data but also a message in which she claims to be Peggy. In security language, the decoder is called the verifier and is named Victor. He is assumed to have some a priori knowledge about Peggy—for instance, in the form of certified reference data—but at the start of the protocol he is not yet sure whether Peggy is present or another person performing an impersonation attack. The outcome of the verification is binary: either "the prover is Peggy" or "the prover is not Peggy."

In identification, the verifier must have access to a database of reference data from all individuals. In verification, this is not necessary and, typically, the reference data of only Peggy suffices. An identification algorithm can, at least in theory, be modified into a verification algorithm by grouping the set of all outputs except "the person is Peggy" into the single outcome "the person is not Peggy." However, in general, the optimization and decision regions are usually chosen differently for identification and verification. Identification systems make the most likely choice, whereas verification systems are designed around false-positive and false-negative probabilities.

*Private verification*, which we will address from Section 4.8 onwards, is a special form of verification in which certain security requirements are also met. In particular, the outcome of private verification can be that the person not only shows biometrics that fit with Peggy, but also that she knows a secret that only Peggy is supposed to know. After the private verification session, Victor preferably doesn't know what the secret is, although Victor can be convinced that the prover knows Peggy's secret.

## 4.3 Model: Biometrics as Random Codewords

Biometrical systems in general involve two phases. In an *enrollment phase* all individuals are observed, and for each individual $p \in \{1, \ldots, M\}$, a record $\mathbf{Y}(p)$ is added to a database. This record is called "reference data," "enrollment data," or "template" and contains $L$ symbols from the alphabet $\mathcal{Y}$. The enrollment data is a noisy version of the biometrical data $\mathbf{X}(p) \in \mathcal{X}^L$ corresponding to the individual $p$. The set of enrollment data for all users is denoted as the entire $M$ by $L$ matrix $\mathsf{Y} = (\mathbf{Y}(1), \mathbf{Y}(2), \ldots, \mathbf{Y}(M))$.

In the *operational phase*, an unknown individual is observed again. The resulting identification data $\mathbf{Z}$, another noisy version of the biometrical data $\mathbf{X}$ of the unknown individual, is compared to (all or a subset of) the enrollment data in the database and the system has to come up with an estimate of the individual. This model is depicted in Fig. 4.1. An essential fact in this procedure is that both in the enrollment phase and in the operational phase, noisy versions of the biometrical data are obtained. The precise biometrical data $\mathbf{X}(p)$ remain unknown.

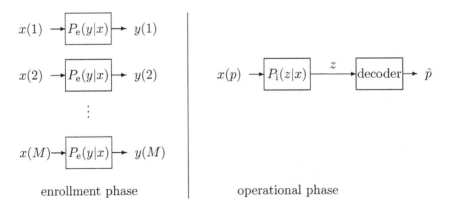

enrollment phase         operational phase

**Fig. 4.1.** Model of a biometrical identification system. Each biometric measurement is represented as a noisy channel.

We use capital notation $\mathbf{X}$, $\mathbf{Y}$, and $\mathbf{Z}$ for random variables and boldface to denote vectors in this section of dimension $L$. Moreover, $\mathbf{x}$, $\mathbf{y}$, and $\mathbf{z}$, denote realizations or the random variables. Each individual has a biometrical data sequence $\mathbf{x} = (x_1, x_2, \ldots, x_L)$ with components $x_i \in \mathcal{X}$ for $i = 1, \ldots, L$. The sequence $\mathbf{x}(p)$ is the sequence for person $p$.

For the development of the theory, preferably we assume that the components of each sequence are independent and identically distributed (IID) and that the biometric source can generate arbitrarily long sequences ($L \to \infty$). In practice, most physical or biological parameters show correlation, but often a set of biometric measurements can be transformed into a sequence of IID random variables. Communication engineers usually consider data to arrive sequentially, and usually speak of a "memoryless source" if $\mathbf{X}$ is IID and of a "memoryless time-invariant channel" if for a memoryless source $\mathbf{Y}$ (resp. $\mathbf{Z}$) is also IID.

The measured output sequence $\mathbf{Z}$ is used by a *decoder*. In identification, the decoder has access to all $M$ enrollment sequences stored in the database $\mathbf{Y}$. The decoder produces an estimate $\hat{p}$ of the index of the unknown individual, $\hat{p} = \mathsf{Dec}(\mathbf{z}, \mathbf{y})$. An erasure $\perp$ is also a valid decoder output. Hence, $\hat{p} \in \{\perp, 1, 2, \ldots, M\}$. Two relevant system parameters are the *maximal error probability* $P_{\max}$ and the *rate* $R$:

$$P_{\max} \overset{\Delta}{=} \max_{1 \leq p \leq M} \mathbb{P}\left[\hat{P} \neq p | P = p\right] \quad \text{and} \quad R \overset{\Delta}{=} \frac{1}{L} \log_2 M. \qquad (4.1)$$

For an ideal binary ($\mathcal{X} = \{0, 1\}$) biometric system, we have $M = 2^L$, so $R = 1$. The *Identification Capacity*, to be defined later, describes asymptotic system properties that theoretically apply only for the case of infinitely long sequences $L \to \infty$. In fact, we will argue that there exists a rate $C_{\mathrm{id}}$ such that $P_{\max}$ is arbitrarily small for rates below capacity ($R < C_{\mathrm{id}}$) and that $P_{\max}$ necessarily tends to unity for rates above $C_{\mathrm{id}}$. This $C_{\mathrm{id}}$ will be called the identification capacity.

## Source and Channel Model

We will denote the probabilities on $\mathbf{X}$ as the source model. We define the "enrollment channel" as the probability of $\mathbf{Y}(p)$ conditioned on the biometric $\mathbf{X}(p)$. Similarly, we define the operational (or identification) channel as the probability of $\mathbf{Z}(p)$ conditioned on $\mathbf{X}(p)$.

In communication systems, the channel is mostly modeled as a statistical operation that is independent of the source. In our generic biometric framework, that is not necessarily the case, although our examples assume this.

## IID Source

Each biometrical data sequence is assumed to be generated by an IID source according to the symbol distribution $Q(\kappa) = \mathbb{P}[x_l(p) = \kappa]$. The probability distribution of the full sequence is

$$P_{\mathbf{X}(p)}(\mathbf{x}) = \mathbb{P}[\mathbf{X}(p) = \mathbf{x}] = \prod_{l=1}^{L} Q(x_l). \tag{4.2}$$

Note that the the distribution $Q$ does not depend on $p$.

## IID Independent Memoryless Channel

In the enrollment phase, all biometrical data sequences are observed via an enrollment channel $\{\mathcal{Y}, P_e(y|x), \mathcal{X}\}$. If we can write

$$\mathbb{P}[\mathbf{Y}(p) = \mathbf{y}|\mathbf{X}(p) = \mathbf{x}] = \prod_{l=1}^{L} P_e(y_l|x_l) \tag{4.3}$$

for any fixed $p \in \{1, \ldots, M\}$, then the channel is memoryless, so we have the same channel $\{\mathcal{Y}, P_e(y_l|x_l), \mathcal{X}\}$ for each symbol number $l$. Moreover, for this channel, $P_e$ does not depend on $p$. In the identification phase, the biometrical data sequence $\mathbf{z}(p)$ of an unknown individual $p$ is observed via a memoryless identification channel $\{\mathcal{Z}, P_i(z_l|x_l), \mathcal{X}\}$. Here $\mathcal{Z}$ is the operational output alphabet. Now

$$\mathbb{P}[\mathbf{Z}(p) = \mathbf{z}|\mathbf{X}(p) = \mathbf{x}] = \prod_{l=1}^{L} P_i(z_l|x_l). \tag{4.4}$$

## 4.4 Identification Capacity

**Definition 4.1.** *The* identification capacity *of a biometrical parameter is the largest value of $C_{id}$ such that for any (arbitrarily small) $\delta > 0$ and sufficiently large L, there exist decoders that achieve a rate $R_{id}$ of*

$$R_{id} \geq C_{id} - \delta \tag{4.5}$$

*at vanishingly small error rate $P_{max} \leq \delta$.*

**Theorem 4.1.** *The* identification capacity *of a biometrical system with IID source and independent IID channel is given by the mutual information*

$$C_{id} = \mathbf{I}(\mathbf{Y}; \mathbf{Z}) \tag{4.6}$$

*for an arbitrary fixed p.*

We use the identity $\mathbf{I}(A; B) = \mathsf{H}(A) + \mathsf{H}(B) - \mathsf{H}(A, B)$. The entropies $\mathsf{H}(\mathbf{Y})$, $\mathsf{H}(\mathbf{Z})$, and $\mathsf{H}(\mathbf{Y}, \mathbf{Z})$ are computed from the probability of the "true" biometric $\mathbf{X}$ and the transition properties over the enrollment and identification channel, where

$$\mathbb{P}[\mathbf{Y}(p) = \mathbf{y}] = \prod_{j=1}^{L} \sum_{x_j \in \mathcal{X}} Q(x_j) P_e(y_j | x_j),$$

$$\mathbb{P}[\mathbf{Z}(p) = \mathbf{z}] = \prod_{j=1}^{L} \sum_{x_j \in \mathcal{X}} Q(x_j) P_i(z_j | x_j),$$

$$\mathbb{P}[\mathbf{Y}(p) = \mathbf{y}, \mathbf{Z}(p) = \mathbf{z}] = \prod_{j=1}^{L} \sum_{x_j \in \mathcal{X}} Q(x_j) P_e(y_j | x_j) P_i(z_j | x_j).$$

Note that none of these probabilities depend on $p$. For an IID (memoryless) source, $\mathsf{H}(\mathbf{X}) = \sum_{l=1}^{L} \mathsf{H}(x_l) = L\mathsf{H}(x_l)$. Similarly, the entropies of $\mathbf{Y}$ and $\mathbf{Z}$ can be calculated componentwise.

## 4.5 Proof Outline for Theorem 4.1

As in communication theory, the proof of the capacity theorem consists of a part that there exist rates that achieve capacity and a part that proves the non-existence of rates above $C_{id}$ with a low average error rate.

Another important step is the random coding argument [66]. This is the observation that we can prove that the average over all randomly chosen sequences achieves an error rate that vanishes. In the development of a theoretical framework for communication systems, this was an innovative step that laid the foundation for several proofs. Here, Shannon's theory apparently fits biometrics naturally, whereas for communication systems, it was a creative, initially believed to be a somewhat artificial assumption to support the derivations of bounds. As first exploited in [292], random coding is a very natural and appropriate model for biometric systems, where the source model is one of randomly generated sequences.[1] In communication systems, an engineer can choose an optimum code sequence for every potential message to be transmitted. Shannon postulated that if the engineer just picks random sequences to represent messages on average, he achieves capacity, so there must be codes that do at least as good. Note that the generation of the IID biometrical data yields the randomness that makes it all work. We get the random code $\{\mathbf{y}(1), \mathbf{y}(2), \dots, \mathbf{y}(M)\}$ by the very nature of biometrics.

---

[1] Yet, the distribution and statistical dependence of biometrics can be questioned.

## 4.5.1 Achievability

In this subsection, we prove that for all $\delta \geq 0$, the rate $R_{\mathrm{id}} \geq \mathbf{I}(\mathbf{X}, \mathbf{Y}) - \delta$ can be achieved.

To prove that there are rates that achieve low error rates, we postulate a decoder that is based on typical sequences for $\mathbf{Y}$, $\mathbf{Z}$ and $\mathbf{Y}, \mathbf{Z}$ jointly. Typical sets are explained in more detail in textbooks such as [66]. The core idea is that a random sequence is with probability 1 a typical sequence. This implies that any typical sequence has a probability that is close to $2^{-\mathsf{H}(\mathbf{Y})}$, $2^{-\mathsf{H}(\mathbf{Z})}$, or $2^{-\mathsf{H}(\mathbf{Y},\mathbf{Z})}$, respectively. More precisely, the jointly typical set $\mathcal{A}_\varepsilon$ is defined as the collection of sequences $(\mathbf{Y}, \mathbf{Z})$ such that $P_{YZ}(\mathbf{y}, \mathbf{z})$ satisfies

$$2^{-L(\mathsf{H}(y_l,z_l)+\varepsilon)} \leq P_{YZ}(\mathbf{y}, \mathbf{z}) \leq 2^{-L(\mathsf{H}(y_l,z_l)-\varepsilon)} \tag{4.7}$$

and similarly for sequences of $\mathbf{Y}$ and $\mathbf{Z}$ separately. An important property is that a sequence $\mathbf{Y}, \mathbf{Z}$ chosen randomly according to the underlying biometric statistical model is a typical sequence with probability higher than $1 - \varepsilon$.

For our proof, we postulate a decoder that generates as its output the unique index $\hat{p}$ satisfying

$$(\mathbf{y}(\hat{p}), \mathbf{z}) \in \mathcal{A}_\varepsilon. \tag{4.8}$$

If no unique $\hat{p}$ exists, the decoder outputs an erasure.

Two kinds of error can occur. An error of the first kind (cf. a false rejection if we had addressed a verification system) occurs when the enrollment sequence of the tested individual $p$ is not jointly typical with his identification sequence resulting from the test. We define the event that the enrollment $\mathbf{Y}(p)$ and an observed identification $\mathbf{Z}$ are jointly typical as

$$E_p = \{(\mathbf{Y}(p), \mathbf{Z}) \in \mathcal{A}_\varepsilon\}.$$

Without loss of generality we denote the test sequence as $p = 1$. Thus, a false rejection corresponds to $\neg E_1$. An error of the second kind (cf. a false acceptance) occurs if the enrollment sequence of some other individual $p' \neq p$ is typical with $p$'s identification sequence. This corresponds to $E_2, E_3, \ldots, E_M$. For errors of the first kind, the probability $\mathbb{P}[(\mathbf{Y}(p), \mathbf{Z}(p)) \notin \mathcal{A}_\varepsilon] \leq \varepsilon$ for all large enough $L$. For errors of the second kind, we calculate the probability that two randomly chosen sequences $\mathbf{Y}$ and $\mathbf{Z}$ match, where the sequences are not necessarily taken from a specific realization of a population but produced by a statistical process that randomly generates sequences over $\mathcal{X}^L$. Let $\mathbf{z}$ be the output of the identification channel that is caused by $\mathbf{X}(p)$. For all $\mathbf{y} \in \mathcal{Y}^L$ and $\mathbf{z} \in \mathcal{Z}^L$ and $p' \neq p$, we have

$$\mathbb{P}[\mathbf{Y}(p') = \mathbf{y}, \mathbf{Z}(p) = \mathbf{z}] = \prod_{l=1}^{L} \sum_{\kappa \in \mathcal{X}} Q(\kappa) P_{\mathrm{e}}(y_l|\kappa) \sum_{\lambda \in \mathcal{X}} Q(\lambda) P_{\mathrm{i}}(z_l|\lambda). \tag{4.9}$$

Using the proporties of typical sequences (e.g., Theorem 8.6.1. in [66]), the false-acceptance probability of two randomly chosen sequences satisfies

$$\mathbb{P}[(\mathbf{Y}(p'), \mathbf{Z}(p)) \in \mathcal{A}_\varepsilon] \leq 2^{-\mathbf{I}(\mathbf{Y}(p); \mathbf{Z}(p)) + 3L\varepsilon}.$$

An error of any kind occurs with probability $\mathbb{P}[e] = \mathbb{P}[e|p=1] = \mathbb{P}[\neg E_1 \cup E_2 \cup E_3 \cup \cdots \cup E_M$. By applying the union bound, one obtains

$$\mathbb{P}[e|p] = \mathbb{P}\left[\neg E_1 \cup \bigcup_{p=2}^{M} E_p\right] \leq \mathbb{P}[\neg E_1] + \sum_{p=2}^{M} \mathbb{P}[E_p].$$

Hence, for sufficiently large $L$, we have

$$\mathbb{P}[e] \leq \varepsilon + \sum_{i=2}^{2^{LR}} 2^{-\mathbf{I}(\mathbf{Y}(p); \mathbf{Z}(p)) + 3L\varepsilon} \leq \varepsilon + 2^{3L\varepsilon} 2^{-[\mathbf{I}(\mathbf{Y}(p); \mathbf{Z}(p)) - LR]} \leq 2\varepsilon.$$

Thus, $\mathbb{P}\left[\hat{P} \neq p | P = p\right]$ can be made smaller than $2\varepsilon$ by increasing $L$.

### 4.5.2 Converse

In this subsection we show that there exists no identification scheme that can identify more than $2^{\mathbf{I}(\mathbf{Y}; \mathbf{Z})}$ persons with negligible error probability:

$$\mathbb{P}\left[\hat{P} \neq P\right] \leq \max_{p=1,\ldots,M} \mathbb{P}\left[\hat{P} \neq p | P = p\right], \tag{4.10}$$

which we require to remain arbitrarily small. Applying Fano's inequality, we get for the entropy in $P$, knowing the database $\mathbf{Y}$ and observation $\mathbf{Z}$,

$$\mathsf{H}(P|\mathbf{Y}, \mathbf{Z}) \leq 1 + \mathbb{P}\left[\hat{P} \neq P\right] \log_2 M. \tag{4.11}$$

Note that we did not assume any a priori distribution over the individuals that are to be identified. Let us see what happens if we assume that $P$ is uniformly distributed over $\{1, 2, \ldots, M\}$. Using inequality (4.11), we obtain

$$\begin{aligned}
\log_2 M &= \mathsf{H}(P) \\
&= \mathsf{H}(P|\mathbf{Y}) \\
&= \mathsf{H}(P|\mathbf{Y}) - \mathsf{H}(P|\mathbf{Z}, \mathbf{Y}) + \mathsf{H}(P|\mathbf{Z}, \mathbf{Y}) \\
&\leq \mathbf{I}(P; \mathbf{Z}|\mathbf{Y}) + 1 + \mathbb{P}\left[\hat{P} \neq P\right] \log_2 M.
\end{aligned} \tag{4.12}$$

Another useful inequality is obtained as follows:

$$\begin{aligned}
\mathbf{I}(P; \mathbf{Z}|\mathbf{Y}) &= \mathsf{H}(\mathbf{Z}|\mathbf{Y}) - \mathsf{H}(\mathbf{Z}|P, \mathbf{Y}) \\
&\leq \mathsf{H}(\mathbf{Z}) - \mathsf{H}(\mathbf{Z}|P, \mathbf{Y}) \\
&= \mathsf{H}(\mathbf{Z}) - \mathsf{H}(\mathbf{Z}(P)|\mathbf{Y}(P)) \\
&= \mathbf{I}(\mathbf{Z}(P); \mathbf{Y}(P)) \\
&= L\mathbf{I}(Y_l; Z_l).
\end{aligned} \tag{4.13}$$

Combining (4.13) and (4.13), we get

$$\log_2 M \leq L\mathbf{I}(Y_l; Z_l) + 1 + \mathbb{P}\Big[\hat{P} \neq P\Big] \log_2 M$$

or

$$\frac{\log_2 M}{L} \leq \frac{\mathbf{I}(Y_l; Z_l) + 1/L}{1 - \mathbb{P}\Big[\hat{P} \neq P\Big]}.$$

When we take the limit $L \to \infty$, we obtain $R_{\mathrm{id}} \leq \mathbf{I}(Y_l; Z_l)(1 + \delta)$. Now as we let $\delta \to 0$ (where $\delta$ is defined in Def. 4.1), which implies $\mathbb{P}\Big[\hat{P} \neq P\Big] \to 0$, we have that $R_{\mathrm{id}} \leq \mathbf{I}(Y; Z)$. By combination with the first part of the proof, it follows that the capacity $C_{\mathrm{id}} = \mathbf{I}(Y; Z)$.

### 4.5.3 Example: Bernoulli Variables

Let us consider a hypothetical biometric that gives balanced IID binary values. Let the biometric $X$ form a Bernoulli random variable ($\mathcal{X} = \{0, 1\}$) with parameter $p = \mathbb{P}[X = 1] = 0.5$. Moreover, let

$$Y = X \oplus N_{\mathrm{e}}, \qquad Z = X \oplus N_{\mathrm{i}}, \tag{4.14}$$

with Bernoulli noise variables $N_{\mathrm{e}}$ and $N_{\mathrm{i}}$ having parameters $d_{\mathrm{e}}$ and $d_{\mathrm{i}}$, respectively. The addition $\oplus$ is modulo 2. Then

$$\mathbb{P}[Y_l \neq Z_l] = d = d_{\mathrm{e}}(1 - d_{\mathrm{i}}) + (1 - d_{\mathrm{e}})d_{\mathrm{i}}. \tag{4.15}$$

The mutual information per symbol is given by

$$\mathbf{I}(Y_l; Z_l) = \mathsf{H}(Z_l) - \mathsf{H}(Z_l | Y_l), \tag{4.16}$$

which yields $\mathbf{I}(\mathbf{Y}, \mathbf{Z}) = L[1 - \mathsf{h}(d)]$, with $\mathsf{h}(d)$ the binary entropy function, defined as $\mathsf{h}(d) = -d \log_2 d - (1 - d) \log_2(1 - d)$. Note that in this example, we can conceptually think of the enrollment process as error-free and the identification process as distorted by the concatenation of the original channels $\mathbf{X} \to \mathbf{Y}$ and $\mathbf{X} \to \mathbf{Z}$, yielding a binary symmetric channel with probability of error $d$.

### 4.5.4 Example: IID Gaussian Variables

As a second example, we consider the case that $\mathbf{X}$ is IID Gaussian, zero mean, with variance $\sigma_0^2$. Moreover, for every dimension $l$, let

$$Y_l = X_l + N_{\mathrm{e}}, \qquad Z_l = X_l + N_{\mathrm{i}}, \tag{4.17}$$

with zero-mean Gaussian noise variables $N_{\mathrm{e}}$ and $N_{\mathrm{i}}$ having variances $\sigma_{\mathrm{e}}^2$ and $\sigma_{\mathrm{i}}^2$, respectively. The covariance matrix $\Sigma_{YZ}$ is given by

$$\Sigma_{YZ} = \begin{pmatrix} \mathbb{E}[Y_l^2] - \mathbb{E}[Y_l]^2 & \mathbb{E}[Y_l Z_l] - \mathbb{E}[Y_l]\mathbb{E}[Z_l] \\ \mathbb{E}[Z_l Y_l] - \mathbb{E}[Z_l]\mathbb{E}[Y_l] & \mathbb{E}[Z_l^2] - \mathbb{E}[Z_l]^2 \end{pmatrix} = \begin{pmatrix} \sigma_0^2 + \sigma_e^2 & \sigma_0^2 \\ \sigma_0^2 & \sigma_0^2 + \sigma_i^2 \end{pmatrix}.$$

$$(4.18)$$

Hence, using $\mathsf{H}(Y_l, Z_l) = \frac{1}{2}\log|\det \Sigma_{YZ}|$, it follows that

$$\mathbf{I}(Y_l; Z_l) = \frac{1}{2}\log_2\left(1 + \frac{\sigma_0^2}{\sigma_e^2 + \sigma_i^2 + \sigma_e^2\sigma_i^2/\sigma_0^2}\right). \qquad (4.19)$$

Note that in this example, in contrast to Section 4.5.3, the combined channel $Y_l \to X_l \to Z_l$ with $\sigma_e^2 > 0$ cannot be represented as a noiseless enrollment followed by an additive Gaussian channel with some noise power depending *only* on $\sigma_e^2$ and $\sigma_i^2$. This phenomenon finds its cause in the fact that, in general, the backward channel of an additive channel is non-additive.

Often, enrollment can be performed under "ideal" circumstances, or can be repeated several times to reduce the noise. Then the noise-free biometric $\mathbf{Y} = \mathbf{X}$ becomes available. In that case, $C_{\mathrm{id}} = 1 - \mathsf{h}(d_i)$ in the example of Bernoulli variables and $C_{\mathrm{id}} = \frac{1}{2}\log(1 + \sigma_0^2/\sigma_i^2)$ for Gaussian variables.

## 4.6 Hypothesis Testing; Maximum Likelihood

We have seen earlier that a decoder that is based on typicality achieves capacity. Nevertheless, such a decoder may not be optimal in the sense of minimizing the maximum error probability for finite $L$. In a more general detection-theoretical setting, we may see our identification problem as a hypothesis testing procedure (i.e., a procedure that aims at achieving the best trade-off between certain error probabilities). An optimal hypothesis testing procedure is based on the likelihoods of the observed data (enrollment data and identification data) given the individual $p$. The *maximum likelihood decoder* selects

$$\hat{p} = \arg\max_p \mathbb{P}[\mathbf{Z}(p) = \mathbf{z}|\mathbf{Y}(p) = \mathbf{y}(p)], \qquad (4.20)$$

where the observation $\mathbf{z}$ is fixed (i.e., not a function of $p$). For the decoder, the relevant probability can be written as

$$\mathbb{P}[\mathbf{Z}(p) = \mathbf{z}|\mathbf{Y}(p) = \mathbf{y}(p)] = \prod_{j=1}^L \frac{\sum_{x \in \mathcal{X}} Q(x) P_e(y_j(p)|x) P_i(z_j|x)}{\sum_{x \in \mathcal{X}} Q(x) P_e(y_j(p)|x)}. \qquad (4.21)$$

Here the sum is over all possible $x$, which is of modest complexity. Particularly if $\mathbf{X}$ contains IID elements and if the channel models $P_e(y_j|x)$ and $P_i(z_j|x)$ are known (e.g., from Sections 4.5.3 and 4.5.4), the complexiy of this calculation is small. Yet this decision variable has to be calculated for all $p$ in the database.

This illustrates how the enrollment output sequences $\mathbf{Y}(1), \mathbf{Y}(2), \ldots,$ $\mathbf{Y}(M)$ act as as codewords. These codewords are observed via a memoryless channel $\{\mathcal{Z}, P(z|y), \mathcal{Y}\}$.

Note that decoding according to our achievability proof involves an exhaustive search procedure. It is not known how an identification scheme can be modified in such a way that the decoding complexity is decreased. However, the helper data proposed in the second half of this chapter has the side effect of accelerating the recognition process.

## 4.7 Private Templates

Identification inherently requires that a verifier searches for matches with the measured $\mathbf{Z}$ in a database Y that contains data about the entire population. This introduces the security and privacy threat that the verifier who steals biometric templates from some (or even all) persons in the database can perform impersonation attacks. This threat was recognized by several researchers [33, 186, 277]. When a private verification system is used on a large scale, the reference database has to be made available to many different verifiers, who, in general, cannot be trusted. Matsumoto et al. [189] showed that information stolen from a database can be misused to construct artificial biometrics to impersonate people. Creation of artificial biometrics is possible even if only part of the template is available. Hill [146] showed that if only minutiae templates of a fingerprint are available, it is still possible to successfully construct artificial biometrics that pass private verification.

To develop an insight in the security aspects of biometrics, we distinguish between verification and private verification. In a typical verification situation, access to the reference template allows a malicious Victor to artificially construct measurement data that will pass the verification test, even if Peggy has never exposed herself to a biometric measurement after the enrollment.

In private verification, the reference data should not leak relevant information to allow Victor to (effectively) construct valid measurement data. Such protection is common practice for storage of computer passwords. When a computer verifies a password, it does not compare the password $\mathbf{Y}$ typed by the user with a stored reference copy. Instead, the password is processed by a cryptographic one-way function $F$ and the outcome is compared against a locally stored reference string $F(\mathbf{Y})$. So $\mathbf{Y}$ is only temporarily available on the system hardware, and no stored data allow calculation of $\mathbf{Y}$. This prevents attacks from the inside by stealing unencrypted or decryptable secrets.

The main difference between password checking and biometric private verification is that during biometric measurements, it is unavoidable that noise or other aberrations occur. Noisy measurement data are quantized into discrete values before these can be processed by any cryptographic function. Due to external noise, the outcome of the quantization may differ from experiment to experiment. In particular, if one of Peggy's biometric parameters has a value close to a quantization threshold, minor amounts of noise can change the outcome. Minor changes at the input of a cryptographic function are amplified and the outcome will bear no resemblance to the expected outcome.

This property, commonly refered to as "confusion" and "diffusion," makes it less trivial to use biometric data as input to a cryptographic function. The notion of *near matches* or *distance* between enrollment and operational measurements vanishes after encryption or any other cryptographically strong operation. Hence, the comparison of measured data with reference data cannot be executed in the encrypted domain without prior precautions to contain the effect of noise.

Furthermore, with increasing $M$ and $L$, the probability that a "randomly created" natural biometric vector lies near a decision boundary goes to unity for any a priori defined digitization scheme. Error correction coding does not help, because the biometrics are generated randomly; thus, they do not naturally lie centered inside decision regions, as codewords would do.

A common misperception is that encryption of $\mathbf{Y}$ and decryption prior to the verification solve this security threat. This would not prevent a dishonest Victor from stealing the decrypted template $\mathbf{Y}$, because Victor knows the decryption key.

The next subsection presents an algorithm to resolve these threats. It is based on a "helper data scheme" that resembles "fuzzy extractors," covered in Chapter 5.

In addition to private verification, a further application can be the generation of a secret key. We illustrate this by the example of access to a database of highly confidential encrypted documents to which only a set of specific users is allowed access. The retrieval system authenticates humans and retrieves a decryption key from their biometric parameters. This system must be protected against a dishonest software programmer Mallory who has access to the biometric reference data from all users. If Mallory downloads the complete reference data file, all encrypted documents, and possibly reads all the software code of the system, she should not be able to decrypt any document.

Meanwhile, it is important to realize that protection of the reference data stored in a database is not a complete solution to the above-mentioned threats. After having had an opportunity to measure operational biometric data, a dishonest Victor uses these measurement data. This can happen without anyone noticing it: Victor grabs the fingerprint image left behind on a sensor. This corresponds to grabbing all keystrokes, including the plain passwords, typed by a user. We do not address this last attack in this chapter.

### 4.7.1 The Helper Data Architecture

We observe that a biometric private verification system does not need to store the original biometric templates. Examples of systems that use other architectures and achieve protection of templates are *private biometrics* [81], *fuzzy commitment* [161], *cancelable biometrics* [231], *fuzzy vault* [159], *quantizing secret extraction* [182], and *secret extraction from significant components* [283]. The systems proposed in [81, 159, 161, 182, 283] are all based on architectures that use helper data.

In order to combine private biometric verification with cryptographic techniques, we derive *helper data* during the enrollment phase. The helper data $\mathbf{W}$ guarantees that a unique string $\mathbf{S}$ can be derived from the biometrics of an individual during the private verification as well as during the enrollment phase. The helper data serves two purposes. On the one hand, it is used to reduce the effects of noise in the biometric measurements. More precisely, it ensures that with high probability, the measured noisy biometric always falls within the same decision region taken by the detector. As a result, exactly the same string $\mathbf{S}$ is always extracted from the same $p$. Since the string $\mathbf{S}$ is not affected by noise anymore, it can be used as input to cryptographic primitives without causing avalanches of errors. Thus, $\mathbf{S}$ can be handled in the same secure manner as computer passwords.

However, since random biometrics are usually not uniformly distributed, the extracted string $\mathbf{S}$ is not guaranteed to be uniform. Therefore, another part of the helper data is used to extract the randomness of the biometric measurements. Usually, this is done by letting the helper data be a pointer to a randomly chosen function from a universal set of hash functions (see Chapter 5). The left-over hash lemma guarantees that the hashed string is indistinguishable from a uniformly random string. The error-correction phase is usually called *information reconciliation* and the randomness extraction is called the *privacy amplification* phase.

Private biometric verification consists of two phases: *enrollment* and *private verification*. During the enrollment phase, Peggy visits a Certification Authority (CA) where her biometrics are measured and reference data (including helper data) are generated. For on-line applications, such protected reference data can be stored in a central database (possibly even publicly accessible), or these data can be certified with a digital signature of the CA, and given to Peggy. In the latter case, it is Peggy's responsibility to (securely) give this certified reference data to Victor. Thus, the reference data consists of two parts: the cryptographic key value $\mathbf{V} = F(\mathbf{S})$ against which the processed measurement data are compared, and the data $\mathbf{W}$ which assist in achieving reliable detection.

Assuming that these data are available as $\mathbf{V}(\text{Peggy}) = \mathbf{v}; \mathbf{W}(\text{Peggy}) = \mathbf{w}$, Peggy authenticates herself as follows:

- When she claims to be Peggy, she sends her identifier message to Victor.
- Victor retrieves the helper data $\mathbf{w}$ from an on-line trusted database. Alternatively, in an off-line application, Peggy could provide Victor with reference data $(\mathbf{v}, \mathbf{w})$ certified by the CA.
- Peggy allows Victor to take a noisy measurement $\mathbf{z}$ of her biometrics.
- Victor calculates $\mathbf{s}' = G(\mathbf{w}, \mathbf{z})$. Here, $G$ is a "shielding" function, to be discussed later.
- *Optional for key establishment:* Victor can extract further cryptographic keys from $\mathbf{s}'$—for instance, to generate an access key.

- Victor calculates the cryptographic hash function $\mathbf{v}' = F(\mathbf{s}')$.
- $\mathbf{v}'$ is compared with the reference data $\mathbf{v}$. If $\mathbf{v}' = \mathbf{v}$, the private verification is successful.

Here, we used lowercase $\mathbf{n}, \mathbf{x}, \mathbf{y}, \mathbf{z}, \mathbf{v},$ and $\mathbf{w}$ to explicitly denote that the protocol operates on realizations of the random variables $\mathbf{N}$, $\mathbf{X}$, $\mathbf{Y}$, $\mathbf{Z}$, $\mathbf{V}$, and $\mathbf{W}$, respectively. The length of these vectors is denoted as $L_N, L_X, L_Y, L_Z, L_V,$ and $L_W$, respectively. Often, the same type of measurement is done for enrollment and for verification; thus, $L_Y = L_Z$ and $\mathcal{Y} = \mathcal{Z}$. Further, $\mathbf{S}$ and $F(\mathbf{S})$ are discrete-valued (typically binary) vectors of length $L_S$ and $L_F$, respectively. Note that here we make an exact match. Checking for imperfect matches would not make sense because of the cryptographic operation $F$. Measurement imperfections (noise) are eliminated by the use of $\mathbf{W}$ and the so-called $\delta$-contracting property of the shielding function $G$.

### 4.7.2 Definitions

During enrollment, $\mathbf{Y}(\text{Peggy}) = \mathbf{y}$ is measured. Some secret $\mathbf{S}(\text{Peggy}) = \mathbf{s} \in \mathcal{S}^{L_S}$ is determined, and the corresponding $\mathbf{V} = F(\mathbf{s}) \in \mathcal{V}^{L_V}$ is computed. In later sections, we will address whether $\mathbf{s}$ can be chosen arbitrarily ($\mathbf{s} \in \mathcal{S}^{L_s}$) by the CA, or that the enrollment algorithm explicitly outputs one specific value of $\mathbf{s}$ based on $\mathbf{y}$. Also, a value for $\mathbf{W}(\text{Peggy}) = \mathbf{w}$ is calculated such that not only $G(\mathbf{w}, \mathbf{y}) = \mathbf{s}$ but also during private verification $G(\mathbf{w}, \mathbf{z}) = \mathbf{s}$ for $\mathbf{z} \approx \mathbf{x}$, more precisely for distances $d(\mathbf{z}, \mathbf{x}) \leq \delta$. We call a function that supports this property $\delta$-contracting.

**Definition 4.2.** *Let $G : \mathcal{W}^{L_w} \times \mathcal{Y}^{L_y} \to \mathcal{S}^{L_S}$ be a function and $\delta > 0$ be a non-negative real number. The function $G$ is called $\delta$-contracting if and only if for all $\mathbf{y} \in \mathcal{Y}^{L_Y}$, there exists (an efficient algorithm to find) at least one vector $\mathbf{w} \in \mathcal{W}^{L_W}$ and one $\mathbf{s} \in \mathcal{S}^{L_S}$ such that $G(\mathbf{w}, \mathbf{y}) = G(\mathbf{w}, \mathbf{z}) = \mathbf{S}$ for all $\mathbf{z} \in \mathcal{Y}^{L_Y}$ such that $d(\mathbf{z}, \mathbf{y}) \leq \delta$.*

We now argue that helper data are an essential attribute to make a secure biometrics system. We show this by contradiction, namely by initially assuming that $\mathbf{W}$ does not depend on $p$.

**Theorem 4.2.** *If $G(\mathbf{w}, \mathbf{z}) = f(\mathbf{z})$ for all $\mathbf{w}$, then either the largest contracting range of $G$ is $\delta = 0$ or $G(\mathbf{w}, \mathbf{z})$ is a constant independent of $\mathbf{z}$.*

Proof. Take $\mathbf{W} = \mathbf{w}_0$. Assume $G$ is $\delta$-contracting, with $\delta > 0$. Choose two points $\mathbf{z}_1$ and $\mathbf{z}_2$ such that $G(\mathbf{w}_0, \mathbf{z}_1) = \mathbf{s}_1$ and $G(\mathbf{w}_0, \mathbf{z}_2) = \mathbf{s}_2$. Define a vector $\mathbf{r} = \lambda(\mathbf{z}_2 - \mathbf{z}_1)$ such that $0 < d(\mathbf{0}, \mathbf{r}) < \delta$. Then $\mathbf{s}_1 = G(\mathbf{w}_0, \mathbf{z}_1) = G(\mathbf{w}_0, \mathbf{z}_1 + \mathbf{r}) = G(\mathbf{w}_0, \mathbf{z}_1 + 2\mathbf{r}) = ... = \mathbf{s}_2$. Thus $G(\mathbf{w}_0, \mathbf{z}_1) = G(\mathbf{w}_0, \mathbf{z}_2)$ is constant.

    **Corrolary.** *The desirable property that biometric data can be verified in the encrypted domain (in an information-theoretic sense) cannot be achieved* *unless person-specific data* **W** *is used. Private biometric verification that attempts to process* **Z** *without such helper data is doomed to store decryptable user templates.*

Any function is 0-contracting. If the radius $\delta$ is properly chosen as a function of the noise power, the $\delta$-contracting property ensures that despite the noise, for a specific Peggy all likely measurements **Z** will be mapped to the same value of **S**. This can particularly be guaranteed if $L \to \infty$. For private verification schemes with large $L_Y = L_Z = L$, $d(\mathbf{Z}, \mathbf{Y}) \to \sigma_n \sqrt{L}$, where $\sigma_n^2$ is the noise power. So one needs to ensure that $\delta$ is sufficiently larger than $\sigma_n \sqrt{L}$.

**Definition 4.3.** *Let $G : \mathcal{W}^{L_W} \times \mathcal{Y}^{L_Y} \to \mathcal{S}^{L_S}$ be a $\delta$-contracting function with $\delta > 0$ and let $\epsilon > 0$ be a non-negative real number. The function $G$ is called $\epsilon$-revealing if and only if for all $\mathbf{y} \in \mathcal{Y}^{L_Y}$, there exists (an efficient algorithm to find) a vector $\mathbf{w} \in \mathcal{W}^{L_W}$ such that $\mathbf{I}(\mathbf{w}; G(\mathbf{w}, \mathbf{y})) < \epsilon$.*

Hence, **W** conceals **S**: it reveals only a well-defined, small amount of information about **S**. Similarly, we require that $F(\mathbf{S})$ conceals **S**. However, we do not interpret this in the information-theoretic sense but in the complexity-theoretic sense; that is, the computational effort to obtain a reasonable estimate of **X** or **S** from $F(\mathbf{S})$ is prohibitive, even though in the information-theoretic sense, $F(\mathbf{S})$ may (uniquely) define **S**.

The above definitions address properties of the shielding function $G$. Efficient enrollment requires an algorithm $\Gamma(\mathbf{Y}) \to (\mathbf{W}, \mathbf{S})$ to generate the helper data and the secret. The procedure $\Gamma$ is a randomized procedure and only used during enrollment.

### 4.7.3 Example: Quantization Indexing for IID Gaussian

Let $\mathbf{X}, \mathbf{Y}, \mathbf{Z}, \mathbf{N_e},$ and $\mathbf{N_i}$ be Gaussian variables as defined in Section 4.5.4. Moreover, $L_X = L_Y = L_Z = L_W = L_S = L$ and $\mathcal{X} = \mathcal{Y} = \mathcal{Z} = \mathcal{W} = \mathbb{R}$. The core idea is that measured data are quantized. The quantization intervals are alternatingly mapped to $s_l = 0$ and $s_l = 1$. The helper data $w_l$ act as a bias in the biometric value to ensure detection of the correct value of $s_l$. This example resembles strategies known in the literature on Quantization Index Modulation (QIM) [62], which is a specific form of electronic watermarking, and on writing on dirty paper. QIM was applied to biometrics in [182].

### Enrollment in QIM

During enrollment, $y_l$ is measured and the CA generates $w_l$ such that the value of $y_l + w_l$ is pushed to the center of the nearest quantization interval that corresponds to the correct $s_l$ value:

$$
w_l = \begin{cases} (2n + \frac{1}{2})q - y_l \text{ if } s_l = 1 \\ (2n - \frac{1}{2})q - y_l \text{ if } s_l = 0, \end{cases} \tag{4.22}
$$

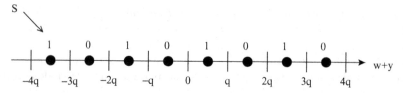

**Fig. 4.2.** Quantization levels for the shielding function $G$ defined in (4.23). The helper data $w$ pushe $y$ toward the center of a quantization interval (indicated by dots).

where $n \in \mathbb{Z}$ is chosen such that $-q < w_l < q$ and $q$ is an appropriately chosen quantization step size. The value of $n$ is discarded, but the values $w_l$ are released as helper data. Figure 4.2 illustrates the quantization.

## Private Verification in QIM

For the $l$-th component of $\mathbf{Z}$, the $\delta$-contracting function is

$$s_l' = G(w_l, z_l) = \begin{cases} 1 \text{ if } 2nq < z_l + w_l \leq (2n+1)q \text{ for any } n \in \mathbb{Z} \\ 0 \text{ if } (2n-1)q < z_l + w_l \leq nq \text{ for any } n \in \mathbb{Z} \end{cases} \quad (4.23)$$

The contraction range $\delta$ equals $q/2$.

## Error Probability in QIM

The probability of a bit error in the component $s_l$ in the case of an honest pair Peggy-Victor is given by

$$P_e = 2 \sum_{b=0}^{\infty} \left\{ Q\left( \left[2b + \frac{3}{2}\right] \frac{q}{\sigma_n} \right) - Q\left( \left[2b + \frac{1}{2}\right] \frac{q}{\sigma_n} \right) \right\}, \quad (4.24)$$

where $Q(x)$ is the $\int_0^x$ integral over the Gaussian probability density function (pdf) with unit variance and $\sigma_n = \sqrt{\sigma_e^2 + \sigma_i^2}$ is the strength of the noise $N_i - N_e$. An error-correcting code can be used to correct the bit errors. The maximum achievable code rate is $1 - h(P_e)$. In practice, this rate is only approached for $L \to \infty$. Large values of $q$ ensure reliable detection, because $P_e$ becomes small. However, we will show now that the information leakage is minimized only if $q$ is small.

## Information Leakage in QIM

Using Bayes' rule, for given $w_l$ we can express the a posteriori probability of the event $S_l = 1$ as

$$\mathbb{P}[S_l = 1 | W_l = w_l] = \frac{f(w_l | S_l = 1)}{f(w_l)} \mathbb{P}[S_l = 1]. \quad (4.25)$$

Here, $f$ is the pdf of $W$. Information leaks whenever $f(w_l|S_l = 1) \neq f(w_l|S_l = 0)$. Since the pdf of $X_l$ is not flat, some values of $w_l$ are more likely than others even within $-q < w_l < q$. This gives an imbalance in the above a posteriori probability.

We now quantify the information leakage given our assumptions on the statistical behavior of the input signal $X_l$. The statistics of $W_l$ are determined by those of $X_l$ and $S_l$. We observe that for $s_l = 1$, $w_l = (2n + 1/2)q - y_l$, so

$$f(w_l|S_l = 1) = \begin{cases} 0 & \text{for } |w_l| \geq q \\ \sum_{n=-\infty}^{\infty} \frac{1}{\sqrt{2\pi\sigma_y^2}} \exp\left(-\frac{([2n+1/2]q - w_l)^2}{2\sigma_y^2}\right) & \text{for } |w_l| < q. \end{cases}$$

(4.26)

Here, we defined $\sigma_y^2 = \sigma_0^2 + \sigma_e^2$. An expression similar to (4.26) is obtained for $f(w_l|S_l = 0)$. We have the symmetry relations $f(w_l|S_l = s) = f(q - w_l|S_l = s)$ and $f(w_l|S_l = 0) = f(-w_l|S = 1)$ [182]. The mutual information follows from

$$\mathbf{I}(W_l; S_l) = \mathsf{H}(S_l) - \int_{-q}^{q} \mathsf{H}(S_l|W_l = w)f(w) \, dw. \tag{4.27}$$

Using Bayes' rule, the symmetry properties of $f$, and the uniformity of $\mathbf{S}$, we obtain

$$\mathbf{I}(W_l; S_l) = \int_{-q}^{q} f(w|S_l = 1) \log_2 f(w|S_l = 1) \, dw - \int_{-q}^{q} f(w) \log_2 f(w) \, dw. \tag{4.28}$$

Fig. 4.3 shows that quantization values as crude as $q/\sigma_y = 1$ are sufficient to ensure small leakage ($< 10^{-4}$). Crude quantization steps are favorable as these allow reliable detection (i.e., a large contracting range).

## 4.8 Secrecy and Identification Capacity

It is natural to ask what the maximum length of the secret key that can be extracted from a biometric measurement is. The size of the secrets is expressed as the rate $R_s$, expressed as the effective key size in bits per biometric symbol (entropy bits/symbol). The maximum achievable rate is defined accordingly by the secrecy capacity $C_s$.

**Definition 4.4 (Secrecy capacity).** *The secrecy capacity $C_s$ is the maximal rate $R_s$, such that for all $\epsilon > 0$, there exist encoders and decoders that, for sufficiently large $L_x$, achieve*

$$\mathbb{P}[\mathbf{S}' \neq \mathbf{S}] \leq \epsilon, \tag{4.29}$$

$$\mathbf{I}(\mathbf{W}; \mathbf{S}) \leq \epsilon, \tag{4.30}$$

$$\frac{1}{L}\mathsf{H}(\mathbf{S}) \geq (R_s - \epsilon). \tag{4.31}$$

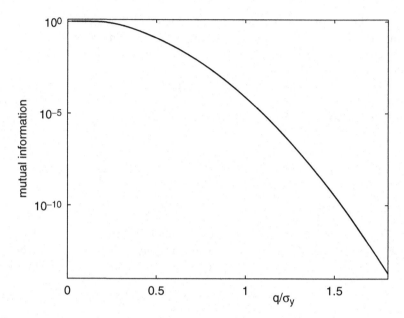

**Fig. 4.3.** Mutual information $\mathbf{I}(W_l; S_l)$ as a function of the quantisation step size $q/\sigma_y$.

Eq. (4.29) ensures correctness of the secret, (4.30) ensures secrecy with respect to eavesdropping of the communication line, and (4.31) guarantees high entropy in the secret. Eq. (4.31) is a stronger requirement than versatility.

If $\mathbf{I}(\mathbf{W}; \mathbf{S})$ is small and H is large, an impersonation attack is based on artificial biometrics that pass an private verification. We remark that, in general, $\mathbf{I}(\mathbf{V}, \mathbf{W}; \mathbf{X})$ is large in the strict information-theoretic sense. In the computational sense, however, it is infeasible to derive information about $\mathbf{S}$ from $\mathbf{V}$. Hence, from a computational point of view, $\mathbf{V}$ does not reveal information about $\mathbf{X}$.

The uncertainty expressed by $H(\mathbf{S}|\mathbf{W}) = H(\mathbf{S}) - \mathbf{I}(\mathbf{W}; \mathbf{S})$ defines a security parameter $\kappa$ for impersonation. It gives the number of attempts that have to be performed in order to achieve successful impersonation. In order to compute the secrecy capacity the following lemma is needed, which we present here for the sake of completeness.

**Lemma 4.1.** *For continuous random variables $X$, $Y$ and $\epsilon > 0$, there exists a sequence of discretized random variables $X_d$ and $Y_d$ that converge pointwise to $X$, $Y$ (when $d \to \infty$) such that for sufficiently large $d$,*

$$\mathbf{I}(X; Y) \geq \mathbf{I}(X_d; Y_d) \geq \mathbf{I}(X; Y) - \epsilon. \tag{4.32}$$

With some modifications to the results from [4, 194], the following theorem can be proven using Lemma 4.1.

**Theorem 4.3.** *The secrecy capacity of a biometric system equals*

$$C_{\mathrm{s}} = \mathbf{I}\left(\mathbf{Y}(p); \mathbf{Z}(p)\right). \tag{4.33}$$

*Proof.* We start with the achievability argument. The proof that $\mathbf{I}(\mathbf{Y}; \mathbf{Z})$ can be achieved if $\mathbf{Y}$ and $\mathbf{Z}$ are discrete variables is analogous to the proof in [4]. In order to prove achievability in the continuous case, we choose $\epsilon \geq 0$ and approximate the random variables $\mathbf{Y}$ and $\mathbf{Z}$ by discretized (quantized) versions, $\mathbf{Y}_d$ and $\mathbf{Z}_d$, respectively, such that $\mathbf{I}(\mathbf{Y}; \mathbf{Z}) - \mathbf{I}(\mathbf{Y}_d; \mathbf{Z}_d) \leq \epsilon$. (The fact that such a quantization exists follows from Lemma 4.1). Then, taking the encoder that achieves the capacity for the discrete case $(\mathbf{Y}_d, \mathbf{Z}_d)$, it follows that we can achieve $\mathbf{I}(\mathbf{Y}_d; \mathbf{Z}_d)$. Since this can be done for any $\epsilon \geq 0$, the proof follows.

The fact that $\mathbf{I}(\mathbf{Y}; \mathbf{Z})$ is an upper bound for $C_{\mathrm{s}}$ for discrete random variables follows from the Fano inequality and some basic entropy inequalities. For the continuous case, this follows again by an approximation argument using Lemma 4.1. □

It was proven in [270] that there exists a biometric private verification algorithm that achieves both the secrecy capacity $C_{\mathrm{s}}$ and the identification capacity $C_{\mathrm{id}}$ at the same time.

**Identification Capacity, Revisited**

We have derived the secrecy capacity for secure private verification systems with helper data. Yet, the identification capacity was up to this section only established for systems without helper data. In this subsection, we show that the identification capacity is equal to the channel capacity of the biometric sensor if helper data and shielding functions are applied.

**Definition 4.5 (Identification capacity).** *The identification capacity $C_{\mathrm{id}}$ is the maximal rate $R_{\mathrm{id}}$, such that for every $\epsilon > 0$, for sufficiently large $L$, there exists an identification strategy that achieves*

$$\mathrm{avg}\ \mathbb{P}[\hat{P} \neq P] \leq \epsilon \quad and \quad \frac{1}{L}\log M \geq R_{\mathrm{id}} - \epsilon, \tag{4.34}$$

*where the average is over all individuals and over all random realizations of all biometrics.*

A private verification scheme with helper data can be used for identification: For a biometric measurement $\mathbf{y}$, the verifier performs an exhausive search over the entire population of candidates $p' \in \{1, \ldots, M\}$ by retrieving from a database the values $\mathbf{w}$ and $\mathbf{v}$ for each candidate and checking if $F(G(\mathbf{w}, \mathbf{y})) = \mathbf{v}$. In practice, such a system can be computationally more efficient than a straightforward identification scheme mentioned in the first part of this chapter: It does not need to consider *near* matches, but only exact matches. The exact matches are performed in the binary domain and therefore are very efficient. The above definition addresses such a system.

For systems without enrollment noise, it can be shown [218, 292] that if the $\delta$-contracting range is chosen such that it matches the sphere that verification noise creates around $\mathbf{X}$, the biometric identification systems, including template-protecting systems, satisfy $C_{\mathrm{id}} = \mathbf{I}(\mathbf{X}; \mathbf{Y})$. This result can be interpreted merely as a statement that helper data do not negatively influence the performance.

## 4.9 Relation with Fuzzy Extractors

In this book, several chapters deal with key extraction from noisy data, in general, and biometrics, in particular. A well-known technique that is treated in Chapter 5 is called *Fuzzy Extractors*. Here, we prove that the helper data technique developed in this chapter is equivalent to that of a fuzzy extractor. We need some details of the construction of a fuzzy extractor. For those details, we refer to Chapter 5. We define

$$\mathsf{Gen}(\mathbf{y}) = \Gamma(\mathbf{y}) \quad \text{and} \quad \mathsf{Rep}(\mathbf{z}, \mathbf{w}) = G(\mathbf{w}, \mathbf{z}).$$

With this definition, the following two theorems have been proven [280].

**Theorem 4.4.** *Suppose that there exists a* $(\mathcal{Y}, m, l, \delta, \epsilon \leq 1/4)$ *fuzzy extractor with generation and reproduction procedures* Gen *and* Rep *constructed by using a secure sketch and with* $K$ *uniformly distributed over* $\{0,1\}^l$ *statistically independent from* $(X, Y)$. *Then, there exists a* $\delta$-*contracting,* $\eta$-*revealing function* $G$, *with counterpart* $\Gamma$, *with*

$$\eta = h(2\epsilon) + 2\epsilon(|\mathsf{Gen}(\mathbf{y})| + |K|) + h(\epsilon) + \epsilon|K|.$$

This theorem proves that a fuzzy extractor implies a helper data algorithm that is $\eta$-revealing. Furthermore, we have the following converse.

**Theorem 4.5.** *Let* $G$ *be a* $\delta$-*contracting,* $\epsilon$-*revealing function creating a uniformly random key* $K$ *on* $\{0,1\}^l$ *wrt to a probability distribution* $P_{XY}$ *with* $\mathsf{H}_\infty(X) > m$. *Then there exists a* $(\mathcal{X}, m, l, \delta, \sqrt{\epsilon})$ *fuzzy extractor.*

For the proofs of Theorems 4.4. and 4.5. we refer the reader to [280].

Theorem 4.5. explains that a helper data algorithm leads to a fuzzy extractor whose key is "only" $\sqrt{\epsilon}$ distinguishable from random if the helper data algorithm was $\epsilon$-revealing. Theorems 4.4. and 4.5. show that fuzzy extractors and helper data algorithms are equivalent up to parameter values.

## 4.10 Conclusion

We have developed an information-theoretic framework for biometrics. We described biometric identification in terms of two communication channels both having the same biometric source $\mathbf{X}$, but with the enrollment data $\mathbf{Y}$ and the operational measurement $\mathbf{Z}$ as destinations. We have shown that it is possible to derive bounds on the capacity of biometric identification systems with relatively simple methods. The main result is that capacity can be computed as the mutual information $\mathbf{I}(\mathbf{Y};\mathbf{Z})$ between a input source $\mathbf{Y}$ and an output source $\mathbf{Z}$ that are related by the concatenation of the backward enrollment channel and the forward identification channel. The base-2 logarithm of the number of persons that can be distinguished reliably is expressed as the number of symbols in the observation, multiplied by the rate $R$. For rates $R$ smaller than $\mathbf{I}(\mathbf{Y};\mathbf{Z})$, this probability can also be made smaller than any $\varepsilon > 0$ by increasing $L$.

We showed that the secrecy capacity measures the entropy available in a key derived from the person. This result has been connected to a protocol that satisfies privacy and security requirements—in particular, the protection of templates to prevent misuse by a dishonest verifier. We have introduced the notion of $\delta$-contracting and $\epsilon$-revealing shielding functions, where the $\delta$-contraction describes the robsutness against noise in the biometric sensor. The $\epsilon$-revelation description the absence of any leakage of information via publicly available templates.

The identification capacity appears to be determined by the "channel capacity" of the biometric sensor, also for schemes that involve template protection. Similarly, the entropy of a secret that can be derived from the biometric measurement depends on the channel capacity of the biometric sensor.

# 5

# Fuzzy Extractors*

Yevgeniy Dodis, Leonid Reyzin, and Adam Smith

## 5.1 Motivation

This chapter presents a general approach for handling secret biometric data in cryptographic applications. The generality manifests itself in two ways: We attempt to minimize the assumptions we make about the data and to present techniques that are broadly applicable wherever biometric inputs are used.

Because biometric data come from a variety of sources that are mostly outside of anyone's control, it is prudent to assume as little as possible about how they are distributed; in particular, an adversary may know more about a distribution than a system's designers and users. Of course, one may attempt to measure some properties of a biometric distribution, but relying on such measurements in the security analysis is dangerous, because the adversary may have even more accurate measurements available to it. For instance, even assuming that some property of a biometric behaves according to a binomial distribution (or some similar discretization of the Normal distribution), one could determine the mean of this distribution only to within $\sim 1/\sqrt{n}$ after taking $n$ samples; a well-motivated adversary can take more measurements and thus determine the mean more accurately.

Rather than assuming that some statistical information about the biometric input is available, we assume only that the input is unpredictable: That if an adversary is allowed a single guess at the value of the input, the likelihood that it is correct is $2^{-m}$ for some $m$. This is a minimal assumption in the applications we consider: Indeed, if the input is easily guessed, then one cannot use it to derive, say, a secret key for encryption or remote authentication. Of course, determining the exact value of $m$ may in itself present a challenge; however, some lower bound on $m$ is necessary for any sort of security claims.

Similarly, although some understanding of errors in biometric measurements is possible, we prefer to minimize the assumptions we make about such

---

* This survey was written while L. Reyzin and A. Smith were visiting the Institute for Pure and Applied Mathematics at UCLA.

errors. We assume only that a subsequent measurement is within a given, allowed distance of the measurement taken at enrollment.

The broad applicability of the approaches presented here stems from the initial observation that many prior solutions for specific security problems based on noisy data (including biometrics) shared essential techniques and analyses. Instead of designing solutions for each particular setting as it arises, it seems worthwhile to consider the properties that such solutions share and to encapsulate them into primitives that can be used in a variety of contexts.

There is a large body of cryptographic literature that can provide security if only there is a secret, uniformly random, reliably reproducible random string (such a string can be used, for example, as a secret key, or as a seed to generate a public/private key pair). Therefore, if biometric inputs can be converted to such strings, a wide array of cryptographic techniques can be used to provide security from biometrics. To do so, we present a primitive termed *fuzzy extractor*. It extracts a uniformly random string $R$ from its input $w$ in a noise-tolerant way: If the input changes to some $w'$ but remains close, the string $R$ can be reproduced exactly. To help in the reproduction of $R$, a fuzzy extractor, when used for the first time, outputs a helper string $P$ that can safely be made public without decreasing the security of $R$.

Fuzzy extractors can be used, for example, to encrypt and authenticate a user's record using his biometric input as a key: One uses $R$ as an encryption/authentication key and stores $P$ in order to recover $R$ from the biometric whenever the record needs to be accessed. Note that $R$ is not stored—thus, the user's biometric itself effectively acts as the key, and the record can be stored encrypted in a nonsecret, even replicated, database with the confidence that only when the correct biometric is presented will the record be decrypted.

As a step in constructing fuzzy extractors, and as an interesting object in its own right, we present another primitive, termed *secure sketch*. It allows precise reconstruction of a noisy input as follows: On input $w$, a procedure outputs a sketch $s$. Then, given $s$ and a value $w'$ close to $w$, it is possible to recover $w$. The sketch is secure in the sense that it does not reveal much about $w$: $w$ retains much of its entropy even if $s$ is known. Thus, instead of storing $w$ for fear that later readings will be noisy, it is possible to store $s$ instead while retaining much of the secrecy of $w$.

Because different biometric information has different error patterns, we do not assume any particular notion of closeness between $w'$ and $w$. Rather, in defining our primitives, we simply assume that $w$ comes from some metric space and that $w'$ is no more than a certain distance $t$ from $w$ in that space. We consider particular metrics only when building concrete constructions, which we provide for the Hamming distance, set difference, and edit distance (these are defined in Section 5.3). Constructions for other notions of distance are possible as well, and some have appeared in the literature (e.g., [58,176]). Of course, biometric measurements often have to be processed before they fall into a convenient metric space; for instance, techniques such as IrisCode [78] convert images of irises into strings in the Hamming space. This processing is non-trivial and is itself an active research area; in particular, Chapter 11 discusses transformations of biometric measurements (feature vectors) into binary strings.

We also present several extensions of secure sketches and fuzzy extractors. In Section 5.4 we consider slight relaxations of the reliability requirement (reducing it from perfect reliability to reliability with high probability or against computationally bounded adversaries), which permit constructions with a significantly higher error tolerance. In Section 5.5 we consider strengthening the privacy requirement, so that not only does $w$ remain unpredictable to an adversary who has $s$ or $P$, but also any adversarially chosen function of $w$ (such as ethnic origin, gender, or diseases revealed by the biometric) remains as hard to compute as without $s$ or $P$. In Section 5.6 we strengthen fuzzy extractors to remain secure even in the face of active adversaries who may modify $P$; in particular, this allows for key-agreement between a user and a server based only on a biometric input.

The techniques presented have applications beyond biometrics to other settings where noisy inputs are used, such as inputs from human memory, drawings used as passwords, keys from quantum channels or noisy channels, and so forth. They share common roots with prior work in these settings, as well as with work on communication-efficient information reconciliation. One unexpected application of fuzzy extractors is the proof of impossibility of certain strong notions of privacy for statistical databases [99].

## 5.2 Basic Definitions

### 5.2.1 Predictability, Min-Entropy, Statistical Distance, Extraction

If $X$ is a random variable, we will also denote by $X$ the probability distribution on the range of the variable. We use $U_\ell$ to denote the uniform distribution $\{0,1\}^\ell$. Two occurrences of the same random variable in a given expression mean that the same value is used in both (rather than two independent samples). If an algorithm (or a function) $f$ is randomized, we denote by $f(x;r)$ the result of computing $f$ on input $x$ with randomness $r$.

For security, one is often interested in the probability that the adversary predicts a random value (e.g., guesses a secret key). The adversary's best strategy is to guess the most likely value. Thus, the *predictability* of a random variable $A$ is $\max_a \mathbb{P}[A = a]$, and the *min-entropy* $\mathsf{H}_\infty(A)$ is $-\log(\max_a \mathbb{P}[A = a])$ (min-entropy can thus be viewed as the "worst-case" entropy [64]). A random variable with min-entropy at least $m$ is called an $m$-source.

Consider now a pair of (possibly correlated) random variables $A$ and $B$. If the adversary finds out the value $b$ of $B$, then the predictability of $A$ becomes $\max_a \mathbb{P}[A = a \mid B = b]$. On average, the adversary's chance of success in predicting $A$ is $\mathbb{E}_{b \leftarrow B}[\max_a \mathbb{P}[A = a \mid B = b]]$. Here, we are taking the *average* over $B$ (which is not under adversarial control), but the *worst case* over $A$ (because the prediction of $A$ is adversarial once $b$ is known). Again, it is convenient to talk about security in log-scale, which is why *conditional min-entropy* of $A$ given $B$ is defined in [90] as simply the logarithm of the above:

$$\widetilde{\mathsf{H}}_\infty(A \mid B) \overset{\text{def}}{=} -\log \mathop{\mathbb{E}}_{b \leftarrow B} \left[ \max_a \mathbb{P}[A = a | B = b] \right] = -\log \mathop{\mathbb{E}}_{b \leftarrow B} \left[ 2^{-\mathsf{H}_\infty(A|B=b)} \right]$$

This measure satisfies a weak chain rule, namely, revealing any $\lambda$ bits of information about $A$ can cause its entropy to drop by at most $\lambda$ [90, Lemma 3.1]: If $B \in \{0,1\}^\lambda$, then $\widetilde{\mathsf{H}}_\infty(A \mid B,C) \geq \widetilde{\mathsf{H}}_\infty(A \mid C) - \lambda$. This definition of conditional min-entropy is suitable for cryptographic purposes and, in particular, for extracting nearly uniform randomness from $A$ (see [90, Appendix C] for a discussion of related entropy measures, such as smooth entropy [237]). The notion of "nearly" here corresponds to the *statistical distance* between two probability distributions $A$ and $B$, defined as $\mathsf{SD}\,[A,B] = \frac{1}{2}\sum_v |\mathbb{P}[A = v] - \mathbb{P}[B = v]|$. We can interpret this as a measure of distinguishability: Any system in which $B$ is replaced by $A$ will behave exactly the same as the original, with probability at least $1 - \mathsf{SD}\,[A,B]$. We sometimes write $A \approx_\varepsilon B$ to say that $A$ and $B$ are at distance at most $\varepsilon$.

Recall the definition of *strong randomness extractors* [215] from a set $\mathcal{M}$.

**Definition 5.1.** *A randomized function* $\mathsf{Ext} : \mathcal{M} \to \{0,1\}^\ell$ *with randomness of length* $r$ *is an* $(m,\ell,\varepsilon)$*-strong extractor if for all* $m$*-sources* $W$ *on* $\mathcal{M}$, $(\mathsf{Ext}(W;I),I) \approx_\varepsilon (U_\ell, U_r)$, *where* $I = U_r$ *is independent of* $W$.

We think of the output of the extractor as a key generated from $w \leftarrow W$ with the help of a seed $i \leftarrow I$. The definition states that this key behaves as if it is independent of the other parts of the system with probability $1 - \varepsilon$.

Strong extractors can extract at most $\ell = m - 2\log(1/\varepsilon) + \mathcal{O}(1)$ bits from (arbitrary) $m$-sources [230]. There has been extensive research on extractors approaching this bound, typically focusing on reducing the length of the seed (see [248] for references). For our purposes, seed length is not too important, and universal hash functions[1] [57] are sufficient. These extract $\ell = m + 2 - 2\log(1/\varepsilon)$ bits (see [262, Theorem 8.1] and references therein), and generalize to conditional min-entropy without any loss: For any $E$ (possibly dependent on $W$), if $\widetilde{\mathsf{H}}_\infty(W|E) \geq m$ and $\ell = m + 2 - 2\log(1/\varepsilon)$, then $(\mathsf{Ext}(W;I),I,E) \approx_\varepsilon (U_\ell, I, E)$ (as shown in [90, Lemma 4.2]). Other extractors also work for conditional min-entropy but may incur additional entropy loss.

### 5.2.2 Secure Sketches and Fuzzy Extractors

We start by presenting the basic definitions of secure sketches and fuzzy extractors from [90], which are illustrated (together with a sample encryption application) in Fig. 5.1. Extensions of these definitions (that handle active

---

[1] $\mathsf{Ext}(w;i)$ with an $\ell$-bit output is universal if for each $w_1 \neq w_2$, $\mathbb{P}_i[\mathsf{Ext}(w_1;i) = \mathsf{Ext}(w_2;i)] = 2^{-\ell}$. If elements of $\mathcal{M}$ can represented as $n$-bit strings, such functions can be built quite easily using seeds of the length $n$: for instance, simply view $w$ and $x$ as members of $\mathrm{GF}(2^n)$ and let $\mathsf{Ext}(w;x)$ be $\ell$ least significant bits of $wx$.

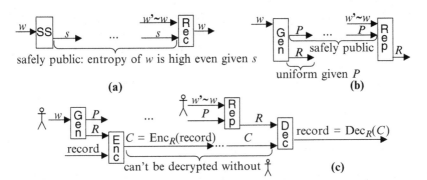

**Fig. 5.1.** (a) Secure sketch; (b) fuzzy extractor; (c) a sample application. The user encrypts a sensitive record using a key $R$ extracted from biometric $w$ via a fuzzy extractor; both $P$ and the encrypted record may be sent or stored in the clear.

attacks, provide more privacy, or refine the notion of correctness) are provided in Sections 5.4, 5.5, and 5.6. Let $\mathcal{M}$ be a metric space with distance function dis. Informally, a secure sketch enables recovery of a string $w \in \mathcal{M}$ from any "close" string $w' \in \mathcal{M}$ without leaking too much information about $w$.

**Definition 5.2.** *An $(m, \tilde{m}, t)$-secure sketch is a pair of efficient randomized procedures* (SS, Rec) *("sketch" and "recover") such that the following hold:*

1. *The sketching procedure* SS *on input $w \in \mathcal{M}$ returns a string $s \in \{0,1\}^*$. The recovery procedure* Rec *takes an element $w' \in \mathcal{M}$ and $s \in \{0,1\}^*$.*
2. *Correctness: If* $\mathsf{dis}(w, w') \leq t$, *then* $\mathsf{Rec}(w', \mathsf{SS}(w)) = w$.
3. *Security: For any $m$-source over $\mathcal{M}$, the min-entropy of $W$ given $s$ is high: For any $(W, E)$, if $\tilde{H}_\infty(W|E) \geq m$, then $\tilde{H}_\infty(W \mid \mathsf{SS}(W), E) \geq \tilde{m}$.*

We will see several examples of secure sketches in the next section. For now, we move on to *fuzzy extractors*, which do not recover the original input but, rather, enable generation of a close-to-uniform string $R$ from $w$ and its subsequent reproduction given any $w'$ close to $w$. The reproduction is done with the help of the helper string $P$ produced during the initial extraction; yet $P$ need not remain secret, because $R$ is nearly uniform even given $P$. Strong extractors are a special case of fuzzy extractors, corresponding to $t = 0$ and $P = I$.

**Definition 5.3.** *An $(m, \ell, t, \varepsilon)$-fuzzy extractor is a pair of efficient randomized procedures (Gen, Rep) ("generate" and "reproduce") such that the following hold:*

1. Gen, *given $w \in \mathcal{M}$, outputs an extracted string $R \in \{0,1\}^\ell$ and a helper string $P \in \{0,1\}^*$.* Rep *takes an element $w' \in \mathcal{M}$ and a string $P \in \{0,1\}^*$.*
2. *Correctness: If* $\mathsf{dis}(w, w') \leq t$ *and $(R, P) \leftarrow \mathsf{Gen}(w)$, then $\mathsf{Rep}(w', P) = R$.*
3. *Security: For all $m$-sources $W$ over $\mathcal{M}$, the string $R$ is nearly uniform even given $P$; that is, if $\tilde{H}_\infty(W \mid E) \geq m$, then $(R, P, E) \approx_\varepsilon (U_\ell, P, E)$.*

*Entropy loss of a secure sketch (resp. fuzzy extractor) is $m - \tilde{m}$ (resp. $m - \ell$).*

We reiterate that the nearly-uniform random bits output by a fuzzy extractor can be used in a variety of cryptographic contexts that require uniform random bits (e.g., for secret keys). The slight nonuniformity of the bits may decrease security, but by no more than their distance $\varepsilon$ from uniform. By choosing $\varepsilon$ sufficiently small (e.g., $2^{-100}$) one can make the reduction in security irrelevant. If more than $\ell$ random bits are needed, then pseudorandom bits can be obtained by inputting $R$ to a pseudorandom generator [31].

### 5.2.3 Secure Sketches Imply Fuzzy Extractors

Given a secure sketch, one can always construct a fuzzy extractor that generates a key of length almost $\tilde{m}$ by composing the sketch with a good (standard) strong extractor. Because universal hash functions extract well even from conditional min-entropy, they incur the least entropy loss, and we state the result for them. Other extractors can also be used but may lose more entropy [90].

**Lemma 5.1 ([90, Lemma 4.1]).** *Suppose we compose an $(m, \tilde{m}, t)$-secure sketch* (SS, Rec) *for a space $\mathcal{M}$ and a universal hash function* Ext : $\mathcal{M} \to \{0,1\}^\ell$ *as follows: In* Gen, *choose a random $i$ and let $P = (\text{SS}(w), i)$ and $R = \text{Ext}(w; i)$; let* $\text{Rep}(w', (s, i)) = \text{Ext}(\text{Rec}(w', s), i)$. *The result is an $(m, \ell, t, \varepsilon)$-fuzzy extractor with $\ell = \tilde{m} + 2 - 2 \log(1/\varepsilon)$.*

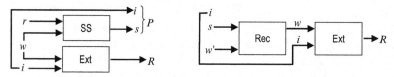

The *random oracle model* is a heuristic for analyzing protocols with cryptographic hash functions. The idea is to mentally replace the hash function by a truly random oracle that can be queried by all parties, but only a bounded number of times. Although this model cannot be instantiated by any real hash function in general [53], it is widely used in situations in which the use of real hash functions is difficult to analyze. In the random oracle model, $\text{Ext}(\cdot, i)$ can be replaced with a random oracle $H(\cdot)$ in Lemma 5.1, and $i$ is not needed. The extracted string can be arbitrarily long and will appear $\varepsilon$-close to uniform to any observer making at most $2^{\tilde{m} - \log 1/\varepsilon}$ queries to $H$. This yields better parameters than Lemma 5.1, at the price of resorting to a heuristic analysis.

## 5.3 Basic Constructions

Secure sketches are related to the problem of information reconciliation, in which two parties holding close values $w \approx w'$ want to reconcile the differences in a communication-efficient manner. A one-message information reconciliation scheme directly yields a secure sketch (with the message being the sketch), which has low entropy loss simply because the message is short. Thus, Constructions 2 and 5 are very similar to information reconciliation constructions of [302, Section VI.C] (citing [256]) and [3]. Other information reconciliation protocols [204] also yield secure sketches. We will occasionally use this communication-based perspective in our analysis.

Because of their error tolerance, constructions of secure sketches are based on error-correcting codes, which we briefly review. Let $\mathcal{F}$ be a finite alphabet of size $F$. For two equal-length strings $w$ and $w'$, let the Hamming distance $\mathsf{dis_{Ham}}(w, w')$ be the number of locations in which these strings differ (these are called "Hamming errors"). A subset $C \subset \mathcal{F}^n$ is an $[n, k, d]_{\mathcal{F}}$ code if it contains $F^k$ elements such that $\mathsf{dis_{Ham}}(v, w) \geq d$ for any $v, w \in C$. A *unique decoding* algorithm, given $w \in \mathcal{F}^n$, finds an element $c \in C$ such that $\mathsf{dis_{Ham}}(c, w) \leq (d-1)/2$ if one exists (if it exists, it is unique by the triangle inequality).

If $\mathcal{F}$ is a field and $C$ is, additionally, a linear subspace of the vector space $\mathcal{F}^n$, then $C$ is known as a *linear* code. In that case, fixing an $(n-k) \times n$ matrix syn over $\mathcal{F}$ whose kernel is $C$, a *syndrome* of a vector $w \in \mathcal{F}^n$ is defined as $\mathsf{syn}(w)$. If the Hamming weight of (i.e., number of non-zero symbols in) $w$ is at most $(d-1)/2$, then $w$ is unique given $\mathsf{syn}(w)$ and can be recovered by the unique decoding algorithm (e.g., by applying it to an arbitrary pre-image $v$ of $\mathsf{syn}(w)$ to get $c \in C$ and computing $w = v - c$).

### 5.3.1 Hamming Distance

To obtain a secure sketch for correcting Hamming errors over $\mathcal{F}^n$, we start with a $[n, k, 2t+1]_{\mathcal{F}}$ error-correcting code $C$. The idea is to use $C$ to correct errors in $w$, even though $w$ may not be in $C$, by shifting the code so that a codeword matches up with $w$ and storing the shift as the sketch. View $\mathcal{F}$ as an additive group (this is automatic if $\mathcal{F}$ is a field; otherwise, use $\mathbb{Z}_F$).

*Construction 1 (Code-offset construction).* On input $w$, select a uniformly random codeword $c \in C$, and set $\mathsf{SS}(w)$ to be the shift needed to get from $c$ to $w$: $\mathsf{SS}(w) = w - c$. To compute $\mathsf{Rec}(w', s)$, subtract the shift $s$ from $w'$ to get $c' = w' - s$, decode $c'$ to get $c$ (note that because $\mathsf{dis_{Ham}}(w', w) \leq t$, so is $\mathsf{dis_{Ham}}(c', c)$), and compute $w$ by shifting back to get $w = c + s$.

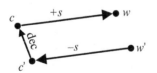

When the code $C$ is linear, the information in $s$ is essentially the syndrome of $w$. Then the scheme can improved to have a shorter sketch, as follows.

*Construction 2 (Syndrome construction).* The sketch algorithm $\mathsf{SS}(w)$ computes $s = \mathsf{syn}(w)$. To compute $\mathsf{Rec}(w', s)$, find the unique vector $e \in \mathcal{F}^n$ of Hamming weight $\leq t$ such that $\mathsf{syn}(e) = \mathsf{syn}(w') - s$, and output $w = w' - e$.

Both Constructions 1 and 2 have appeared in other contexts, some closely related to ours (e.g., [26, 70, 161]). They were analyzed as secure sketches in [90] (where it is also pointed out [90, Section 4.2] that the first construction generalizes to other so-called "transitive" metric spaces).

**Theorem 5.1 ([90]).** *For any $m$, given an $[n, k, 2t + 1]_{\mathcal{F}}$ error-correcting code, Construction 1 (and Construction 2 if the code is linear) is an $(m, m - (n - k) \log F, t)$ secure sketch for the Hamming distance over $\mathcal{F}^n$. Combined with Lemma 5.1, these constructions give, for any $\varepsilon$, an $(m, m - (n - k) \log F + 2 - 2 \log(1/\varepsilon), t, \varepsilon)$ fuzzy extractor for the same metric.*

For the syndrome construction, the analysis of entropy loss follows easily from the fact that the length of the sketch is $(n - k) \log F$ bits. A slightly more involved proof is needed for the code-offset construction.

The trade-off between the error tolerance and the entropy loss depends on the choice of error-correcting code. For large alphabets ($\mathcal{F}$ is a field of size $\geq n$), one can use Reed-Solomon codes to get the optimal entropy loss of $2t \log F$. No secure sketch construction can have a better trade-off between error tolerance and entropy loss than Construction 1, as searching for better secure sketches for the Hamming distance is equivalent to searching for better error-correcting codes.[2] Better secure sketches, however, can be achieved if one is willing to slightly weaken the guarantee of correctness (Section 5.4).

Although the syndrome construction may seem like only a mild improvement over the code-offset construction, the difference is crucial for the set difference metric considered in the next subsection.

### 5.3.2 Set Difference

We now turn to the case when inputs are relatively small subsets of a huge universe $\mathcal{U}$; let $n = |\mathcal{U}|$. This corresponds to representing an object by a list of its features. Examples include "minutiae" (ridge meetings and endings) in a fingerprint, short strings that occur in a long document, and lists of favorite movies. We stress that $\mathcal{U}$ may be very large (e.g., all 100-character strings); we consider work polynomial in $\log n$ to be feasible, but anything polynomial in $n$ to be too expensive (for a discussion of small $\mathcal{U}$, see [90]). The distance between two sets $w, w' \subseteq \mathcal{U}$ is the size of their symmetric difference: $\mathsf{dis}_{\mathsf{Set}}(w, w') \stackrel{\text{def}}{=} |w \triangle w'|$.

Here, we describe the "PinSketch" construction of [90]. Other constructions [159, 204] have also been proposed and are analyzed as secure sketches (with improvements to the first one) in [90]. However, the PinSketch construction is the most efficient and flexible of them; it is also linear over GF(2),

---

[2] This follows from Lemma A.1 of [90], which applies to secure sketches that work for the uniform distribution. We do not know of a result that rules out constructions of secure sketches that work better for lower entropy levels, although by Lemma B.1 of [90] they would not work as well for the uniform case.

which will be useful when we turn to robust extractors in Section 5.6. A set $w$ can be represented by its *characteristic vector* $x_w \in \{0,1\}^{\mathcal{U}}$, with 1 at positions $a \in \mathcal{U}$ if $a \in w$, and 0 otherwise. The symmetric difference of two sets is exactly the Hamming distance of their characteristic vectors. Thus, we may try applying solutions designed for the Hamming distance. In our setting, where $\mathcal{U}$ is large, this representation is too large to be written down explicitly. Nonetheless, this view of sets leads to a good construction of secure sketches.

Recall that Construction 2 for the Hamming metric results in secure sketches that are $n - k$ characters long. Thus, it is possible that the sketches will be of reasonable length even for very large $n$, as long as we choose a linear code for the binary alphabet with $k$ close to $n$. Indeed, binary BCH codes (see, e.g., [281]) fit the bill: They are a family of $[n, n - t\alpha, 2t + 1]_2$ linear codes for any $t, \alpha$, and $n = 2^\alpha - 1$. (These codes are optimal for $t \ll n$ by the Hamming bound, which implies that $k \leq n - \log \binom{n}{t}$ [281].) Using these codes in Construction 2 results in sketches that correct up to $t$ set-difference errors and consist of $t$ values of length $\alpha$ bits each. It is impossible to do much better, since the reconstruction algorithm may get $w'$ that is simply missing $t$ elements of $w$ and would have to find them from the information in the sketch $s$. The entropy loss of this secure sketch will be $t\lceil \log(n + 1) \rceil$.

The only problem is that the scheme appears to require computation time $\Omega(n)$, since we must compute the linear function $s = \mathsf{syn}(x_w)$ and, later, run a decoding algorithm on $\mathsf{syn}(x_{w'}) \oplus s$ to find error vector $e$. For BCH codes, this difficulty can be overcome [90].

The resulting construction works for $w$ and $w'$ of any size, as long their symmetric difference has at most $t$ elements. To use it, one needs to view the universe $\mathcal{U}$ as a set of all strings of length $\alpha$, except the string $0^\alpha$ (this may mean enlarging the actual universe—for instance, going from movie titles to all non-zero strings of a certain length, whether or not they are titles of actual movies). $\mathcal{U}$ is then identified with the non-zero elements of the field $\mathrm{GF}(2^\alpha)$.

**Construction 3 (PinSketch).**    To compute $\mathsf{SS}(w) = \mathsf{syn}(x_w)$:

1. Let $s_i = \sum_{a \in w} a^i$ (computations in $\mathrm{GF}(2^\alpha)$).
2. Output $\mathsf{SS}(w) = (s_1, s_3, s_5, \ldots, s_{2t-1})$.

To recover $\mathsf{Rec}(w', (s_1, s_3, \ldots, s_{2t-1}))$:

1. Compute $(s'_1, s'_3, \ldots, s'_{2t-1}) = \mathsf{SS}(w') = \mathsf{syn}(x_{w'})$.
2. Let $\sigma_i = s'_i - s_i$ (in $\mathrm{GF}(2^\alpha)$, so "−" is the same as "+").
3. Use the sublinear BCH decoding algorithm of [90] to find a set $v$ of size at most $t$ such that $\mathsf{syn}(x_v) = (\sigma_1, \sigma_3, \ldots, \sigma_{2t-1})$.
4. Output $w = w' \triangle v$.

An implementation of this construction, including the reworked BCH decoding algorithm, is available [143].

**Theorem 5.2 ([90]).** *For all $m$, $t$, and $\alpha$, Construction 3 is an $(m, m - \alpha t, t)$ secure sketch for set difference over $\mathrm{GF}(2^\alpha)^*$. Combined with Lemma 5.1, this* *construction gives, for any $\varepsilon$, an $(m, m-t\alpha+2-2\log(1/\varepsilon), t, \varepsilon)$ fuzzy extractor for the same metric.*

### 5.3.3 Edit Distance

In this subsection, we are interested in the space of $n$-character strings over some alphabet $\mathcal{F}$, with distance between two strings $\mathsf{dis_{Edit}}(w, w')$ defined as the smallest number of character insertions and deletions needed to get from one string to the other. It comes up, for example, when the password is entered as a string, due to typing errors or mistakes made in handwriting recognition.

It is difficult to work with this space directly. Instead, the constructions below proceed by constructing *embeddings* of edit distance into the set difference or Hamming metric that approximately preserve distance, that is, given a string $w$, they compute a function $\psi(w)$ with output in a simpler space and apply one of the previous constructions to $\psi(w)$.

First, we consider the low-distortion embedding of Ostrovsky and Rabani [217]. It is an injective, polynomial-time computable mapping $\psi_{\mathsf{OR}} : \{0,1\}^n \to \{0,1\}^d$, which "converts" edit to Hamming distance; namely if $\mathsf{dis_{Edit}}(w, w') \leq t$, then $\mathsf{dis_{Ham}}(\psi_{\mathsf{OR}}(w), \psi_{\mathsf{OR}}(w')) \leq tD_{\mathsf{OR}}$, where $D_{\mathsf{OR}} = 2^{\mathcal{O}(\sqrt{\log n \log \log n})}$.

We now apply Construction 2, using BCH codes, to get a fuzzy extractor for the edit distance over $\{0,1\}^n$. (A secure sketch can also be constructed, but to have an efficient Rec, we would need an efficient algorithm for $\psi_{\mathsf{OR}}^{-1}$, whose existence is currently unknown.)

***Construction 4.*** Let $\mathsf{Gen}'$ and $\mathsf{Rep}'$ be from Construction 1 or 2, instantiated with a $[d', k, 2tD_{\mathsf{OR}} + 1]_2$ error-correcting code. Let $\mathsf{Gen}(w) = \mathsf{Gen}'(\psi_{\mathsf{OR}}(w))$ and $\mathsf{Rep}(w', P) = \mathsf{Rep}'(\psi_{\mathsf{OR}}(w'), P)$.

**Theorem 5.3 ([90]).** *Construction 4 is an $(m, \ell, t, \varepsilon)$-fuzzy extractor for the edit metric over $\{0,1\}^n$ for any $n, t, m, \varepsilon$, and $\ell = m - t2^{\mathcal{O}(\sqrt{\log n \log \log n})} - 2\log(1/\varepsilon)$.*

This construction works well when the fraction of errors is small, particularly if the number of errors $t = n^{1-\Omega(1)}$, because the entropy loss is $tn^{o(1)}$.

An observation that allows one to handle larger error rates (and also create a much simpler construction) is that the stringent conditions traditionally placed on embeddings are not necessary to build fuzzy extractors. Informally, all that is needed is a mapping $\psi$ that (1) does not have too many points $w_1 \neq w_2$ for which $\psi(w_1) = \psi(w_2)$ (thus causing entropy loss) and (2) for which $\mathsf{dis_{Edit}}(w_1, w_2) \leq t$ implies $\mathsf{dis}(\psi(w_1), \psi(w_2)) \leq t'$ for some $t'$ and some notion of distance that already-known fuzzy extractors can handle. Moreover, if $\psi$ is invertible given a relatively small amount of extra information, then it can be used to build secure sketches, which will simply store the extra information as part of the sketch. The precise requirements for such $\psi$ are spelled out in [90], where they are called *biometric embeddings*.

We construct such an embedding $\psi_{\mathsf{SH}}$ as follows. A *c-shingle* is a length-$c$ consecutive substring of a given string $w$. A *c-shingling* [44] of a string $w$ of length $n$ is the set (ignoring order or repetition) of all $(n - c + 1)$ $c$-shingles of $w$. (For instance, a 3-shingling of "abcdecdegh" is {abc, bcd, cde, dec, ecd, deg, egh}). Our $\psi_{\mathsf{SH}}(w)$ is simply the $c$-shingling of the string $w$ for some parameter $c$; its output is a nonempty subset of $\mathcal{F}^c$ of size at most $n - c + 1$. A single edit error adds at most $2c - 1$ to the set difference.

In order to invert the map $\psi_{\mathsf{SH}}$, we need to add information on how to reconstruct the string $w$ from its shingles. This information, denoted by $g_c(w)$, can be computed as follows: Sort $\psi_{\mathsf{SH}}(w)$ alphabetically, and let $g_c(w)$ be the list of $\lceil n/c \rceil$ indices into the set $g_c(w)$ that tell which shingle gives the first $c$ characters, the next $c$ characters, and so on. This leads to the following construction of secure sketches. (Note that there are no limitations on the lengths of $w$ and $w'$ in the constructions, although the resulting entropy loss will depend on $n = |w|$; in particular, it may be that $|w| \neq |w'|$.)

***Construction 5.*** Fix a parameter $c$. Let $\mathsf{SS'}$ and $\mathsf{Rec'}$ be from Construction 3. Let $\mathsf{SS}(w) = (s', g)$, where $s' = \mathsf{SS'}(\psi_{\mathsf{SH}}(w))$ and $g = g_c(w)$. Let $\mathsf{Rec}(w', (s', g))$ be computed as the reconstruction of $w$ from the alphabetically ordered shingles in $\mathsf{Rec'}(\psi_{\mathsf{SH}}(w'), s')$ using the indexes in $g$.

***Construction 6.*** One can build a fuzzy extractor from Construction 5 using Lemma 5.1. However, it is simpler to use the fuzzy extractor for set difference (given by Construction 3 and Lemma 5.1), applying $\mathsf{Gen}$ to $\psi_{\mathsf{SH}}(w)$ and $\mathsf{Rep}$ to $\psi_{\mathsf{SH}}(w')$. This saves the computation of $g_c(w)$, which is not needed, because fuzzy extractors, unlike secure sketches, do not require reconstruction of $w$.

***Theorem 5.4.*** *For any $n, m, c$, and $\varepsilon$, Construction 5 is an $(m, \tilde{m}, t)$-secure sketch, where $\tilde{m} = m - \lceil n/c \rceil \log_2(n - c + 1) - (2c - 1)t \lceil \log(F^c + 1) \rceil$, and Construction 6 is an $(m, \tilde{m} + 2 - 2\log(1/\varepsilon), t, \varepsilon)$-fuzzy extractor.*

The optimal choice of $c$, analyzed in [90], results in entropy loss $m - \tilde{m} \approx 2.38(t \log F)^{1/3}(n \log n)^{2/3}$. If the original string has a linear amount of entropy $\theta(n \log F)$, then this construction can tolerate $t = \Omega(n \log^2 F / \log^2 n)$ insertions and deletions while extracting $\theta(n \log F) - 2\log(1/\varepsilon)$ bits. The number of bits extracted is linear; if the string length $n$ is polynomial in the alphabet size $F$, then the number of errors tolerated is linear also.

## 5.3.4 Other Distance Measures

There have been several works constructing secure sketches (or variants thereof) for other distance measures. We list here a few examples: Chang and Li [58] constructed the first non-trivial sketches for "point-set difference," an abstraction of several distance measures commonly used for matching fingerprints. Linnartz and Tuyls [182] (see also [270, 283] and Chapter 11) considered key extraction primitives for continuous metrics, assuming the biometric is distributed according to a known multidimensional Gaussian distribution. Li et al. [176] explored the question of building secure sketches for discrete distributions in continuous spaces. They showed that a large class of quantizers are equivalent from the entropy point of view, simplifying the design of sketches for such spaces.

## 5.4 Improving Error-Tolerance via Relaxed Notions of Correctness

So far, we required *perfect correctness*; that is, the primitives worked for *every* $w'$ within distance $t$ of $w$, with no probability of error. We now show how the number of tolerated errors $t$ can be significantly increased by insisting only that errors with very high probability be corrected. In other words, we allow that for an unlikely choice of $w'$, the correction will fail.

As an illustration, consider binary Hamming errors. The Plotkin bound from coding theory implies that no secure sketch with residual entropy $\tilde{m} \geq \log n$ can correct $n/4$ errors with probability 1 [90]. However, under a relaxed notion of correctness (made precise below), one can construct secure sketches that tolerate arbitrarily close to $n/2$ errors; that is, correct $n(\frac{1}{2} - \gamma)$ errors for any constant $\gamma > 0$, and still have residual min-entropy $\tilde{m} = \Omega(n)$ (provided the original min-entropy $m \geq (1 - \gamma')n$, for some $\gamma' > 0$ dependent on $\gamma$).

We discuss relaxed correctness arising from considering the following error models: random errors, input-dependent errors, and computationally bounded errors. For simplicity, we limit our discussion to binary Hamming errors.

### 5.4.1 Random Errors

Assume there is a *known* distribution on the errors that occur in the data. The most common distribution is the binary symmetric channel $\mathrm{BSC}_p$: Each bit of the input is flipped with probability $p$ and left untouched with probability $1 - p$. In that case, error-correcting codes and, by extension, the code-offset construction can correct an error rate up to Shannon's bound on noisy channel coding, and no more (see, e.g., [66] for a textbook coverage of Shannon's coding bounds). If $p \in (0, 1/2)$, there are deterministic sketches with entropy loss $n\mathrm{h}(p) - o(n)$, where $\mathrm{h}$ is the binary entropy function $\mathrm{h}(p) = -p \log p - (1 - p) \log(1 - p)$. In particular, if $m \geq n(\mathrm{h}(\frac{1}{2} - \gamma) + \varepsilon)$, which is strictly less than $n$ for a small enough $\varepsilon$, one can tolerate the $(\frac{1}{2} - \gamma)$-fraction of errors and still have residual min-entropy $m' \geq \varepsilon n$.

The assumption of a known noise process is, for our taste, far too strong: There is no reason to believe that we understand the exact distribution on errors that occur in complex data such as biometrics.[3] However, it provides a useful baseline by which to measure results for other models.

---

[3] Since the assumption here only plays a role in correctness, it is still more reasonable than assuming that we know exact distributions on the data in proofs of

### 5.4.2 Input-dependent Errors

Here, the errors are adversarial, subject only to the conditions that (a) the error $\mathsf{dis}(w, w')$ is bounded to a maximum magnitude of $t$ and (b) the corrupted word *depends only on the input* $w$, not on the secure sketch $\mathsf{SS}(w)$. (In particular, this means that the sketch must be probabilistic; thus, the assumption states that the errors are independent of the randomness used to compute $\mathsf{SS}(w)$.) Here, we require that for any pair $w, w'$ at distance at most $t$, we have $\mathsf{Rec}(w', \mathsf{SS}(w)) = w$ with high probability over the random choices made by the randomized sketching algorithm $\mathsf{SS}$.

This model encompasses any complex noise process that has been observed to never introduce more than $t$ errors. Unlike the assumption of a particular distribution on the noise, the bound on magnitude can be checked experimentally. For binary Hamming errors, perhaps surprisingly, in this model we can tolerate exactly the same error rate $t/n$ as in the model of random errors; that is, we can tolerate an error rate up to Shannon's coding bound and no more. Thus, *removing the assumption of a known distribution comes at no cost*.

The basic idea, originally due to Lipton [183], is to prepend a random permutation $\pi : [n] \rightarrow [n]$ to the sketch, which acts on the bit positions of the word $w = (w_1, ..., w_n) \in \{0, 1\}^n$; that is, define $\mathsf{SS}(w; \pi) = (\pi, \mathsf{syn}_C(w_{\pi(1)}, w_{\pi(2)}, ..., w_{\pi(n)}))$. If the difference between $w$ and $w'$ does not depend on the sketch, then the errors that the code $C$ is asked to correct will in fact be randomly distributed (subject only to having a fixed number of bits flipped). Thus, one can use codes for random errors and reduce the entropy loss to near the Shannon limit. One can in fact further reduce the total size of the sketch by choosing $\pi$ pseudo-randomly [183, 258].

### 5.4.3 Computationally-Bounded Errors

Here, the errors are adversarial and may depend on both $w$ and the publicly stored information $\mathsf{SS}(w)$. However, we assume that the errors are introduced by a process of bounded computational power; that is, there is a probabilistic circuit of polynomial size (in the length $n$) that computes $w'$ from $w$. Results proved in this model are extremely powerful: Unless the process introducing errors — natural or artificial — is, say, capable of forging digital signatures, then the sketch will successfully recover from the errors. It is not clear, however, whether this model allows correcting binary Hamming errors up to the Shannon bound, as in the two models above. As we explain below, the question is related to some open questions regarding the constructions of efficiently *list-decodable* codes. These codes enlarge the radius of tolerated errors in return for generating a list of not one, but polynomially many codewords. However, when the error rate $t/n$ is either very high or very low, then the appropriate list-decodable codes exist and we can indeed match the Shannon bound.

---

*secrecy*. However, in both cases, we would like to enlarge the class of distributions for which we can provably satisfy the definition of security.

The main technique is to use the syndrome of a list-decodable code in the code-offset construction, as opposed to the usual, uniquely decodable code. Appending a short hash or a digital signature of the original input $w$ to the syndrome allows the recovery algorithm to disambiguate the (polynomially long) list and decide which of the possibilities leads to the correct value of $w$. This allows tolerating arbitrary errors as long as the process introducing the errors is unable to "break" (i.e., find a collision for) the hash function or the digital signature. This idea of sieving is fundamental to almost all applications of list-decoding. See [258, Table 1] for a summary of these ideas as they apply to information reconciliation and secure sketches.

## 5.5 Strong Privacy Guarantees

Although secure sketches leave entropy in $w$, and fuzzy extractors even extract uniform randomness from it, they may leak (through the string $s$ or $P$) sensitive information about $w$: An adversary may learn a function $f(w)$ such as the user's eye color, ethnicity, or risk of diabetes. Moreover, when the very process that generates $w$ is secret (this does not happen when $w$ is just a user's biometric, but happens in example applications considered at the end of this section), $s$ or $P$ may leak information about that process itself, with undesirable consequences for the future. We therefore ask if it is possible to design fuzzy extractors that leak "no information" about $w$.

To get some intuition, let us first consider the noiseless case (i.e., when $t = 0$). Strong extractors directly yield fuzzy extractors whose helper string $P = i$ (the seed to a strong extractor) is independent of $w$. However, for $t > 0$, such a construction is impossible: The mutual information between $w$ and $P$ has to be non-trivial (and to grow roughly proportionally to $t$) [92]. In other words, $P$ must leak *some* information about $w$ in order to help correct errors in $w$. In contrast, it turns out that one can correct errors in $w$ without leaking anything "useful" about $w$. We need the following definition:

**Definition 5.4.** *([93]). A probabilistic map $Y()$ **hides all functions of** $W$ with leakage $\varepsilon$ if for every adversary $\mathcal{A}$, there exists an adversary $\mathcal{A}_*$ such that for all functions $f : \{0,1\}^* \to \{0,1\}^*$,*

$$\big| \Pr[\mathcal{A}(Y(W)) = f(W)] - \Pr[\mathcal{A}_*() = f(W)] \big| \leq \varepsilon.$$

*The map $Y()$ is called $(m, \varepsilon)$-entropically secure if $Y()$ hides all functions of $W$, for all $m$-sources $W$.*

In our context, a natural choice for the variable $Y(W)$ should be the helper string $P = P(W)$. In fact, we can do better and set $Y = \mathsf{Gen}(W) = (R, P)$. As long as $W$ has sufficient min-entropy, it is nearly as hard to predict $f(W)$ given *both $R$ and $P$* as it is without $(R, P)$, regardless of the adversary's computing power. This strengthening is important since the "outside" application that uses $R$ as its secret key may leak $R$ (think of a one-time pad, for example). We ensure the *information-theoretic* privacy of $w$ even if $R$ is eventually leaked or used as a key in a computationally secure scheme:

**Definition 5.5.** *A* $(m, \ell, t, \varepsilon)$ *fuzzy extractor for* $\mathcal{M}$ *is called* $(m, \varepsilon')$*-private if the pair* $(R, P)$ *is* $(m, \varepsilon')$*-entropically secure.*

Entropic security should not be confused with the much stronger notion of statistical "Shannon" secrecy, which requires that $(R, P)$ and $W$ be (almost) statistically independent. Entropic security only states that $(R, P)$ does not help in predicting $f(W)$, for any function $f$ *specified in advance*. For example, after seeing any particular realization $(r, p)$ of $(R, P)$, one might learn many functions $f_{(r,p)}$ of $W$. Nonetheless, entropic security is quite strong: No particular function $f$ is likely to be one of them for random $(r, p)$. Shannon security is impossible to achieve in our context, and entropic security provides an alternative that is sufficient in several applications.

### 5.5.1 Uniform Fuzzy Extractors.

A seemingly weaker definition than entropic security is that of $(m, \varepsilon)$-indistinguishability [93]: A (probabilistic) map $Y()$ is $(m, \varepsilon)$-*indistinguishable* if for all pairs of $m$-sources $W_1$, $W_2$, the distributions $Y(W_1)$ and $Y(W_2)$ are $\varepsilon$-close. For example, extractors for $m$-sources are trivially $(m, 2\varepsilon)$-indistinguishable. Entropic security is essentially equivalent to indistinguishability: Hiding all functions of $W$ is nearly the same as Hiding the distribution of $W$.

**Theorem 5.5 ([93]).** *If* $Y()$ *is* $(m, \varepsilon)$*-entropically secure, then it is* $(m - 1, 4\varepsilon)$*-indistinguishable. Conversely, if* $Y()$ *is* $(m, \varepsilon)$*-indistinguishable, then it is* $(m + 2, 8\varepsilon)$*-entropically secure. In particular, extractors for min-entropy* $m$ *hide all functions for sources of min-entropy* $m + 2$.

Applying this characterization to the case of private fuzzy extractors, we see that it is enough to construct what we call a $(m, \varepsilon)$-*uniform* fuzzy extractor, which is defined by the constraint $(R, P) \approx_{\varepsilon} (U_{\ell}, U_{|P|})$. A uniform extractor automatically satisfies the security requirement on fuzzy extractors. By Theorem 5.5, it is also $(m + 2, 8\varepsilon)$-private. Thus, we focus our attention on uniform fuzzy extractors.

### 5.5.2 Extractor-Sketches

Similar to the definitions of private and uniform fuzzy extractors, we can also define private or uniform secure sketches. For our purposes, however, it will be convenient to define the following special case of uniform (and, therefore, private) secure sketches.

**Definition 5.6.** *A $(m, \tilde{m}, t, \varepsilon)$-extractor-sketch (for $\mathcal{M}$) is given by two efficient randomized procedures $(\mathsf{Ext}, \mathsf{Rec})$ s.t. (a) $\mathsf{Ext}$ is a $(m, \lambda, \varepsilon)$-strong extractor (for some $\lambda$, typically equal to $m - \tilde{m}$; see below), and (b) $(\mathsf{SS}, \mathsf{Rec})$ is a $(m, \tilde{m}, t)$-secure sketch, where $\mathsf{SS}(W; I) \stackrel{\text{def}}{=} (\mathsf{Ext}(W; I), I)$.*

As the definition states, extractor-sketches are simultaneously strong extractors and secure sketches. On the one hand, the output of the sketch looks uniform: $(\mathsf{Ext}(W; I), I) \approx_\varepsilon U_{|\mathsf{SS}(W)|}$. In particular, an extractor-sketch of $W$ hides the distribution and all of the functions of $W$. On the other hand, $w$ can be recovered from $\mathsf{Ext}(w; i)$, the seed $i$, and any $w'$ close to $w$. Unlike the standard rationale for extractors, however, the objective of such extractor-sketches is to *minimize* their output length $\lambda$, since this length corresponds to the length of the secure sketch, which directly bounds the entropy loss $m - \tilde{m} \leq \lambda$ of the sketch (in fact, in most constructions, $\lambda = m - \tilde{m}$). In other words, the purpose of extractor-sketches is the recovery of $w$ using the minimal amount of information and not randomness extraction. The latter property only serves to argue privacy via Theorem 5.5.

We now make a few observations. First, every $(m, \tilde{m}, t, \varepsilon)$-extractor-sketch is $(m + 2, 8\varepsilon)$-private by Theorem 5.5, meaning that no function about a source of min-entropy $m+2$ is leaked. Second, unlike ordinary secure sketches, extractor-sketches must be probabilistic (otherwise they cannot be entropically secure). Third, fuzzy extractors constructed from secure sketches via Lemma 5.1 will be $(m, \varepsilon + \varepsilon')$-uniform if an $(m, \tilde{m}, t, \varepsilon')$-extractor-sketch is composed with an ordinary universal hash function to extract $\ell = \tilde{m} + 2 - 2\log(1/\varepsilon)$ bits. Thus, in the sequel we will only need to construct extractor-sketches. We limit our discussion to the Hamming metric.

### 5.5.3 Constructing Extractor-Sketches

Dodis and Smith [92] constructed extractor-sketches for the Hamming space $\mathcal{F}^n$, where $|\mathcal{F}| = F$. The actual construction of extractor-sketches in [92] uses a special family $\{C_i\}_i$ of $[n, k, d = 2t + 1]$-codes (for "appropriate" $k$) over $\mathcal{F}^n$ and sets $\mathsf{SS}(w; i) = (i, \mathsf{syn}_{C_i}(w))$. Thus, it replaces the fixed $[n, k, d = 2t + 1]$-code in Construction 2 from Section 5.3.1 by a carefully chosen family of codes $\{C_i\}_i$. The challenge was to obtain the largest possible dimension $k$ such that for a random code $C_I$ and for any $m$-source $W$, the pair $(I, \mathsf{syn}_{C_I}(W))$ is $\varepsilon$-close to uniform.

When the alphabet size $F > n$, the family of codes used by [92] is straightforward. We start from a fixed code $C$ equal to the $[n, n - 2t, 2t + 1]$-Reed-Solomon code. Given an index $i = (a_1, \ldots, a_n)$ consisting of *non-zero* elements of $\mathcal{F}$, we define $C_i = \{(a_1 \cdot c_1, \ldots, a_n \cdot c_n) \in \mathcal{F}^n \mid (c_1, \ldots, c_n) \in C\}$. (Restricting $a_j$'s to be non-zero ensures that each $C_i$ still has minimal distance $2t + 1$.) The resulting family[4] is $\{C_{(a_1,\ldots,a_n)} \mid a_1 \neq 0, \ldots, a_n \neq 0\}$. For

---

[4] The code families use in the Dodis-Smith construction are sometimes called "generalized Reed-Solomon" codes.

general alphabets, including the binary alphabet $\mathcal{F} = \{0,1\}$, the construction is somewhat more complicated, and we do not include it here.

**Theorem 5.6 ([92]).** *There exists families of efficiently encodable and decodable codes* $\{C_i\}_i$ *such that the above "randomized" syndrome construction yields* $(m, \tilde{m}, t, \varepsilon)$*-extractor-sketches for* $\mathcal{F}^n$ *with the following parameters:*

**(Binary alphabet; $F = 2$)** *For any min-entropy* $m = \Omega(n)$, *one achieves* $\tilde{m}$, $t$, *and* $\log(1/\varepsilon)$ *all* $\Omega(n)$, *and* $|\mathsf{SS}(w)| < 2n$.

**(Large alphabet; $F > n$)** *For* $m > 2t \log F$, *we have* $\tilde{m} = m - 2t \log F$ *and* $\varepsilon = \mathcal{O}(2^{-\tilde{m}/2})$. *Both of these parameters are optimal. The total length of the sketch is* $|\mathsf{SS}(w)| = (n + 2t) \log F$.

Thus, extractor-sketches for high alphabets can achieve the same entropy loss $\lambda = 2t \log F$ as "non-private" sketches, at the price of increasing the length of the sketch from $2t \log F$ to $(n + 2t) \log F$. Moreover, they achieve the same error $\varepsilon = \mathcal{O}(2^{-\tilde{m}/2})$ as the best strong extractors for a given output length $\lambda = m - \tilde{m}$. Thus, their only disadvantage comes from the fact that the length of the sketch is greater than the length of the message. For binary alphabets, the construction of [92] loses significant constant factors as compared to the best non-private sketches, although it is still asymptotically optimal. In particular, using Theorem 5.6 we obtain $(m, \varepsilon)$-private $(m, \ell, t, \varepsilon)$-fuzzy extractors for the Hamming space $\{0,1\}^n$, where $\ell$, $\log(1/\varepsilon)$, and $t$ are $\Omega(n)$ as long as $m = \Omega(n)$.

### 5.5.4 Applications

As we already stated, extractor-sketches immediately yield corresponding uniform (and, therefore, private) secure sketches and fuzzy extractors.

As another application of extractor-sketches, [92] showed how to use them to construct so-called $(m, t, \varepsilon)$-*fuzzy perfectly one-way* hash functions for the binary Hamming metric. Such functions come with a fixed verification procedure Ver and allow one to publish a probabilistic hash $y$ of the secret $w$ such that (a) Ver$(w', y)$ will accept any $w'$ within distance $t$ from $w$, (b) it is computationally infeasible to find $y$ and secrets $w$ and $w'$ of distance greater than $2t$ from each other, such that Ver$(w, y)$ and Ver$(w', y)$ both accept, and (c) the map $W \mapsto Y$ is $(m, \varepsilon)$-entropically secure. Thus, publishing $y$ allows anybody to test (without either false positives or false negatives!) whether some input $w'$ is *close* to the "correct" secret input $w$, and yet without leaking any particular function of $w$. The construction of [92] achieved, for any entropy level $m = \Omega(n)$, an $(m, t, \varepsilon)$-fuzzy perfect one-way family where both $t$ and $\log(1/\varepsilon)$ are $\Omega(n)$.

We next present two applications of private fuzzy extractors to situations when the very process that generates high entropy $w$ must remain secret. In the approach proposed in [55] for mitigating dictionary attacks against password-protected local storage [55], one stores on disk many different puzzles solvable only by humans (so-called "CAPTCHAs" [285]). A short password specified by the user selects a few puzzles to be manually solved by the user; their solutions are $w = w_1, \ldots, w_n$. The string $w$ is then used to derive a secret key $R$ (e.g., used to encrypt the local hard drive). The security of the system rests on the fact that the adversary does not know which puzzles are selected by the user's password: thus, the process that generates $w$ must remain secret. In order to tolerate a few incorrectly solved puzzles, one would like to use a fuzzy extractor to derive $R$ from $w$. However, an ordinary fuzzy extractor does not suffice here, because although it will not leak too much information about $w$ it may leak *which puzzles* are used to construct $w$ and thus allow the adversary to focus on solving them and obtain $w$ on its own. A private fuzzy extractor, however, will work.

In a similar vein, [92] showed that entropically secure sketches can be used to simultaneously achieve error correction, key reuse, and "everlasting security" in the so-called bounded storage model (BSM) [195]. This resolved the main open problem of [86]. We refer to [92] for more details and references regarding this application.

## 5.6 Robustness and Protection Against Active Attacks

So far in this survey we have implicitly focused on situations with a *passive* adversary: Specifically, we assumed that the adversary could not tamper with the helper string $P$ output by the fuzzy extractor. This is not representative of all of the situations where biometrics are used: Users may be connected by an insecure (i.e., unauthenticated) channel, and the recovery algorithm Rep may receive an input $\tilde{P} \neq P$. Such situations call, essentially, for *authentication* based on noisy secrets $W \approx W'$. The literature has considered a variety of settings. These fall into two broad categories.

> Authenticated Key-Agreement: Here, a trusted server stores the "actual" biometric data $W$ of a user; periodically, the user obtains a fresh biometric scan $W'$ that is close, but not identical, to $W$. The server and user then wish to mutually authenticate and agree on a key $R$ over a network controlled by an adversary.
>
> Key Encapsulation: Here, a user (on his own) uses his biometric data $W$ to generate a random key $R$ along with some public information $P$ and then stores $P$ on an untrusted disk. The key $R$ may then be used, say, to encrypt some file for long-term storage. At a later point in time, the user obtains a fresh biometric scan $W'$. After retrieving $P$ from the disk, the user recovers $R$ (with which he can decrypt the file). The challenge here is that the value $P$ provided by the disk may not be the same as what the user originally stored. In this second setting, the user is essentially running a key-agreement protocol with *himself* at two points in time, with the (untrusted) disk acting as the network. This inherently requires

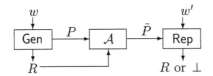

Fig. 5.2. Robust extractors.

a *non-interactive* (i.e., one-message) key-agreement protocol, since $W$ is no longer available at the later point in time. Any solution for the second scenario is also a solution for the first.

### 5.6.1 Robust Fuzzy Extractors

One can construct protocols for both of these settings using a common abstraction, a *robust* fuzzy extractor, which recovers $R$ if and only if it is fed the original helper string $P$ produced by Gen. In all other cases, it rejects with high probability and outputs a special symbol $\perp$. The definition is illustrated in Fig. 5.2. It is inspired by the definition of chosen-ciphertext security of standard key encapsulation mechanisms [95]: If all variations in $P$ are rejected, the adversary $\mathcal{A}$ is essentially constrained to behave passively. Note that the adversary is given access to the extracted key $R$ when attempting to forge a valid $\tilde{P} \neq P$. This guarantee is necessary, for example, in the second setting above since the adversary may attempt to forge $\tilde{P}$ after seeing how $R$ is used to encrypt a possibly known file. See [88] for a statement of the definition and discussion of the variations considered in the literature. In the remainder of this section, we sketch two constructions of robust fuzzy extractors.

### 5.6.2 A Construction Using Ideal Hash Functions

In the random oracle model (described in Section 5.2.3), there is a simple, generic construction of a robust extractor from any secure sketch. Assume that we are given two hash functions $H_1, H_2 : \{0,1\}^* \to \{0,1\}^\ell$ (the pair can be simulated given a single random oracle by prepending a bit to the input).

*Construction 7 ([42]).*

- Gen($w$): Let $s = \mathsf{SS}(w)$. Output $P = (s, H_1(w,s))$ and $R = H_2(w,s)$.
- Rep($w', \tilde{P}$): Parse $\tilde{P}$ as $(\tilde{s}, \tilde{h})$ and set $\tilde{w} = \mathsf{Rec}(w', \tilde{s})$. If $\mathrm{dis}(\tilde{w}, w') \leq t$ and $\tilde{h} = H_1(\tilde{w}, \tilde{s})$, then output $H_2(\tilde{w}, \tilde{s})$, else output $\perp$.

We formulated the above security definitions for the case of computationally unbounded adversaries, and we are now discussing a protocol that is only computationally secure. Nonetheless, in the random oracle model the definitions make sense; it suffices to restrict the number of calls the adversary makes to the random oracle.

Let $\mathsf{Vol}_t^{\mathcal{M}}$ be the maximum volume of a ball of radius $t$ in the space $\mathcal{M}$. The following statement captures the basic properties of the construction; see [42] for a more detailed statement and proof.

**Proposition 5.1 ([42, Theorem 1]).** *Suppose that* SS *is a* $(m, \tilde{m}, t)$*-secure sketch. An adversary that makes at most* $q$ *queries to the random oracle has forgery probability at most* $\delta = q^2/2^{\ell} + 3q + 2\mathsf{Vol}_t^{\mathcal{M}}/2^{\tilde{m}}$, *and advantage at most* $q/2^{\tilde{m}}$ *in distinguishing* $R$ *from random.*

### 5.6.3 Unconditionally Secure Constructions

Analyses of protocols in the random oracle model are fraught with peril: They yield at best a heuristic estimate of the protocols' security (at worst, a drastic overestimate [53]). At the cost of some loss of parameters, for specific metrics one can in fact construct unconditionally-secure robust fuzzy extractors.

If we consider the above random oracle construction slightly more abstractly, we can view the first hash value (appended to $P$) as some kind of message authentication code (MAC) applied to the sketch $s$, using $w$ as a key. We may try to emulate this in the standard model by replacing the random oracle with a regular MAC. The problem with analyzing such a scheme is that the key used by Rep to verify the MAC actually depends on the message whose authenticity is being tested. In the language of cryptanalysis, the adversary can mount a specific kind of *related key attack*. The circularity is broken in the above random oracle construction since the dependency goes through a large random table to which the adversary does not have complete access. It turns out that we can also break the circularity in the standard model by looking carefully at the class of relations the adversary can induce on the keys and tailoring the MAC to this particular application.

The second major problem comes from the fact that the MAC key is itself non-uniform, and there is no shared perfect randomness with which one can extract. Again, in the above random oracle construction, one circumvents this difficulty because the key space is irrelevant; each key essentially defines a completely random function. It turns out that this difficulty, too, can be circumvented for a class of information-theoretic MACs by looking carefully at the set of constraints on the key space defined by the adversary's view and showing that the remaining set of keys is rich enough to make forgery unlikely.

The full construction of a robust extractor based on these ideas is quite delicate, and we refer the reader to [88] for details. Note, however, that the construction has a fundamental limit: One cannot extract robustly if the entropy $m$ is less than $n/2$. This limit holds for any information-theoretically secure scheme, but not for the above random oracle construction. Finding a scheme that breaks this bound in the standard (computational) model remains an open question.

### 5.6.4 Remarks on Extensions and Other Models

1. As mentioned earlier, constructing robust extractors gives non-interactive protocols for both of the settings mentioned at the beginning of the section. However, it is possible to get considerably better solutions in the interactive setting. By modifying known password-authenticated key exchange protocols, one can get solutions which are in fact secure against "off-line" attacks without the large entropy requirements of information-theoretically secure solutions [42].

2. The problem of authentication based on noisy secrets arises in the so-called "bounded storage model" when the long, shared string is noisy [86]. In that setting, it is reasonable to assume that the two parties Gen and Rep additionally share a short, truly random secret key. This does not trivialize the problem, since Gen extracts a much longer key than the small shared key with which it starts. Also, we require the output of Gen to leak no information about the small shared key, so that the small key can be reused. One can construct very good robust fuzzy extractors in that model, and, combined with extractor-sketches of Section 5.5, these yield the first stateless protocols for the bounded storage model with noise that are secure against active adversaries [88].

3. The issue of robustness is closely related to the issue of reusability, introduced by Boyen [41] and discussed in a different chapter of this volume. Essentially, we have considered a setting in which the public information $P$ is generated once, and then possibly reused many times. One runs into much more difficult questions if many copies of $P$ are generated *independently*. Many of those questions remain open. For example: can one construct reusable entropically secure extractors [92]?

# 6

# Robust and Reusable Fuzzy Extractors

Xavier Boyen

## 6.1 Introduction

The use of biometric features as key material in security protocols has often been suggested to relieve their owner from the need to remember long cryptographic secrets. The appeal of biometric data as cryptographic secrets stems from their high apparent entropy, their availability to their owner, and their relative immunity to loss. In particular, they constitute a very effective basis for user authentication, especially when combined with complementary credentials such as a short memorized password or a physical token. However, the use of biometrics in cryptography does not come without problems. Some difficulties are technical, such as the lack of uniformity and the imperfect reproducibility of biometrics, but some challenges are more fundamental.

The first challenge is that each person is given a limited supply of non-renewable biometric entropy that has to last a lifetime. Technological refinements of feature extraction methods should expand the accessible pool of biometric entropy in the future, but in the meantime one must use what is avaialable. Often, this will require us to stretch the limits of conventional cryptographic wisdom beyond the requirement that key material be fresh and never reused. The second challenge has to do with the lack of any storage on the user side other that his or her noisy biometric data, which complicates the design of protocols over adversarially controlled channels. These are the issues that are addressed in this chapter.

Cryptographic fuzzy extractors, discussed in the previous chapter, provide an elegant mechanism for dealing with two technical difficulties regarding the use of biometrics in protocols. First, the actual distribution of biometric features is not known precisely and is certainly far from being uniform. In order to obtain provable security guarantees, it is thus necessary to apply a hash function, which can be viewed either as a random oracle [21] or a strong extractor [214]. The second and more delicate problem is that biometric features are inherently noisy and cannot be reproduced exactly; this problem has been addressed when the channel is public but authenticated [25, 27, 196] or adversarially controlled [193,234]. Dealing with both issues at once requires a noise-tolerant randomness extractor, called a fuzzy extractor [91].

A large body of work has focused on overcoming these two problems in an effort to develop secure techniques for the use of biometric data in various settings [81,159,161,205,273], or, from a more theoretical angle, how to derive uniformly distributed cryptographic keys from noisy data [91]. The work of Dodis et al. [91] defines two primitives: a secure sketch that allows recovery of a shared secret given a close approximation thereof, and a fuzzy extractor that extracts a uniformly distributed string $s$ from a shared secret in an error-tolerant manner.

Secure sketches and fuzzy extractors work by constructing from an initial reading of the biometric data a public string $P$ to be stored on a server for later use; the role of $P$ is to encode enough information to reconstruct the initial reading exactly given a sufficiently close approximation of it (e.g., obtained from a second reading). Once an exact reconstruction has been obtained, it is easy to derive a key using a hash function. Both primitives are designed to withstand eavesdropping attacks by a passive adversary who can read the public string $P$ but cannot modify it. An asymmetric generalization of these notions has also been proposed in [43]. See Chapter 5 for precise definitions.

### 6.1.1 Robust Fuzzy Extractors

Unfortunately, ordinary fuzzy extractors do not address the issue of an active adversary that can modify $P$ maliciously, either on the storage server or while in transit to the user. Consequently, fuzzy extractors alone do not provide secure authentication in the presence of an active adversary that may interfere with the messages exchanged by the server and the user, in an attack model where the user's only authenticated (and private) storage is for her biometrics.

This vulnerability is not merely theoretical: Depending on the fuzzy extractor's design, an adversary who maliciously alters the public string before it is sent back to a user may be able to trick the user into revealing his or her secret biometric data. This problem would not exist if the error-correction string $P$ were stored locally rather than on a remote server, or authenticated by a trusted third party before use; however, one of the purposes of biometric authentication is to alleviate the need for user-side cryptographic storage, and it is good practice not to rely on trusted infrastructures.

Robust fuzzy extractors [42] provide an elegant answer to the above difficulty. They enable a user and a server to achieve mutual authentication and/or authenticated key exchange over a completely insecure channel, based only on biometric information on the user's side. To obtain this result, we add a layer of authentication to the public string $P$, thanks to which the user can reject and abort the protocol in case of tampering. The difficulty stems from the need to authenticate $P$ based on the noisy biometric data itself, since no other information can be trusted.

A generic construction from any secure sketch or fuzzy extractor was given by Boyen et al. [42] in the random oracle model. By making judicious use of cryptographic hashes, their construction can protect any black-box secure sketch or fuzzy extractor against modification of the public value $P$, in any context in which secure sketches or fuzzy extractors are used. This solution may be viewed as a drop-in replacement that transforms any protocol secure under the assumption that $P$ is transmitted reliably into one that is secure even when $P$ might be tampered with; it also quite practical. We study this generic construction in some detail in the first part of this chapter.

### 6.1.2 Reusable Fuzzy Extractors

The other difficultly of using biometrics for authentication is that of reusing the same private data in many applications without compromising its secrecy. In this setting, we consider a single user who wants to authenticate with many, unrelated servers. Conceivably, the user could provide the same value of $P$ to all servers, or publish it where all servers find it. However, in reality the servers have no reason to trust the published value of $P$ and may insist that the user reconstruct it from a fresh biometric reading in a controlled environment. In this setting, the user is forced to derive multiple public strings $P_1, \ldots, P_n$ from various readings of the same biometric data, which could lead to exposure of the private data under a collusion attack. Ordinary and robust fuzzy extractors provide no protection against this possibility, as has been demonstrated [41] for various types of construction.

Reusable fuzzy extractors [41] have been introduced to address this issue. In the general case, protecting a fuzzy extractor against a reuse attack is a tough challenge because of two contradictory requirements. On the one hand, $P$ must contain some amount of cleartext information in order for the user to use his or her biometric features in any protocol. On the other hand, publishing more than one instance of $P$ from the same biometric data is likely to reveal too much information about it when the instances are studied in combination. This is especially true if the creation of $P$ is randomized or if it is performed on non-identical inputs—which is naturally to be expected in biometric applications.

Because of these contradictory requirements, reuse of biometric data appears infeasible in the general case, at least for information-theoretic security requirements. Nevertheless, it can be achieved [41] under appropriate restrictions on the type of error that can affect the biometrics. The crucial notion for cryptographic reusability is one of symmetry or regularity, in the sense that all inputs should be affected by it in a uniform manner by the noise process. The results of [41] show that it is desirable for the biometric readers, encodings of features, and error-correcting codes to be as uniform and symmetric as possible. We briefly discuss these in the second part of this chapter.

We note that reusable fuzzy extractors are but one approach for preserving the long-term secrecy of biometrics. Recent work on (biometric) template protection [268, 270, 283] has focused on the physical acquisition of biometric readings, both from a liveness angle to ensure human presence at the reader and from a privacy aspect to make the relevant biometrics hard to clone [287].

## 6.2 Background and Definitions

For completeness of exposition, we briefly review a few notions that we will find useful. We refer the reader to Chapter 5 for further details.

Let $(\mathcal{M}, d)$ be a finite metric space equipped with an integer distance $d$. For biometric applications, we will assume that the biometric readings belong in some metric space with an appropriate distance function, although we do not necessarily impose what such a space may be, as long as the space supports a basic secure sketch or fuzzy extractor construction.

All stochastic events belong in a finite discrete probability space $(\Omega, \mathbb{P})$. The min-entropy of a random variable $A : \Omega \to \mathcal{A}$ is denoted $\mathsf{H}_\infty(A)$, and its average min-entropy given a variable $B : \Omega \to \mathcal{B}$ is denoted $\bar{\mathsf{H}}_\infty(A \mid B)$:

$$\mathsf{H}_\infty(A) = -\log(\max_{a \in \mathcal{A}} \mathbb{P}[A = a]),$$

$$\bar{\mathsf{H}}_\infty(A \mid B) = -\log(\mathbb{E}_{b \leftarrow B}[2^{-\mathsf{H}_\infty(A \mid B=b)}]).$$

Secure sketches provide a way to recover a shared secret $w$ from any sufficiently close approximation $w'$ of $w$, without leaking too much information about $w$. They are defined as follows.

**Definition 6.1.** *An $(m, m', t)$-secure sketch over $(\mathcal{M}, d)$ consists of a pair of procedures* $\mathsf{Sk} : \mathcal{M} \to \{0,1\}^*$ *and* $\mathsf{Rec} : \mathcal{M} \times \{0,1\}^* \to \mathcal{M} \cup \{\bot\}$*, such that the following hold:*

*(Security) For all random variables $W : \Omega \to \mathcal{M}$ satisfying $\mathsf{H}_\infty(W) \geq m$, it holds that $\bar{\mathsf{H}}_\infty(W \mid \mathsf{Sk}(W)) \geq m'$.*
*(Error tolerance) For all values $w, w' \in \mathcal{M}$ with $d(w, w') \leq t$, it holds that $\mathsf{Rec}(w', \mathsf{Sk}(w)) = w$.*

*It is well formed if $\forall w' \in \mathcal{M}, \forall P', \mathsf{Rec}(w', P') \neq \bot \Rightarrow d(w', \mathsf{Rec}(w', P')) \leq t$.*

Well-formedness is a technical condition on $\mathsf{Rec}$ that confines error correction within the claimed correction capability; it is easily enforced by testing that $d(w', w) \leq t$ before outputting $w$, otherwise outputting the error symbol $\bot$.

Fuzzy extractors extend the notion of secure sketch by further addressing the issue of the non-uniformity of $W$.

**Definition 6.2.** *An $(m, \ell, t, \epsilon)$-fuzzy extractor over $(\mathcal{M}, d)$ consists of a randomized extraction algorithm* $\mathsf{Ext} : \mathcal{M} \to \{0,1\}^\ell \times \{0,1\}^*$ *and a reproduction procedure* $\mathsf{Rep} : \mathcal{M} \times \{0,1\}^* \to \{0,1\}^\ell$*, such that the following hold:*

*(Security) For a random variable* $W : \Omega \to \mathcal{M}$ *with* $\mathsf{H}_\infty(W) \geq m$, *if* $(R, P) \leftarrow \mathsf{Ext}(W)$, *then* $\mathsf{SD}((R, P), (U_\ell, P)) \leq \epsilon$, *where* $U_\ell$ *is uniform over* $\{0, 1\}^\ell$.
*(Error tolerance) For all pairs of points* $w, w' \in \mathcal{M}$ *with* $d(w, w') \leq t$, *if* $(R, P) \leftarrow \mathsf{Ext}(w)$, *then* $\mathsf{Rep}(w', P) = R$.

It is well known from [91] that any secure sketch can be turned into a fuzzy extractor in the same metric space simply by applying a strong extractor [214] to the secret $w$ using a random key that is then added to the public string $P$. Starting with an $(m, m', t)$-secure sketch and with an appropriate choice of extractor, one obtains an $(m, m' - 2 \log \epsilon^{-1}, t, \epsilon)$-fuzzy extractor.

## 6.3 Flexible Error Models

As error tolerance is a primary goal of fuzzy extractors, it is necessary to develop formal models of the types of error that may occur. This is especially true since our interest in robustness and reusability stem from the threat of active adversaries that was not a concern with (non-robust) fuzzy extractors.

The error models we use are not universal and depend on the application. Clearly, if an adversary is given full control over the error process that affects the secret biometric data before they are fed into the fuzzy extractor algorithms, it will not remain secret for long. For reusable extractors, errors can be arbitrarily large and under adversarial control, but must be a symmetric operator in the sense that they cannot depend on the secret value they are affecting. In the case of robust extractors, errors must be small but can be otherwise arbitrary, which seems to correspond better to the physical reality.

### 6.3.1 Bounded Arbitrary Errors

The error model we consider for robust extractors allows errors to be data dependent and hence correlated not only with each other but also with the biometric secret itself. We allow these errors to be arbitrary within a certain amplitude bound, to account for our lack of knowledge of the physical processes that cause fluctuations in the biometric measurements. Indeed, the only restriction we make is that the errors be less than the desired error-correction bound. This seems to be a reasonable restriction since in a real-world application, one would select the error-correction capability to overcome any measurement error with high probability. This is formally captured by the notion of a bounded distortion ensemble. Recall that a random variable taking values in $\mathcal{M}$ is a map from an underlying probability sample space $\Omega$ to $\mathcal{M}$.

**Definition 6.3.** *We call a* $t$-*bounded distortion ensemble* $\mathcal{W} = \{W_i\}_{i=0,1,...}$ *a sequence of random variables* $W_i : \Omega \to \mathcal{M}$ *such that* $d(W_0, W_i) \leq t$ *for all* $i$, *where* $d(W_0, W_i) \leq t$ *is shorthand for* $d(W_0(r), W_i(r)) \leq t$ *for all states* $r \in \Omega$.

In context, $W_0$ can represent the biometric features as first read when a user initially registers with a server, and $W_i$ can represent the subsequent reading by the user on his or her $i$th authentication attempt.

### 6.3.2 Errors as Computable Functions

In spite of its appeal, the error model above is too strong to permit the construction of reusable fuzzy extractors in the information-theoretic sense, because errors can be arbitrary (bounded) functions of the data. When many values $P$ based on arbitrary functions of the data are published, one cannot expect the data to remain secret in the information-theoretic sense. To have a better grasp on this possibility, we model errors as explicit functions of the data that they are affecting; unlike the previous model, the resulting errors need not be small.

**Definition 6.4.** *A* perturbation *is a function* $\phi : \mathcal{M} \to \mathcal{M}$ *assumed to be efficiently computable. A* perturbation family *is a finite set* $\Phi$ *of such functions.*

These perturbation functions are defined in the metric space $(\mathcal{M}, d)$. The identity perturbation corresponds to a perfect measurement without error. By restricting which functions are allowable and which ones are not, we can restrict our attention to error functions that are sufficiently well behaved. In the context of reusable fuzzy extractors, well-behaved perturbation functions are those that cause similar perturbations regardless of the input value. An example of such a physically plausible well-behaved perturbation family is that of an additive random noise process distributed independently of the data it affects.

## 6.4 Practical Robustness

As discussed in Section 6.1, the security guarantees provided by ordinary secure sketches and fuzzy extractors no longer hold if the public string $P$ can be modified before it is used by the recovery mechanism. Robust sketches and robust fuzzy extractors provide a very effective protection against this attack, by requiring that the recovery algorithm abort with high probability in case of tampering. We first formalize these notions and then give generic conversions from secure sketch to robust sketch and then to robust fuzzy extractor, in the random oracle model.

Robust sketches and robust fuzzy extractors are defined similarly as ordinary sketches and fuzzy extractors, except for the added security requirement that the recovery function be protected against corruptions of the string $P$. Security against active attacks is best captured by an interactive game.

**Definition 6.5.** *A* $(m, m', t, n, \delta)$-robust sketch *is a well-formed* $(m, m', t)$-secure sketch $(\mathsf{Sk}, \mathsf{Rec})$ *such that for all adversaries* $\mathcal{A}$ *and all* $t$-bounded distortion ensembles $\mathcal{W} = \{W_0, W_1, \ldots, W_n\}$, *where* $\mathsf{H}_\infty(W_0) \geq m$, *the advantage of* $\mathcal{A}$ *in the following game,* $\mathbb{P}(\text{Success})$, *is* $\leq \delta$:

*Registration: $\mathcal{A}$ is given a string $P \leftarrow \mathsf{Sk}(w_0)$, where $w_0 \leftarrow W_0$.*
*Trials: $\mathcal{A}$ outputs $n$ strings $P_1, \ldots, P_n$.*
*Success: $\mathcal{A}$ wins if $\exists i$, $(P_i \neq P) \wedge \mathsf{Rec}(w_i, P_i) \neq \bot$, where $w_i \leftarrow W_i$.*

**Definition 6.6.** *A $(m, \ell, t, \epsilon, n, \delta)$-robust fuzzy extractor is a $(m, \ell, t, \epsilon)$-fuzzy extractor $(\mathsf{Ext}, \mathsf{Rep})$ such that for all adversaries $\mathcal{A}$ and all $t$-bounded distortion ensembles $\mathcal{W} = \{W_0, W_1, \ldots, W_n\}$, where $\mathsf{H}_\infty(W_0) \geq m$, the advantage of $\mathcal{A}$ in the following game, $\mathbb{P}(Success)$, is $\leq \delta$:*

*Registration: $\mathcal{A}$ is given a pair $(R, P) \leftarrow \mathsf{Ext}(w_0)$, where $w_0 \leftarrow W_0$.*
*Trials: $\mathcal{A}$ outputs $n$ strings $P_1, \ldots, P_n$.*
*Success: $\mathcal{A}$ wins if $\exists i$, $(P_i \neq P) \wedge \mathsf{Rep}(w_i, P_i) \neq \bot$, where $w_i \leftarrow W_i$.*

We consider the adversary to win as soon as some $P_i$ is accepted, since even an incorrectly reproduced value might leak information about $w_i$ and thus $w_0$.

### 6.4.1 Generic Robust Sketches

Any well-formed secure sketch $(\mathsf{Sk'}, \mathsf{Rec'})$ can be transformed into a robust sketch $(\mathsf{Sk}, \mathsf{Rec})$ using a hash function $H : \{0,1\}^* \to \{0,1\}^k$ viewed as a random oracle.

| $\mathsf{Sk}(w)$ | $\mathsf{Rec}(w, P)$ |
|---|---|
| 1. $P' \leftarrow \mathsf{Sk'}(w)$ | 1. parse $P$ as $(P', h)$ |
| 2. $h = H(w, P')$ | 2. $w' \leftarrow \mathsf{Rec'}(w, P')$ |
| 3. return $P = (P', h)$ | 3. if $w' = \bot$ output $\bot$ |
| | 4. if $H(w', P') \neq h$ output $\bot$ |
| | 5. otherwise, output $w'$ |

The intuition behind the generic construction should be clear: The hash function output $h$ acts as a secret-key authenticator for the public string $P$, thanks to which any tampering will be detected with overwhelming probability. The key for the authenticator is none other than the secret input $w$ itself, which is the only available option given the constraints. It is because $w$ can be reconstructed exactly by the honest user on the recovery side that we can use it as authentication key.

Let $\mathsf{Vol}_t^{\mathcal{M}} = \max_{x \in \mathcal{M}} |\{x' \in \mathcal{M} : d(x, x') \leq t\}|$ be the maximum number of points in any ball of radius $t$. The exact security of the construction is bounded by the following theorem [12].

**Theorem 6.1.** *If $(\mathsf{Sk'}, \mathsf{Rec'})$ is a well-formed $(m, m', t)$-secure sketch in the metric space $(\mathcal{M}, d)$ and $H : \{0,1\}^* \to \{0,1\}^k$ is a random oracle, then $(\mathsf{Sk}, \mathsf{Rec})$ is an $(m, m'', t, n, \delta)$-robust sketch in $(\mathcal{M}, d)$ for any adversary that makes at most $q_H$ queries to $H$, where*

$$\delta = (q_H^2 + n) \cdot 2^{-k} + (3q_H + 2n \cdot \mathsf{Vol}_t^{\mathcal{M}}) \cdot 2^{-m'},$$
$$m'' = m' - \log(3q_H + 2).$$

At a high level, the theorem is proved along these lines. Let $W = \{W_0, \ldots\}$ be a sequence of random variables, with $W_0$ the initial biometric reading and each $W_i$ a subsequent reading. For a well-formed secure sketch $(\mathsf{Sk}', \mathsf{Rec}')$, it can be shown that the min-entropy of $W_i'$ remains high given any value $P_i' \neq P' = \mathsf{Sk}'(W_0)$ chosen by the adversary. The adversary is thus unable to output the correct value $h_i = H(W_i', P_i')$ from the random oracle $H$ with probability better than $2^{-\mathsf{H}_\infty(W_i')}$ at the $i$th iteration. Since, furthermore, the published value $h = H(W_0, P')$ does not significantly affect the entropy of $W_0$ in this reasoning, again because $H$ is a random oracle, the theorem follows. See [42] for additional details.

### 6.4.2 Generic Robust Fuzzy Extractors

Given any robust sketch $(\mathsf{Sk}, \mathsf{Rec})$, one easily obtains a robust fuzzy extractor $(\mathsf{Ext}, \mathsf{Rep})$ by applying a second hash function $G : \mathcal{M} \rightarrow \{0,1\}^\ell$, viewed as an independent random oracle, to the recovered value $w$. If the robust sketch rejected the input, then the robust extractor rejects it as well.

| $\mathsf{Ext}(w)$ | $\mathsf{Rep}(w, P)$ |
|---|---|
| 1.  $P \leftarrow \mathsf{Sk}(w)$ | 1.  $w' \leftarrow \mathsf{Rec}(w, P)$ |
| 2.  $R = G(w)$ | 2.  if $w' = \bot$ output $\bot$ |
| 3.  return $(R, P)$ | 3.  otherwise, output $G(w')$ |

A similar hashing idea was used in [91] to construct ordinary fuzzy extractors from sketches using pairwise independent hash functions. We remark that pairwise independent hashing will not work in general for robust extractors because the hash parameters must be specified as part of $P$, which the adversary can modify at will. Giving $R$ to $\mathcal{A}$ as required by Definition 6.6 would further reduce the residual entropy if pairwise independent hashing were used.

### 6.4.3 Remote Biometric Authentication

It is straightforward to achieve mutual authentication and authenticated key exchange based on biometrics over an insecure channel, thanks to robust fuzzy extractors. Suppose that $\Pi$ is a protocol that performs mutually authenticated key exchange based on uniformly distributed shared secrets of length $\ell$, along the lines of [19, 20]. Suppose also that a user possesses a biometric entropy source $W_0$ with min-entropy $\mathsf{H}_\infty(W_0) \geq m$ and whose subsequent readings are distributed differently (due to distortions in the measurement mechanisms or the biometric itself). Using any $(m, \ell, t, \epsilon, n, \delta)$-robust fuzzy extractor $(\mathsf{Ext}, \mathsf{Rec})$, we construct a new protocol $\Pi'$:

> *Initialization.* The user obtains $w_0 \leftarrow W_0$ (i.e., from the initial biometric reading) and computes $(R, P) \leftarrow \mathsf{Ext}(w_0)$. The user registers $(R, P)$ at the server.

*Protocol execution.* The $i$th time the user wants to run the protocol, the server sends $P$ back to the user. The user obtains $w_i \leftarrow W_i$ (i.e., from a fresh biometric reading) and computes $\hat{R} = \mathsf{Rep}(w_i, P)$. If $\hat{R} = \perp$, the user aborts; otherwise, the user and server proceed by executing protocol $\Pi$ using respective keys $\hat{R}$ and $R$.

The correctness of $\Pi'$ is easily verified under the assumption that $\mathcal{W} = \{W_0, W_1, \ldots\}$ is a $t$-bounded distortion ensemble: Since $d(w_0, w_i) \leq t$, the user will always recover $\hat{R} = R$ provided that he received the correct $P$ from the server; from there, the parties will execute $\Pi$ using the same key.

The security of $\Pi'$ is ensured against an active adversary who controls all communications and who can run the protocol concurrently with many user or server instances, for the following reasons. All user instances who receive $P' \neq P$ will abort with overwhelming probability before executing $\Pi$ and thus without leaking any information. By our robustness definition, this remains true even against an adversary that constructs $P'$ with knowledge of $R$ (which the adversary might gain by observing the messages of $\Pi$ between user and server instances allowed to run the protocol without interference). As for user instances who are forwarded the correct $P$, they will end up executing $\Pi$ with a key $R$ within statistical difference $\epsilon$ from a uniformly distributed $\ell$-bit key, in which case the security guarantees of $\Pi$ apply.

### 6.4.4 Robustness Without Random Oracles

The above constructions are well suited for practical use, due to their generality, simplicity, and relatively modest entropy loss. Robustness against active attacks is achieved by authenticating the public string using cryptographic hash functions viewed as random oracles.

For authenticated key exchange applications, it is possible to retain even more of the available biometric entropy and avoid random oracles, by using a different mechanism for authenticating the public string $P$ that does not involve hashing. In a solution proposed by Boyen et al. [42], the public string is authenticated by including it as part of the user's and server's names in a regular authenticated key exchange protocol, such as the protocol of [166] in the common reference string model. The intuition is that such protocols will fail gracefully whenever the authenticating parties do not agree on each other's names. This solution provides robustness without the extra hashing and the associated loss of entropy. Its main drawbacks are that it serves a special purpose only and it requires the user to give his or her actual biometric reading $w_0 \leftarrow W_0$ to the server upon registration.

Another line of work has focused on the direct construction of robust fuzzy extractors in the standard model. Dodis et al. [88] presented a specific such construction for the metric space $GF(2^k)$ and the Hamming distance. Their solution is very elegant and is optimal for that space in the sense that it meets the lower bound of [94] on entropy loss for strong extraction in the standard model, namely $k/2$ bits for $k$ bits of input. Unfortunately, this lower bound is a challenge for biometric applications, because many biometric feature sets encoded over $k$ bits tend to have much less than $k/2$ bits of min-entropy and are hard to compress without good knowledge of the distribution (e.g., the estimated entropy of a 4000-bit iriscode is only 250 bits [157]). The generic random oracle extractors presented earlier do not suffer from this limitation.

## 6.5 Toward Reusability

Whereas robustness is concerned with malicious modifications of $P$, reusability is about extracting multiple instances of $P$ from different readings of the same biometric. As people only have a limited number of biometric features at their disposal, there is a strong motivation for reusing the same ones with multiple servers. For a variety of reasons, such as user convenience, evidence of liveness, and the servers' mutual mistrust, users will often be forced to rederive new instances of their public strings from fresh biometric readings. In this context, we define reuse as the application of Sk or Ext on multiple inputs $\{w_i\}_{i=0,1,\dots}$ that are somehow related.

Reusability poses a delicate challenge, since each instance $P_i$ obtained from a new reading $w_i \leftarrow W_i$ of the secret biometric will reveal additional information about it, thanks to which $w_0$ can be reconstructed and the user impersonated. To guard against this possibility in the information-theoretic sense, it is necessary to ensure that additional public strings $P_i \leftarrow \mathsf{Sk}(w_i)$ do not exhibit new information that was not already present in $P_0 \leftarrow \mathsf{Sk}(w_0)$. For this purpose, we view the $w_i$ not as realizations of dependent random variables, but as deterministic functions $w_i = \phi_i(w)$ of some secret $w$. Here, the perturbation functions $\phi_i$ are members of a perturbation family $\Phi$ that determines what errors can possibly affect the biometric readings.

The choice of error functions $\phi_1, \phi_2, \dots$ affecting the successive readings of $w$ can be arbitrary; they can even be chosen by the adversary. The security of an (ordinary or robust) reusable secure sketch is then defined with respect to a chosen perturbation attack limited to the perturbation family $\Phi$.

**Definition 6.7.** *A secure sketch* (Sk, Rec) *is* $(m, m', t, \Phi)$-*secure against a chosen perturbation attack if the advantage of any adversary $\mathcal{A}$ in the following game,* $\mathbb{P}(Success)$, *is* $\leq 2^{-m'}$:

> *Preparation: $\mathcal{A}$ publishes an efficient sampling procedure for a random variable $W : \Omega \to \mathcal{M}$ of its choice. The challenger secretly samples $w \leftarrow W$.*
> *Sketching: For $i = 1, 2, 3, \dots$, adaptively, $\mathcal{A}$ designates a perturbation function $\phi_i \in \Phi$ and receives the (possibly randomized) sketch $P_i \leftarrow \mathsf{Sk}(\phi_i(w))$.*
> *Guessing: When $\mathcal{A}$ is ready, he outputs $w' \in \mathcal{M}$. We have Success if $w' = w$.*

Chosen perturbation security for reusable fuzzy extractors is defined similarly; the changes are that $\mathcal{A}$ receives $P_i$ from $(R_i, P_i) \leftarrow \mathsf{Ext}(\phi_i(w))$ in response to queries and is to guess the value of $R_0$ such that $(R_0, P_0) = \mathsf{Ext}(w)$.

### 6.5.1 Barriers to Reusability

Before proceeding with a construction, it is useful to substantiate the earlier claim that no sketching function $\mathsf{Sk}$ can withstand an active attack with an unrestricted perturbation family. For concreteness, let $\mathcal{M}$ be the Hamming space of $k$-bit binary strings and suppose that $\mathsf{Sk}$ is non-trivial in the sense that there exist two inputs $a, b \in \mathcal{M}$ on which $\mathsf{Sk}$ behaves differently. Without restrictions on $\Phi$, $\mathcal{A}$ can recover $w$ in $k$ queries, by letting, for $i = 1, \ldots, k$,

$$\phi_i : w \mapsto \begin{cases} a & \text{if } w|_i = 0 \quad \text{(the $i$th bit of $w$ is 0)} \\ b & \text{if } w|_i = 1 \quad \text{(the $i$th bit of $w$ is 1).} \end{cases}$$

To avoid giving such unfair advantages to the adversary, we need to restrict the perturbation functions to those that treat their input in a uniform manner. A natural notion of uniformity is to require the perturbations to be isometric (to preserve distances). Isometric perturbations are physically plausible for data-independent errors such as caused by additive noise processes.

### 6.5.2 Reusable Sketches from Symmetries

We now show how to construct reusable secure sketches (and fuzzy extractors) for families of isometric perturbations, based on error-correcting codes that satisfy certain (rather weak) notions of symmetry.

Let $\mathcal{C}' \subset \mathcal{M}$ be an error-correcting code. Let $\mathcal{Q}$ be a group of permutations in $\mathcal{M}$ (i.e., a set of permutations $\pi : \mathcal{M} \to \mathcal{M}$ that is closed under composition and inversion). We say that an element $p_{\mathcal{Q}} \in \mathcal{C}'$ is a $\mathcal{Q}$-pivot if $\forall \pi \in \mathcal{Q}$, $\pi(p_{\mathcal{Q}}) \in \mathcal{C}'$. It follows that all of the images $\pi(p_{\mathcal{Q}})$ under all of the permutations $\pi \in \mathcal{Q}$ form a subcode $\mathcal{C} \subseteq \mathcal{C}'$ that is closed under $\mathcal{Q}$ and on which $\mathcal{Q}$ acts transitively (i.e., mapping any element of $\mathcal{C}$ to any other). Equipped with this weak notion of symmetry, we can construct a generic secure sketch that is unconditionally secure against chosen perturbation attacks. The construction is based on any transitive group of isometric permutations $\mathcal{Q}' \supseteq \mathcal{Q}$ and any error-correcting code $\mathcal{C}' \supseteq \mathcal{C}$ such that $\mathcal{C}$ and $\mathcal{Q}$ have the above properties.

Let $(E \circ D) : \mathcal{M} \to \mathcal{C}$ be the function that maps elements of $\mathcal{M}$ to the closest codeword in $\mathcal{C}'$ (e.g., obtained by applying the decoding function of $\mathcal{C}'$ followed by its encoding function). Fix a $\mathcal{Q}$-pivot $p_{\mathcal{Q}} \in \mathcal{C}'$ and construct:

| $\mathsf{Sk}(w)$ | $\mathsf{Rec}(w, P)$ |
|---|---|
| 1. pick $\pi_1 \in \mathcal{Q}'$ such that $\pi_1(w) = p_{\mathcal{Q}}$ | 1. interpret $P$ as $\pi \in \mathcal{Q}'$ |
| 2. pick $\pi_2 \in \mathcal{Q}$ at random | 2. let $\pi' = \pi^{-1} \circ E \circ D \circ \pi$ |
| 3. construct $\pi = \pi_2 \circ \pi_1 \in \mathcal{Q}'$ | 3. output $w' = \pi'(w)$ |
| 4. output a canonical representation of $\pi$ | |

The preceding construction can be viewed as an active-attack analogue to a permutation-based secure sketch construction from [91]. The following theorem [41] relates the entropy loss achieved by the generic fuzzy sketch to the relative sizes of $\mathcal{Q}$ and $\mathcal{Q}'$, for any perturbation family $\Phi \subseteq \mathcal{Q}'$.

**Theorem 6.2.** *Let $\mathcal{C}'$ be a code with correction radius $t$ in the metric space $\mathcal{M}$. Let $\mathcal{Q}'$ be a transitive isometric permutation group. Assume that $\mathcal{C}'$ admits a $\mathcal{Q}$-pivot $p_{\mathcal{Q}} \in \mathcal{C}'$ for some subgroup $\mathcal{Q} \subseteq \mathcal{Q}'$. Then $(\mathsf{Sk}, \mathsf{Rec})$ constitutes a $(m, m', t, \Phi)$-secure sketch against chosen perturbation attacks for any perturbation family $\Phi \subseteq \mathcal{Q}'$, provided that $m - m' \geq \log|\mathcal{Q}'| - \log|\mathcal{Q}|$.*

It is advantageous to use a code $\mathcal{C}'$ with enough symmetry to allow the sub-code $\mathcal{C}$ and subgroup $\mathcal{Q}$ to be as large as possible, which lessens the loss of entropy. However, this requires the code $\mathcal{C}$ to be large, which places a bound on its correction radius $t$. Ordinary secure sketches face similar compromises.

## 6.6 Summary

We studied two information-theoretic security notions that address two kinds of active attack against cryptographic fuzzy extractors. The two notions—robustness and reusability—are essentially orthogonal and the same primitive can, in principle, defend against both.

# Fuzzy Identities and Attribute-Based Encryption

Amit Sahai and Brent Waters

We introduce a new type of Identity-Based Encryption (IBE) scheme that we call Fuzzy Identity-Based Encryption. In fuzzy IBE, we view an identity as a set of descriptive attributes. A fuzzy IBE scheme allows for a private key for an identity, $\omega$, to decrypt a ciphertext encrypted with an identity, $\omega'$, if and only if the identities $\omega$ and $\omega'$ are close to each other as measured by the "set overlap" distance metric. A fuzzy IBE scheme can be applied to enable encryption using biometric inputs as identities; the error-tolerance property of a fuzzy IBE scheme is precisely what allows for the use of biometric identities, which inherently will have some noise each time they are sampled. Additionally, we show that fuzzy IBE can be used for a type of application that we term "attribute-based encryption."

In this paper we present two constructions of fuzzy IBE schemes. Our constructions can be viewed as an IBE of a message under several attributes that compose a (fuzzy) identity. Our IBE schemes are both error-tolerant and secure against collusion attacks. Additionally, our basic construction does not use random oracles. We prove the security of our schemes under the selective-ID security model.

## 7.1 Introduction

In the previous chapters we have seen how to apply the entropy in biometrics toward the generation of secret keys that can be used for encryption and remote authentication. All of these techniques will require that a user keep his biometric a secret. In practice, it might be quite difficult to find biometrics that are both easy to scan when required and difficult for an adversary to obtain; fingerprints are regularly left by people during activities in their daily lives and high-resolution cameras are able to capture detailed images of an iris from a distance. Once a user's biometric is captured by an adversary, it is gone forever; a user cannot obtain a new biometric.

In addition to the above problems, there is a movement in some systems to use biometrics as *identities*. The largest example of this is the effort of the International Civil Aviation Organization (ICAO) to standardize methods for integrating passports with chips containing the biometric readouts of its holder. Clearly, such biometrics cannot serve both as identities for foreign customs inspections and as secret keys for highly sensitive materials. Currently, it is unclear exactly what biometric information will be embedded into which passports. However, given the the importance of this application, it appears that designers of cryptographic protocols using biometrics may need to adapt to the reality implied by these standards.

In this chapter we examine applications for biometrics in cryptography if a user's biometric is known by the attacker, and even possibly used as a public identity. The ideas presented in this chapter are based on [242].

### 7.1.1 Context: Identity-Based Encryption

Identity-based encryption [250] allows for a sender to encrypt a message to an identity without access to a public-key certificate. The ability to do public-key encryption without certificates has many practical applications. For example, a user can send an encrypted mail to a recipient (e.g., bobsmith@gmail.com) without requiring either the existence of a Public-Key Infrastructure or that the recipient be on-line at the time of creation.

One common feature of all previous IBE systems is that they view identities as a string of characters. In this chapter we propose a new type of IBE that we call *Fuzzy Identity-Based Encryption* or, more generally, *Attribute-Based Encryption*, in which we view identities as a set of descriptive attributes. In a fuzzy IBE scheme, a user with the secret key for the identity $\omega$ is able to decrypt a ciphertext encrypted with the public key $\omega'$ if and only if $\omega$ and $\omega'$ are within a certain distance of each other as judged by some metric. Therefore, our system allows for a certain amount of error tolerance in the identities.

The most natural application of fuzzy IBE is an IBE system that uses biometric identities; that is, we can view a user's biometric (e.g., an iris scan) as that user's identity described by several attributes and then encrypt to the user using their biometric identity. Since biometric measurements are noisy, we cannot use existing IBE systems. However, the error-tolerance property of a fuzzy IBE allows for a private key (derived from a measurement of a biometric) to decrypt a ciphertext encrypted with a slightly different measurement of the same biometric.

We further discuss the usefulness of using biometrics in IBE and then discuss our contributions.

### Using Biometrics in Identity-Based Encryption

In many situations, using biometric-based identity in an IBE system has a number of important advantages over "standard" IBE. We argue that the use of biometric identities fits the framework of IBE very well and is a very valuable application of it.

First, the process of obtaining a secret key from an authority is very natural and straightforward. In standard IBE schemes a user with a certain identity (e.g., "Bob Smith") will need to go to an authority to obtain the private key corresponding to the identity. In this process, the user will need to "prove" to the authority that he is indeed entitled to this identity. This will typically involve presenting supplementary documents or credentials. The type of authentication that is necessary is not always clear and robustness of this process is questionable (the supplementary documents themselves could be subject to forgery). Typically, there will exist a trade-off between a system that is expensive in this step and one that is less reliable.

In contrast, if a biometric is used as an identity, then the verification process for an identity is very clear. The user must demonstrate ownership of the biometric under the supervision of a well-trained operator. If the operator is able to detect imitation attacks (e.g., playing the recording of a voice), then the security of this phase is only limited by the quality of the biometric technique itself. We emphasize that the biometric measurement for an individual need *not* be kept secret. Indeed, it is not if it is used as a public key. We must only guarantee that an attacker cannot fool the key authority into believing that an attacker owns a biometric identity that he does not.

Also, a biometric identity is an inherent trait and will always remain with a person. Using biometrics in IBE will mean that the person will always have their public key handy. In several situations, a user will want to present an encryption key to someone when they are physically present. For example, consider the case when a user is traveling and another party encrypts an ad hoc meeting between them.

Finally, using a biometric as an identity has the advantage that identities are unique if the underlying biometric is of a good quality. Some types of standard identity, such as the name "Bob Smith" will clearly not be unique or change owners over time.

**Security Against Collusion Attacks**

In addition to providing error tolerance in the set of attributes composing the identity, any IBE scheme that encrypts to multiple attributes must provide security against collusion attacks. In particular, no group of users should be able to combine their keys in such a way that they can decrypt a ciphertext that none of them alone could. This property is important for security in both biometric applications and "attribute-based encryption."

**Our Contributions**

We formalize the notion of fuzzy IBE and provide a construction for a fuzzy IBE scheme. Our construction uses groups for which an efficient bilinear map exists, but for which the computational Diffie-Hellman problem is assumed to be hard.

Our primary technique is that we construct a user's private key as a set of private-key components, one for each attribute in the user's identity. We use Shamir's method of secret sharing [249] to distribute shares of a master secret in the exponents of the user's private-key components. Shamir's secret sharing within the exponent gives our scheme the crucial property of being error tolerant since only a subset of the private-key components is needed to decrypt a message. Additionally, our scheme is resistant to collusion attacks. Different users have their private-key components generated with different random polynomials. If multiple users collude, they will be unable to combine their private-key components in any useful way.

In the first version of our scheme, the public-key size grows linearly with the number of potential attributes in the universe. The public parameter growth is manageable for a biometric system where all of the possible attributes are defined at the system creation time. However, this becomes a limitation in a more general system where we might like an attribute to be defined by an arbitrary string. To accommodate these more general requirements, we additionally provide a fuzzy IBE system for large universes, where attributes are defined by arbitrary strings.

We prove our scheme secure under an adapted version of the selective-ID security model first proposed by Canetti et al. [54]. Additionally, our construction does not use random oracles. We reduce the security of our scheme to an assumption that is similar to the decisional bilinear Diffie-Hellman assumption.

### 7.1.2 Related Work

**Identity-Based Encryption**

Shamir [250] first proposed the concept of IBE. However, it was not until much later that Boneh and Franklin [37] presented the first IBE scheme that was both practical and secure. Their solution made novel use of groups for which there was an efficiently computable bilinear map.

Canetti et al. [54] proposed the first construction for IBE that was provably secure outside the random oracle model. To prove security, they described a slightly weaker model of security known as the selective-ID model, in which the adversary declares which identity he will attack before the global public parameters are generated. Boneh and Boyen [36] gave two schemes with improved efficiency and proved security in the selective-ID model without random oracles.

**Biometrics**

Other work in applying biometrics to cryptography has focused on the derivation of a secret from a biometric  [41, 81, 91, 161, 205–207]. This secret can be then used for operations such as symmetric encryption or UNIX-style password authentication.

The distinguishing feature of our work from the above related work on biometrics is that we view the biometric input as potentially *public* information instead of a secret. Our only physical requirement is that the biometric cannot be imitated such that a trained human operator would be fooled. We stress the importance of this, since it is much easier to capture a digital reading of someone's biometric than to fool someone into believing that someone else's biometric is one's own. Simply capturing a digital reading of someone's biometric would (forever) invalidate approaches where symmetric keys are systematically derived from biometric readings.

**Attribute-Based Encryption**

Yao et al. [306] showed how an IBE system that encrypts to multiple hierarchical identities in a collusion-resistant manner implies a forward secure hierarchical IBE scheme. They also noted how their techniques for resisting collusion attacks are useful in attribute-based encryption. However, the cost of their scheme in terms of computation, private-key size, and ciphertext size increases exponentially with the number of attributes.

### 7.1.3 Organization

The rest of the chapter is organized as follows. In Section 7.2 we formally define a fuzzy IBE scheme including the selective-ID security model for one. Then we describe our security assumptions. In Section 7.3 we show why two naive approaches do not work. We follow with a description of our construction in Section 7.4. We describe our second construction in Section 7.5. Finally, we conclude in Section 7.6.

## 7.2 Preliminaries

We begin by presenting our definition of security. We follow with a brief review of bilinear maps and then state the complexity assumptions we use for our proofs of security.

### 7.2.1 Definitions

In this subsection we define our selective-ID models of security for fuzzy IBE. The fuzzy selective-ID game is very similar to the standard selective-ID model for IBE with the exception that the adversary is only allowed to query for secret keys for identities that have less than $d$ overlap with the target identity.

*Fuzzy Selective-ID*

Init    The adversary declares the identity, $\alpha$, that he wishes to be challenged.

Setup    The challenger runs the setup phase of the algorithm and tells the adversary the public parameters.

Phase 1    The adversary is allowed to issue queries for private keys for many identities $\gamma_j$, where $|\gamma_j \cap \alpha| < d$ for all $j$.

Challenge    The adversary submits two equal length messages $M_0$ and $M_1$. The challenger flips a random coin, $b$, and encrypts $M_b$ with $\alpha$. The ciphertext is passed to the adversary.

Phase 2    Phase 1 is repeated.

Guess    The adversary outputs a guess $b'$ of $b$.

The advantage of an adversary $\mathcal{A}$ in this game is defined as $\Pr[b' = b] - \frac{1}{2}$.

**Definition 7.1 (Fuzzy selective-ID).** *A scheme is* secure *in the fuzzy selective-ID model of security if all polynomial-time adversaries have at most a negligible advantage in the above game.*

### 7.2.2 Bilinear Maps

We briefly review the facts about groups with efficiently computable bilinear maps. We refer the reader to previous literature [37] for more details.

Let $\mathbb{G}_1$ and $\mathbb{G}_2$ be groups of prime order $p$ and let $g$ be a generator of $\mathbb{G}_1$. We say $\mathbb{G}_1$ has an admissible bilinear map, $e : \mathbb{G}_1 \times \mathbb{G}_1 \to \mathbb{G}_2$, into $\mathbb{G}_2$ if the following two conditions hold. The map is bilinear; for all $a$ and $b$ we have $e(g^a, g^b) = e(g, g)^{ab}$. The map is non-degenerate; we must have that $e(g, g) \neq 1$.

### 7.2.3 Complexity Assumptions

We state our complexity assumptions.

**Definition 7.2 (Decisional bilinear Diffie-Hellman (BDH) assumption).** *Suppose a challenger chooses $a, b, c, z \in \mathbb{Z}_p$ at random. The decisional BDH assumption is that no polynomial-time adversary is to be able to distinguish the tuple $(A = g^a, B = g^b, C = g^c, Z = e(g, g)^{abc})$ from the tuple $(A = g^a, B = g^b, C = g^c, Z = e(g, g)^z)$ with more than a negligible advantage.*

**Definition 7.3 (Decisional modified bilinear Diffie-Hellman (MBDH) assumption).** *Suppose a challenger chooses $a, b, c, z \in \mathbb{Z}_p$ at random. The decisional MBDH assumption is that no polynomial-time adversary is to be able to distinguish the tuple $(A = g^a, B = g^b, C = g^c, Z = e(g, g)^{ab/c})$ from $(A = g^a, B = g^b, C = g^c, Z = e(g, g)^z)$ with more than a negligible advantage.*

## 7.3 Other Approaches

Before describing our scheme we first show three potential approaches to building a Fuzzy Identity-Based Encryption scheme and show why they fall short. This discussion additionally motivates our approach to the problem.

### 7.3.1 Correcting the Error

We consider the feasibility of "correcting" the errors of a biometric measurement and then use standard IBE to encrypt a message under the corrected input. However, this approach relies upon the faulty assumption that each biometric input measurement is slightly deviated from some "true" value and that the set of possible "true" values are well known. In practice, the only reasonable assumption is that two measurements sampled from the same person will be within a certain distance of each other. This intuition is captured by previous work. Dodis et al. [91] used what they call a *fuzzy sketch* that contains information of a first sampling of a biometric that allows subsequent measurements to be corrected to it. If the correction could be done without any additional information, then we could simply do away with the fuzzy sketch.

### 7.3.2 Key per Attribute

The second naive approach we consider is for an authority to give a user a different private key for each of the attributes that describe the user. Such a system easily falls prey to simple collusion attacks where multiple users combine their keys to form identities that are a combination of their attributes. The colluders are then able to decrypt ciphertexts that none of them individually were able to decrypt.

### 7.3.3 Several Keys

Suppose a key authority measures an input $\omega$ for a particular party. The authority could create a separate standard IBE private key for every $\omega'$ such that $|\omega \cap \omega'| \geq d$ for some error-tolerance parameter $d$. However, the private key storage will grow exponentially in $d$ and the system will be impractical for even modest values of $d$.

## 7.4 Our Construction

Recall that we view identities as sets of attributes and we let the value $d$ represent the error tolerance in terms of minimal set overlap. When an authority is creating a private key for a user, he will associate a random $(d-1)$ degree polynomial $q(x)$ with each user, with the restriction that each polynomial have the same valuation at point 0 (i.e., $q(0) = y$).

For each of the attributes associated with a user's identity, the key generation algorithm will issue a private-key component that is tied to the user's random polynomial $q(x)$. If the user is able to "match" at least $d$ components of the ciphertext with his private-key components, then he will be able to perform decryption. However, since the private-key components are tied to random polynomials, multiple users are unable to combine them in any way that allows for collusion attacks.

A detailed description of our scheme follows.

### 7.4.1 Description

Recall that we wish to create an IBE scheme in which a ciphertext created using identity $\omega$ can be decrypted only by a secret key $\omega'$, where $|\omega \cap \omega'| \geq d$.

Let $\mathbb{G}_1$ be a bilinear group of prime order $p$ and let $g$ be a generator of $\mathbb{G}_1$. Additionally, let $e : \mathbb{G}_1 \times \mathbb{G}_1 \rightarrow \mathbb{G}_2$ denote the bilinear map. A security parameter, $\kappa$, will determine the size of the groups. We also define the Lagrange coefficient $\Delta_{i,S}$ for $i \in \mathbb{Z}_p$ and a set, $S$, of elements in $\mathbb{Z}_p$:

$$\Delta_{i,S}(x) = \prod_{j \in S, j \neq i} \frac{x - j}{i - j}.$$

Identities will be element subsets of some universe, $\mathcal{U}$, of size $|\mathcal{U}|$. We will associate each element with a unique integer in $\mathbb{Z}_p^*$. (In practice, an attribute will be associated with each element so that identities will have some semantics.) Our construction follows.

### Setup($d$)

First, define the universe $\mathcal{U}$ of elements. For simplicity, we can take the first $|\mathcal{U}|$ elements of $\mathbb{Z}_p^*$ to be the universe, namely the integers $1, \ldots, |\mathcal{U}|$ (mod $p$). Next, choose $t_1, \ldots, t_{|\mathcal{U}|}$ uniformly at random from $\mathbb{Z}_p$. Finally, choose $y$ uniformly at random in $\mathbb{Z}_p$. The published public parameters are

$$T_1 = g^{t_1}, \ldots, T_{|\mathcal{U}|} = g^{t_{|\mathcal{U}|}}, \quad Y = e(g, g)^y.$$

The master key is

$$t_1, \ldots, t_{|\mathcal{U}|}, y.$$

### Key Generation

To generate a private key for identity $\omega \subseteq \mathcal{U}$, the following steps are taken. A $(d - 1)$st-degree polynomial $q$ is randomly chosen such that $q(0) = y$. The private key consists of components $\{D_i\}_{i \in \omega}$, where $D_i = g^{q(i)/t_i}$ for every $i \in \omega$.

**Encryption**

Encryption with the public key $\omega'$ of a message $M \in \mathbb{G}_2$ proceeds as follows. First, a random value $s \in \mathbb{Z}_p$ is chosen. The ciphertext is then published as

$$E = (\omega', E' = MY^s, \{E_i = T_i^s\}_{i \in \omega'}).$$

Note that the identity, $\omega'$, is included in the ciphertext.

**Decryption**

Suppose that a ciphertext, $E$, is encrypted with a key for identity $\omega'$ and we have a private key for identity $\omega$, where $|\omega \cap \omega'| \geq d$. Choose an arbitrary $d$-element subset, $S$, of $\omega \cap \omega'$. Then, the ciphertext can be decrypted as

$$E' / \prod_{i \in S} (e(D_i, E_i))^{\Delta_{i,S}(0)}$$

$$= Me(g,g)^{sy} / \prod_{i \in S} \left( e(g^{q(i)/t_i}, g^{st_i}) \right)^{\Delta_{i,S}(0)}$$

$$= Me(g,g)^{sy} / \prod_{i \in S} \left( e(g,g)^{sq(i)} \right)^{\Delta_{i,S}(0)}$$

$$= M.$$

The last equality is derived from using polynomial interpolation in the exponents. Since the polynomial $sq(x)$ is of degree $d - 1$, it can be interpolated using $d$ points.

### 7.4.2 Efficiency and Key Sizes

The number of exponentiations in the group $\mathbb{G}_1$ to encrypt to an identity will be linear in the number of elements in the identity's description. The cost of decryption will be dominated by $d$ bilinear map computations.

The number of group elements in the public parameters grows linearly with the number attributes in the system (elements in the defined universe). The number of group elements that compose a user's private key grow linearly with the number of attributes associated with her identity. Finally, the number of group elements in a ciphertext grows linearly with the size of the identity to which we are encrypting.

### 7.4.3 Flexible Error Tolerance

In this construction, the error tolerance is set to a fixed value $d$. However, in practice, a party constructing a ciphertext might want more flexibility. For example, if a biometric input device happens to be less reliable, it might be desirable to relax the set overlap parameters. In the example of attribute-based encryption, we would like to have flexibility in the number of attributes required to access a document.

There are two simple methods for achieving flexible error tolerance. First, we can create multiple systems with different values of $d$ and the party encrypting a message can choose the appropriate one. For $m$ different systems, the size of the public parameters and private keys both increase by a factor of $m$. In the second method, the authority will reserve some attributes that it will issue to every keyholder as part of their identity. The party encrypting the message can increase the error tolerance by increasing the number of these "default" attributes it includes in the encryption identity. In this approach, ciphertexts must be at least as long as the maximum number of attributes that can be required in an encryption. Additionally, we can combine the above two techniques and explore trade-offs between ciphertext size and public parameter and private key size.

## 7.5 Large-Universe Construction

In the previous construction, the size of the public parameters grows linearly with the number of possible attributes in the universe. We describe a second scheme that uses all elements of $\mathbb{Z}_p^*$ as the universe, yet the public parameters only grow linearly in a parameter $n$, which we fix as the maximum size identity to which we can encrypt.

In addition to decreasing the public parameter size, having a large universe allows us to apply a collision-resistant hash function $H : \{0,1\}^* \rightarrow \mathbb{Z}_p^*$ and use arbitrary strings as attributes. We can now use attributes that were not necessarily considered during the public-key setup. For example, we can add any verifiable attribute, such as "Ran in N.Y. Marathon 2005," to a user's private key.

Our large-universe construction is built using concepts similar to the previous scheme and uses an algebraic technique of Boneh and Boyen [36]. Additionally, we reduce the security of this scheme to the decisional BDH problem. We now describe our construction and give our proof of security.

### 7.5.1 Description

Let $\mathbb{G}_1$ be a bilinear group of prime order $p$, and let $g$ be a generator of $\mathbb{G}_1$. Additionally, let $e : \mathbb{G}_1 \times \mathbb{G}_1 \rightarrow \mathbb{G}_2$ denote the bilinear map. We restrict encryption identities to be of length $n$ for some fixed $n$. We define the Lagrange coefficient $\Delta_{i,S}$ for $i \in \mathbb{Z}_p$ and a set, $S$, of elements in $\mathbb{Z}_p$:

$$\Delta_{i,S}(x) = \prod_{j \in S, j \neq i} \frac{x - j}{i - j}.$$

Identities will be sets of $n$ elements of $\mathbb{Z}_p^*$.[1] Alternatively, we can describe an identity as a collection of $n$ strings of arbitrary length and use a collision resistant hash function, $H$, to hash strings into members of $\mathbb{Z}_p^*$. Our construction follows.

## Setup$(n, d)$

First, choose $g_1 = g^y, g_2 \in \mathbb{G}_1$. Next, choose $t_1, \ldots, t_{n+1}$ uniformly at random from $\mathbb{G}_1$. Let $N$ be the set $\{1, \ldots, n+1\}$ and we define a function, $T$, as

$$T(x) = g_2^{x^n} \prod_{i=1}^{n+1} t_i^{\Delta_{i,N}(x)}.$$

We can view $T$ as the function $g_2^{x^n} g^{h(x)}$ for some $n^{\text{th}}$-degree polynomial $h$. The public key is published as $g_1, g_2, t_1, \ldots, t_{n+1}$ and the private key is $y$.

## Key Generation

To generate a private key for identity $\omega$, the following steps are taken. A $(d-1)$st-degree polynomial $q$ is randomly chosen such that $q(0) = y$. The private key will consist of two sets. The first set is $\{D_i\}_{i\in\omega}$, where the elements are constructed as

$$D_i = g_2^{q(i)} T(i)^{r_i},$$

where $r_i$ is a random member of $\mathbb{Z}_p$ defined for all $i \in \omega$. The other set is $\{d_i\}_{i\in\omega}$, where the elements are constructed as

$$d_i = g^{r_i}.$$

## Encryption

Encryption with the public key $\omega'$ and message $M \in \mathbb{G}_2$ proceeds as follows. First, a random value $s \in \mathbb{Z}_p$ is chosen. The ciphertext is then published as

$$E = (\omega', E' = Me(g_1, g_2)^s, E'' = g^s, \{E_i = T(i)^s\}_{i\in\omega'}).$$

## Decryption

Suppose that a ciphertext, $E$, is encrypted with a key for identity $\omega'$ and we have a key for identity $\omega$, where $|\omega \cap \omega'| \geq d$. Choose an arbitrary $d$-element

---

[1] With some minor modifications to our scheme, which we omit for simplicity, we can encrypt to all identities of size $\leq n$.

subset, $S$, of $\omega \cap \omega'$. Then the ciphertext can be decrypted as

$$M = E' \prod_{i \in S} \left( \frac{e(d_i, E_i)}{e(D_i, E'')} \right)^{\Delta_{i,s}(0)}$$

$$= Me(g_1, g_2)^s \prod_{i \in S} \left( \frac{e(g^{r_i}, T(i)^s)}{e(g_2^{q(i)} T(i)^{r_i}, g^s)} \right)^{\Delta_{i,s}(0)}$$

$$= Me(g_1, g_2)^s \prod_{i \in S} \left( \frac{e(g^{r_i}, T(i)^s)}{e(g_2^{q(i)}, g^s) e(T(i)^{r_i}, g^s)} \right)^{\Delta_{i,s}(0)}$$

$$= Me(g, g_2)^{ys} \prod_{i \in S} \frac{1}{e(g, g_2)^{q(i)s \Delta_{i,s}(0)}}$$

$$= M.$$

The last equality is derived from using polynomial interpolation in the exponents. Since the polynomial $sq(x)$ is of degree $d - 1$, it can be interpolated using $d$ points.

### 7.5.2 Efficiency and Key Sizes

Again, the number of exponentiations in the group $\mathbb{G}_1$ to encrypt to an identity will be linear in the number of elements in the identity's description. The cost of decryption will be dominated by $2 \cdot d$ bilinear map computations.

The key feature of the scheme is that the number of group elements in the public parameters only grows linearly with $n$, the maximum number of attributes that can describe an encryption identity. The number of group elements that compose a user's private key grows linearly with the number of attributes associated with her identity. Finally, the number of group elements in a ciphertext grows linearly with the size of the identity to which we are encrypting.

## 7.6 Conclusions

We introduced the concept of fuzzy IBE, which allows for error tolerance between the identity of a private key and the public key used to encrypt a ciphertext. We described two practical applications of fuzzy IBE: encryption using biometrics and attribute-based encryption.

We presented our construction of a fuzzy IBE scheme that uses set overlap as the distance metric between identities. Finally, we proved the security of our scheme under the selective-ID model by reducing it to an assumption that can be viewed as a modified version of the bilinear decisional Diffie-Hellman assumption.

This work motivates a few interesting open problems. The first is whether it is possible to create a fuzzy IBE scheme in which the attributes come from multiple authorities. Although it is natural for one authority to certify all attributes that comprise a biometric, in attribute-based encryption systems there will often not be one party that can act as an authority for all attributes. Also, a fuzzy IBE scheme that hides the public key that was used to encrypt the ciphertext [17] is intriguing. Our scheme uses set overlap as a similarity measure between identities. (We note that a Hamming-distance construction can also be built using our techniques.) An open problem is to build other fuzzy IBE schemes that use different distance metrics between identities.

## 7.7 Applications Beyond Biometrics

Beyond using biometrics in security applications, fuzzy IBE can be generalized to what we call "attribute-based encryption." In this application, a party will wish to encrypt a document to all users that have a certain set of attributes. For example, in a computer science department, the chairperson might want to encrypt a document to all of its systems faculty on a hiring committee. In this case, it would encrypt to the identity {"hiring-committee", "faculty", "systems"}. Any user who has an identity that contains all of these attributes could decrypt the document. The advantage to using fuzzy IBE is that the document can be stored on a simple untrusted storage server instead of relying on a trusted server to perform authentication checks before delivering a document. For more, see [137].

# 8

## Unconditionally Secure Multiparty Computation from Noisy Resources

Stefan Wolf and Jürg Wullschleger

## 8.1 Introduction

Two old friends, who have both become millionaires, want to find out who is richer without, however, any one of them having to reveal any (additional) information about their wealth. Is it possible in principle to fulfill this task?

Alice and Bob, the two main characters of contemporary cryptography, speak on the telephone and would like to do a fair coin flip. Is this possible at all? Clearly, the obvious way of one party throwing a coin and telling the result to the other is useless by reasons that should be all too obvious: "I am sorry, but *you lost....*"

The worldwide cryptographers' union would like to elect a new president by e-mail in a fair way (i.e., such that nobody can influence the outcome of the vote beyond delivering her proper ballot).

Clearly, all of these tasks are easy to fulfill as long as a *trusted third party* (i.e., a distinct player that would carry out the computation for them) is present. It is a natural goal to simulate such a party by a protocol between the involved players. This is called *multiparty computation* (MPC) and was introduced by Yao [305] in 1982. The general setting is that a number of parties or *players* want to collaborate in a secure way in order to achieve a common goal, although they mutually distrust each other and do not want to make use of a trusted third party.

In this chapter, we will only look at the special case of *secure function evaluation*; that is, every party holds an input to a function, and the output should be computed in a way such that no party has to reveal unnecessary information about her input. A complete solution for this problem with respect to computational security was given in [133]. In [22,60], it was shown that in a model with only pairwise secure channels, MPC unconditionally secure against an active adversary is achievable if and only if $t < n/3$ players are corrupted. In [14, 229], it was shown that this bound can be improved to $t < n/2$, if global broadcast channels are additionally given—and this bound was shown tight. A more efficient protocol than those in [14, 229] was given in [68].

For the case $n = 2$, there cannot exist a protocol that is unconditionally secure, as we will see later. However, if a primitive called *oblivious transfer* is assumed, then *any* function can be calculated unconditionally securely, as has been shown by Kilian [171].

In this chapter we will present several protocols that implement the basic primitives of bit commitment, oblivious transfer, and broadcast based on noisy resources such as imperfect channels or distributed randomness.

### 8.1.1 Models for Physical Resources

We will consider two different models for physical resource, namely distributed randomness and noisy channels. For simplicity, we will assume that the physical resources *perfectly* implement these resources (i.e., without any error). In the last section, we will discuss some more realistic models.

*Distributed Randomness.* The two players receive values $X$ and $Y$, distributed according to a certain distribution $P_{XY}$, from a resource outside their control. Such a source could, for example, be a satellite (see Chapter 2).

*Noisy Channel.* The two players are connected by a *noisy channel* (i.e., a resource where one player can choose an input $X$ and the other player receives an output $Y$, distributed according to some conditional distribution $P_{Y|X}$).

### 8.1.2 Basic Functionalities

We will now present the basic functionalities in multiparty computation and how they relate to each other.

### Bit Commitment

Bit commitment was introduced in [30]—together with distributed coin-flipping among two players. Bit commitment is a cryptographic primitive in which, at some point, Alice has to commit to a value of her choice that Bob does not get to know. Later, Alice can open her commitment to Bob. It is guaranteed that she cannot reveal any other value than the committed one. Bit commitment is used as a building block of identification schemes, zero-knowledge proofs, and general MPC.

*Bit commitment implies coin toss.*

A basic application of bit commitment is that it can be used to execute a distributed coin toss. This is not hard to achieve: Alice commits to a random bit, then Bob sends her a random bit, and, finally, Alice opens her commitment. It can easily be verified that the exclusive OR (XOR) of the two bits will always be random if one of the two players is honest.

## Oblivious Transfer

Oblivious transfer, or OT for short, was introduced by Wiesner [290] (under the name of "multiplexing") and Rabin [228]. We will be using the variant of OT introduced in [290] and later in [103], called *chosen one-out-of-two oblivious transfer*, $\binom{2}{1}$–OT for short, which is the most important version of OT. Here, the sender sends two bits $b_0$ and $b_1$, and the receiver's input is a choice bit $c$; the latter then learns $b_c$ but gets no information about the other bit $b_{1-c}$.

*OT implies bit commitment.*

Bit commitment can easily be implemented using $n$ instances of OT. To commit to a value $v$, the committer sends random bits using the $n$ instances of OT in parallel, where the XOR of each input pair equals $v$. The verifier chooses, for each instance, one of the two bits randomly. To open the commitment, the committer sends all the bits he has sent earlier. The verifier checks whether the values match the values he had chosen to see. It is easy to see that the verifier does not get any information about the value $v$ in the commit phase, as he only receives $v$ xored with a random bit. On the other hand, the committer cannot change the value he is committed to with probability larger than $2^{-n}$, since he would need to be able to change the value the verifier did not receive, but since he does not know the choice bits $c_i$ used by the verifier, he will fail to do so with probability $1/2$ for every instance.

## Pseudo-signature Schemes

Much less known than classical *digital signatures* [85,173] are so-called *pseudo-signature schemes* (PSSs) that guarantee, in contrast to the former, *unconditional* security. The inherent price for their higher security, however, is that a signature can only be transfered[1] a limited number of times. After prior work in [61, 229], the first complete PSS was proposed in [224]. This scheme allows for any (constant) transferability $\lambda$ (i.e., number of possible transfers) and any number of corrupted players.

## Broadcast (Byzantine Agreement)

The *broadcast problem* (Byzantine agreement) was introduced by Lamport et al. [174]. A protocol where one player can send a value and all players receive a value achieves broadcast if all honest players receive the value sent by an honest sender, and always receive identical values, even if the sender is

---

[1] We say that a signature, generated by $A$ and known to $B$, can be *transfered to $C$ by $B$* if it allows $B$ to convince $C$ that the original signature was indeed generated by $A$. Note that the transferability of "ordinary" digital signatures is unlimited since, here, no conclusiveness is "lost along the way."

malicious. In [174], it was shown that in the model of secure channels between each pair of players, but without the use of a signature scheme, broadcast is achievable if and only if the number $t$ of cheaters satisfies $t < n/3$. Furthermore, it was shown that when, additionally, a signature scheme is given among the $n$ players, then computationally secure broadcast is achievable for any number of corrupted players. The first efficient such protocol was given in [96]. In [224], an efficient protocol was given with unconditional security based on a PSS with transferability $t + 1$.

### 8.1.3 Definition of Security

We will assume that the adversary is unlimited in computing power and memory space and that his behavior may deviate from the protocol specification in an arbitrary way. Today's standard definition of security was given in [201] and [15], which is based on the so-called *real versus ideal* paradigm. The idea behind the definition is that anything an adversary can achieve in the *real-life protocol*, he could also achieve by an attack in an *ideal world* (i.e., where he only has black-box access to the functionality to be achieved). Such a protocol is secure if for any adversary in the real life, there exists an adversary in the ideal model such that both situations produce the same output distribution. A very important property of this definition is that it implies that the *sequential composition* of secure protocols is again a secure protocol, a fact that was shown in [50]. This greatly simplifies proofs of protocols, as only small parts need to be shown secure.

### 8.1.4 Impossibility of Bit Commitment and Oblivious Transfer from Scratch

It would be preferable to have an implementation of unconditionally secure bit commitment and OT protocols only using (noiseless) communication. Unfortunately, such protocols cannot exist, as we will show now. Assume that there exists a bit commitment protocol, unconditionally secure for both players. It must be secure for the receiver, which means that after the commit phase, given all of the communication between the two players, there can only exist *one* possible opening for the sender. However, this means that the receiver is able, at least in principle, to calculate that value. Hence, such a protocol would not be unconditionally secure for the sender. It follows that OT as well is impossible to achieve from scratch, since OT implies bit commitment.

## 8.2 Preliminaries

In this section, we introduce some information-theoretic notions of central importance in the rest of this chapter.

### 8.2.1 Common Part

The *common part* of two random variables $X$ and $Y$ was first introduced in [118]. We denote it by $X \wedge Y$. It is the maximal random variable that two players Alice and Bob knowing the random variables $X$ and $Y$, respectively, can commonly extract, without any error; that is, there exist functions $f_X$ and $f_Y$ with $X \wedge Y = f_X(X) = f_Y(Y)$.

### 8.2.2 Sufficient Statistics

The *sufficient statistics* of a random variable $X$ with respect to $Y$ is the part of $X$ that is dependent on $Y$. We will use the notion $X \searrow Y$, as in [111, 298, 299], where it was called the *dependent part*. It was also used in [151, 296], where it was called *non-redundant*. $X \searrow Y$ can be calculated very easily in the following way: $X \searrow Y := f(X)$ for $f(x) = P_{Y|X=x}$. It is obtained by collapsing all values $x_1$ and $x_2$, for which $Y$ has the same conditional distribution, to a single value.

   Lemma 8.1 shows an important property of the sufficient statistics. Roughly speaking, the sufficient statistics of $X$ with respect to $Y$ cannot be changed by a player that only knows $X$, without also changing the joint distribution with $Y$.

**Lemma 8.1 [111].** *Let $X$ and $Y$ be random variables, and let $K = X \searrow Y$. Let $\overline{K} = f(X)$ for a randomized function $f$. If $P_{KY} = P_{\overline{K}Y}$, then we have $\overline{K} = K$.*

This property will be very useful in our application, as it allows the player holding $Y$ to verify whether the other player really sent him $X \searrow Y$ by doing a statistical test over many instances of $X$ and $Y$.

### 8.2.3 Universal Hashing and Randomness Extraction

The *statistical distance* of two random variables $X$ and $Y$ over the same domain $\mathcal{V}$ is $\mathrm{SD}[X, Y] := \frac{1}{2} \sum_{v \in \mathcal{V}} |P_X(v) - P_Y(v)|$. A function $h : \mathcal{R} \times \mathcal{X} \rightarrow \{0, 1\}^m$ is called a *2-universal hash function* [57] if for all $x_0 \neq x_1 \in \mathcal{X}$, the probability that they are mapped to the same value is at most $2^{-m}$; more precisely, we have

$$\mathbb{P}[h(R, x_0) = h(R, x_1)] \leq 2^{-m}$$

if $R$ is uniform over $\mathcal{R}$. We measure the *uncertainty* of a random variable $X$, given a random variable $Y$, as the *conditional min-entropy*, which is defined as

$$\mathsf{H}_{\min}(X \mid Y) = \min_{x,y:P_{XY}(x,y)>0} \log \frac{1}{P_{X|Y}(x \mid y)} \ .$$

Note that for independent and identically distributed (*i.i.d.*) random variables, the conditional min-entropy converges to the *conditional Shannon entropy*, which is

$$H(X \mid Y) = \sum_{x,y:P_{XY}(x,y)>0} P_{XY}(x,y) \log \frac{1}{P_{X|Y}(x \mid y)} \,,$$

with an error that vanishes exponentially fast in the number of i.i.d. variables. (See [147] for explicit bounds.)

The following two facts (Lemmas 8.2 and 8.3) are often used in information-theoretic protocols in cryptography. The first one is called the *leftover hash lemma* [152]. It tells us that we can extract roughly $H_{\min}(X \mid Y)$ bits from a random variable $X$ that are uniformly distributed and independent of $Y$. In other words, an adversary who knows $Y$ will have almost no knowledge about the extracted value: This is why the process has also been called *privacy amplification* [25, 27].

**Lemma 8.2 (Leftover hash lemma [27, 152]).** *Let $X$ and $Y$ be random variables over $\mathcal{X}$ and $\mathcal{Y}$ and let $m > 0$. Let $h : \mathcal{S} \times \mathcal{X} \rightarrow \{0,1\}^m$ be a 2-universal hash function. If $m \leq H_{\min}(X|Y) - 2\log(1/\varepsilon)$, then for $S$ uniform over $\mathcal{S}$, we have $\mathsf{SD}[(h(S,X),S,Y),(U,S,Y)] \leq \varepsilon$, where $U$ is uniform over $\{0,1\}^m$ and independent of $S$ and $Y$.*

Often, certain pieces of information are leaked to the adversary during a protocol. Lemma 8.3 gives us a lower bound on the remaining min-entropy: Roughly speaking, it states that with high probability, the min-entropy decreases by at most the logarithm of the alphabet size of the leaked information.

**Lemma 8.3 [49, 193].** *For all random variables $X$ and $Y$ and for all $\varepsilon > 0$, the probability that $Y$ takes on a value $y$ for which*

$$H_{\min}(X \mid Y = y) \geq H_{\min}(XY) - \log|\mathcal{Y}| - \log(1/\varepsilon)$$

*holds is at least $1 - \varepsilon$.*

### 8.2.4 Basic Reductions for OT

We will discuss two basic reductions for OT. The first implements OT from a randomized version of it. The protocol is due to Bennett et al. [26].

**Protocol 1 (OT from randomized OT).** *The sender has inputs $b_0, b_1 \in \{0,1\}$ and the receiver has $c \in \{0,1\}$. Furthermore, the sender has the uniformly random values $\overline{B}_0, \overline{B}_1 \in \{0,1\}$, the receiver has the uniformly random value $\overline{C} \in \{0,1\}$, and $\overline{Y} = \overline{B}_{\overline{C}}$.*

1. *The receiver sends $m = c \oplus \overline{C}$.*
2. *The sender sends $r_0 = b_0 \oplus \overline{B}_m$ and $r_1 = b_1 \oplus \overline{B}_{1-m}$.*
3. *The receiver outputs $y = r_c \oplus \overline{Y}$.*

Intuitively, the protocol is secure because, first, the sender only gets the value $c$ one-time padded by a random value $\overline{C}$ and, hence, will not learn any information about $c$. Furthermore, the receiver will only receive either $\overline{B}_0$ or $\overline{B}_1$, but not both. Therefore, he will only be able to decrypt one one-time pad, the one of his choice, and he will remain ignorant about the other value.

Note that one way to obtain the values $\overline{B}_0 \, \overline{B}_1$, $\overline{C}$, and $\overline{Y}$ is to give random inputs to an instance of OT. This gives us a method to *precompute OT* [16]. This can be very useful in our application, as an implemented OT may not be available when the OT is needed.

The following protocol is due to Crépeau and Kilian [71]. It shows that many instances of OT, all of which are secure for the sender but only one of them (where it is unknown to both players which one this is) is secure for the receiver, can be combined to achieve a secure implementation of OT.

**Protocol 2 (R-Combiner).** *The sender has inputs* $b_0, b_1 \in \{0,1\}$ *and the receiver has* $c \in \{0,1\}$. *Furthermore, they have* $k$ *implementations of OT.*

1. *Alice chooses the values* $b_{01}, \dots, b_{0k-1}$ *uniformly at random and sets* $b_{0k} := \bigoplus_{i=1}^{k-1} b_{0i} \oplus b_0$ *and* $b_{1i} := b_{0i} \oplus b_0 \oplus b_1$, *for* $i \in [k]$.
2. *Bob chooses the values* $c_1, \dots, c_{k-1}$ *uniformly at random and sets* $c_k := \bigoplus_{i=1}^{k-1} c_i \oplus c$.
3. *They execute the* $k$ *implementations of OT, using* $b_{0i}, b_{1i}$, *and* $c_i$ *as input to the* $i$th *execution. Bob receives* $y_i$.
4. *Bob outputs* $y := \bigoplus_{i=1}^{k} y_i$.

It is easy to verify that the output is correct. If the sender gets the receiver's input in $k-1$ instances, he will not learn $c$, as it is still one-time padded with a random value. On the other hand, if all instances of OT are secure for the sender, then the receiver will not get any information about $b_0 \oplus b_1$, a fact that implies that the resulting OT is secure for the sender.

## 8.3 Monotones

It was shown in [299] that the following three quantities are *monotones* for two-party computation—that is, cannot increase during the execution of any protocol based on (noiseless) communication and (lossless) processing (where $X$ and $Y$ are the random variables summarizing the entire information accessible to $A$ and $B$, respectively):

$$H(Y \searcok X \mid X), \qquad H(X \searcok Y \mid Y), \qquad I(X;Y \mid X \wedge Y).$$

These monotones can now be used to show the impossibility of certain reduction protocols or at least to derive lower bounds on the efficiency of such protocols.

Since OT is equivalent to a randomized version OT (see Protocol 1), which is simply distributed randomness, we can directly apply these monotones: For $\binom{2}{1}$–OT, all three monotones are equal to 1. However, if the players do not have any distributed randomness to start with, all three monotones have the value 0 at the beginning. Since they cannot be increased, we get another proof for the impossibility of OT from scratch! However, we can now also easily conclude that OT cannot be duplicated; that is, it is impossible to make $n + 1$ instances of OT out of $n$ instances, or we can derive lower bounds on the number of instances needed for a certain reduction. For example, to produce one instance of $\binom{2}{1}$–OT out of distributed randomness that is distributed according to $P_{XY}$, we need at least

$$\max \left( \frac{1}{\mathsf{H}(Y \searchsmall X \mid X)}, \frac{1}{\mathsf{H}(X \searchsmall Y \mid Y)}, \frac{1}{\mathsf{I}(X;Y \mid X \wedge Y)} \right)$$

instances of this randomness.

## 8.4 Bit Commitment from Noise

Bit commitment based on common randomness was introduced in [239]. In [296], the *commitment capacity* of two correlated random variables is defined. It is the supremum of all rates (bits per instance) that can be achieved with an arbitrarily small error. Note that in this model, all bits are committed to and opened *simultaneously*. It was proved in [296] that the commitment capacity of $X$ and $Y$, where the committer holds $X$ and the verifier holds $Y$, is

$$\mathsf{H}(X \searchsmall Y \mid Y).$$

The protocol of [296] (see also [151]) is based on a code that has been introduced by Wyner [303] for the *wire-tap channel*, but that is inefficient. An efficient (and also simpler) protocol was given in [298]; it only relies on universal hashing [57] and Lemma 8.2 and works as follows. Let Alice have $X^n = X_1, \ldots, X_n$ and Bob $Y^n = Y_1, \ldots, Y_n$. Assume that Alice wants to commit to a value $d \in \{0,1\}^\ell$. Let $h : \{0,1\}^* \times \mathcal{K}^n \to \{0,1\}^m$ and $\text{ext} : \{0,1\}^* \times \mathcal{K}^n \to \{0,1\}^\ell$ be 2-universal hash functions.

**Protocol 3.** *Commit to a value $d \in \{0,1\}^\ell$.*

1. *Bob chooses $r_1 \in \{0,1\}^*$ and sends it to Alice.*
2. *Alice calculates[2] $K^n := (X_1 \searchsmall Y_1, \ldots, X_n \searchsmall Y_n)$. She chooses $r_0 \in \{0,1\}^*$ and sends $c := (r_0, h(r_1, K^n), d \oplus \text{ext}(r_0, K^n))$ to Bob.*

**Protocol 4.** *Open the commitment.*

1. *Alice sends $(d, K^n)$ to Bob.*
2. *Bob accepts $d$ if $(K^n, Y^n)$ is distributed according to $P_{X \searchsmall Y, Y}$ and $c = (r_0, h(r_1, K^n), d \oplus \text{ext}(r_0, K^n))$, but rejects otherwise.*

---

[2] Recall that $K_i = f(X_i)$ for $f(x) = P_{Y \mid X = x}$.

Since Alice has to send the sufficient statistics $K^n$ to Bob, we know by Lemma 8.1 that she cannot change the value $K^n$ without changing the joint statistics of $K^n$ with $Y^n$. Therefore, she can only change $s = O(\sqrt{n})$ values in $K^n$ without being detected. Therefore, Alice can only choose from

$$\binom{n}{s}|\mathcal{K}|^s \le (n|\mathcal{K}|)^s$$

different values. Let us choose $m = s\log(n|\mathcal{K}|) + \log(1/\varepsilon)$. Now, the probability that among the values Alice can choose from, there exist two values with the same hash value is at most

$$2^{-s\log(n|\mathcal{K}|) - \log(1/\varepsilon)}(n|\mathcal{K}|)^s = (n|\mathcal{K}|)^{-s}\varepsilon(n|\mathcal{K}|)^s = \varepsilon .$$

Therefore, with probability of at least $1 - \varepsilon$ Alice will not be able to change her commitment, which implies that it is binding. To ensure that Bob has no information about Alice's secret, she applies the function ext on $K^n$, where $\ell \le \mathsf{H}_{\min}(K^n \mid Y^n) - m - 3\log(1/\varepsilon)$. Lemma 8.3 implies that the min-entropy of Bob about $K^n$ after he has received $h(r_1, K^n)$ is at least $\mathsf{H}_{\min}(K^n \mid Y^n) - m - \log(1/\varepsilon)$ with probability at least $1 - \varepsilon$. Lemma 8.2 states now that given Bob's information, the extracted string is $\varepsilon$-close to uniform. Therefore, with a probability of at least $1 - 2\varepsilon$, Bob has no information about $d$ in the commitment phase. Since $m = O(\sqrt{n}\log(n))$ is sublinear in $n$ and $\mathsf{H}_{\min}(K^n \mid Y^n)$ converges to $n\mathsf{H}(X \searrow Y \mid Y)$, it follows that our scheme achieves the commitment rate $\mathsf{H}(X \searrow Y \mid Y)$.

**Noisy Channels**

The same protocol c an also be applied to the model where the two players are connected by a noisy channel: We let the sender give a random input, according to a specified distribution, to the noisy channel and then apply the above protocol. Additionally, we have to make sure that the receiver can verify whether the sender has used the specified input distribution [296]. It turns out that bit commitment is possible for any non-trivial channel, the same condition as for OT, which we will see in the following section.

## 8.5 Oblivious Transfer from Noise

We will describe the protocol of [72] showing that OT can be achieved from *any non-trivial channel* $P_{Y|X}$, a result that generalizes the results of [70]. A channel is non-trivial if there exist two inputs $x_1$ and $x_2$ such that $P_{Y|X=x_1} \ne P_{Y|X=x_2}$ holds and there exists $y \in \mathcal{Y}$ such that $P_{Y|X=x_1}(y) > 0$ and $P_{Y|X=x_2}(y) > 0$ both hold. Furthermore, we require that $x_1$ and $x_2$ be *extremal neighbors*, meaning, in particular, that the distributions $P_{Y|X=x_1}$ and $P_{Y|X=x_2}$ cannot be produced by any linear combination of other inputs.

OT can now be achieved in several steps. First, the channel is used to implement a *binary-symmetric erasure channel* (BSEC). Let $(y_1, y_2)$ be the *most informative pair* (i.e., the values that give the best estimate over the input, given that the input is uniform over $x_1$ and $x_2$).

**Protocol 5 (BSEC).** *The sender has input* $r \in \{0, 1\}$.

1. *The sender sends* $x_1 x_2$ *if* $r = 0$ *and* $x_2 x_1$ *if* $r = 1$ *over* $P_{Y|X}$.
2. *The receiver returns* 0 *if he receives* $y_1 y_2$, 1 *if he receives* $y_2 y_1$, *and otherwise the erasure symbol* $\Delta$.

In this protocol, the sender who correctly chooses the inputs will get no information about whether the receiver outputs $\Delta$ or not. The receiver will get some information about the input of the sender even if he receives $\Delta$, but this information will be smaller than in the case when he receives a value in $\{0, 1\}$. Note that the channel might make some errors; that is, the receiver could get output 1, even though the sender has sent 0.

We can now use this protocol to construct an OT that is secure if the sender follows the protocol. The protocol makes use of *one-way key-agreement* (i.e., key agreement by unidirectional communication [4, 73]).

**Protocol 6 (Passively secure OT).** *The sender has inputs* $b_0, b_1 \in \{0, 1\}$ *and the receiver* $c \in \{0, 1\}$.

1. *The sender picks* $2n$ *random bits* $r_i$ *and sends them to the receiver using the BSEC; the receiver gets* $r'_i$.
2. *The receiver picks and sends two disjoint sets* $I_0$ *and* $I_1$ *of the same size* $n'$, *such that* $r_i \neq \Delta$ *for all* $i \in I_c$.
3. *The sender and the receiver execute twice a one-way key-agreement protocol, once for the values in* $I_0$ *and once for the values in* $I_1$. *The sender gets two key bits,* $k_0$ *and* $k_1$. *The receiver gets* $k_c$.
4. *The sender sends* $m_0 = b_0 \oplus k_0$ *and* $m_1 = b_1 \oplus k_1$. *The receiver outputs* $m_c \oplus k_c$.

The parameter $n'$ has to be as large as possible, but such that the honest player can construct a set $I_c$ that does not contain any $r'_i = \Delta$ with high probability. Then a malicious player does not receive enough values to construct two such sets and, therefore, has some disadvantage against the honest player in at least one of the two sets. The key-agreement protocol then ensures that the honest player gets the key while the dishonest does not get any information about it for the string about which he has some disadvantage.

We have to ensure that the sender cannot actively cheat the protocol by not choosing the input values to the channel as he should. To do so, we apply the above protocol $k = \lceil n^{1+\varepsilon} \rceil$ times on a random input and use Protocol 2 to combine them to one instance of OT. In order to be able to cheat in this OT, the sender would have to cheat in every instance of the $k$ OTs at least once, which means that he would have to choose a different input in at least $n^{1+\varepsilon}$ instances of BSEC of the total $n^{2+\varepsilon}$ instances. However, this would bias the statistical distribution of the outputs of the BSECs since $n^{1+\varepsilon} = (\sqrt{n^{2+\varepsilon}})^{1+\Theta(1)}$. We let the sender apply a statistical test to prevent this. Then we end up with a secure implementation of OT.

It has been shown in [212, 298] that these results for noisy channels carry over to the distributed-randomness scenario.

## 8.6 Pseudo-Signatures and Broadcast from Noise

It was shown in [224] how to set up a PSS using global broadcast channels, using the *dining-cryptographers protocol* [38,59]. Obtaining a PSS from a common random source was considered in [109,110], but only with respect to three players and *one particular* probability distribution.

In [111], the following implementation of a PSS among three players is presented, assuming that the players have access to some distributed randomness. Let the signer know $X^n$, the intermediate player know $Y^n$, and the receiver know $Z^n$. These random variables are i.i.d. according to $P_{XYZ}$. Furthermore, let us assume that $\mathbf{I}(X \searchar Y; Z \mid Y) > 0$.

**Protocol 7.** *Let $v \in \{0,1\}$ be the value $P_1$ wants to sign.*

1. *$P_1$ calculates $K_i := X_i \searchar Y_i$ and sends $(v, K_{1+(n/2)v}, \dots, K_{n/2+(n/2)v})$ to $P_2$.*
2. *$P_2$ checks whether the received $K_i$ and the corresponding $Y_i$ have the correct joint distribution $P_{X \searchar Y,Y}$. If so, he accepts, calculates $L_i := (K_i, Y_i) \searchar Z_i$, and sends $(v, L_{1+(n/2)v}, \dots, L_{n/2+(n/2)v})$ to $P_3$.*
3. *$P_3$ checks whether the received $L_i$ and the corresponding $Z_i$ have the correct joint distribution $P_{(X \searchar Y,Y) \searchar Z,Z}$. If so, he accepts.*

First the signed bit from a correct sender $P_1$ is accepted by $P_2$ except with exponentially small probability. Because of Lemma 8.1, even a malicious signer has to send the correct values $K_i$ if he wants the intermediate player to accept. If an honest intermediate player accepts, then only $O(\sqrt{n})$ values of $K^n$ can be false. Therefore, he can be sure that the receiver accepts his message. (Note that the receiver has to be somewhat more tolerant about the errors he accepts.) If the intermediate player tries to transfer $1-v$, he needs to calculate the values $L_i$ only using his values $Y_i$. It can now be shown that he will not be able to do that if $\mathbf{I}(X \searchar Y; Z \mid Y) > 0$.

### Broadcast from Pseudo-signatures

We will now present a protocol for broadcast among the three players $P_1$, $P_2$, and $P_3$, where $P_1$ is the sender, using the above PSS, with $P_1$ as signer. We assume that signatures can be transfered along the path $P_1 \to P_2 \to P_3$. The following protocol is adapted from [110].

**Protocol 8.** *Let $v \in \{0, 1\}$ be the value $P_1$ wants to send.*

1. *$P_1$ signs $v$ and sends it to $P_2$. He also sends $v$ (unsigned) to $P_3$.*
2. *$P_2$ receives $v'$ and checks the signature. If it is correct, he transfers it to $P_3$ and outputs $v'$. If not, he sends $\perp$ to $P_3$.*
3. *$P_3$ receives a value $v''$ from $P_2$ and $u$ from $P_1$. If the signature of $v''$ is correct, then he outputs $v''$. Otherwise, he outputs $u$ and sends $u$ to $P_2$.*
4. *If $P_2$ has not output a value yet, he outputs what $P_3$ sends to him.*

If $P_1$ is honest, then an honest $P_2$ will identify the signature as correct and output $v$. $P_2$ can now correctly transfer $v$ and its signature to $P_3$, who will be able to verify the signature and output $v$. However, he cannot send any other value to $P_3$ that will be accepted since he is not able to forge signatures. Hence, an honest $P_3$ will also output $v$, and the protocol is correct if the sender is honest. Now let $P_2$ and $P_3$ be honest. If $P_2$ has received a correctly signed value $v'$, then he will output $v'$, but he will also be able to transfer the signature to $P_3$, who will also output $v'$. If $P_2$ did not receive a correctly signed value $v'$, then he will finally output what $P_3$ sent him (i.e., the same value as $P_3$ outputs). Hence, the protocol is also correct if the sender is malicious.

Using our PSS, we can achieve broadcast among three players having $X$, $Y$, and $Z$, where the sender holds $X$, if

$$\mathbf{I}(X \searize Y; Z \mid Y) + \mathbf{I}(X \searize Z; Y \mid Z) > 0 .$$

It was shown in [111] that this bound is tight; that is, no such protocol can exist if $\mathbf{I}(X \searize Y; Z \mid Y) + \mathbf{I}(X \searize Z; Y \mid Z) = 0$.

## 8.7 More Realistic Models

The results of the previous sections seem very promising: Almost *any* noise can be used to achieve tasks that would otherwise be impossible. Unfortunately, the assumptions used are not as weak as one might think.

Let us, for example, look at the *binary noisy channel*. This is a model that is often used in communication, because, *there*, it *is* a very weak resource. It is only required that the receiver obtains a bit that is correlated enough with the bit the sender has sent. However, in cryptography, this condition does not suffice, because the receiver (or the sender) must not receive too much information. This means that the error has to be *exactly* as specified, and the sender or receiver must not get *any* information about whether an error occurred or not. It seems to be very hard to come up with a physical implementation that satisfies these specifications.

If it is possible to physically implement a primitive such as a binary noisy channel, it will probably not be perfect, but will only approximate the binary noisy channel with an error that cannot be chosen arbitrarily small but that is constant. However, then, the protocols we have seen will give us an implementation of OT with a constant error that, depending on the application, might not be sufficiently small. One possibility to reduce the error is to *amplify* the quality of our implementation. For oblivious transfer, it was shown in [75] that a weak version of oblivious transfer can be amplified for certain parameters. These results were corrected and improved in [301].

To get a more realistic model of a physical noisy channel, the notion of so-called *unfair noisy channels* was introduced in [75]. Such a channel is binary-symmetric with error probability $\delta$ if both players are honest. However, if one of the player cheats, he may reduce the error to $\gamma < \delta$ and use the additional knowledge to his advantage. It has been proved in [75] and [74] that for a certain range, oblivious transfer is still possible.

# 9

## Computationally Secure Authentication with Noisy Data

Berry Schoenmakers and Pim Tuyls

In this chapter we discuss authentication techniques involving data such as biometrics, which are assumed to be typical (essentially unique) for a particular person (or physical object). The data are captured by a sensor or measuring device, which is an imperfect process introducing some noise. Upon enrollment of a user, a sample of the noisy data is captured and stored as a template. Later, during authentication, another sample of the noisy data is captured and matched against the stored template.

The object is to achieve authentication while keeping the noisy data private. To this end, the problem of authentication is considered in the setting of secure multiparty computation. In particular, we will focus on the so-called cryptographic model, where privacy is guaranteed subject to a computational assumption.

## 9.1 Introduction

The basic idea of biometric authentication is to perform a measurement on a given person and to compare the result to a previously obtained measurement (biometric template) for this person. Such a measurement is done using a sensor or a more involved measurement device, which we will call the *biometric sensor* throughout this chapter.

The aim of privacy-preserving biometric authentication is to minimize the leakage of potentially sensitive information obtained in these measurements. Obviously, the biometric sensors will get to "see" biometric data, so the goal is to prevent any other parts of the system from having access to any information on the biometrics. In particular, it is desirable that no biometric templates need to be stored in a central database.

In previous chapters, an approach to privacy-preserving biometric authentication of an information-theoretic nature has been considered. There a new primitive, called Fuzzy Extractor or Helper Data Algorithm was introduced.

It allows one to extract a secret key from a biometric measurement. This primitive works in two steps: During *enrollment*, a measurement is performed and helper data and a secret key are generated. The secret key or its hash are then stored together with an identifier in a database. The helper data serves two goals: (1) It will help in correcting the noise during the authentication phase and (2) it allows one to extract an almost uniformly random string from the biometric measurement. Later, during the *authentication* phase, a noisy measurement is used together with the helper data to extract the same key. Using this technique, biometric data can be stored in a privacy-preserving way in a database. It was shown in [91, 182] that no full privacy can be achieved from a pure information-theoretic point of view. Although the helper data leak no information on the extracted key, they leak some information on the underlying biometrics. In this chapter we consider an approach that is computationally secure. The presented protocol allows for biometrics-based authentication without leaking *any* information about the biometric data involved, under a computational assumption. This is the major advantage of computationally secure authentication.

The scenario is as follows. Assume that a public key $pk$ is given for a suitable public-key cryptosystem and that the corresponding private key is shared among a group of servers. When a user enrolls in the system, a biometric sensor is used to determine a biometric template $x$ for the user, which is subsequently encrypted using public key $pk$. The encrypted template $x$ is stored in a central database. Later, whenever the user needs to be authenticated, a sensor will perform another measurement $y$, which will be a noisy version of the template $x$—if indeed the same user is present.

To authenticate the user, the measurement $y$ needs to be compared (matched) with the encrypted template $x$. This can be done in essentially two different ways, where the sensor either takes part in the matching protocol or it does not. If the sensor takes part in the protocol, the sensor will use $y$ as a private input, the servers will use their shares of the private key as private input, and the encrypted template $x$ will be the common input. In the other case, the sensor may outsource the matching protocol completely to the servers by releasing an encryption of $y$ (under public key $pk$). The servers perform a matching protocol given the encryptions of $x$ and $y$.

We will focus on the latter case; hence, consider the case of a multiparty computation among the servers for determining if the encrypted values $x$ and $y$ match (i.e., are sufficiently close wrt a given similarity measure).

In this chapter, we will use the matching of iris scans as our running example. The biometric templates for iris scans are basically bit strings that can be matched using a suitable Hamming distance. Concretely, we consider authentication based on iris scans as put forth by Daugman [77–79]. He uses the so-called *fractional* Hamming distance, which allows matching of iris scans that are incomplete (e.g., due to an eyelash in front of the iris).

We will both consider methods in which the Hamming distance is computed exactly (before comparing it with a given threshold) and methods in which only an approximation of the Hamming distance is computed such that the comparison with the threshold can still be done with sufficient precision. For exact matching, we will take the private profile matcher as described in [246] as a starting point. For approximate[1] matching, we take the framework introduced in [105] as a starting point.

We note that the setting of computationally secure authentication with noisy data has been considered in various places in the literature. The case of biometric data has been considered by Atallah et al. in a number of papers, in which techniques for private biometric authentication are described, also with the option of outsourcing this task. See, for example, [97] for an overview and also the paper on biometric authentication based on fingerprints [168] and references therein. As another example, we note that related problems of private matching (set intersection) have been considered in [113].

## 9.2 Exact Secure Matching

In this section we consider the problem of securely matching iris scans as a main example of computationally secure authentication. We adopt the setting developed and put forth by Daugman in a series of papers, starting with [77], and summarized in [78]. First, an overview is given of reliable methods for matching iris scans, followed by an implementation of these methods as a secure multiparty computation.

### 9.2.1 Iris Recognition

The work by Daugman has shown that iris scans indeed give a reliable method for recognizing individuals (ignoring the issue of liveness detection, which is a non-trivial problem for iris scans; especially, when the system is required to be non-intrusive, thus excluding the use of retina scans, for instance). Large-scale deployment of these techniques in the United Arab Emirates, involving a "watch-list" of about 316,250 persons as of June 2005 (with 632,500 different iris scans), is described in [79].

For our purposes, it suffices to focus on the way iris scans are represented as biometric templates and what it means when two iris scans form a sufficiently close match. A major advantage of Daugman's methods is that an iris scan is simply represented as a bitstring; see Fig. 9.1. More precisely, an iris scan is represented as a 4096-bit string (512 bytes) of a standardized structure

---

[1] In recent literature, the usage of the terms "exact" versus "approximate" matching of strings is used in two ways: (1) to distinguish whether two strings are identical versus close in Hamming distance and (2) to distinguish whether the Hamming distance between two strings is computed exactly versus approximately before it is compared with a given threshold. These different uses of exact versus approximated also apply when edit distance or any other suitable distance measure is used instead of Hamming distance.

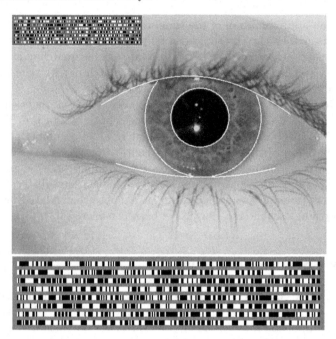

**Fig. 9.1.** Top: Iris pattern example (bit encoding in top left corner); bottom: enlarged iris image part of an IrisCode. Source: Daugman [78].

called IrisCode. Such an IrisCode is divided into two parts of equal length, corresponding to the actual iris image and a mask. The iris image is represented by a monochrome bitmap consisting of 2048 black and white pixels. Each pair of (consecutive) pixels represents 2 bits of information indicating to which quadrant the angle of the phasor of the corresponding local region of the iris belongs. The mask (also consisting of 2048 bits) then indicates which pixels of the iris image are considered valid and, hence, which bits should be ignored.

More formally, an IrisCodes is a vector $(x, a)$, where $x \in \{0, 1\}^{2048}$ is the iris image and $a \in \{0, 1\}^{2048}$ is the mask. The *fractional Hamming distance* between two such IrisCodes $(x, a)$ and $(y, b)$ is defined by

$$d((x,a),(y,b)) := \frac{\sum_{i=1}^{m}(x_i \oplus y_i)a_i b_i}{\sum_{i=1}^{m} a_i b_i}, \qquad (9.1)$$

where $\oplus$ denotes exclusive or Two IrisCodes are said to match if their fractional Hamming distance is below a certain threshold $t$, $0 < t < 1$. So, two IrisCodes match if the number of differences is relatively low, for the pixels that are considered valid, as indicated by the masks. A typical value for the threshold is $t = 0.32$, in which case the probability of a false match ("false positive") is about 1 in a 1,000,000.[2]

### 9.2.2 Recap of Threshold Homomorphic Cryptosystems

Threshold homomorphic cryptosystems provide a basis for secure multiparty computation in the cryptographic model, as described in a series of papers [69,76,112,158,245]. For a given $n$-ary function $f$, one composes a circuit $C$ of elementary gates that, given encryptions of $x_1, \ldots, x_\ell$ on its input wires, produces an encryption of $f(x_1, \ldots, x_\ell)$ on its output wire. The elementary gates operate in the same fashion. The wires of the entire circuit $C$ are all encrypted under the same public key; the corresponding private key is shared among a group of parties. It is customary to distinguish addition gates and multiplication gates. Addition gates can be evaluated without having to decrypt any value, taking full advantage of the homomorphic property of the cryptosystem. Multiplication gates, however, require at least one threshold decryption to succeed even for an honest-but-curious (passive) adversary. To deal with a malicious (active) adversary, multiplication gates additionally require the use of zero-knowledge proofs.

A major advantage of secure computation based on threshold homomorphic cryptosystems is the fact that it results in particularly efficient solutions, even withstanding active adversaries. The communication complexity, which is the dominating complexity measure, is $O(nk|C|)$ bits, where $n$ is the number of parties, $k$ is a security parameter, and $|C|$ is the number of gates of circuit $C$.

We use $[\![m]\!]$ to denote a (probabilistic) encryption under an understood public key $pk$ for a threshold homomorphic cryptosystem. Typically, such a cryptosystem is based on the ElGamal cryptosystem [101], the Paillier cryptosystem [220], or the Goldwasser-Micali cryptosystem [134]. We briefly describe the details for the ElGamal cryptosystem.

Let $\langle g \rangle = \{1, g, g^2, \ldots, g^{q-1}\}$ denote a cyclic group of prime order $q$ for which the discrete log problem is assumed to be intractable: Given $h \in \langle g \rangle$, it is hard to find the discrete log $\alpha \in \mathbb{Z}_q$ of $h$ to the base $g$ satisfying $g^\alpha = h$. An ElGamal key pair consists of a public key $h \in \langle g \rangle$ and the corresponding private key $\alpha = \log_g h$. A message $m \in \mathbb{Z}_q$ is encrypted as a pair $[\![m]\!] = (g^r, h^r g^m)$ for a random $r \in \mathbb{Z}_q$. An ElGamal ciphertext $[\![m]\!] = (a, b)$ is decrypted by calculating $b/a^\alpha = g^m$ and then solving for $m \in \mathbb{Z}_q$.

A few remarks are in order. First, note that encryption is *additively* homomorphic: Given encryptions $(a, b)$ and $(a', b')$ of messages $m$ and $m'$, respectively, an encryption of $m + m'$ is obtained as $(a, b) \star (a', b') := (aa', bb')$

---

[2] Here, we ignore the aspect of renormalization, which is actually required to compensate for matches based on relatively few bits (i.e., when $\sum_{i=1}^{m} a_i b_i$ is small). For the database of 632,500 irises reported in [79], the number of false matches drops to 1 in 200 billion when the threshold is set to $t = 0.26$ and a proper renormalization is used.

$= (g^{r+r'}, g^{m+m'}h^{r+r'})$. This homomorphic property ensures that addition gates can be implemented essentially for free. However, since decryption involves solving for $m$, given $g^m$, we must see to it that whenever a value is decrypted that we know that $m$ belongs to a subset of $\mathbb{Z}_q$ of limited size, such that $m$ can be found efficiently. An extreme, but very useful, case is when $m$ can take on two values only (e.g., $m \in \{0, 1\}$ or $m \in \{-1, 1\}$). Finally, note that for $(t, n)$-threshold ElGamal, the private key $\alpha$ is not known to any single party but shared among $n$ parties in such a way that any $t$ or more of them can decrypt messages, whereas $t - 1$ or less parties cannot obtain any information on the plaintext.

For achieving general secure multiparty computation in this setting, the hard nut to crack is to implement multiplication gates securely. On inputs $[\![x]\!]$ and $[\![y]\!]$, the problem is to compute an encryption $[\![xy]\!]$, such that no information is leaked at all on the values of $x$ and $y$. The parties executing the protocol must use their shares of the private key of the underlying cryptosystem. In many cases, the values $x$ and $y$ are actually bits, but this is not necessarily so (e.g., [69] covers arithmetic modulo $N$ for an RSA modulus $N$, when the Paillier cryptosystem is used).

In the remainder of this chapter, we will use secure protocols for basic tasks like integer addition, multiplication, and comparison as building blocks. For the details of these protocols, we will refer to the literature. Note that, depending on the context, integer values will either be represented as (encrypted) numbers modulo the size of the plaintext space or as strings of (encrypted) bits.

### 9.2.3 Secure Matching of IrisCodes

To determine securely whether $d((x, a), (y, b)) \leq t$, given $(x, a)$ and $(y, b)$ in encrypted form, we first rewrite this inequality such that both sides are integral numbers. Assuming that $t$ is a rational number this can always be done. A typical value for the threshold $t$ is $t = 0.32$ (see [78]), for which the inequality becomes

$$25 \sum_{i=1}^{m} (x_i \oplus y_i) a_i b_i < 8 \sum_{i=1}^{m} a_i b_i. \tag{9.2}$$

To perform this integer comparison, we will first compute the binary representations of the sums on both sides.

The vectors $(x, a)$ and $(y, b)$ are assumed to be encrypted bitwise, hence of the form $([\![x_1]\!], \ldots, [\![x_m]\!], [\![a_1]\!], \ldots, [\![a_m]\!])$ and $([\![y_1]\!], \ldots, [\![y_m]\!], [\![b_1]\!], \ldots, [\![b_m]\!])$, where $[\![\cdot]\!]$ denotes probabilistic public-key encryption for a threshold homomorphic cryptosystem. Using $3m$ secure multiplication gates, the first step is to compute the terms $[\![a_i b_i]\!]$, $[\![x_i \oplus y_i]\!]$, and $[\![(x_i \oplus y_i) a_i b_i]\!]$, for $i = 1, \ldots, m$, using the fact that $x_i \oplus y_i = x_i + y_i - 2x_i y_i$. Subsequently, the terms $[\![a_i b_i]\!]$ may be added using a $\log_2 m$-depth tree of adders, producing the value of this sum, represented in binary. Each adder takes as input two numbers of equal bit length $s$ say, encrypted bitwise, and produces the sum of these two numbers, which is of bit length $s + 1$ and is also encrypted bitwise. The terms $[\![(x_i \oplus y_i)a_i b_i]\!]$ are summed in the same fashion.

The multiplication by 8 in inequality (9.2) is done for free, whereas the multiplication by 25 requires two further adders. As an intermediate result, we thus obtain the binary representations of both sides of inequality (9.2), which are subsequently used as input to a secure integer comparison. For this task, an efficient log-depth circuit has been presented in [121].

*Remark 9.1.* A mask does not contain sensitive information; therefore, one may consider making the masks public. If masks $a$ and $b$ are publicly known, matching $(x, a)$ and $(y, b)$ simplifies to comparing the Hamming distance between two vectors $x'$ and $y'$ with a public threshold value. However, knowing mask $b$, it may be easier to pass verification by using an (almost) disjoint mask $a$ (and seeing to it that $x_i = y_i$ at the positions that are still included). In this case, only few positions need to match. Requiring that the sensor take a new reading until $\sum_{i=1}^{m} a_i b_i$ is sufficiently large (or, simply, until $\sum_{i=1}^{m} a_i$ is sufficiently large) helps to reduce this.

## 9.3 Approximate Secure Matching

Exact matching as described earlier can be very computationally demanding. This is mainly caused by the high number of secure multiplications required, which, in turn, each require several modular exponentiations for each party involved. For large inputs (e.g., consisting of hundreds up to thousands of bits), the computational complexity of exact secure matching may thus be impractical (e.g., when the result must be available in (near) real time).

Some experiments with a prototype implementation of a private profile matching protocol show that secure matching of IrisCodes takes a long time even when PCs are used as hardware for the clients [197]. For example, for the case of two (possibly malicious) parties matching 1024-bit strings wrt Hamming distance, the running time is 9.5 minutes, on an Intel Pentium 4, 2-GHz CPU. Hence, matching two IrisCodes would take a considerable amount of time. As it turns out, most of the time is spent on modular exponentiations (once suitable optimizations are done); each party simply needs to evaluate thousands of modular exponentiations.

To circumvent this bottleneck, we consider the use of approximate matching instead of exact matching, where one expects that the performance of approximate matching actually improves as the inputs get larger. The important question is what the breakeven point is, beyond which approximate matching outperforms exact matching. Moreover, as explained in the work by Feigenbaum et al. [105], the use of approximations in the context of secure multiparty computation raises further issues, basically because the approximation of a function value may reveal more information on the inputs to the function than the exact function value would.

In the framework of [105] (also elaborated upon in later papers such as [153]), an approximation is thus required not to reveal any information on the inputs beyond what can be derived from the exact output value. More precisely, for a secure approximation $\hat{f}$ of $f$, it is not only required that $\hat{f}(x_1, \ldots, x_n)$ be in some sense close to $f(x_1, \ldots, x_n)$ but also that the value of $\hat{f}(x_1, \ldots, x_n)$ not reveal more information about the inputs $x_1, \ldots, x_n$ than $f(x_1, \ldots, x_n)$ does. A simple example of a bad approximation is the function $\hat{f}(x_1, \ldots, x_n) = \sum_{i=1}^{n} x_i + (\sum_{i=1}^{n} x_i + x_1) \bmod 2$, which approximates the function $f(x_1, \ldots, x_n) = \sum_{i=1}^{n} x_i$ closely but at the same time leaks the parity of $x_1$.

A good approximation in the above sense is called *functionally private* in [105]. Using secure multiparty computation to evaluate a functionally private approximation thus yields the desired result. For the special case of approximating Hamming distance, [105] gives an interesting protocol with sublinear communication complexity (essentially proportional to $\sqrt{m}$ for $m$-bit strings). The basic idea is to use two subprotocols: one for the case of a small Hamming distance and one for the case of a large Hamming distance.

If the Hamming distance is assumed to be large (say, larger than $\sqrt{m}$), it suffices to sample both strings at roughly $\sqrt{m}$ positions to get an approximation of the Hamming distance between the entire strings. In the other case, if the Hamming distance is assumed to be sufficiently small, it is possible to partition both strings into buckets such that with high probability, there will be at most one position per bucket in which the two strings differ. Whether there is a difference is then determined by hashing the contents of the buckets and comparing the results for equality. Here, the idea is that such a hash value (viewed as a bitstring) is substantially shorter than the size of a bucket.

Asymptotically the performance of the above approximation protocol is proportional to $\sqrt{m}$. The breakeven point at which the approximation protocol outperforms an exact matching protocol, however, is way beyond input sizes of several thousands of bits. For instance, in case of a small Hamming distance less than $\sqrt{m}$, the total number of buckets used is something on the order of $\sqrt{m}k^3 \log_2^2 m$, where $k$ is a security parameter. Even if we set $k = 10$, which corresponds to a low level of security, we see that the breakeven point is reached only when $m = 1000\sqrt{m} \log_2^2 m$, which means that $m > 10^{12}$.

Similarly, asymptotic improvements of [105], such as reported in [153], do not give better results for the range of input lengths relevant in our case. Only when considering *massive* datasets do these asymptotic methods start to pay off.

## 9.4 Conclusion

Techniques from secure multiparty computation allow for methods of biometric authentication that are both secure and private. The use of threshold homomorphic cryptosystems as described in this chapter enables an easy way of outsourcing the matching task to a set of servers, some of which may behave maliciously. As long as the number of malicious servers does not exceed a certain threshold value, the privacy of the biometric data is ensured.

As matching of biometric templates involves a substantial amount of data, secure and private biometric authentication protocols are rather costly. More efficient ways of matching the biometric templates are therefore desirable. One avenue for achieving this goal is to use randomized (probabilistic) methods for computing an *approximation* of the Hamming distance between two given bitstrings. The apparent disadvantage is that the currently known approximation methods only beat straightforward exact matching for inputs of huge sizes, far beyond what is relevant for biometric authentication.

Another avenue is to use a different approach to secure multiparty computation (e.g., using [22], which is based on verifiable secret sharing (VSS) instead of threshold homomorphic cryptosystems (THCs)). By using VSS, one may avoid the heavy use of modular exponentiations, which is typical for protocols based on THCs. A disadvantage of methods based on VSS, however, is that each pair of parties must communicate privately when performing secure multiplications, hence this may become the bottleneck. A detailed performance comparison between the various approaches to secure multiparty computation has never been done.

# Part II

## Applications of Security with Noisy Data

# Privacy Enhancements for Inexact Biometric Templates©

Nalini Ratha, Sharat Chikkerur, Jonathan Connell, and Ruud Bolle

## 10.1 Introduction

Traditional authentication schemes utilize tokens or depend on some secret knowledge possessed by the user for verifying his or her identity. Although these techniques are widely used, they have several limitations. Both token- and knowledge-based approaches cannot differentiate between an authorized user and an impersonator having access to the tokens or passwords. Biometrics-based authentication schemes overcome these limitations while offering usability advantages in the area of password management. However, despite its obvious advantages, the use of biometrics raises several security and privacy concerns.

1. Biometrics is secure but not secret: Passwords and cryptographic keys are known only to the user and, hence, secrecy can be maintained. In contrast, biometrics such as voice, face, signature, and even fingerprints can be easily recorded and potentially misused without the user's consent. There have been several instances where artificial fingerprints [189] have been used to circumvent biometric security systems. Face and voice biometrics are similarly vulnerable to being captured without the user's explicit knowledge.
2. Biometrics cannot be revoked or canceled: Passwords, crypto-keys and PINs can be changed if compromised. When tokens such as credit cards and badges are stolen, they can be replaced. However, biometrics is permanently associated with the user and cannot be revoked and replaced if compromised.

---

©Figures 10.2, 10.3, 10.4. 10.5. and 10.6 appeared in Nalini K. Ratha, Sharat Chikkerur, Jonathan H. Connell, Ruud M. Bolle, "Generating Cancelable Fingerprint Templates", IEEE Transactions on Pattern Analysis and Machine Intelligence, Vol. 29, No. 4, April 2007, pp. 561–572.

3. If a biometric is lost once, it is compromised forever: If a biometrics is compromised in one application, then it can be used to compromise all applications where the biometrics is used.
4. A biometric retains its uniqueness over time (Persistence) and this can be a security issue when it needs to be changed. Note that even though the signal as well as the template can look different, the uniqueness contained in them is still the same.
5. Cross-matching can be used to track individuals without their consent: Since the same biometric is used across all applications and locations, the user can be potentially tracked if one or more organizations collude and share their respective biometric databases.

In the information security area, there has been significant progress made in the area of design of one-way hash functions that compute a digest from a message and also match in the hash domain for exactly reproduced input. These hash functions have been shown to be almost impossible to invert. However, these functions also produce a significantly different digest even with minor changes in the input. This is one of the challenges that biometrics faces. The templates are never the same except when a stored image is replayed. Two samples of a biometric collected in quick succession in which the features still are quite different and thus the hash digests are also quite different are shown in Fig. 10.1. Therefore, these functions cannot used directly despite being theoretically very strong, as they apply only to exact data.

In this chapter we present several methods for constructing multiple identities from a fingerprint template. The basic minutiae features are used in the template. In Section 10.2, we review the literature in this area. Hashing or encryption of biometric data is reviewed in Section 10.3. The key requirements in constructing a cancelable template without losing too much accuracy are presented in Section 10.4. Finally, we compare our approach against the published techniques in Section 10.5.

## 10.2 Related Work

Solutions to enhance privacy and security come from both the cryptographic and biometric research communities. The cryptographic community's interest is in combining cryptography authentication with biometrics. The approaches mostly consist of deriving a very error-tolerant binary representation of biometrics, which can be treated as any password/secret key and can be stored securely using traditional hashing or encryption techniques. The first reference to such work can be found in the German patent by Bodo [32] (the link between revocable templates and privacy is not established in this patent). The biometric community, on the other hand, is interested in privacy-preserving authentication and relied upon developing alternate feature representations of the original biometric. This dichotomy is somewhat

| Minutiae Points | Minutiae Points |
|---|---|
| 209 300 214 | 204 192 175 |
| 160 286 319 | 148 350 11 |
| 171 265 121 | 218 331 185 |
| 150 287 312 | 146 313 339 |
| 270 284 228 | 96 335 344 |
| 198 150 201 | 186 299 199 |
| 143 182 316 | 107 299 322 |
| 312 117 61 | 155 249 125 |
| 61 254 312 | 233 291 218 |
| 258 203 241 | 193 228 90 |
| 94 224 303 | 203 215 78 |
| 227 156 235 | 252 311 212 |
| 223 100 41 | 155 198 124 |
| 179 105 355 | 173 215 124 |
| 96 132 309 | 191 192 139 |
| 71 185 127 | 159 228 292 |
| 281 144 239 | 204 192 175 |
| 253 79 216 | 92 322 330 |
| 291 120 59 | 180 263 68 |
| 155 52 339 | 183 280 250 |
| 105 22 312 | 179 248 101 |
| 304 28 228 | |

Hash Values
**SHA-1:18169f54d631be1c20a13baa3bf9fa06a9b774a1**
**MD-5: 696f3da57d0a71e78acb65e2b2c64c0**

| Minutiae Points | Minutiae Points |
|---|---|
| 252 245 139 | 328 192 68 |
| 158 347 319 | 192 229 303 |
| 208 292 119 | 250 191 199 |
| 286 335 224 | 113 299 319 |
| 244 272 84 | 312 246 239 |
| 207 243 125 | 145 274 303 |
| 225 259 117 | 275 202 228 |
| 240 240 139 | 228 152 350 |
| 210 276 290 | 317 188 235 |
| 223 310 119 | 270 144 30 |
| 203 331 316 | 125 232 136 |
| 228 290 107 | 146 185 299 |
| 264 344 210 | 304 119 214 |
| 216 332 348 | 202 98 326 |
| 234 308 73 | 251 44 11 |
| 236 324 239 | 290 23 23 |
| 252 245 139 | 154 74 319 |
| 255 260 78 | 138 43 316 |
| 254 250 44 | 96 336 334 |
| 261 228 214 | |

Hash Values
**SHA-1:a73b48defcbf86ecd0b523255874b375a515b0be**
**MD-5: 2bdb66ccedc8773eea5dfb232c37e602**

**Fig. 10.1.** Even with two fingerprint (biometric) impressions collected in quick succession, it is impossible to compute a one-way cryptographic hash using standard hash functions such as MD-5 or SHA-1. The hash function has been applied on the fingerprint features shown in the figure also.

oversimplified and we will present a detailed survey of both of these approaches in the next section.

Observing this as an important future research area, a 2003 NSF Workshop on a Biometrics Research Agenda identified "anonymous biometrics" as a privacy-enhancing technology of great interest. The techniques that can meet these requirements have interchangeably been called "cancelable," "anonymous," and "revocable." Although conceptual frameworks for cancelable biometrics have been presented when these problems were first identified [34,231], working solutions emerged only recently. Biometric cryptosystems [276] are equivalent to cancelable biometrics, since the error-tolerant binary/cryptographic key derived in the process can be made privacy-preserving by simply hashing them in a manner similar to passwords. A recent paper [39] demonstrates how robust facial features coupled with encryption can be used to address privacy issues in face biometric domain.

Monrose et al. were the first to outline a technique to "harden" traditional passwords by adding error-tolerant bits derived from biometrics. In [205] they used keystroke dynamics observed over multiple sessions to derive a robust binary vector. Furthermore, a similar technique for voice biometrics was proposed by Monrose et al. in [207]. Recently, Davida et al. [81] outlined a procedure to extract cryptographic keys from iris biometrics. The strength of the keys derived using these techniques are limited by the entropy of the biometrics used. Additional entropy and error tolerance can be introduced by combining the biometric with user-specific random information. Goh and Ling [132] developed techniques to derive cryptographic keys from face biometrics. In this technique, they combined the biometric information with user-specific random vectors to derive an error-tolerant representation. Subsequently, the same technique was also applied to palm prints [65] and to fingerprints [155]. An additional advantage of their technique is the use of *two-factor* authentication (biometrics + token-based user-specific information). Savvides et al. [243] proposed an alternative approach where user information is added by convolving the face image with user-specific random kernels to generate cancelable templates. Another approach for constructing cancelable templates involves the use of auxiliary information (also called helper data, shielding functions) that is combined with biometric information to reduce the intrauser variation. Constructions that follow this approach can be found in [161,182] and are implemented for fingerprint biometrics in [268]. A more theoretical treatment of these cryptographic constructions can be found in [91,270]. An alternate approach relies upon hiding secret information within fingerprint features. Soutar et al. [261] first proposed embedding information within fingerprint features. A more rigorous construction called 'Fuzzy Vault' with provable security bounds was proposed by Juels and Sudan [159] and was implemented by Uludag et al. [275] recently.

There has been some work in the biometrics community on hiding data in biometrics signals. This type of steganographic technique enhances security in terms of preventing replay attacks on biometric systems. However, these methods do not address the core issues of revocation and cross-matching. Hence, we will not review papers in this area. The prior work in the general area of key generation involving biometric systems can be studied under four broad classes: (1) biometric hardening; (2) biometric keying; (3) hashing and (4) fuzzy schemes.

## 10.3 Hashing or Encrypting Biometric Data

In order to derive an error-tolerant key or a binary representation directly from a biometric, the following problems have to be solved:

1. Distortion tolerance: Biometric signals from the same user result in the same key and signals from different users should produce different keys. and,
2. Security: The key has to be non-invertible. Even if the key is compromised, the biometric signal or the embedded key should be unrecoverable.

The wide range of techniques that satisfy these requirements can be coarsely divided into the following categories: (i) Combining the biometric with pseudo-random user-specific data to produce a redundant binary representation. We call this method *biometric hardening*. (ii) Generating an error-tolerant binary representation directly from the features extracted from the biometric data. We call this method *biometric keying*. (iii) Combining a biometric measurement with error-correcting codes and storing the *hashed* value of the result. (iv) *Fuzzy schemes* that recover a cryptographic key given "sufficiently" close biometric representations form the third category. The ensuing subsections provide a detailed description and implementations of each of these approaches.

### 10.3.1 Biometric Hardening

This is similar to password "salting" in conventional crypto-systems. In this approach, before hashing the password $P$ of the user, it is concatenated with a pseudo-random string $S$ and the resulting hash $H(P + S)$ is stored in the database. The addition of the random sequence increases the entropy and therefore the security of the user password. Biometric hardenining is based on the same principle.

Goh and Ling [132] developed techniques to derive cryptographic error tolerant binary keys from face biometrics. Analogous to password hashing, this is called bio-hashing. In their approach, the computation consists of three distinct phases: (i) feature extraction: Face features are represented using Eigenfaces coefficients $\mathbf{a} = (a_1, a_2, \ldots, a_n)$; (ii) Biometric discretization: In this step, a random-user specific set of orthogonal vectors $\mathbf{b_i} = (b_1, b_2, \ldots, b_n)$ is generated. The Eigenfaces coefficients are projected onto this set of vectors to yield dot products $s_i = \mathbf{a} \cdot \mathbf{b_i}$. The vector $\mathbf{s} = (s_1, s_2, \ldots, s_n)$ is reduced to a binary string $\mathbf{x} \in [0,1]^n$ through quantization. (iii) Cryptographic interpolation: The resulting binary string $\mathbf{x}$ along with a user specific hash string $h(\mathbf{x})$ are used as key shares in a Shamir secret sharing scheme to encode a secret key $\mathbf{S}$. The token stores $h(x), y$, and $c$, where $y = h(x)f(x)/(h(x) - x)$, and $c = f(h(x))$. Here all arithmetic is defined over a finite field and the vectors $\mathbf{x}$ and $\mathbf{S}$ can be treated as numbers. During verification, given the biometric $\mathbf{x}$, the secret can be recovered using $S = cx/(x - h(x)) + y$.

The entire process is a transformation from high-dimensional and high-uncertainty data to a lower or even zero-uncertainty representation. This process serves two purposes. First, the bitstrings from the same user are highly correlated, resulting in lower error rates during recognition. Second, by combining the high-uncertainty and low-entropy biometric data with user-specific keys, the inherent entropy of the resulting template is increased. Hence, we term this process *biometric hardening*. Soutar et al. [261] proposed an approach where the key is embedded in the biometric template (Bioscrypt$^{\mathrm{TM}}$) itself at a very fundamental level. Following [261], an input fingerprint is denoted by $f(x)$ and its Fourier transform by $F(u)$. The enrollment process requires a set of $T$ input fingerprints and a pre-specified random signal $r(x)$ or its transform $R(u)$. The transform $C(u) = F(u).R(u)$ and, more specifically, its corresponding signal $c(x)$ are used to encode a secret key $K$. Using the $T$ training images, a filter $G(u)$ is constructed such that when used instead of $F(u)$, it minimizes the intrauser variations of $c(x)$. The Bioscrypt$^{\mathrm{TM}}$ consists of the function $c(x)$ and the phase component of $G(u)$ (The magnitude part is discarded to improve security.) During encoding, for each bit $b_i$ of the key $K$, $L$ specific locations where $c(x) = b_i$ are recorded. This redundant lookup table is stored as part of the template. During verification, fingerprint image $f'(x)$ is combined with the Bioscrypt$^{\mathrm{TM}}$ $G(u)$ to regenerate $c'(x)$, which is an approximate version of the original output $c(x)$. After quantizing the output, the lookup table is used to recover the bit values $b_i$ of the key $K$ from the $L$ specified locations. The cryptographic key is then regenerated using majority decoding. The Bioscrypt$^{\mathrm{TM}}$ meets the requirements of distortion tolerance, discriminability, and security.

### 10.3.2 Biometric Keying

Generally speaking, in this approach the binary representation is derived directly from the biometric signal. In very early work, Davida et al. [81] proposed methods to generate cryptographic keys using iriscodes. Iriscodes can be represented directly in binary form as a 256-bit string. In the approach proposed by Davida et al., user-specific Hamming codes are stored on tokens and are used to offset the errors caused during acquisition and feature representation. Error-correction schemes have formal and rigorous bases and are an improvement over Soutar's table lookup methods. Also, in this approach the token has no security requirements. However, due to this allowance, the error-correcting codes leak certain information about the template, reducing the entropy of the template to an extent.

Monrose et al. [205] outlined a technique to match from keystroke dynamics data. In this method, the key-holding duration and latency between keystrokes is measured and used as a biometric to identify the user. The resulting $m = 15$ biometric features $\phi_i, i = 1, ..., m$, is quantized into an error-tolerant bit representation. The importance of each feature is measured as the user repeatedly logs into the system. For each feature $\phi_i$, the system maintains $t_i, \mu_i,$ and $\sigma_i$, which correspond to a fixed threshold, mean, and standard deviation of the feature. Feature $\phi_i$ is said to be a distinguishing feature if $|\mu_i - t_i| > k\,\sigma_i$ across different attempts; that is, the user consistently measures below $t_i$ or above $t_i$. The key itself is chosen at random and $2m$ shares are created using a secret sharing scheme such that $m$ shares can be used to reconstruct the key. These shares are arranged in a $m \times 2$ lookup table. During the first logins after initialization, for each feature $\phi_i$ a share from either the first or second column of each row works equally well to reconstruct the key. As the consistent features develop over time, the login program perturbs the share in the other column of the lookup table. Therefore, even if an adversary has access to the lookup table and the text password, it is still difficult to guess the password. A similar technique is proposed by Monrose et al. [207] for speech data using cepstral features.

The advantage of this approach is that it does not require user-specific keys or tokens as required by *biometric hardening* methods and is therefore scalable. However, the strong association between the key and the biometric means that if the key is compromised, the use of the biometric is lost forever. However, this can be easily avoided if we store the hash $H(B, K)$ parameterized by the biometric and a user-specific key instead of the actual biometric itself. During verification, we check if $H(B', K) = H(B, K)$. The major problem in this approach is achieving error tolerance in the binary representation of the biometric.

### 10.3.3 Hashing

The paper by Davida et al. [80] investigated a new authentication technology by binding a biometric template with authorization information on a token. This article, to the best of our knowledge, is the first to use error-correcting codes in biometric encryption. In the initialization phase, an algebraic code $(N, K, D)$ is constructed. The biometric used is a $K$-bit template (i.e., an iriscode [77]). This $K$-bit biometric template is concatenated with $N - K$ check bits. The bounded distance decoding now can correct up to $(D - 1)/2$ errors. During enrollment, $M$ biometric templates of length $K$ are acquired and majority decoded giving the template $\mathbf{T}$. An $N$-bit codeword $\mathbf{E} = \mathbf{T}||\mathbf{C}$ with $N - K$ check bits $\mathbf{C}$ is defined. It is this code, along with some other information, that is hashed $H(\mathbf{E})$ and stored in a database or on a token. There is no security requirement imposed on the resulting value since it is irreversible. At verification time, another $M$ samples are used to construct a template $\mathbf{T}'$. Subsequently, error correction is performed on a string to obtain the closest codeword $\mathbf{T}''\|\mathbf{C}$. The user is authenticated if for the resulting string $\mathbf{E}'$, the hash generated by the $H(\mathbf{E}')$ is the same as the one stored in the database. It is to be noted that the public $(N, K, D)$ code leaks $N - K$ bits of information about the template. Therefore, this scheme can only be used if the biometric has sufficient inherent entropy to tolerate the loss due to the public code.

### 10.3.4 Fuzzy Schemes

Juels and Wattenberg [161] proposed a construction known as fuzzy commitment that can be used to encrypt a biometric in an error-tolerant way. The biometric itself is not stored. Let $C$ be the set of codewords of some error-correcting code. To encrypt the biometric $B$, which represents the biometric template ($B \in \{0, 1\}^n$), a codeword $c$ is randomly chosen and the offset $\delta = c - B$ is computed. (The symbols $-$ and $+$ denote the bitwise exclusive OR (XOR) of bitstrings.) The biometric representation then consists of the public pair $(\delta, y)$, where $y = h(c)$ is some suitable one-way function. Now, given a sufficiently close biometric template $B'$, the system computes $\delta + B'$ and decodes it to the nearest codeword $c'$. The user is authenticated if $h(c') = y$. This is similar to the approach of Davida et al. in which $\delta$ can be identified as the user-specific error-correcting code. Dodis et al. [91] suggested a very similar construction called *secure sketch* that is based on the same paradigm. A drawback of these approaches is that biometric data are often subject to reordering spurious features and erasures that cannot be handled by such a simple bio-cryptology method.

Juels and Sudan [159] introduced the idea of a *fuzzy vault*, which is more compatible with partial, reordered, and spurious data. Suppose a secret $S$ is to be locked under set $A$. A polynomial $p$ in a single variable $x$ is chosen such that $p$ encodes $S$. Now, taking the elements of $A$ as distinct $x$-coordinate values, the polynomial is evaluated at the elements of $A$. Further, a number of random chaff points that do not lie on $p$ are generated. Another user who has sufficient points overlapping with the first user will be able to decode the polynomial inexactly in the presence of the chaff points. Error-correcting codes can then be used to recover the exact polynomial. The security of the scheme is based on the infeasibility of the polynomial reconstruction problem. This scheme securely stores secret data $S$ that can be retrieved using sufficiently similar keys $A$ and $B$ even though they may not be identical (here, keys are actually unordered sets such as a collection of favorite movies, minutia points, etc.). A *fuzzy vault* constructs a polynomial $p(x)$ that embeds the secret data $S$ in some way (maybe by embedding $S$ is the coefficients of $p$). Using the polynomial, the user generates points $y(i) = p\{x(i)\}, x(i) \in A$. In addition, the user inserts several points $(c(i), y(i))$ not on $p$ that are not generated by the polynomial. These chaff points serve to hide the real points and the polynomial $p(x)$. Now, let us unlock $S$ with the help of set $B$. If $B$ significantly overlaps with $A$, then $B$ identifies many points in $R$ that lie on $p$. With error-correction, $p$ and thereby $S$ are reconstructed exactly.

This work provides the first construction using a metric other than the Hamming distance, namely the set-difference metric. According to Dodis et al. [91], the informal notion of a fuzzy fault is very closely related to secure sketches.

## 10.4 Cancelable Biometrics

Cancelable Biometrics is one of the original solutions for privacy-preserving biometric authentication. Instead of storing the original biometric, the biometric is transformed using a one-way function. This transformation can be performed either in the signal domain or in the feature domain [231]. This construct preserves privacy since it will not be possible (or computationally very hard) to recover the original biometric using such a transformed version. If a biometric is compromised, it can be simply re-enrolled using another transformation function, thus providing revocability. The construct also prevents cross-matching between the databases, since each application using the biometric uses a different transformation. In Fig. 10.2, the key idea of this approach is explained. Another advantage of this approach is that the feature representation is not changed (in both signal and feature domain

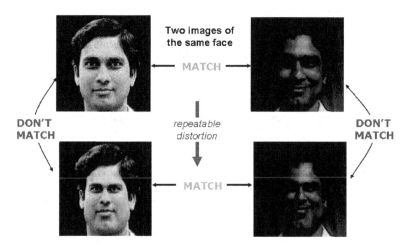

**Fig. 10.2.** Illustration of cancelable biometrics for face recognition. In this case, the face is distorted in the signal domain prior to feature extraction. The distorted version does not match with the original biometric, whereas the two instances of distorted features match between themselves. © 2006 IEEE

transformation). This will allow one to use existing feature extraction and matching algorithms and be backward compatible with legacy systems.

There are several challenges to be overcome before successfully designing a cancelable transform:

1. **Registration:** One way to ensure that the transformation is repeatable is to cast the signal into a canonical form each time before applying the transform. For geometry-based biometrics, this requires that an absolute registration be done for each biometric signal acquired prior to the transformation.
2. **Entropy retention:** The transformed version should not lose any individuality while we generate multiple templates from the same template.
3. **Error tolerance:** Another problem to contend with, even after registration, is the intrauser variability that is present in biometric signals. The features obtained after transformation should be robust wrt to this variation.
4. **Transformation function design:** The transform has to further satisfy the following conditions:
   a) The transformed version of the fingerprint should not match the original. Furthermore, the original should not be recoverable from the transform. This property helps in preserving the privacy of the transformed template.
   b) Multiple transforms of the same fingerprint should not match oneanother. This property of the transform prevents cross-matching between databases.

### 10.4.1 Cancelable Transforms

In this subsection, we will describe the design of three cancelable transforms. In particular, we will focus on fingerprint biometrics here. Once a global registration has been achieved using a singular-point location (see [63] for more details), the minutiae feature points can be transformed consistently across multiple samples collected at different times. The three transform methods, namely Cartesian, polar, and surface folding transformation, will be described in detail next.

### 10.4.2 Cartesian Transformation

In the Cartesian transformation, the minutiae positions are measured in rectangular coordinates with reference to the position of the singular point. The $x$-axis is aligned with the orientation of the singular point. This coordinate system is divided into *cells* of fixed size (with a total of $H \times W$ cells, as illustrated in Fig. 10.3). The cells are numbered in a fixed sequence. The process of transformation consists of exchanging the cell positions (see Fig. 10.3). Alternatively, the cell may be rotated in multiples of $90°$ after transposition.

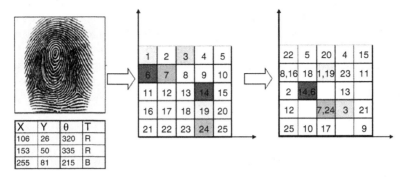

**Fig. 10.3.** In a Cartesian transformation, the space is divided into cells of equal size. The transformation maps each cell into some random cell within the feature space. © 2006 IEEE

However, we consider only position displacement in our experiments. When the cell positions are changed, all of the minutiae within the cells retain their relative position.

The transformation is not a strict permutation, since the condition of irreversability requires that more than one cell be mapped into the same cell after transformation. In our case, the cell mapping is governed by a mapping matrix $M$. For instance, consider a simplified process where the coordinates are divided into just $2 \times 2$ cells. The transformation through the matrix M is

$$\begin{bmatrix} 1 \, 2 \, 3 \, 4 \end{bmatrix} \begin{bmatrix} 0 \, 0 \, 0 \, 0 \\ 0 \, 1 \, 0 \, 0 \\ 1 \, 0 \, 0 \, 1 \\ 0 \, 0 \, 1 \, 0 \end{bmatrix} = \begin{bmatrix} 3 \, 2 \, 4 \, 2 \end{bmatrix}. \tag{10.1}$$

It can be seen that both cells 2 and 4 have been mapped to cell 2 after transformation. A similar transformation is also applied to minutiae angles. (The angles are quantized into four or eight distinct sectors and the same type of mapping is applied.) The positions of the cells, before ($C$) and after ($C'$) transformation can be written simply as

$$CM = C'. \tag{10.2}$$

An example of the transformation process is shown in Fig. 10.3. The binary representation of the exchange matrix is convenient from a storage perspective. It also gives us a first-order approximation of the information embedded in the key matrix $C$. Each column of the matrix encodes $\log_2(HW)$ bits. Thus, the total information content has an upper bound of $HW\log_2(HW)$ bits. This is a very loose upper bound since, in reality, we cannot expect all cells to be occupied. If we consider the approximate strength of the transformation process, each resulting cell after the transformation could have originated from $HW$ possible source cells. Therefore, a brute-force attack would have to try roughly $HW^{(HW)}$ possibilities (corresponding to $HW\log_2(HW)$ bits).

In Cartesian transformation, there is a high probability of cell exchanges that may cause performance trade-off. Also, note that due to the nature of the transformation itself, the discontinuities and non-linear transformations alter the regular distribution of the minutiae within the fingerprint image. Furthermore, the transformation does not prevent formation of clusters that could degrade performance.

### 10.4.3 Radial Transformation

In order to preserve the natural distribution of the minutiae within the fingerprint, a radial transformation function is proposed. In this method, the minutiae positions are measured in radial coordinates with reference to the core position. The angles are measured with reference to the orientation of the core. The coordinate space is now divided into radial *sectors* ($L$ levels and $S$ angles) that are numbered in some sequence (see Fig. 10.4). The process of transformation consists of exchanging the sector positions. The minutiae angles change in accordance to the difference in the sector positions before and after transformation.

In the radial transformation case, the sector mapping is governed by a translation key matrix $M$ ($1 \times LS$) that relates the cell transformation. The positions of the sectors before and after transformation is written simply as

$$C' = C + M. \tag{10.3}$$

For instance, consider a simplified transformation where $L = 2$ and $S = 2$. The transformation through the matrix $M$ is

$$\begin{bmatrix} 1\ 2\ 3\ 4 \end{bmatrix} + \begin{bmatrix} +3\ -1\ +1\ -2 \end{bmatrix} = \begin{bmatrix} 4\ 1\ 4\ 2 \end{bmatrix}. \tag{10.4}$$

This mapping is many-to-one (in the example, both sectors 1 and 3 are mapped to 4 after transformation). The translation is constrained to prevent

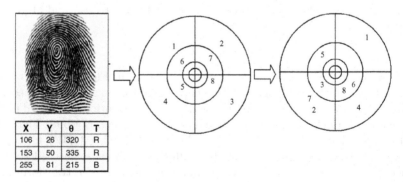

| X | Y | θ | T |
|---|---|---|---|
| 106 | 26 | 320 | R |
| 153 | 50 | 335 | R |
| 255 | 81 | 215 | B |

**Fig. 10.4.** During radial transformation, the feature space is divided into sectors. Each sector is mapped into some other random sector after transformation. © 2006 IEEE

performance (error rate) degradation. Unlike the Cartesian transformation, this does not alter the natural distribution of minutiae points to a large extent (see Fig. 10.4).

### 10.4.4 Surface Folding Transformation

In the third class of transforms called "surface folding transforms" (see Fig. 10.5), we try to design transforms that preserves local smoothness in the minutia regions; that is, for minor perturbation in the minutia location, the transformed position does not change significantly. In addition, we require that this smooth transformation be largely unconstrained and be a many-to-one mapping to satisfy the invertibility condition. In this subsection, we explore a family of functions that have locally smooth transformation of the minutiae position. The transformation has a parametric form that is governed by a random key. As earlier, the transformation is applied after aligning the fingerprint using the core location and orientation. The requirement of cancelability puts several constraints on the parametric function such as the following:

1. Minutiae-based matchers tolerate a certain amount of uncertainty in the minutiae position and orientation to account for the feature extraction inaccuracies. The minutiae position has to be pushed outside the tolerance limit of the matcher after transformation. Thus, we need to ensure that there is a minimum amount of translation during the transformation.
2. The transformation should be locally smooth to ensure that small changes in the minutiae position before transformation should lead to small changes in the minutiae position after transformation.
3. The transformation should not be globally smooth, since the minutiae positions after transformation are highly correlated to minutiae positions after transformation and hence can be inverted easily.

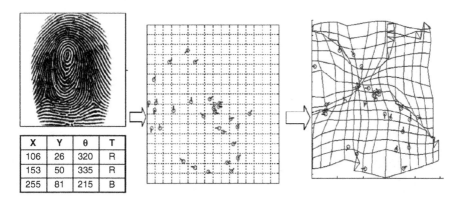

| X | Y | θ | T |
|---|---|---|---|
| 106 | 26 | 320 | R |
| 153 | 50 | 335 | R |
| 255 | 81 | 215 | B |

**Fig. 10.5.** Illustration of the functional transformation. Both the position and the orientation of the minutiae are changed by some parametric transfer function. The function is locally smooth but globally not smooth. © 2006 IEEE

Using such "locally smooth but globally not smooth" functions, we alter the position and orientation of the minutiae using

$$X' = X + f_X(X, Y),$$ (10.5)
$$Y' = Y + g_Y(X, Y),$$ (10.6)
$$\Theta' = \mathrm{mod}\,(\Theta + h_\Theta(X, Y), 2\pi).$$ (10.7)

Here, $\{X, Y, \Theta\}$ and $\{X', Y', \Theta'\}$ represent the original and transformed minutiae coordinates, respectively. $f_X(X, Y)$ is a non-invertible function of the original coordinates that is used to generate the new minutiae position. In a similar fashion, the non-invertible functions $g_Y(X, Y)$ and $h_\Theta(X, Y)$ are used to map the $Y$ coordinate and minutia angle.

### 10.4.5 Results

Some performance results of the three transforms is presented in the Receiver Operating Characteristic (ROC) curve shown in Fig. 10.6. With the Cartesian transform, the unconstrained mapping alters the natural distribution of the minutiae points in the image. Also, due to many-to-one-mapping, there is some reduction in the distinctiveness of the resulting feature distribution. Since it is

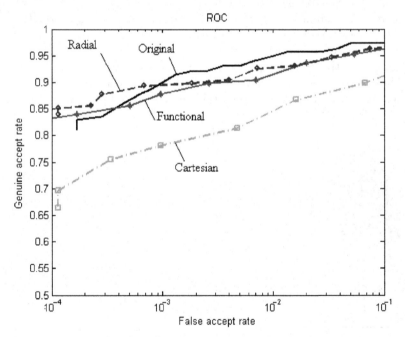

**Fig. 10.6.** Comparison of the matching performance without transformation and with three different classes of cancelable transform. These performance curves were generated using 188 pairs of fingerprints and a tolerance-box matcher. © 2006 IEEE

relatively complicated to analytically express the effect of the transformation on the individuality, we resort to empirical evaluation of the matching performance, before and after the transformation. We performed the evaluation using 180 pairs of images drawn from the IBM optical database (since the matcher was primarily optimized over this). It can be seen that the overall accuracy of the matcher has reduced.

The relatively poor performance of the Cartesian transform can be explained in terms of the additional intrauser variability introduced due to cell swapping between instances. Since the transformation function is not smooth, if a minutiae close to the border of the cell crosses over between instances (due to intrauser variation), then it will not match with the corresponding minutiae after transformation. The probability of cell exchanges is proportional to the number of minutiae that fall at the border of the cell boundaries. If we assume that the minutiae can shift $\Delta$ pixels in either direction, $1 - (X - 2\Delta)^2/X^2$ fraction of the area corresponds to border areas, where the cell exchanges can occur. In our case, the cell width is chosen to be $X = 32$. If we chose to $\Delta = 4$, the cell-exchange probability will close to 42%, and with $\Delta = 8$, the cell-exchange probability will be close to 75%. Due to the non-linear and discontinuous nature of the transformation, small changes in the minutiae location before transformation gets translated to very large changes in position after transformation, causing loss in accuracy.

Similar to the Cartesian transformation, for the radial transform we expect that there will be some performance overhead due to the many-to-one mapping. However, our experimental evaluation shows that it performs better than the Cartesian transformation.

## 10.5 Discussion

In this chapter we extensively reviewed related literature and also presented three transforms to achieve cancelability in fingerprint templates. The revocability of the templates can be employed should there be a loss of privacy in an application.

There are several factors to assess such bio-crypto systems. The following parameters have been used to compare our approach with others: (i) robustness of the transform to variation in the registration process; (ii) how the accuracy depends on the transformation; (iii) how many transforms are possible; (iv) whether the transforms are dependent on noise in feature measurements; and (v) whether the entropy is retained. Our proposed method is compared with other published method using these factors in Table 10.1.

In approaches that utilize discretization in order to increase the robustness of the biometric representation (e.g., [205,207]), the entropy or distinctiveness of the original biometric is lost. Therefore, it is usually combined with some user-specific "salt" or randomness to maintain the distinctiveness. Therefore, when we design the one-way transformation function to distort the minutiae

**Table 10.1.** Summary of the Comparative Merits of Various Privacy Preserving Authentication Techniques

| Technique | Ideal | Cancelable Biometrics | Biometric Hardening | Biometric Keying | Fuzzy Techniques |
|---|---|---|---|---|---|
| Applicable for fingerprints (minutiae data)? | YES | YES | NO | NO | YES |
| Preserves representation? | YES/NO | YES | YES | YES | NO |
| Preserves entropy of original biometric? | YES | YES | NO | NO | YES |
| Is the template revokable/cancelable? | YES | YES | YES | NO | NO |

information, we have to take care that the entropy is not reduced drastically. Our claim about the robustness of our cancelable biometrics was obtained through empirical experiments (such as results shown in Fig. 10.6).

# 11

# Protection of Biometric Information

Tom Kevenaar

## 11.1 Introduction

The field of biometrics is concerned with recognizing individuals by means of unique physiological or behavioral characteristics. In practical systems, several biometric modalities are used, such as fingerprint, face, iris, hand geometry, and so forth. Recently, biometric systems are becoming increasingly popular because they potentially offer more secure solutions than other identification means such as PIN codes and security badges because a biometric is tightly linked to an individual. For the same reason, biometrics can prevent the use of several identities by a single individual. Finally, biometrics are also more convenient because, unlike passwords and PIN codes, they cannot be forgotten and are always at hand.

In this chapter we describe how biometrics can be combined with cryptographic techniques described in Part I of this book in order to, for example, derive cryptographic keys from biometric measurements or to protect the privacy of information stored in biometric systems.

In order to do so, this chapter is organised as follows. The remainder of this section gives an overview of a general biometric verification system. The privacy threats introduced by traditional biometric systems are presented in Section 11.2 and requirements for a private biometric system are given in Section 11.3. Section 11.4 gives a general architecture and Section 11.5 gives several implementations of an important building block in the architecture (the quantizer). Then, in Section 11.6, security and privacy consideration are discussed and the chapter concludes with a number of application examples that are based on biometric template protection techniques.

### 11.1.1 Overview of Biometric Systems

In this subsection we describe biometric systems and introduce terminology that is required in subsequent sections of this chapter.

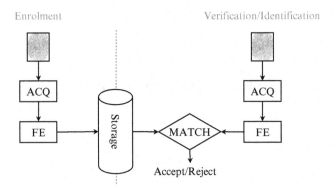

**Fig. 11.1.** An overview of a biometric system.

A biometric system can be used for *verification* and *identification* of individuals. In verification, a person claims to have a certain identity and the biometric system performs a 1:1 comparison between the offered biometric and the biometric reference information that is linked to the claimed identity and stored in the biometric system. In identification, a 1:$N$ comparison is performed between the offered biometric template and all available reference information stored in the biometric system to reveal the identity of an individual. Without loss of generality we will only consider verification systems as the 1:$N$ comparison in an identification system is, in general, implemented as a sequence of 1:1 comparisons. Figure 11.1 gives a high-level overview of a biometric system. During *enrollment*, an acquisition device ACQ (e.g. a fingerprint sensor) measures a biometric. After processing the measurement data and extracting relevant features in the feature extraction (FE) block, a *template* representing the measurement is stored in the biometric system. During *verification*, an individual claims an identity, and a biometric measurement from this individual is obtained. This measurement is transformed into a template and compared (matched) with the template stored in the biometric system corresponding to the claimed identity and an "Accept" or "Reject" message is generated.

In the following subsection, the matching process (MATCH) will be explained in more detail.

### 11.1.2 Statistical Classification

In biometric applications, the measurements and the resulting templates are inherently noisy. Apart from the noise present in the measurement system, this is mainly due to varying interaction of the biometric with the acquisition device (sensor). For example, a different pressure on a finger when offering it to a fingerprint sensor will lead to distortion of the fingerprint image. Likewise, different lighting conditions in a face recognition systems will result in variations in the acquired measurements. Although a large proportion of the variations can be eliminated in the feature extraction phase (FE), the generated biometric templates will always contain a certain amount of noise.

Consequently, comparison or matching of biometric templates must be treated as a *statistical classification* process that determines if a measured template is drawn from the probability distribution of the claimed identity (the *genuine distribution*) or from the distribution describing all other individuals (the *impostor distribution* or *background distribution*). To this purpose we assume that a biometric template can be represented as a *feature vector* $\mathbf{f} \in \mathbb{R}^l$ that is an observation of the stochastic variable $\mathbf{F}$. We have two classes $\omega_I$ and $\omega_G$ with probability density functions $p(\mathbf{F}|\omega_I)$ and $p(\mathbf{F}|\omega_G)$, respectively. Thus, given $p(\mathbf{F}|\omega_I)$ and $p(\mathbf{F}|\omega_G)$, the classifier (or matcher) must assign the observation $\mathbf{f}$ to $\omega_I$ or $\omega_G$ so as to minimize the probability of assigning $\mathbf{f}$ to the wrong class. In other words, a decision criterion or classification boundary must be determined against which $\mathbf{f}$ must be tested in order to assign $\mathbf{f}$ to $\omega_I$ or $\omega_G$.

A decision criterion based on a posteriori probabilities [115] chooses the class $\omega_i, i \in \{I, G\}$ that is most probable for this given $\mathbf{f}$, or

$$\mathbb{P}(\omega_I|\mathbf{f}) \gtrless \mathbb{P}(\omega_G|\mathbf{f}) \rightarrow \mathbf{f} \in \begin{cases} \omega_I \\ \omega_G \end{cases} . \tag{11.1}$$

If $\mathbb{P}(\omega_i)$ denotes the a priori probability that an event from class $\omega_i$ occurs, then we can use Bayes' rule

$$\mathbb{P}(\omega_i|\mathbf{f}) = \frac{p(\mathbf{f}|\omega_i)\mathbb{P}(\omega_i)}{p(\mathbf{f})} \tag{11.2}$$

to rewrite (11.1) as

$$p(\mathbf{f}|\omega_I)\mathbb{P}(\omega_I) \gtrless p(\mathbf{f}|\omega_G)\mathbb{P}(\omega_G) \rightarrow \mathbf{f} \in \begin{cases} \omega_I \\ \omega_G \end{cases} \tag{11.3}$$

or

$$l(\mathbf{f}) = \frac{p(\mathbf{f}|\omega_G)}{p(\mathbf{f}|\omega_I)} \gtrless \frac{\mathbb{P}(\omega_I)}{\mathbb{P}(\omega_G)} \rightarrow \mathbf{f} \in \begin{cases} \omega_G \\ \omega_I \end{cases} . \tag{11.4}$$

The term $l(\mathbf{f})$ is called the *likelihood ratio* and is the basic quantity in hypothesis testing. From (11.4) it is clear that the classification *boundary* is given by

$$l(\mathbf{F}) = \frac{p(\mathbf{F}|\omega_G)}{p(\mathbf{F}|\omega_I)} = \frac{\mathbb{P}(\omega_I)}{\mathbb{P}(\omega_G)}; \tag{11.5}$$

so depending on which side of the boundary the observation $\mathbf{f}$ is located, it is assigned to $\omega_I$ or $\omega_G$. Eq. (11.4) is called the *Bayes test for minimum error*.

In general, for any classification boundary, there will be occurrences that the observation $\mathbf{f}$ is assigned to the wrong class, leading to a classification error. In order to evaluate the performance of a given decision rule or classification boundary, the probability of error $\epsilon$ must be determined. Let us denote by $\Gamma_G$ and $\Gamma_I$ the regions where $p(\mathbf{f}|\omega_G)/p(\mathbf{f}|\omega_I) > \mathbb{P}(\omega_I)/\mathbb{P}(\omega_G)$ and $p(\mathbf{f}|\omega_G)/p(\mathbf{f}|\omega_I) < \mathbb{P}(\omega_I)/\mathbb{P}(\omega_G)$, respectively. Note that if $\mathbf{f} \in \Gamma_I$, it will be assigned to class $\omega_I$ (likewise for $\Gamma_G$ and $\omega_G$). In general, we have

$$\epsilon = \Pr(\text{error}) = \mathbb{P}(\omega_G)\Pr\{\text{error}|\omega_G\} + \mathbb{P}(\omega_I)\Pr\{\text{error}|\omega_I\}. \tag{11.6}$$

The term $\Pr\{\text{error}|\omega_I\}$ is the probability that $\mathbf{f}$ originated in class $\omega_I$ but is assigned to $\omega_G$ (likewise for $\Pr\{\text{error}|\omega_G\}$) so we have that the probability of a wrong classification of an observation $\mathbf{f}$ is

$$\epsilon = \mathbb{P}(\omega_G) \int_{\Gamma_I} p(\mathbf{F}|\omega_G) \, d\mathbf{F} + \mathbb{P}(\omega_I) \int_{\Gamma_G} p(\mathbf{F}|\omega_I) \, d\mathbf{F}. \tag{11.7}$$

In biometrics, often the expressions False Accept Rate (FAR) and False Reject Rate (FRR) are used. The setting in which these entities are used is closely related to two-class classification described earlier. In our notation, $\omega_G$ is associated with "Accept" and $\omega_I$ with "Reject" and we have

$$\text{FAR} = \int_{\Gamma_G} p(\mathbf{F}|\omega_I) \, d\mathbf{F} \tag{11.8}$$

and

$$\text{FRR} = \int_{\Gamma_I} p(\mathbf{F}|\omega_G) \, d\mathbf{F}. \tag{11.9}$$

An example for two one-dimensional Gaussian distributions is given in Fig. 11.2. Where (11.8) and (11.9) give the FAR and FRR for a single individual, most commonly FAR and FRR are reported as an average over all available individuals.

In many practical situations including biometrics, the a priori probabilities $\mathbb{P}(\omega_I)$ and $\mathbb{P}(\omega_G)$ are not known and (11.4) cannot be used as a decision criterion. An alternative is to choose a decision rule based on the required FAR

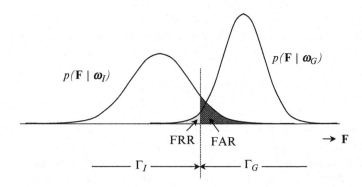

**Fig. 11.2.** A one-dimensional illustration of FAR and FRR.

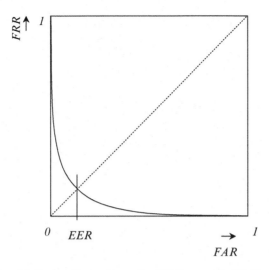

**Fig. 11.3.** An illustration of a ROC curve (solid line).

and FRR. One could, for example, minimize FRR over all possible decision rules under the constraint that FAR $\leq \alpha$, where $\alpha$ is a value chosen depending on the application. The solution of this constrained optimization problem is known as the Neyman-Pearson criterion [115] and defines the decision rule based on the likelihood ratio as

$$l(\mathbf{f}) = \frac{p(\mathbf{f}|\omega_G)}{p(\mathbf{f}|\omega_I)} \gtrless \eta \rightarrow \mathbf{f} \in \begin{cases} \omega_G \\ \omega_I \end{cases}, \tag{11.10}$$

where $\eta$ is chosen such that

$$\int_{\forall \mathbf{F}|l(\mathbf{F})>\eta} p(\mathbf{F}|\omega_I)\, d\mathbf{F} = \alpha. \tag{11.11}$$

By modifying the threshold $\eta$, a trade-off between FAR and FRR can be achieved. The quality of a classifier can be represented as a Receiver Operating Characteristic (ROC) curve that gives a trade-off between FAR and FRR (see Fig. 11.3). In order to represent the quality of such curve by a single number, usually the Equal Error Rate (EER) is chosen, defined as the point where the FAR equals the FRR.

Due to complexity reasons or the fact that $p(\mathbf{F}|\omega_G)$ and $p(\mathbf{F}|\omega_I)$ cannot be accurately estimated, one sometimes resorts to simpler decision rules such as Euclidean distance, defined as

$$|\mathbf{f} - \boldsymbol{\mu}|^2 \gtrless \eta \rightarrow \mathbf{f} \in \begin{cases} \omega_I \\ \omega_G \end{cases}, \tag{11.12}$$

where $\boldsymbol{\mu}$ is the mean of $p(\mathbf{F}|\omega_G)$.

In the following sections, biometric templates $\mathbf{f}$ will be represented as binary strings $\mathbf{z} \in \{0,1\}^*$ such that they can more easily be combined with the techniques in Part I. A common decision rule for these binary templates is based on the Hamming distance such that

$$d_{HD}(\mathbf{z} - \boldsymbol{\mu}_z) \gtrless \eta \rightarrow \mathbf{z} \in \begin{cases} \omega_I \\ \omega_G \end{cases}, \tag{11.13}$$

where $\boldsymbol{\mu}_z$ is the binary string representation of the biometric of an individual. Most biometric modalities are not naturally represented as binary strings and, therefore, in Section 11.5 some methods will be given to transform feature vectors into binary strings.

From the explanation given above it follows that biometric systems store biometric reference information in the form of biometric templates. In the following section we discuss privacy issues that arise when there is a widespread use of biometric systems.

## 11.2 Privacy Threats of Biometrics

A biometric template is a representation of a unique characteristics of an individual, and as such, it contains privacy-sensitive information. Especially when biometric systems store this information without any precaution in centralized databases or on unsecure devices, privacy problems will arise.

The first problem is that biometrics might contain information on the health condition of an individual [35, 223]. Second, when an attacker obtains a biometric template, he might impersonate the rightful owner of the template by spoofing the biometric because it is well known that based on biometric templates, fake biometric identifiers can be produced that pass the identification test [186]. This will lead to identity theft. This problem becomes even more serious if we realize that biometric templates cannot be renewed or reissued (e.g., [244]) because people have only ten fingers, two eyes, and so forth. This stands in sharp contrast to situations where passwords and tokens are used for verification because they can easily be reissued. Third, when the biometric templates are stored without adequate protection in a database, they can be used to perform cross-matching between databases and track people's behavior. A malicious employee of a bank can, for instance, find out that some biometric templates in his database also appear in the database of a night club. The underlying notion is that it is not possible to obtain an "alias" of a biometric template as is possible with, for example, names and addresses. Finally, in many countries, legislation obliges institutions to properly protect the stored personal information and to properly regulate who has access to which kind of information.

The above-mentioned privacy problems become less severe if we assume that a database owner (or a verifier) can be trusted, in which case the privacy protection of biometric information hinges on employees correctly following procedures, but in practical situations, this is difficult to maintain. In the past years, much research has been carried out to protect the privacy of biometric information using technological means rather than procedural means. These technical methods are collectively referred to as biometric *template protection* techniques. An elaborate overview of such techniques is given in Chapter 10 as well as a possible approach known as Cancelable Biometrics. In this chapter we describe how biometrics can be combined with cryptographic techniques described in Part I of this book, but we start by giving an overview of the requirements for template protection.

## 11.3 Requirements for Template Protection

In this section we first consider two approaches that might be considered to achieve template protection. From the drawbacks of these approaches and the discussion in Section 11.2 we then will derive the security requirements for template protection.

### 11.3.1 Naive Approaches

One might think that encryption of biometric templates before storing them in a biometric system solves the problem. We show here that a straightforward application of encryption does not solve the privacy problem with respect to the verifier.

Assume that we use a symmetric key encryption scheme (the system works similarly for a public-key scheme). All sensors get a secret key $K$ that is equal to the secret key of the verifier. During enrollment, a biometric template $\mathbf{f}$ of a person is obtained, $\mathbf{f}$ is encrypted with the key $K$, and $E_K(\mathbf{f})$ is stored in the biometric system. During verification, the measurement of the same biometric results in the value $\mathbf{f}'$ (close but not identical to $\mathbf{f}$ due to noise). The verification system (e.g., the sensor) encrypts the value $\mathbf{f}'$ with the key $K$ and sends $E_K(\mathbf{f}')$ to the verifier. The verifier is faced with the problem of comparing $E_K(\mathbf{f})$ with $E_K(\mathbf{f}')$. However, encryption functions have the property that $E_K(\mathbf{f})$ and $E_K(\mathbf{f}')$ are very different even when $\mathbf{f}$ and $\mathbf{f}'$ are very close (but not equal). Hence, given only the values $E_K(\mathbf{f})$ and $E_K(\mathbf{f}')$, the verifier cannot decide whether $\mathbf{f}$ and $\mathbf{f}'$ originate from the same person. This implies that the verifier must decrypt $E_K(\mathbf{f})$ and $E_K(\mathbf{f}')$ to obtain $\mathbf{f}$ and $\mathbf{f}'$ and find out whether they are sufficiently similar. However, in that case, the verifier knows $\mathbf{f}$ and, hence, the system does not provide privacy with respect to the verifier. Furthermore, in practical situations, the need for a cryptographic key infrastructure will severely inhibit a wide acceptance of this approach.

The problem of storing reference information also exists with password authentication. In order to protect passwords against the owner of the database and eavesdropping, the following measures are taken. During *enrollment*, a cryptographic hash function $H$ is applied to a chosen password $pwd$ and the hash of the password $H(pwd)$ together with the username or identity $ID$ is stored in the (public) database for authentication. For example, in the UNIX system, this database can be found in the directory /etc/passwd. During authentication, the identity $ID$ and the password $pwd'$ are entered and $(ID, H(pwd'))$ is sent to the verifier. The verifier then compares $H(pwd')$ with $H(pwd)$, and when $H(pwd) = H(pwd')$, access is granted to the computer, otherwise access is denied. The security of this system follows from the fact that $H$ is a one-way function: Given $H(pwd)$, it is *very hard* to compute $pwd$. Hence, for the owner of the database as well as for the eavesdropper, it is infeasible to retrieve $pwd$ from $H(pwd)$.

In essence, one would like to mimic the password authentication scheme in the case of biometrics. The problem is, as explained in Section 11.1, that biometrics are inherently noisy and that $H$ is a one-way function. These functions are very good for security purposes but have no continuity properties. Applying the password authentication scheme implies that $H(\mathbf{f})$ is stored in the reference database. During authentication, the value $\mathbf{f}'$ is obtained, which is typically close to $\mathbf{f}$ when $\mathbf{f}$ and $\mathbf{f}'$ originate from the same person, but, in general, they are *not* equal due to noise. Therefore, due to the one-way property of $H$, even when $\mathbf{f}$ and $\mathbf{f}'$ are very close, $H(\mathbf{f})$ and $H(\mathbf{f}')$ will be very different.

In the remainder of this chapter it will be explained how the various techniques explained in Part I can be used to protect biometric information. Before that, we give some security assumptions and requirements for template protection systems.

### 11.3.2 Security Assumptions and Requirements

The scenarios in the previous subsections illustrate that an encryption approach to template protection does not work because the verifier must be trusted. Hashing biometric templates is not feasible because biometric measurements are inherently noisy. In order to come up with a template protection system, the following security assumptions are made:

- Enrollment is performed at a Trusted Authority (TA). The TA enrolls all users by capturing their biometrics, performing additional processing and adding a protected form of the user data to a database.
- The storage is vulnerable to attacks both from the outside and from the inside (malicious verifier).
- During the authentication phase, an attacker is able to present artificial biometrics at the sensor.
- All capturing and processing during authentication is tamper-resistant; for example, no information about biometrics can be obtained from the sensor. The sensor is assumed to be trusted; it does not distribute measured information.

- The communication channel between the sensor and the authentication authority is public; that is, the line can be eavesdropped by an attacker.

In essence, this means that template protection methods protect the *storage* of biometric systems against attackers. The requirements for an architecture that does not suffer from the threats mentioned in Section 11.2 are given as follows:

- The information that is stored in the biometric system does not give sufficient information to make successful impersonation possible.
- The information in the biometric system provides the least possible information about the original biometrics; in particular, it reveals no sensitive information about the persons whose biometrics are stored.
- During matching, a verifier should not have access to (unprotected) biometric templates. This means that, at the verifier, a *secure sensor* is used that does not output unprotected biometric information.
- It is possible to generate several representations of a single biometric template.
- When a biometric measurement of the same person is contaminated with noise, verification (or identification) should still be successful if the noise is not too large.

Note that an approach that meets those requirements guarantees that the biometric cannot be compromised, it prevents cross-matching, and it can handle noisy biometric measurements. In the following section it is explained how template protection, in principal, can be achieved using some of the methods given in Part I.

## 11.4 An Architecture for Biometric Template Protection

Some of the methods in Part I derive cryptographic keys from noisy binary strings. In the key derivation process, side information $W$ is stored (or published), which makes it possible to retrieve the key from a noisy version of the original binary string. For binary strings with certain properties of their probability distribution (e.g., a minimum value for the min-entropy), bounds can be derived for the number of secure key bits that can be extracted and the amount of information leakage.

As explained in Section 11.1.2, most biometrics can be represented as real-valued feature vectors $\mathbf{f}$ in a high-dimensional space $\mathbb{R}^l$. If it would be possible to represent these feature vectors $\mathbf{f}$ accurately enough as binary strings, these methods could be used to protect biometric information stored in biometric systems.

A high-level architecture of a template protected biometric system is given in Fig. 11.4. As compared to Fig. 11.1, a quantizer Q, a key extractor EXTR, and a cryptographic protocol PROT is added. The quantizer Q transforms

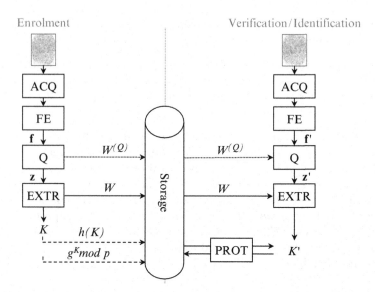

**Fig. 11.4.** A high-level architecture of biometric template protection.

feature vectors $\mathbf{f} \in \mathbb{R}^l$ into binary strings $\mathbf{z} \in \{0,1\}^*$, which can serve as an input for the extractor. These quantizers are not commonly used in traditional biometric systems nor are they part of the theory of (fuzzy) extractors, which assumes that binary strings with a certain probability distribution are given. Therefore, in Section 11.5 some quantizers will be discussed. In order to work properly, some quantizers generate side information $W^{(Q)}$ during enrollment, which is used during verification. This is indicated by a dotted line in Fig. 11.4. Given the binary representation of a biometric, the extractor EXTR can extract a key $K$. The extractor EXTR will generate *exactly* the same key $K$ if for two successive inputs $\mathbf{z}$ and $\mathbf{z}'$, the distance $d(\mathbf{z}, \mathbf{z}') < t$, where $d$ is some metric and $t$ is a user-defined threshold incorporated in EXTR. Therefore, in order to perform a biometric verification, the key $K$ generated during enrollment should be matched *exactly* with the key $K'$ generated during verification. Note that if the metric $d$ used in the extractor is the Hamming distance, matching the binary strings $\mathbf{z}$ and $\mathbf{z}'$ is in effect a Hamming distance classifier (see also (11.13)).

The fact that $K$ and $K'$ must be compared exactly makes it possible to use the large range of cryptographic authentication protocols (PROT in Fig. 11.4) for biometric authentication. Depending on the attack model, one could simply store the hash $h(K)$ and, during authentication, compare $h(K)$ and $h(K')$. An other possibility is to use zero-knowledge protocols. Choosing, for example, Schnorr's zero-knowledge protocol implies that $g^K \bmod p$ is stored in the biometric system, where $p$ is a prime and $g$ is a generator of a multiplicative subgroup of $\mathbb{Z}_p^*$, and during verification, the sensor proves knowledge of $K$. The essence of privacy protection of biometric information is that the public information required for the cryptographic authentication protocol (such as $h(K)$ or $g^K \bmod p$) does not leak information about $K$. Thus, provided that $W^{(Q)}$ and $W$ do not leak information, the privacy of the biometric information is protected.

Most extractors EXTR are or can be changed into randomized functions. This means that from a single input $\mathbf{z}$, it is possible to derive several different keys that also results in different side information stored in the biometric system. This means that several representations of a biometric can be generated. The randomization information is considered to be part of $W$.

Provided the side information for the quantizers $W^{(Q)}$ and the side information $W$ for the key derivation process only leak a limited amount of information about $\mathbf{f}$ or $\mathbf{z}$ and provided that the algorithms during verification are executed on a secure sensor, this architecture fulfills the requirements mentioned in Section 11.3.2. The issue of information leakage will be discussed in Section 11.6.

## 11.5 Quantization of Biometric Measurements

The architecture explained in Section 11.4 requires a quantizer that transforms feature vectors $\mathbf{f} \in \mathbb{R}^l$ into binary strings $\mathbf{z} \in \{0,1\}^*$ while allowing some "noise" or "fuzziness" in the input. More specifically, during *enrollment*, one or more biometric measurements are used to derive a binary string $\mathbf{z}$ that is stored in the biometric system in a protected form. During *verification*, a binary string $\mathbf{z}'$ is derived from a biometric measurement and compared with the string $\mathbf{z}$. The general notion is that methods such as fuzzy extractors are insensitive to noise (e.g., derive the same cryptographic key) as long as the noise is smaller, in terms of the Hamming distance, than some preset threshold.

In the context of binary strings derived from biometric measurements, this means that the Hamming distance between $\mathbf{z}$ and $\mathbf{z}'$ should be small enough. Moreover, the binary templates should lead to proper classification results in terms of FAR, FRR, and EER (see Section 11.1.2). In this section we will discuss methods from the literature that transform feature vectors $\mathbf{f}$ into binary strings.

### 11.5.1 Shielding Functions

One of the first methods to extract binary strings from continuous distributions was given in [182] and the method was inspired by a method called Quantization Index Modulation to embed a watermark in an audio or video stream [62]. It will be illustrated how a single bit is generated for the $t$-th feature $(\mathbf{f}_i)_t$ in the feature vector $\mathbf{f}_i$ of user $i$. The complete binary string $\mathbf{z}_i$ is obtained by repeating the procedure for all entries in $\mathbf{f}$, followed by concatenation of all the bits derived from the individual features.

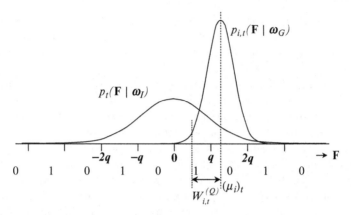

**Fig. 11.5.** An illustration of the shielding function approach for a feature for which a "1" should be embedded.

### Enrollment

For enrollment of user $i$, we assume that an estimate for the genuine distribution $p_{i,t}(\mathbf{F}|\omega_G)$ (with mean $(\mu_i)_t$) and the background distribution $p_t(\mathbf{F}|\omega_I)$ is available as depicted in Fig. 11.5. In most practical situations, these estimates are obtained from a number of measurements of user $i$ and a number of measurements of other users, respectively. Note that the feature axis is uniformly quantized using a fixed quantization step $q$ and that every other interval is labeled using a "0" or a "1". In order to embed a bit $(\mathbf{z}_i)_t$, the value $W_{i,t}^{(Q)}$ is computed as

$$W_{i,t}^{(Q)} = \begin{cases} (2n + \frac{1}{2})q - (\mu_i)_t & \text{if } (\mathbf{z}_i)_t = 1 \\ (2n - \frac{1}{2})q - (\mu_i)_t & \text{if } (\mathbf{z}_i)_t = 0, \end{cases} \tag{11.14}$$

where $n \in \mathbb{Z}$ such that $-q < W_{i,t}^{(Q)} < q$. To finalize the enrollment, the binary string $\mathbf{z}_i$ for user $i$ is defined as the concatenation of the bits $(\mathbf{z}_i)_t, t = 1, \ldots, l$, and the values $W_{i,t}^{(Q)}, t = 1, \ldots, l$, are stored in the biometric system and used to extract $(\mathbf{z}_i')_t$ during verification.

### Verification

During verification, a feature $(\mathbf{f}_i')_t$ is obtained and the extracted bit $(\mathbf{z}_i')_t$ is computed as

$$(\mathbf{z}_i')_t = \begin{cases} 1 & \text{if } 2nq \leq (\mathbf{f}_i')_t + W_{i,t}^{(Q)} < (2n+1)q \\ 0 & \text{if } (2n-1)q \leq (\mathbf{f}_i')_t + W_{i,t}^{(Q)} < 2nq, \end{cases} \tag{11.15}$$

for all $n \in \mathbb{Z}$.

It can be seen that a bit error contributes to the FRR of the system. The bit error probability for the shielding function approach is

$$\text{FRR}_{i,t} = \sum_{n=-\infty}^{\infty} \int_{(2n+\frac{1}{2})q}^{(2n+\frac{3}{2})q} p_{i,t}(\mathbf{F} - (\boldsymbol{\mu}_i)_t | \omega_G) \, d\mathbf{F}. \tag{11.16}$$

Likewise, the probability that an impostor generates the proper bit contributes to the FAR and equals $\text{FAR}_{i,t} = 0.5$.

## 11.5.2 Reliable Components

An alternative method also extracts a single bit per feature and was first published in [268]. It uses the estimate of the error probability of an extracted bit to select the most *reliable* bits to be incorporated in the binary string $\mathbf{z}$. As in Section 11.5.1, the bit extraction process for the $t$-th feature $(\mathbf{f}_i)_t$ of user $i$ will be explained first which is followed by an explanation on how to select the most reliable bits.

### Enrollment

Again, we assume that for enrollment of user $i$, an estimate for the genuine distribution $p_{i,t}(\mathbf{F} | \omega_G)$ (with mean $(\mu_i)_t$ and standard deviation $\sigma_{i,t}$) and the background distribution $p_t(\mathbf{F} | \omega_I)$ (with mean $(\boldsymbol{\mu})_t$) is available as depicted in Fig. 11.6. Given $(\mu_i)_t$, $\sigma_{i,t}^2$, and $(\boldsymbol{\mu})_t$, a (candidate) bit $(\mathbf{q}_i)_t$ is extracted according to

$$(\mathbf{q}_i)_t = \begin{cases} 0 & \text{if } (\boldsymbol{\mu_i})_t \leq (\boldsymbol{\mu})_t \\ 1 & \text{if } (\boldsymbol{\mu_i})_t > (\boldsymbol{\mu})_t. \end{cases} \tag{11.17}$$

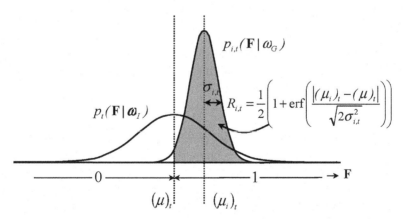

**Fig. 11.6.** An illustration of extracting a bit from the $t$-th feature of user $i$, including the reliability $R_{i,t}$ of this bit.

Next, the *reliability* of a bit $(\mathbf{q}_i)_t$ is estimated as

$$R_{i,t} = \frac{1}{2}\left(1 + \mathrm{erf}\left(\frac{|(\boldsymbol{\mu}_i)_t - (\boldsymbol{\mu})_t|}{\sqrt{2\sigma_{i,t}^2}}\right)\right), \tag{11.18}$$

where erf is the error function.

Finally, the binary string $\mathbf{z}_i$ for user $i$ is generated by choosing the most reliable components from the candidate bits $(\mathbf{q}_i)_t$. The ordered set $W_i^{(Q)}$ contains the indexes of the reliable bits in $\mathbf{q}_i$ and is stored in the biometric system and used to derive $\mathbf{z}_i'$ during verification.

## Verification

During verification, a feature vector $\mathbf{f}_i'$ is measured, and for every entry $(\mathbf{f}_i')_t$, a candidate bit $(\mathbf{q}_i')_t$ is generated according to

$$(\mathbf{q}_i')_t = \begin{cases} 0 & \text{if } (\mathbf{f}_i')_t \leq (\boldsymbol{\mu})_t \\ 1 & \text{if } (\mathbf{f}_i')_t > (\boldsymbol{\mu})_t. \end{cases} \tag{11.19}$$

Finally, using $W_i^{(Q)}$, the appropriate bits are selected from the candidate bits $(\mathbf{q}_i')_t$ to form the string $\mathbf{z}'$.

Clearly, the estimated error probability equals $\mathrm{FRR}_{i,t} = 1 - R_{i,t}$ and the probability that an impostor generates the same bit equals $\mathrm{FAR}_{i,t} = 0.5$.

### 11.5.3 Multiple-Bit Extraction

The methods explained in the previous sections extract one bit per feature. In some cases,—for example, when the standard deviation $\sigma_{i,t}$ of $p_{i,t}(\mathbf{F}|\omega_G)$ is much smaller than the standard deviation $\sigma_t$ of $p_t(\mathbf{F}|\omega_I)$—extracting more than one bit per feature might lead to better classification results (see also Section 11.5.4). In [309], the authors discussed an approach to extract more than one bit per feature and this method will be discussed in this subsection.

## Enrollment

Like the methods discussed earlier, for enrollment of user $i$, the current method assumes that an estimate for the genuine distribution $p_{i,t}(\mathbf{F}|\omega_G)$ (with mean $(\mu_i)_t$ and standard deviation $\sigma_{i,t}$) and the background distribution $p_t(\mathbf{F}|\omega_I)$ is available, as depicted in Fig. 11.7. Based on these distributions, a parameterized acceptance interval $A_{i,t}^{(0)}$ is defined as

$$A_{i,t}^{(0)} = [(\mu_i)_t - k_{i,t}\sigma_{i,t}, (\mu_i)_t + k_{i,t}\sigma_{i,t}] \tag{11.20}$$

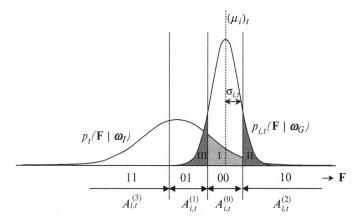

**Fig. 11.7.** Multiple-bit extraction from the $t$th feature of user $i$.

as well as some other intervals $A_{i,t}^{(1)}, A_{i,t}^{(2)}, \ldots$ If there are $a_{i,t}$ intervals, every interval can be encoded using a bitstring $(\mathbf{z}_i)_t$ containing $\lceil \log_2(a_{i,t}) \rceil$ bits. For every feature, the interval boundaries and the binary codes per interval are stored in the biometric system. However, before storing the intervals, an optimal value for $k_{i,t}$ must be determined as explained below.

Area I in Fig. 11.7 indicates the false accept rate ($\mathrm{FAR}_{i,t}$) and areas II and III together depict the false reject rate ($\mathrm{FRR}_{i,t}$). Thus, the parameter $k_{i,t}$ allows for a trade-off between $\mathrm{FAR}_{i,t}$ and $\mathrm{FRR}_{i,t}$, as it defines the width of the acceptance interval.

If we assume that all $l$ features in the vector $\mathbf{f}$ are independent, the total FAR and FRR are given as

$$\mathrm{FAR}_i = \prod_{t=1}^{l} \mathrm{FAR}_{i,t} \tag{11.21}$$

and

$$(1 - \mathrm{FRR}_i) = \prod_{t=1}^{l} (1 - \mathrm{FRR}_{i,t}). \tag{11.22}$$

In order to find optimal values for $\mathrm{FAR}_i$ and $\mathrm{FRR}_i$ for user $i$, optimal values for the parameters $k_{i,t}, t = 1, \ldots, l$, can be obtained by solving the following optimization problem:

$$\max_{k_{i,t}, t=1..l} \quad (1 - \mathrm{FRR}_i) \tag{11.23}$$

$$\text{subject to} \quad \mathrm{FAR}_i \le \alpha, 0 \le \alpha \le 1. \tag{11.24}$$

Using (11.21) and (11.22) and setting the Lagrange multiplier $\lambda \ge 0$, this optimization problem can be formulated as

$$\max_{k_{i,t},\; t=1,\ldots,l} [\log(1 - \mathrm{FRR}_i) - \lambda \log(\mathrm{FAR}_i)] \tag{11.25}$$

$$= \max_{k_{i,t},\; t=1,\ldots,l} \sum_{t=1}^{l} [\log(1 - \mathrm{FRR}_{i,t}) - \lambda \log(\mathrm{FAR}_{i,t})] \tag{11.26}$$

$$= \sum_{t=1}^{l} \max_{k_{i,t}} [\log(1 - \mathrm{FRR}_{i,t}) - \lambda \log(\mathrm{FAR}_{i,t})]. \tag{11.27}$$

By choosing a value for $\lambda$ and maximizing the expressions $\log(1 - \mathrm{FRR}_{i,t}) - \lambda \log(\mathrm{FAR}_{i,t})$ individually, the optimal values for $k_{i,t}, i = 1, \ldots, l$, are obtained along with the optimal values for $(1 - \mathrm{FRR}_{i,t})$ and $\mathrm{FAR}_{i,t}$. Using (11.21) and (11.22), one thus obtained a single point on the optimal total ROC curve of $(1 - \mathrm{FRR}_i)$ versus $\mathrm{FAR}_i$. By varying $\lambda$ and repeating this procedure, different points on this optimal ROC curve can be computed from which a point of operation can be chosen.

Finally, the binary representation $\mathbf{z}_i$ of the vector $\mathbf{f}_i$ is defined as the concatenation of the binary codes $(\mathbf{z}_i)_t, t = 1, \ldots, l$, coding for the acceptance intervals $A_{i,t}^{(0)}, t = 1, \ldots, l$.

## Verification

During verification, a feature vector $\mathbf{f}_i'$ is measured and every entry $(\mathbf{f}_i')_t$ is assigned to one of the intervals $A_{i,t}^{(0)}, A_{i,t}^{(1)}, A_{i,t}^{(2)}, \ldots$. The corresponding binary code is looked up in the biometric system. All $l$ binary codewords are concatenated to yield the string $(\mathbf{z}_i')_t$, the binary representation of $\mathbf{f}_i'$.

### 11.5.4 Discussion on Classification Results

In the previous subsections, methods were presented to transform an enrollment feature vector $\mathbf{f}$ and a verification feature vector $\mathbf{f}'$ into binary strings $\mathbf{z}$ and $\mathbf{z}'$, respectively. These binary strings can be used in the general architecture for biometric template protection depicted in Fig. 11.4, where a biometric verification is successful if $K = K'$. If we assume that the extractor EXTR will generate the same key $K$ if, for two successive inputs $\mathbf{z}$ and $\mathbf{z}'$, the distance $d(\mathbf{z}, \mathbf{z}') < t$, where $d$ is the Hamming distance and $t$ is a user-defined threshold incorporated in EXTR, then matching the binary strings $\mathbf{z}$ and $\mathbf{z}'$, is in effect a Hamming distance classifier (see also (11.13)).

From the viewpoint of a biometric system it is important to consider the classification results (e.g., in terms of EER) for the system in Fig. 11.4. At first sight one might expect that the methods in Sections 11.5.1–11.5.3, which quantize every feature to one or a few bits, will significantly deteriorate the classification results. However, simulations using several real databases (see Table 11.1 and [309]), suggest that quantization does not have a major impact on classification quality. Nevertheless, further research has to be done to

**Table 11.1.** Some classification results for real fingerprint and face databases

| EER | Feature Vector | Binary String |
|---|---|---|
| Fingerprints Database 1 (see [268]) | 1.4% | 4.0% |
| Fingerprints Database 2 (see [268]) | 1.6% | 3.5% |
| Face Database 1 (see [170]) | 1.5% | 2.5% |
| Face Database 2 (see [170]) | 0.25% | 0.25% |

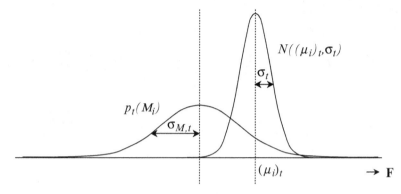

**Fig. 11.8.** Distributions for the assumption of a Gaussian channel.

enhance the quality of the binary strings and thus the classification performance of the template protected biometric system.

There are two intuitions supporting the relatively good classification results of the binary strings. The first one is concerned with the information content of the individual features. Let us assume that the $t$th feature of individual $i$ is denoted by $(\mu_i)_t$ and that the distribution of the values $(\mu_i)_t$ over the whole population is given by $p_t(M_i)$ with variance $\sigma_{M,t}^2$. Further assume that for every user $i$, the genuine (noise) distribution is Gaussian according to $\mathcal{N}((\mu_i)_t, \sigma_t^2)$ such that every user for this feature has the same variance but a different mean (see Fig. 11.8). Under these assumptions, we have a Gaussian channel and the maximum amount of information that can be transmitted over this channel is limited by [66]

$$\frac{1}{2} \log \left( 1 + \frac{\sigma_{M,t}^2}{\sigma_t^2} \right). \tag{11.28}$$

As an illustration, Fig. 11.9 gives the results for the FVC2000 database [185] containing 8 gray-scale images of 110 different fingers captured at 500 dpi, resulting in an image size of $256 \times 364$ pixels. Feature vectors **f** were derived containing 1536 entries using methods described in [11–13]. It can be seen that the channel capacity varies between 0.2 and 1.9 bits, with an average of 0.79 bits. Although this clearly is not a scientific proof and the assumption for a Gaussian genuine distribution does not always hold, it gives an intuition why

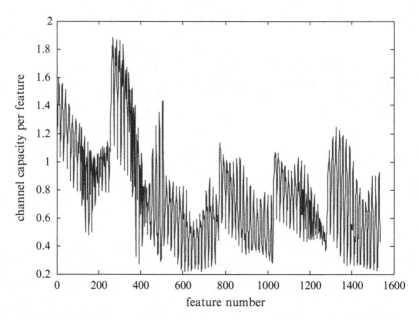

**Fig. 11.9.** Simulation results for the channel capacity for each of 1536 features derived from fingerprint images.

quantizing a feature to a single or a few bits does not necessarily deteriorate the classification results.

The second intuition is related to a phenomenon known as *overtraining*, which might occur when a model is used that has too many parameters compared to the number of training data available. If the redundancy in the parameters is not properly dealt with, the model will not behave well for observations that were not in the training set. As explained in Section 11.1.2, in traditional systems, often an estimate for the high-dimensional probability distributions $p(\mathbf{F}|\omega_I)$ and $p(\mathbf{F}|\omega_G)$ must be obtained using, in general, a limited amount of training data. This might result in inaccurate estimates of the distributions and, thus, in an overtrained and non-optimal classifier. The quantization methods described in Sections 11.5.1–11.5.3 assume that all of the features are independent such that only scalar distributions have to be estimated. Although the assumption of independent features is, in general, not correct, practical simulations show that this assumption can be less severe than assuming that an accurate estimate of distributions is available.

## 11.6 Security and Privacy Considerations

In discussing the privacy and security of biometric systems, *privacy* refers to the required effort to obtain the biometric information of an individual. This is related to the amount of information in the biometric itself (e.g., expressed as the mutual information $\mathbf{I}$ between $\mathbf{z}$ and $\mathbf{z}'$) and the information leakage (or entropy loss) due to the data stored in the biometric system (e.g., $W$ and $W^{(Q)}$ in Fig. 11.4). On the other hand, *security* refers to the required effort to be accepted by a biometric system as a certain individual without having access to the biometric of this individual.

The discussions on the privacy and security of *practical* template-protected biometric systems are mostly complicated by the fact that up until now, little is known about the statistical properties of biometric templates and, in our case, about the binary templates $\mathbf{z}$ derived from feature vectors $\mathbf{f}$ in terms of, for example, Shannon entropy, min-entropy, dependency of the bits in $\mathbf{z}$, and so forth. In several publications, security and privacy bounds are given assuming some (statistical) properties of the binary strings $\mathbf{z}$. If the strings $\mathbf{z}$ are of finite length but independent and identically distributed (i.i.d.), it can be shown [270] that the information leakage equals $nh(p)$, where $h$ is the Shannon entropy function and $p$ is the probability that two corresponding bits in $\mathbf{z}$ and $\mathbf{z}'$ are different. Other authors [90] assume that the probability distribution of the strings $\mathbf{z}$ has a certain min-entropy and give constructions (*secure sketches*) for which the information leakage (entropy loss) of the data stored in the biometric system is bounded by the redundancy in the Error-Correcting Code used in the secure sketch. Under the same assumption, they also derive bounds regarding the number of secure key bits that can be extracted from a biometric measurements.

Unfortunately, in practical biometric systems the assumptions do not hold or it is not known if they hold. Furthermore, known bounds on entropy loss and maximum possible key length are not always tight and this is especially problematic in situations in which sources have limited information content, as is the case with biometrics. This is in contrast to other practical applications such as Physical Unclonable Functions (PUFs) described in Chapters 12 and 13, which can be designed to have a high information content. Therefore, for example, bounds on entropy loss do not necessarily lead to practically relevant results about the entropy that remained in the biometric after observing its secure sketch.

Therefore, first, it is important to further study the properties of the binary strings $\mathbf{z}$ that are derived from biometric measurements. Initial work in [46] estimates min-entropy values for binary strings derived from continuous distributions—for example, obtained by methods discussed in Sections 11.5.1–11.5.3 thus linking real-life continuous biometric distributions to methods like fuzzy extractors. The authors further aim to relate the min-entropy of the strings $\mathbf{z}$ to the FAR, thus formalizing the intuition that the min-entropy of an extracted key (in bits) cannot be larger than $-\log_2(\text{FAR})$.

This last point motivates research into improving the FAR (i.e., the classification results) of biometric systems, especially related to the strings $\mathbf{z}$, at acceptable FRR values. Currently, most biometric modalities (except irises) have EERs in the order of 1% (see, e.g., [187]), which is too high to derive PIN codes, passwords, or keys of sufficient length. Still, it is probably not to be expected that the information content of most biometric modalities is more than, say, 100 bits. This means that tighter bounds are required on entropy loss and maximum achievable key lengths in order to get meaningful results.

## 11.7 Application Examples of Template-Protected Biometric Systems

This section discusses three practical application examples [169] based on the architecture given in Fig. 11.4. In principle, the techniques for template protection only store side information $W$ and but do not store biometric information nor the key that is derived from it. This gives rise to architectures that are different from the architectures when traditional, non-protected biometric systems are used.

### 11.7.1 A Server Access Token

#### Introduction and Problem Definition

Corporate computing is becoming increasingly mobile as can be seen, for example, from an increase in the notebook to desktop shipment ratio of PCs [167]. This means that an increasing number of employees connect to their corporate network from a remote location. Traditionally, access to these corporate networks has been protected using a so-called server access token. These tokens, often implemented as a small keyring device, typically contain a secret key, an accurate time reference, and a small LCD display. Based on the key and the time reference, some (cryptographic) function generates random access codes that appear in the display of the token. The corporate network also knows the secret key, and using an accurate time reference, it can verify if a proper token is used. In combination with a PIN code assigned to the owner of the token, access will be allowed to the corporate network.

In order to increase the convenience of using such a token, biometrics could be used rather than PIN codes. A preferred implementation would be to equip the token with a biometric sensor such that any PC could be used to log onto the corporate network.

A straightforward approach is to store biometric templates in the token, and if the offered biometric is close enough to the reference information, the token will send a random access code derived from the key and the time reference to the display. This approach has the drawback that biometric information and the secret key are stored in the token and both can, in principle, be retrieved by reverse engineering. Another possibility is to attack the point in the device where the decision on the similarity of the stored and measured biometric is made.

The following subsection gives a solution for these problems using Fig. 11.4.

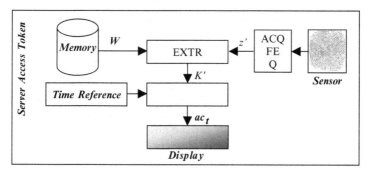

**Fig. 11.10.** Architecture for a secure server access token.

## Deriving the Secret Key from the Biometric

In this subsection, we propose an architecture for securing the server access token using biometrics. The solution is such that neither biometric reference information nor the secret key is stored on the device. In order to obtain a personalized server access token, an employee goes to the corporate IT department, where the following steps are performed (enrollment):

- A biometric (e.g., fingerprint) is measured several times, resulting in a enrollment string $\mathbf{z}$.
- The extractor EXTR internally chooses a random value and generates $W$, which is stored on the token.
- The extractor EXTR generates a key $K$ that is stored in the database of corporate IT. The time reference of the token is synchronized with the reference of corporate IT.

When the employee wants to log onto the corporate network, he puts the proper finger on a sensor on the token and a binary string $\mathbf{z}'$ is obtained (see Fig. 11.10). The token computes $K'$ using $W$ and and $\mathbf{z}'$ and combines this with a time reference to form a random access code $ac_t$ that is shown on the display of the token.

At the moment of log-on, corporate IT combines the stored value $K$ with a local time reference giving an access code $ac_c$. If $\mathbf{z}' \approx \mathbf{z}$, we have $ac_t = ac_c$ and log-on is allowed. The proposed architecture enhances the security of the token because the secret key is not stored on the token but derived from a biometric, thus thwarting a physical attack on the token.

### 11.7.2 Three-Way Check for Biometric ePassport

#### Introduction and Problem Definition

Nowadays, most biometric applications store biometric reference information on a personal smartcard. An example is the Privium system [227] used for automatic border passage at Schiphol Airport; reference information of an iris scan is stored on a personal Privium card.

However, many applications would benefit from storing biometric reference information on a central server or in a centralized database. One of the reasons is that this might lead to more secure applications because not all reference information is placed in the hands of possibly malicious individuals. The International Civil Aviation Organization (ICAO) [149] recently proposed an optional three-way check for the new biometric ePassport, for which a live biometric measurement is not only checked against the information on the passport but also against reference information stored in a database. In many countries, legislation allows storing biometric information in centralized databases provided that (complicated) procedures are put in place regulating access to the stored information. However, public opinion and privacy interest groups still can delay or prevent the use of databases.

In the following subsection we propose an architecture for a three-way check around the biometric ePassport, for which the reference information stored in a database contains no information on the biometric. Although the architecture will be explained for the ePassport, many other applications could benefit from this architecture. One could imagine an aircraft boarding system for which the boarding card contains secure biometric information and for which a three-way check is performed against the passenger list. Another example is a soccer stadium entrance system for which supporters are checked against a list of hooligans.

**Architecture for a Three-Way Check**

The architecture for the three-way check is given in Fig. 11.11, where Kiosk represents the location where a passport is checked. In order to explain the architecture, we assume that when the passport is issued, secure biometric information of the form $(h(K_c), W)$ is stored in the passport and reference information of the form $h(K)$ is stored in a database. A three-way check then proceeds as follows:

- The Kiosk reads $(h(K_c), W)$ from the passport and sends $W$ to the Sensor.
- The Sensor performs a biometric measurement resulting in a binary string $\mathbf{z}'$ and combines this with $W$ to generate a key $K_s$. The hash $h(K_s)$ is sent to the Kiosk.
- If $h(K_s) \neq h(K_c)$, authentication fails, otherwise the individual is considered to be the owner of the passport.
- Next, the Kiosk verifies if $h(K_s)$ is in the database. Depending on the response, the Kiosk allows or denies the individual's access.

Note that $K$ is chosen independently from the biometric measurement $\mathbf{z}$ and, thus, $h(K)$ can reveal no information on $\mathbf{z}$. Clearly, it is possible to add additional information, such as name and address, to a stored value $h(K_i)$, but for the biometric part of the system, this is not required.

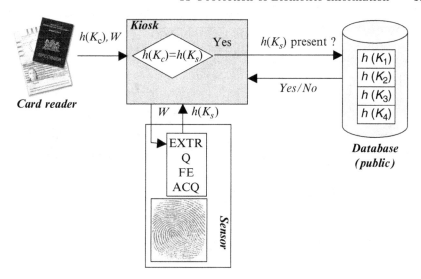

**Fig. 11.11.** Architecture for ePassport three-way check.

Summarizing, we have presented a biometric system in which biometric reference information can be stored in a central database without violating the privacy of individuals.

### 11.7.3 A Secure Password Vault

**Introduction and Problem Definition**

Nowadays, people have to remember a large number of passwords and PIN codes. In addition to PIN codes for bank accounts, the average computer user has to remember several different passwords for access to e-mail, internet accounts, web services, and so forth. Remembering all of these passwords is inconvenient, especially when systems also require passwords to be changed frequently. Moreover, strong passwords are random sequences in which all allowed characters have an equal probability of being used. This, however, makes them inherently hard to remember for humans.

In order to make life easier, a user often chooses passwords that are easy to remember or writes passwords on a piece of paper that is kept close to the log-in terminal. Both methods are insecure: Easy-to-remember passwords can be guessed without much effort and using a piece of paper allows a malicious individual to just read the passwords from the paper such that all of the user's passwords are compromised at once.

We propose to solve these problems by introducing a Secure Password Vault (SPV) that uses biometrics and the architecture of Fig. 11.4.

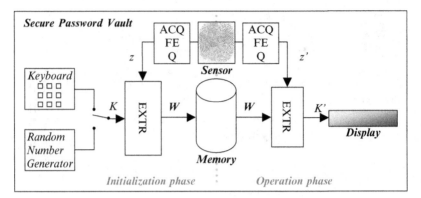

**Fig. 11.12.** Architecture for Secure Password Vault.

## Architecture for a Secure Password Vault

The SPV is a small device that is easily carried by the user and consists of the following components: a biometric sensor (e.g., a fingerprint sensor), a small display for showing a password or PIN to the user, some memory for storing helper data, and a processing unit to process the biometric data that are read from the sensor. Optionally, the SPV contains input means (e.g., a keyboard) allowing the user to choose a password and/or a random generator to generate random passwords. An example architecture of an SPV with keyboard and random generator is given in Fig. 11.12.

The basic idea behind the SPV is that it displays its user's password or PIN code whenever the user presents his biometric to the sensor. This is achieved by storing the appropriate $W$ in the memory of the SPV during the initialization phase, which contains the following steps:

- The user presents his biometric to the sensor (resulting in a binary string $\mathbf{z}$) and enters the desired password $K$ via the keyboard (alternatively, the SPV could use its Random Number Generator to generate a (strong) PIN or password $K$);
- Given $\mathbf{z}$ and $K$, the SPV generates $W$ and stores it in memory (in many practical implementations of Fig. 11.4, it is possible to derive $W$ given $K$ and $\mathbf{z}$).

Clearly, the SPV could also connect to an external device that enrolls the user, computes the appropriate helper data $W$, and stores it in the SPV's memory.

During operation, the user presents his biometric to the sensor and the SPV obtains a string $\mathbf{z}'$. Subsequently, the SPV combines $\mathbf{z}'$ and $W$, resulting in a reconstructed password or PIN code $K'$, and, finally, $K'$ is displayed on the display of the SPV such that the user can read the result.

Note that the actual password $K$ is not stored in the memory of the SPV but is reconstructed from stored information $W$ and an offered biometric, $\mathbf{z}'$.

For any offered biometric, the device will produce a password, but only for the genuine biometric will it generate the correct password.

Obviously, by storing different values $W$ in the SPV, multiple passwords can be retrieved for different applications and the user could select the required password by choosing the application. Finally, as a practical implementation, the SPV could be built into another personal device such as a mobile phone or Personal Digital Assistant (PDA).

## 11.8 Conclusions

In this chapter we described how biometrics can be combined with some of the cryptographic techniques described in Part I of this book. A general architecture was given to derive PIN codes, passwords, or cryptographic keys from (noisy) biometric measurements. An important block in the architecture, the quantizer, was treated in some more detail, and, based on the proposed architecture, some practical application examples were given. A discussion on the privacy and security properties of the general architecture showed that the limited knowledge on the statistical properties of biometrics and the fact that bounds are not always tight makes it hard to give realistic quantative results on privacy and security properties of practical systems. However, with the current classification performance for most biometric modalities, it is not to be expected that that sufficiently long cryptographic keys can be derived. This motivates further research into the (statistical) properties of biometrics, tighter bounds, and better classifications results.

# On the Amount of Entropy in PUFs[©]

Boris Škorić and Pim Tuyls

## 12.1 Introduction

The aim of this chapter is to provide an information-theoretic framework for the analysis of physical unclonable function (PUF) security. We set up this framework and then apply it to optical PUFs and coating PUFs. From the description of PUFs in Chapter 1 some obvious questions arise in the context of the security primitives discussed in Part I.

- How much information does a PUF contain?
- How much of this information can be used for security purposes?
- How hard is it for an attacker to extract enough information to launch an effective attack?
- How do we define a quantitative security parameter?

We address the first two questions by introducing the notions of "intrinsic entropy," "measurement entropy," and "measurable entropy." All of these entropies depend on the random process of creating the PUF. In addition, the latter two also depend on the resolution of measurements. The intrinsic entropy is the entropy of the PUF creation process. The measurement entropy (also referred to as response entropy) gives the lack of knowledge about the outcome of a single (predetermined) measurement. The measurable PUF entropy does the same, but for all possible combinations of "relevant" measurements. By "relevant" we mean those measurements that are relevant for the operation of the security system. For instance, if the installed challenging devices probe PUF structures down to a length scale of a micrometer, then submicrometer measurements are not relevant. Hence, even though a PUF may contain an infinite amount of information, the amount that can actually be used, the measurable entropy, is limited by the resolution of the measurements.

To address the last two questions, we work with the following attack model. The PUF is unprotected, meaning that there is no access control of the type discussed in Chapter 14, but it takes finite time to perform a measurement. The attacker gets hold of the PUF for a finite amount of time. (For instance, while the owner of the PUF is sleeping or otherwise unable to notice the attack.) During this time, the attacker subjects the PUF to as many challenges as he can and stores the Challenge-Response Pairs (CRPs) in a database. He is allowed to do so in an adaptive way. We assume that the attacker has infinite computation power. We say that the attack is successful if the obtained information enables him to predict, with significant probability, the response to a new random challenge.

We define the PUF security parameter $C$ as the maximum number of *independent* CRPs. We call a set of CRPs independent if none of the responses can be predicted, in the information-theoretic sense, from the other CRPs in the set. From the maximum set of independent CRPs, all responses can be predicted in theory. Hence, we have an *information-theoretic* security parameter, representing the minimum number of measurements that is required for the computationally unbounded adversary to extract all measurable entropy from the PUF. (For a computationally bounded adversary, the attack is, of course, much harder, especially if the interactions in the PUF are complex.) Assuming equivalence of all responses, we show that $C$ is given by the ratio of measurable entropy and measurement entropy.

Our framework can be applied to all types of PUF. In Sections 12.3 and 12.4 we analyze the case of optical PUFs and coating PUFs. For optical PUFs, the measurable entropy is easily estimated as the number of "voxels" (wavelength-sized cubes) in the PUF. The response entropy is computed using the waveguide model of multiple scattering and the quantization of light [272]. The security parameter is typically of order $10^4$ per square millimeter of PUF surface.

The situation is completely different for coating PUFs. For one sensor and one challenge frequency, there is only one possible measurement. The measurable entropy is equal to the measurement entropy when there is almost no noise, and $C = 1$. Hence, a coating PUF should never be unprotected, but used as a controlled PUF (see Chapter 14). The extracted key is sometimes referred to as a *physically obfuscated key* (POK). The POK entropy is equal to the measurement entropy. We compute the measurement entropy in a simplified parallel-plate model, where the dielectric particles are cubes on a grid. We distinguish between two cases: noiseless and noisy measurements. In the noiseless case, the measurable entropy is equal to the measurement entropy. We show how to partition the PUF space into equivalence classes of equal capacitances. In the noisy case, the measurement entropy is determined by the signal-to-noise ratio, where the "signal" is the variance of the capacitance. When the particles are made smaller, the measurable entropy grows, but the noisy measurement entropy decreases due to averaging effects. Because of these counteracting trends, there is (at fixed noise power) an optimum particle size where the measurement entropy is maximal. We study this optimal point.

## 12.2 Information-Theoretic Framework

### 12.2.1 Definitions

A PUF can be modeled as a function mapping challenges to responses. The function is parameterized by the physical configuration of the PUF, in the same way that a keyed hash function is parameterized by a key. The internal structure is the result of a stochastic process (e.g., mixing). Hence, we describe the structure by a stochastic variable $K$. The space of all possible PUF configurations is denoted as $\mathcal{K}$. We assume $|\mathcal{K}| < \infty$, even though the space can be very large. The probability measure on $\mathcal{K}$ is denoted as $\eta$:

$$\mathbb{P}[K = k] = \eta_k. \tag{12.1}$$

**Definition 12.1.** *The intrinsic or creation entropy of a PUF with configuration space $\mathcal{K}$ and probability measure $\eta$ is*

$$\mathsf{H}(K) = -\sum_{k \in \mathcal{K}} \eta_k \log \eta_k.$$

The intrinsic entropy is not always a useful concept for security purposes. Many "microstates" $k$ that lie close together are completely equivalent in practice, since the differences are unnoticeable in the macroscopic world. To deal with this, we introduce a formal definition of measurements (see Fig. 12.1).

**Definition 12.2.** *A measurement $M$ is a function on $\mathcal{K}$ giving rise to the partition $\mathcal{K}^M = \{\mathcal{K}_1^M, \mathcal{K}_2^M, \ldots, \mathcal{K}_m^M\}$ of $\mathcal{K}$. Here, $\mathcal{K}_j^M$ is the set in $\mathcal{K}$ containing all PUFs that produce outcome $j$ upon measurement $M$, and $m$ is the number of possible outcomes.*[1]

It is possible to model noise non-stochastically as a modification of the partition $\mathcal{K}^M$. The number of possible outcomes of the measurement is reduced by an amount depending on the noise power. However, it is more usual to model noise as a separate channel through which $M(K)$ is communicated.

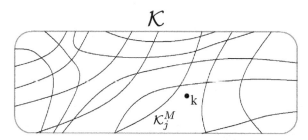

**Fig. 12.1.** Schematic visualisation of the PUF space $\mathcal{K}$ and its partitioning by a measurement $M$. The configuration $k$ gives response $j$ and hence belongs to the region $\mathcal{K}_j^M$.

---

[1] Note that the definition does not depend on the actual outcomes.

**Definition 12.3.** *Let $\eta$ be the probability measure on the PUF configuration space $\mathcal{K}$ and let $M$ be a measurement according to Definition 12.2; then the measurement entropy of $M$ is*

$$\mathsf{H}(M(K)) = -\sum_{j=1}^{m} \eta_j^M \log \eta_j^M,$$

*where we have used the notation*

$$\eta_j^M = \sum_{k \in \mathcal{K}_j^M} \eta_k.$$

Two measurements give more information than one (i.e., a more fine-grained partition of $\mathcal{K}$). The formal notation is as follows.

**Definition 12.4.** *The composition of two measurements $M_1$ and $M_2$ is denoted as $M_1 \vee M_2$ and is defined as the following partition:*

$$\mathcal{K}^{M_1 \vee M_2} = \{\mathcal{K}_i^{M_1} \cap \mathcal{K}_j^{M_2}\}_{i,j=1}^m.$$

By induction, this definition extends to composition of more than two measurements. It is easy to prove the monotonicity property

$$\mathsf{H}\left((M_1 \vee M_2)(K)\right) \geq \mathsf{H}(M_1(K)). \tag{12.2}$$

In particular, we will consider the combination of all PUF challenges that are possible with a certain challenging apparatus. This results in the most fine-grained PUF space partitioning achievable with that apparatus (i.e., the maximum resolving power).

**Definition 12.5.** *Let $\mathcal{M}$ be the set of PUF challenges. The measurable PUF entropy, given that all measurements belong to $\mathcal{M}$, is given by*

$$\mathsf{H}_{\mathcal{M}}(K) := \mathsf{H}(\mathcal{M}(K)) = \sup_{M_1,\ldots,M_q \in \mathcal{M};\ 0 < q \leq |\mathcal{M}|} \mathsf{H}\left((M_1 \vee \cdots \vee M_q)(K)\right).$$

*Here, $\mathcal{M}(K)$ denotes the set of responses to all measurements in $\mathcal{M}$.*

### 12.2.2 Security Parameter for Unprotected PUFs

Our aim is to define an information-theoretic security parameter that indicates how costly an attack is for a computationally unbounded adversary. The PUF is unprotected, but it takes finite time to perform a measurement. The attacker is allowed to measure CRPs adaptively. The attack is considered successful if the obtained information enables him to predict, with significant probability, the response to a new randomly generated challenge.

We define the security parameter $C$ as the minimum number of measurements required to extract all measurable information from a PUF. In order to compute this number, we first determine how much information is revealed by one measurement $M$. This is given by the mutual information between the response and the (measurable) PUF configuration:

$$\mathbf{I}(M(K), \mathcal{M}(K)) = \mathsf{H}(\mathcal{M}(K)) - \mathsf{H}(\mathcal{M}(K)|M(K)) \tag{12.3}$$
$$= \mathsf{H}(\mathcal{M}(K), M(K)) - \mathsf{H}(\mathcal{M}(K)|M(K)) = \mathsf{H}(M(K)).$$

In the second equality, we have used the fact that $\mathcal{M}(K)$ contains $M(K)$. We see that the revealed information is precisely the entropy of the response.

Next, we define *independent measurements* as measurements that reveal independent information about the PUF.

**Definition 12.6.** *Measurements $M_1, \ldots, M_t$ are called mutually independent iff*
$$\mathsf{H}\left((M_1 \vee \cdots \vee M_t)(K)\right) = \mathsf{H}(M_1(K)) + \cdots + \mathsf{H}(M_t(K)).$$

Independent measurements are also called *independent CRPs* since measurements are characterized by their responses in Definition 12.2.

Finally, we make the assumption that all responses reveal the same amount of information. In most PUF setups, all responses in $\mathcal{M}$ are of the same type (e.g., a speckle pattern). Given this symmetry and the PUF's complexity, the assumption is reasonable. It then follows that $\mathsf{H}\left((M_1 \vee \cdots \vee M_t(K)\right) = t \cdot \mathsf{H}(M_1(K))$. The security parameter can now be formulated in terms of independent CRPs:

**Definition 12.7.** *Under the assumption that all responses reveal the same amount of information, the security parameter $C$ of an unprotected PUF with configuration $K$ and challenge set $\mathcal{M}$ is defined as the maximum number of mutually independent CRPs:*
$$C = \frac{\mathsf{H}(\mathcal{M}(K))}{\mathsf{H}(M(K))}.$$

*Here, $M$ is an arbitrary measurement.*

We stress that this parameter is information-theoretic and, hence, independent of the attacker's capabilities. If computational constraints are taken into account, then the attacker may need many more than $C$ measurements, for the following reasons:

- Finding a set of independent CRPs requires computation. In practice, the independent challenges may turn out to be complicated combinations of basic challenges.
- Even after all information $\mathsf{H}(\mathcal{M}(K))$ has been extracted, predicting a response requires computation. Ideally, the PUF and the physical interactions are so complex that this is a difficult problem.

We expect security parameters based on computational complexity to be linear in $C$.

In practice, many mutually *dependent* challenges may be used safely by the verifier. Even if some mutual information exists between the responses, the information is computationally hard to exploit, since that would require a characterization of the physical function. It is not a priori clear how much mutual information between responses can be tolerated before the system becomes insecure, only that the answer depends on the capabilities of the attacker and that the "safe" number of challenges is proportional to $C$.

## 12.3 Information Theory of Optical PUFs

### 12.3.1 Measurable Entropy

Optical PUFs are probed with a laser beam of fixed wavelength $\lambda$, and the responses are speckle patterns. In the terminology of Section 12.2, $\mathcal{M}$ consists of all challenges that an attacker can apply at wavelength $\lambda$ (e.g., beam location, different angles of incidence, and different focal distances). The configuration $K$ represents the locations, orientations, refractive indexes, and so forth of all of the scattering particles in the PUF.

Even though we cannot compute $\mathsf{H}_{\mathcal{M}}(K)$ exactly, we can give a good estimate. By applying all challenges in $\mathcal{M}$ one characterizes the PUF at length scale $\lambda$. Smaller details are hard to resolve [116]. Hence, we can think of the PUF as being a collection of cubes of size $\lambda \times \lambda \times \lambda$, so-called "voxels." We further simplify matters by assuming that a voxel carries only 1 bit of information, namely whether a scatterer is present or not. The measurable entropy is then simply given by the number of voxels, $N_{\mathrm{vox}}$.[2] Taking a slab geometry with area $A$ and thickness $d$, we get

$$\mathsf{H}_{\mathcal{M}}(K) \approx N_{\mathrm{vox}} = \frac{Ad}{\lambda^3}. \tag{12.4}$$

### 12.3.2 Entropy of a Speckle Pattern

We determine the information content $\mathsf{H}(M)$ of a speckle pattern in transmission. We investigate the physics of multiple coherent scattering and speckle formation. Based on the physics, we turn this problem into a counting problem of the distinguishable photon states in the light leaving the PUF.

#### Waveguide Model

The illuminated piece of the PUF can be modeled as a strongly scattering waveguide of thickness $d$, cross section $W^2$, and scattering length $\ell$, satisfying

---

[2] It is possible to refine this model, taking into account the number of photons taking part in the measurement process. This gives rise to an extra factor proportional to the log of the number of photons. We will not discuss this refinement here.

$\lambda \ll \ell \ll d$. The waveguide allows a number of transversal modes $N_{\mathrm{mod}} = \pi W^2/\lambda^2$.[3] Each mode is characterized by a transversal momentum $(k_x, k_y) = 2\pi/W(a_x, a_y)$ with $a_x, a_y \in \mathbb{Z}$ and $k_x^2 + k_y^2 < (2\pi/\lambda)^2$. The angular distance between outgoing modes corresponds to the correlation length present in the speckle pattern as derived in [136]. The scattering process is represented by an $N_{\mathrm{mod}} \times N_{\mathrm{mod}}$ complex random matrix $S$, whose elements map incoming electric field states to outgoing states:

$$\tilde{E}_a^{\mathrm{out}} = \sum_{b=1}^{N_{\mathrm{mod}}} S_{ab} \tilde{E}_b^{\mathrm{in}}. \tag{12.5}$$

The distribution function of $S$ has mode symmetry. We introduce $T_{ab} = |S_{ab}|^2$, the scattering coefficient from mode $b$ to mode $a$, which specifies how much light *intensity* is scattered. This is a natural quantity to study, since the light sensors measure only the light intensity, not the phase. Given a basic challenge, consisting of a single incoming mode $b$, a speckle pattern corresponds to an $N_{\mathrm{mod}}$-component vector $\mathbf{v}(b)$, namely the $b$th column of the $T$ matrix:

$$v_a(b) = T_{ab}. \tag{12.6}$$

Hence, the entropy of the response is given by $\mathsf{H}(\mathbf{v}(b))$. Because of the mode symmetry in the distribution of $S$, the entropy does not depend on $b$. In the more general case where the challenge is a linear combination of basic challenges, one can always perform a unitary transformation on the modes such that the challenge is given by a single mode in the new basis. The response is then a single column of the transformed matrix $S'$. Since $S'$ has the same probability distribution as $S$, the entropy contained in one column of $S'$ is the same as the entropy of one column of $S$. Hence, the entropy of $\mathbf{v}$ (12.6) is the correct result for composite challenges as well.

Given a single incoming mode, the speckle pattern is fully determined by one column of the $S$ matrix. Hence, the question is: How much information is contained in one such column?

We first calculate the speckle pattern entropy in the case where all $S$-matrix elements are independent. This yields an upper bound on $\mathsf{H}(M)$. In this calculation, the finiteness of the speckle pattern entropy is ultimately based on the discretization of light in terms of photons. Then we take correlations between the matrix elements into account to compute a lower bound on $\mathsf{H}(M)$.

**Weak PUFs: Upper Bound on $\mathsf{H}(M)$**

We start with a simplified situation, assuming the outgoing modes to be independent. This is generally not true, but it gives an upper bound on $\mathsf{H}(M)$ and, hence, a lower bound on $C$. For this reason we refer to such a PUF as a *weak* PUF.

---

[3] If polarization is taken into account, the number of modes doubles. We will not consider polarization degrees of freedom.

We estimate the information content of $N_{\mathrm{mod}}$ light intensity states. Although the physics of multiple scattering is classical, we need the quantum description of light in terms of photons for our computation.[4] We have to count the number of *distinguishable* ways in which $N_\varphi$ photons can be distributed over $N_{\mathrm{mod}}$ outgoing modes. To this end, we estimate the number of distinguishable photon states (energy levels) $N_{\mathrm{states}}$ in one mode. The energy in the mode is $Nh/\lambda$,[5] where $N$ is the number of photons in the mode. We restrict ourselves to the case of photon number statistics governed by Poisson statistics, $\mathbb{E}\left[N^2\right] - \mathbb{E}\left[N\right]^2 = \mathbb{E}\left[N\right]$. This Poisson relation holds for lasers and thermal light at room temperature. The more general case is treated in [116]. The energy states have a width of approximately $2\sqrt{N}$. Given the level density $1/(2\sqrt{N})$, the number of distinguishable energy levels with photon number lower than $N$ is

$$N_{\mathrm{states}} \approx \int_0^N \frac{dx}{2\sqrt{x}} = \sqrt{N}. \tag{12.7}$$

The energy level of the $i$th mode is denoted by the integer $L_i$ and the corresponding number of photons by $n_i \approx L_i^2$. We assume that all configurations $\{n_i\}$ have the same probability of occurring, as long as they satisfy the conservation $\sum_i n_i = N_\varphi$. From (12.7) we see that this translates to $\sum_i L_i^2 = N_\varphi$. Hence, the number of distinguishable configurations is given by the area of a section of an $N_{\mathrm{mod}}$-dimensional sphere of radius $\sqrt{N_\varphi}$ (the section with $L_i \geq 0$ for all $i$). The area of an $n$-sphere is $2\pi^{n/2}r^{n-1}/\Gamma(n/2)$. Thus, our upper bound on $\mathsf{H}(M)$ becomes

$$\mathsf{H}_{\mathrm{up}}(M) \approx \log\left[(\tfrac{1}{2})^{N_{\mathrm{mod}}} 2\pi^{N_{\mathrm{mod}}} 2\sqrt{N_\varphi}^{N_{\mathrm{mod}}-1}/\Gamma(\tfrac{1}{2}N_{\mathrm{mod}})\right]. \tag{12.8}$$

Since $N_{\mathrm{mod}}$ is large, we can use Stirling's approximation for the Gamma function and obtain

$$\mathsf{H}_{\mathrm{up}}(M) \approx \tfrac{1}{2}N_{\mathrm{mod}} \log\left(\tfrac{1}{2}\pi e N_\varphi/N_{\mathrm{mod}}\right). \tag{12.9}$$

We have assumed $N_\varphi > N_{\mathrm{mod}}$, so the log in (12.9) is positive. The entropy increases with the number of photons, but only in a logarithmic way. Hence, errors in estimating $N_\varphi$ have a small effect on $\mathsf{H}_{\mathrm{up}}(M)$. The number of participating photons is proportional to the measurement time $\triangle t$:

$$N_\varphi = P\triangle t \cdot \lambda/(hc), \tag{12.10}$$

where $P$ is the laser power and $c$ is the speed of light. In principle, it is possible to completely characterize the PUF by performing a single, very long measurement. However, as seen from (12.9) and (12.10), the information extracted from the PUF is logarithmic in $\triangle t$. Information can be extracted much faster, namely linearly in $\triangle t$, by doing many fast measurements.

---

[4] A similar situation arises in statistical mechanics, where a discretization of classical phase space, based on quantum physics, is used to count the number of microstates.

[5] $h$ denotes Planck's constant.

## Strong PUFs: Lower Bound on $H(M)$

In multiple-scattering PUFs, the modes at the outgoing surface are correlated. In [108], a correlation function was obtained for the elements of the $T$ matrix:

$$\frac{\mathbb{E}\left[\delta T_{ab}\delta T_{a'b'}\right]}{\mathbb{E}\left[T_{ab}\right]\mathbb{E}\left[T_{a'b'}\right]} = D_1\delta_{\triangle\mathbf{q}_a,\triangle\mathbf{q}_b}F_1\left(\frac{d}{2}|\triangle\mathbf{q}_b|\right) \tag{12.11}$$

$$+\frac{D_2}{4gN_{\mathrm{mod}}}\left[F_2\left(\frac{d}{2}|\triangle\mathbf{q}_a|\right) + F_2\left(\frac{d}{2}|\triangle\mathbf{q}_b|\right)\right] + \frac{D_3}{(4gN_{\mathrm{mod}})^2},$$

where $\delta T_{ab} = T_{ab} - \mathbb{E}\left[T_{ab}\right]$, $\mathbb{E}\left[\cdot\right]$ is the average over all scatterer configurations, and

$$F_1(x) = x^2/\sinh^2 x; \quad F_2(x) = 2/(x\tanh x) - 2/\sinh^2 x, \tag{12.12}$$

with $\triangle\mathbf{q}_a = \mathbf{q}_{a'} - \mathbf{q}_a$, $g$ the transmittance $N_{\mathrm{mod}}^{-1}\sum_{ab}T_{ab} \approx \ell/d$, and $D_i$ constants of order unity. Due to the correlations, the number of degrees of freedom $N_{\mathrm{dof}}^{\mathrm{out}}$ in the speckle pattern is less than $N_{\mathrm{mod}}$. We calculate $N_{\mathrm{dof}}^{\mathrm{out}}$ following the approach of [82], but we make use of (12.11). We sum over the correlations in the vector $\mathbf{v}$ to obtain the *effective cluster size* $\mu$. $\mu$ represents the number of variables correlated to a given $v_a$ (for arbitrary $a$). The vector $\mathbf{v}$ can be imagined to consist of uncorrelated clusters of size $\mu$, where each cluster contains exactly one degree of freedom. This means that we approximate $\mathbf{v}$ by a vector of $N_{\mathrm{dof}}^{\mathrm{out}} = N_{\mathrm{mod}}/\mu$ independent cluster-size entries. Denoting the variance of $v_a$ as $\sigma_a$ and neglecting the $D_3$ term, the correlations within $\mathbf{v}$, obtained from (12.11), are given by

$$C_{aa'} = \langle\delta v_a\,\delta v_{a'}\rangle/(\sigma_a\sigma_{a'}) = \delta_{aa'} + D_2/(D_14gN_{\mathrm{mod}})\left[\tfrac{4}{3} + F_2(\tfrac{1}{2}d|q_a - q_{a'}|)\right]. \tag{12.13}$$

The $D_2$ term consists of the sum of a short-range ($F_2$) term and a long-range contribution $(4/3)$. From (12.13) we obtain $\mu$ and the number of degrees of freedom:

$$\mu = \sum_a C_{aa'} \approx \frac{D_2}{3D_1}\frac{d}{\ell}; \quad N_{\mathrm{dof}}^{\mathrm{out}} = \frac{N_{\mathrm{mod}}}{\mu} \approx \frac{3D_1}{D_2}\frac{\pi W^2}{\lambda^2}\frac{\ell}{d}. \tag{12.14}$$

Here, we have neglected the summation over the $F_2$ term, since $F_2(x)$ asymptotically falls off as $2/x$ for large $x$. We have also neglected the contribution $\sum_a \delta_{aa'} = 1$ with respect to $d/\ell$.

The speckle entropy is calculated by repeating the level counting computation of the Weak PUFs subsection, but now with modified parameters. Every output mode within a cluster of size $\mu$ emits exactly the same amount of light. Consequently, the problem of distributing $N_\varphi$ photons over $N_{\mathrm{mod}}$ modes is equivalent to the problem of distributing $N_\varphi/\mu$ bunches of $\mu$ photons over $N_{\mathrm{mod}}/\mu$ clusters. Substituting $\{N_{\mathrm{mod}} \to N_{\mathrm{mod}}/\mu, N_\varphi \to N_\varphi/\mu\}$ into (12.9) we obtain

$$H_{\text{low}}(M) = \frac{N_{\text{dof}}^{\text{out}}}{2} \log \left( \frac{\pi e}{2} \frac{N_\varphi}{N_{\text{mod}}} \right) = \frac{3\pi D_1}{2D_2} \frac{W^2 \ell}{\lambda^2 d} \log \left( \frac{\pi e}{2} \frac{N_\varphi}{N_{\text{mod}}} \right). \quad (12.15)$$

By assuming that several modes carry the same photon state, we have underestimated $N_{\text{dof}}^{\text{out}}$. Therefore, the result (12.15) is indeed a lower bound on $H(M)$. Furthermore, we have assumed that all of the information present in the outcoming light is recorded by an ideal detector, capturing all of the light in a half-sphere surrounding the PUF. This is the optimal situation for an attacker. Hence, we err on the side of safety.

### 12.3.3 The Security Parameter for Optical PUFs

We now use the results of Section 12.3.2 to estimate the security parameter. We have $C = H_{\mathcal{M}}(K)/H(M)$, and after substitution of the upper bound (12.9) and the lower bound (12.15) for $H(M)$, we find that $C$ lies in the interval

$$\left( \min \left\{ \frac{2}{\pi} \cdot \frac{A/W^2}{\log(\pi e/2)(N_\varphi/N_{\text{mod}})} \cdot \frac{d}{\lambda}, \frac{\pi A}{\lambda^2} \right\}, \min \left\{ \frac{2}{3\pi} \cdot \frac{A/W^2}{\log(\pi e/2)(N_\varphi/N_{\text{mod}})} \cdot \frac{d^2}{\lambda \ell}, \frac{\pi A}{\lambda^2} \right\} \right).$$

$$(12.16)$$

The $\min\{\ldots, \pi A/\lambda^2\}$ function reflects the fact that there cannot be more than $N_{\text{mod}} \cdot A/W^2$ basic challenges. The result (12.16) has the following properties:

- $C$ grows with increasing $d/\lambda$, since the PUF entropy is proportional to $d/\lambda$.
- Furthermore, the upper bound on $C$ grows with increasing $d/\ell$. This is a measure for the number of scattering events $N_{\text{sc}}$ taking place before a photon exits the PUF. (Assuming a random walk, $d/\ell \propto \sqrt{N_{\text{sc}}}$.) Hence, multiple scattering increases the cryptographic strength of a PUF.

Finally, we compare our result (12.16) to [221,222]. Their approach is based on the memory angle $\delta\theta \propto \lambda/d$ [108] and does not take the density of scatterers into account. Dividing the half-sphere into pieces of solid angle $\delta\theta^2$, they obtain a number of CRPs proportional to $d^2/\lambda^2$, representing the number of obtainable responses that look mutually uncorrelated. This number is larger than our upper bound for $C$ by a factor $\propto \ell/\lambda$. The two approaches give comparable results only in the limit of extremely strong scattering, $\ell \approx \lambda$.

### Numerical Example

We give example numbers for the optical PUF setup described in Chapter 15 (see Table 12.1). Again, we stress that $C$ is an *information-theoretical* parameter. Thus, although numbers of the order $10^4$ seem low, it is important to realize that identifying those $10^4$ challenges and then exploiting the obtained knowledge will be extremely difficult in practice.

**Table 12.1.** Typical parameter values for an optical PUF

| $\lambda$ | $A$ | $d$ | $N_{\text{vox}}$ | $W$ | $N_{\text{mod}}$ | $\ell$ | $\Delta t$ | $N_\varphi$ | $C_{\text{weak}}$ | $C_{\text{strong}}$ |
|---|---|---|---|---|---|---|---|---|---|---|
| $0.5\,\mu\text{m}$ | $25\,\text{mm}^2$ | $1\,\text{mm}$ | $2 \times 10^{11}$ | $1\,\text{mm}$ | $1 \times 10^7$ | $10\,\mu\text{m}$ | $1\,\text{ms}$ | $3 \times 10^{12}$ | $2 \times 10^3$ | $5 \times 10^4$ |

**Slow and Limited-Challenge PUFs**

We conclude this section with some remarks on how to strengthen unprotected PUFs. In [272], the concept of a "slow PUF" was introduced. The principle is very simple: Construct the PUF in such a way that a measurement inevitably takes a long time to perform. For optical PUFs, this can be realized by making the PUF dark. It takes time to collect enough photons to distinguish between different photon states. An obvious attack is to use a high-power laser, but this attack can be thwarted by choosing materials that degrade under strong illumination.

Another defense was introduced, exploiting the difference between ordinary usage and a brute-force attack[6]: The number of measurements in a brute force attack is orders of magnitude larger than in ordinary day-to-day use. A structure that degrades a little each time it is challenged will remain intact if used normally, but it will be destroyed by a brute force attack. In the case of Optical PUFs this is easily implemented. The PUF has to be shielded off between measurements, and a material should be chosen that slowly degrades when illuminated.

## 12.4 Information Theory of Coating PUFs

We introduce a model of a coating PUF measurement at one location in the sensor array by describing each sensor as a parallel-plate capacitor. The geometry is simplified, but the effects of finite particle size are incorporated, as well as the insensitivity of the capacitance to particle permutations.

Using our model, we compute the measurable entropy. It turns out that the measurable entropy scales as $\sqrt{n}(\ln n)^{3/2}$, with $n$ the number of particles that fits linearly between the capacitor plates. We also compute the measurement entropy for noisy measurements. It is determined by the ratio of capacitance variance to noise power.

There are two counteracting effects at work. On the one hand, smaller particle size leads to higher measurable entropy. On the other hand, smaller particles imply better mixing, which leads to a reduced variance of the capacitance. (This is a "law of large numbers" effect proportional to $1/\sqrt{\#\text{particles}}$). The latter puts a lower bound on the useful particle size, since a large capacitance variance is needed in order to obtain a good signal-to-noise ratio. We

---

[6] Here, a brute-force attack is an attempt to measure a large fraction of all possible CRPs.

derive an optimum particle size (at fixed noise power) that yields the highest measurement entropy. In the regime of noisy measurements, the measurement entropy is largest if (1) the relative dielectric constants of the two coating materials differ strongly and (2) the mixture contains only a small fraction of the substance with the low dielectric constant, namely of the order of the ratio of the two constants.

If the measurement noise $\Delta$ is very small, of the order 1/(density of states), individual capacitance states may be resolved. The density of states has a sharp peak, but the capacitances most likely to be measured lie outside this peak. Hence, if $\Delta$ is made so small that individual states can just be resolved, one enters into a regime where the finite density of states limits the measurement entropy, while the measurement entropy is still far smaller than the measurable entropy. This complicates the analysis, but we show that it only leads to logarithmic corrections.

### 12.4.1 The Model

For the sake of simplicity, we model the sensor wires and the coating above them (Fig. 15.1 in Chapter 15) as an ordinary capacitor consisting of two parallel electrode plates with a dielectric substance between them. This simplification will, of course, fail to represent the spatially varying electric field produced by the wires. However, we are interested only in the statistical properties of particle distributions within the region that contains most of the electric field density. As a first approximation, we idealize the geometry of the field.

As a first step, we study the capacitor shown in Fig. 12.2a, a parallel-plate capacitor filled with layers $1, \ldots, n$ of equal thickness $a/n$ with dielectric constants $\varepsilon_1, \ldots, \varepsilon_n$, respectively. It is well known (see, e.g., [138]) that its capacitance is given by

$$C_{n \text{ layers}} = C_{\text{ref}} \cdot \left( \frac{1}{n} \sum_{s=1}^{n} \frac{1}{\varepsilon_s} \right)^{-1} ; \quad C_{\text{ref}} = \frac{A\varepsilon_0}{a}, \tag{12.17}$$

where $A$ is the plate area, $\varepsilon_0$ is the permittivity of the vacuum, and $C_{\text{ref}}$ is the capacitance of the system with vacuum between the plates, which we will use as a reference value throughout this chapter. The result (12.17) has several invariance properties. A reordering of the layers does not change the capacitance. Additionally, $C$ remains unchanged even if we split up a layer, so that we have more than $n$ layers, and then reorder. In fact, as long as we make changes in the vertical direction only, the capacitance depends just on the average value of $1/\varepsilon$.

As a second step, we look at the capacitor shown in Fig. 12.2b, with $m$ columns of different dielectric material. This capacitor can, in good approximation, be considered as $m$ parallel components; hence, its total capacitance is the sum of the parts:

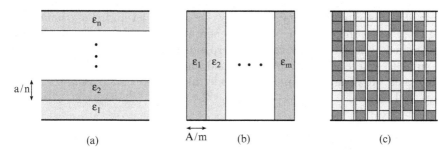

**Fig. 12.2.** Motivation of the model. **(a)** A capacitor consisting of several dielectric layers parallel to the plates. **(b)** Dielectric columns perpendicular to the plates. **(c)** Combination of layers and columns. The volume between the plates is filled with random dielectric building blocks.

$$C_{m \text{ columns}} = C_{\text{ref}} \cdot \frac{1}{m} \sum_{j=1}^{m} \varepsilon_j. \tag{12.18}$$

We observe that only the average dielectric constant matters. This leads us to the construction of our model (see Fig. 12.2c). Between the plates there is a mixture of two substances that have different dielectric constants $\varepsilon_1$ and $\varepsilon_2$. Without loss of generality, we will always assume that $\varepsilon_2 < \varepsilon_1$.

The volume is discretized: There are $m$ columns of $n$ "voxels." We will always assume that $n \gg 1$ and $m \gg 1$. When the mixture is produced, the probability that a voxel will be occupied by substance 1 is denoted as $p$, and the probability of having substance 2 is $q = 1 - p$. The intrinsic entropy according to Definition 12.1 is given by $mn \cdot (-p \log p - q \log q)$. However, the measurable entropy is much smaller, since capacitance measurements give the same response for many microstates.

The number of voxels in the $j$th column that ends up filled with substance 1 is denoted as $N_j$. Writing the total capacitance as a sum of parallel column capacitances, we have

$$C = \sum_{j=1}^{m} C_j; \qquad C_j = \frac{C_{\text{ref}}}{m} \cdot n \left( \frac{N_j}{\varepsilon_1} + \frac{n - N_j}{\varepsilon_2} \right)^{-1}. \tag{12.19}$$

Note that $C$ is invariant under swaps of complete columns and under voxel shifts within a column.

For convenience later on, we introduce the following notation. The number of columns containing precisely $k$ particles of substance 1 ($k = 0, \ldots, n$) is denoted as $\alpha_k$. The set $\{\alpha_k\}$ satisfies $\sum_{k=0}^{n} \alpha_k = m$, since the total number of columns is $m$. The capacitance is then expressed as

$$C = \sum_{k=0}^{n} \alpha_k \chi_k; \qquad \chi_k = \frac{C_{\text{ref}}}{m} \cdot n \left( \frac{k}{\varepsilon_1} + \frac{n - k}{\varepsilon_2} \right)^{-1}. \tag{12.20}$$

Note that discrepancies may arise between our model and the geometry of Fig. 15.1 when the dielectric constants become very large. In our model, the electric field lines are forced to move perpendicular to the plates, through the "columns," whereas in Fig. 15.1, the field lines are free to avoid the coating altogether. However, we expect our model to be useful for reasonable values of $\varepsilon_1$ and $\varepsilon_2$.

### 12.4.2 The Density of States

First, we examine the density of states (d.o.s.) in our model. The d.o.s. is the number of states that exist per infinitesimal interval on the capacitance axis, and we will denote it as $D(C)$. The total number of capacitance values in the model is given by the number of points in the $\alpha$-lattice; that is, the number of ways to partition $m$ into $n+1$ non-negative integers, where the ordering is important:

$$N_{\text{states}} = \sum_{\alpha_0=0}^{m} \sum_{\alpha_1=0}^{m-\alpha_0} \cdots \sum_{\alpha_{n-1}=0}^{m-\alpha_0-\cdots-\alpha_{n-2}} 1 = \binom{n+m}{n}. \tag{12.21}$$

The d.o.s. must satisfy $\int_{C_{\text{ref}}\varepsilon_2}^{C_{\text{ref}}\varepsilon_1} D(C)\, dC = N_{\text{states}}$. The states are distributed non-uniformly over the $C$-axis. In [286], the shape of $D(C)$ was estimated based on a *typical set* argument. The highest concentration of states occurs at $C = C_{\text{peak}}$. For symmetry reasons, this point occurs when all the $\alpha_k$ are equal (i.e., $\alpha_k = m/(n+1)$ for all $k$). The corresponding capacitance $C_{\text{peak}}$ is given by

$$C_{\text{peak}} \approx \frac{C_{\text{ref}}}{\varepsilon_2^{-1} - \varepsilon_1^{-1}} \ln \frac{\varepsilon_1}{\varepsilon_2}. \tag{12.22}$$

Here, terms of relative order $1/n$ have been neglected, as $n \gg 1$. In the vicinity of this peak, the d.o.s. turns out to have an almost Gaussian distribution with variance $\Sigma$:

$$\Sigma^2 \approx \Gamma^2 \frac{1}{n} \cdot \left\{ C_{\text{ref}}^2 \varepsilon_1 \varepsilon_2 - C_{\text{peak}}^2 \right\}, \tag{12.23}$$

where $\Gamma$ is a constant of order unity. Figure 12.3 shows that (12.23) has good correspondence with simulation results. However, the typical set approximation is only valid close to the peak. The tails of the d.o.s. are not Gaussian.

### 12.4.3 The Probability Distribution of the Capacitance

Without loss of generality, we assume that the ratio $\varepsilon_2/\varepsilon_1$ is chosen such that the numbers $\{\chi_k\}$ are rationally independent; that is, for all pairs $(k,l)$, we have $\chi_k/\chi_l \notin \mathbb{Q}$. In this way, the mapping from $\{\alpha_k\}$ to $C$ is bijective; that is, the capacitance is uniquely determined by the set $\{\alpha_k\}$. This means that the probability distribution of $C$ is equivalent to the probability distribution

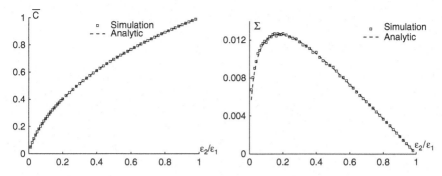

**Fig. 12.3.** Density of states for $n = 180$, $m = n$. **Left:** Location of the peak as a function of $\varepsilon_2/\varepsilon_1$. **Right:** Width of the peak as a function of $\varepsilon_2/\varepsilon_1$. The squares are numerical simulation results. The dashed curve in the left graph corresponds to (12.22). The dashed curve in the right graph is the estimate (12.23) with $\Gamma = 0.9$. All capacitances have been expressed in units of $C_{\text{ref}}\varepsilon_1$.

of $\{\alpha_k\}$. The latter is obtained as follows. First, we introduce the notation $x_k$ for the probability of finding $k$ voxels with substance 1 in a given column. This is the binomial distribution

$$x_k = \binom{n}{k} p^k q^{n-k}. \tag{12.24}$$

Then we note that the total probability of a configuration $\{\alpha_k\}$ is a multiplication of probabilities $x_k$, one for each column. Finally, the capacitance is invariant under column permutations; hence, the number of such permutations must be taken into account. This brings us to the following expression:

$$P_\alpha = \binom{m}{\alpha} \prod_{k=0}^{n} x_k^{\alpha_k}; \qquad \binom{m}{\alpha} = \frac{m!}{\alpha_0! \cdots \alpha_n!}. \tag{12.25}$$

Here, we have used the shorthand notation $\alpha = \{\alpha_k\}$ with the implicit constraint $\sum_{k=0}^{n} \alpha_k = m$. It is easily verified that the probabilities $P_\alpha$ add up to unity using the following general identity (see, e.g., [241]):

$$\sum_\alpha \binom{m}{\alpha} \prod_{k=0}^{n} Y_k^{\alpha_k} = (Y_0 + \cdots + Y_n)^m. \tag{12.26}$$

A useful identity (for the computation of moments) can be derived from (12.26) by taking the derivative $\partial/\partial Y_s$ and multiplying by $Y_s$:

$$\sum_\alpha \alpha_s \binom{m}{\alpha} \prod_{k=0}^{n} Y_k^{\alpha_k} = m Y_s (Y_0 + \cdots + Y_n)^{m-1}. \tag{12.27}$$

### 12.4.4 Measurable Entropy of a Coating PUF

**Analytic part of the calculation**

The measurable entropy of a coating PUF in our model is given by the Shannon entropy of the distribution (12.25). We denote this entropy as $H_\alpha$. The first steps can be done analytically. We start by expanding $\ln P_\alpha$:

$$H_\alpha = -\sum_\alpha P_\alpha \ln P_\alpha = -\sum_{k=0}^n \ln x_k \sum_\alpha P_\alpha \alpha_k - \sum_\alpha P_\alpha \ln \binom{m}{\alpha}. \quad (12.28)$$

The $\alpha$-sum in the first right-hand-side term is evaluated using the identity (12.27) with $Y_k \to x_k$, yielding $\sum_\alpha P_\alpha \alpha_k = m x_k$. Rewriting the logarithm of the multinomial in the last term as a sum of logarithms, we get

$$H_\alpha = -m \sum_{k=0}^n x_k \ln x_k - \ln m! + \sum_{k=0}^n \sum_\alpha P_\alpha \ln(\alpha_k!). \quad (12.29)$$

All three terms in (12.29) have a combinatorial interpretation. The first term is $m$ times the entropy of the binomial distribution $x_k$. This represents the measurement entropy of $m$ separate *distinguishable* columns. (Note that the capacitance measurement in our model does not "see" the locations of columns.)

The second term is the entropy of permuting the $m$ columns. The third term is the average entropy of permuting only those columns that have the same filling value $k$, for all $k$ separately. The second and third terms together represent the average entropy of the $\binom{m}{\alpha}$ distinct column configurations that are consistent with a given set $\alpha$.

The last term in (12.29) can be further evaluated. The $\alpha$-sum averages a quantity that depends only on one component, $\alpha_k$, of the set $\alpha$. Hence, the average with respect to the probability $P_\alpha$ can be replaced by the average with respect to the marginal distribution $P_{\alpha_k}$ of the component $\alpha_k$:

$$H_\alpha = -m \sum_{k=0}^n x_k \ln x_k - \ln m! + \sum_{k=0}^n \sum_{\alpha_k=0}^m P_{\alpha_k} \ln(\alpha_k!). \quad (12.30)$$

The marginal distribution was derived in [286] and is given by

$$P_{\alpha_k} = \binom{m}{\alpha_k} x_k^{\alpha_k} (1 - x_k)^{m-\alpha_k}. \quad (12.31)$$

Note that $P_{\alpha_k}$ is a binomial distribution corresponding to $\alpha_k$ out of $m$ events with base probability $x_k$. This is what one would intuitively expect. As $x_k$ itself is a binomial in $k$, we have "nested" binomial distributions.

## Approximation

Eq. (12.30) is hard to evaluate exactly. However, we can obtain a good approximation for $n \gg 1$, $m \gg \sqrt{n}$. (We remind the reader that $m \propto n$ in the 2-D case and $m \propto n^2$ in the 3-D case). We make use of the fact that both binomial distributions $P_{\alpha_k}$ and $x_k$ are sharply peaked, and that $x_k$ can be approximated by a Normal distribution $\mathcal{N}_{np,\sigma}(k)$ in the vicinity of its peak, with $\sigma = \sqrt{npq}$. Furthermore, we define a constant $c$ and an interval $I_c = (np - c\sigma, np + c\sigma)$ such that $mx_k > 1$ for $k \in I_c$. The details of the calculation are given in [286]. The result is

$$\mathsf{H}_\alpha \approx \tfrac{1}{3}c^3\sigma + c\sigma \ln\sqrt{2\pi} + 3\sigma/c; \qquad c = f\sqrt{\ln\frac{m^2}{2\pi npq}}, \qquad (12.32)$$

where $f$ is a numerical constant of order 1. Figure 12.4 shows that the approximation is quite accurate.

There is an intuitive way of understanding the scaling $\mathsf{H}_\alpha \propto c^3\sigma$. The entropy is approximately the log of the number of lattice points in the $\alpha$-configuration lattice that carry substantial probability. The probability is concentrated around a sharp peak at $\mathbb{E}\,[\alpha_k] = mx_k$. In each of the $n + 1$ dimensions, the standard deviation is $\sqrt{mx_k}$. However, in most of these

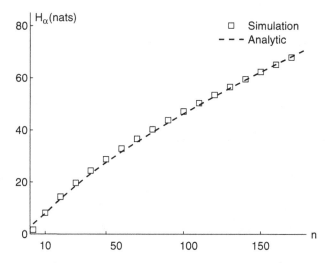

**Fig. 12.4.** Measurable entropy of a capacitor for $m = n$, $p = \frac{1}{2}$. The squares show the result of numerical evaluation of (12.30). The dotted curve is the approximation (12.32) with $f = 1.27$. The entropy is expressed in "natural units", that is, the logarithm with base $e$ is used.

dimensions, $\sqrt{mx_k}$ is far less than one lattice point; hence, these hardly contribute to the entropy. In the contributing dimensions ($k \in I_c$), the standard deviation is of order $\sqrt{mx_{np}}$. Since $|I_c| = 2c\sigma$, we then get $\mathsf{H}_\alpha \propto \ln(\sqrt{mx_{np}})^{2c\sigma} \approx c\sigma \ln(m/\sqrt{n}) \approx c^3\sigma$.

In the case of a 2-D capacitor, $m \propto n$, where the proportionality constant depends on the length and the width of the capacitor. In the 3-D case, $m$ will scale as $m \propto n^2$. In both cases, we have $\ln m \propto \ln n$ and, therefore, $\mathsf{H}_\alpha$ scales as

$$\mathsf{H}_\alpha \propto \sqrt{n}(\ln n)^{3/2}. \tag{12.33}$$

This equation for the entropy $\mathsf{H}_\alpha$ is the main result of this section.

### 12.4.5 Entropy of a Noisy Measurement

In the case of a noisy measurement, the noise is larger than the effects caused by the finiteness of the particle size. For all intents and purposes, the capacitance can be treated as a continuous variable (i.e., a stochastic variable $C$ with a smooth probability distribution function $\rho(C)$). In order to obtain reproducible measurements in spite of the noise, the $C$-axis is divided into bins of size $\Delta$, where $\Delta$ is chosen proportional to the noise amplitude.

The entropy $\mathsf{H}^\Delta[\rho]$ of the thus discretized distribution is given by (see, e.g., [66])

$$\mathsf{H}^\Delta[\rho] = h[\rho] - \ln \Delta, \tag{12.34}$$

where we have introduced the differential entropy $h[\rho] = -\int dC\rho(C) \ln \rho(C)$. If the noise level is reduced, $h[\rho]$ remains constant, but the term $-\ln \Delta$ grows, and hence $\mathsf{H}^\Delta$ grows. If the noise is made very small, the dielectric particle size becomes noticeable and (12.34) becomes invalid. Then one has to use the results of Section 12.4.4.

The differential entropy $h[\rho]$ is readily estimated. In [286], the average capacitance $\mu_c$ and the variance $\sigma_c$ were estimated for the model of Section 12.4.1 and the capacitance distribution $P_\alpha$ was estimated by (12.25). For $n \gg 1$, the result is

$$\mu_c \approx \frac{C_{\text{ref}}}{p\varepsilon_1^{-1} + q\varepsilon_2^{-1}}; \quad \sigma_c \approx C_{\text{ref}}\sqrt{\frac{pq}{nm}} \cdot \frac{|\varepsilon_1^{-1} - \varepsilon_2^{-1}|}{(p\varepsilon_1^{-1} + q\varepsilon_2^{-1})^2}. \tag{12.35}$$

Figure 12.5 compares (12.35) to numerical simulations. The error in $\sigma_c$ is 2%, and the error in $\mu_c$ is 0.2%.

Note that $\sigma_c$ is a *decreasing* function of $n$ and $m$. This can be understood as follows. When the number of random particles between the plates is large, the probability of deviating from the average value $\mathbb{E}[k] = np$ is small for all columns. A finer-mixing process allows for a better approximation of perfectly uniform mixing of the two substances.

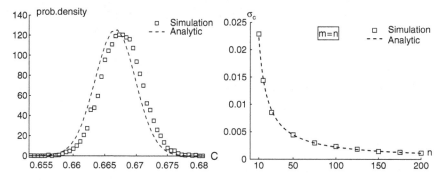

**Fig. 12.5. Left:** Probability distribution of the capacitance. **Right:** $\sigma_c$ as a function of $n$. The dotted line represents the estimate (12.35). The squares show the statistical result of $10^4$ randomly generated fillings. The parameters are $m = n = 70$, $p = \frac{1}{2}$, $\varepsilon_2 = \varepsilon_1/2$, and capacitances have been normalized wrt $C_{\text{ref}}\varepsilon_1$.

If the capacitance distribution is sharply peaked ($\sigma_c/\mu_c \ll 1$), then we can replace it with a Gaussian distribution without much loss of accuracy. The differential entropy of the Gaussian distribution $\mathcal{N}_{\mu_c,\sigma_c}$ is given by [66]:

$$h[\mathcal{N}_{\mu_c,\sigma_c}] = \ln(\sigma_c\sqrt{2\pi e}).  \quad (12.36)$$

Combining (12.34) and (12.36), we can write the entropy of the discretised distribution as

$$\mathsf{H}^{\Delta}[\rho] = \ln(\frac{\sigma_c}{\Delta}\sqrt{2\pi e}).  \quad (12.37)$$

This equation has the form of a channel capacity for a noisy channel with signal-to-noise ratio $(\sigma_c/\Delta)^2$.

### 12.4.6 Optimal Choice of Parameters

Our aim is to determine which choice of parameters $n$, $m$, $\varepsilon_1$, $\varepsilon_2$, and $p$ gives the highest measurement entropy for fixed noise $\Delta$. First, we try a naive approach based only on (12.37). Then we refine it, taking into account the density of states. We introduce the notation $\varepsilon := \varepsilon_2/\varepsilon_1 \ll 1$ and $C_{\text{max}} := C_{\text{ref}}\varepsilon_1$. We normalize all capacitances with respect to $C_{\text{max}}$.

### Naive Approach

The expression for the noisy measurement entropy (12.37) suggests that we have to increase $\sigma_c$ as much as possible. The result (12.35) can be written as

$$\frac{\mu_c}{C_{\text{max}}} \approx \frac{\varepsilon}{q + p\varepsilon}; \quad \frac{\sigma_c}{C_{\text{max}}} \approx \sqrt{\frac{pq}{nm}}\frac{\varepsilon}{(q + p\varepsilon)^2}.  \quad (12.38)$$

For fixed $n$, $m$, and $\varepsilon$, we choose $q$ such that $\sigma_c$ is maximal. In doing this, we have to satisfy $q > 1/(nm)$, otherwise there is no substance 2 present. There are two regimes, yielding different results:

1. The case $\varepsilon \ll 1/(nm)$. The optimal choice is to take $q$ as small as possible. We have $p \approx 1$ and $q \gg p\varepsilon$, yielding

$$\frac{\mu_c}{C_{\max}} \approx \frac{\varepsilon}{q}; \qquad \frac{\sigma_c}{C_{\max}} \approx \frac{\varepsilon}{q^{3/2}\sqrt{nm}}. \tag{12.39}$$

2. The case $\varepsilon \gg 1/(nm)$. In this case, it is possible to make $q$ so small that it no longer dominates the term $p\varepsilon$. The optimal choice is $q = \tau\varepsilon$, with $\tau$ a constant, yielding

$$\frac{\mu_c}{C_{\max}} \approx \frac{1}{1+\tau}; \qquad \frac{\sigma_c}{C_{\max}} \approx \frac{\sqrt{\tau}(1+\tau)^{-2}}{\sqrt{nm\varepsilon}}. \tag{12.40}$$

Case 2 is clearly more favorable than case 1. Next, for fixed $\varepsilon$ and freely choosable $n$ and $m$, we set $nm = G/\varepsilon$, with $G$ a large constant. This makes sure that case 2 applies, yielding $\sigma_c/C_{\max} \approx \sqrt{\tau}(1+\tau)^{-2}/\sqrt{G}$. Finally, the optimal choice for $\varepsilon$ is to make $\varepsilon$ as small as possible, since this results in a large $C_{\max}$.

### Why the Naive Approach Does Not Work

Setting $q = \mathcal{O}(\varepsilon)$ is problematic because the measurable entropy $\mathsf{H}_\alpha$ in (12.32) vanishes. This is seen as follows. Assuming we are in the regime $m \gg \sqrt{n}$ (necessary for the derivation of (12.32)), we have $m \propto n^\gamma$, with $\gamma > 1/2$. Then the above-mentioned choice $nm = G/\varepsilon$ implies $n \propto \varepsilon^{-1/(1+\gamma)}$. As $\mathsf{H}_\alpha$ is proportional to $\sqrt{npq}$, the asymptotic behavior of $\mathsf{H}_\alpha$ is

$$\mathsf{H}_\alpha \propto \varepsilon^{\gamma/(2+2\gamma)} \times \{\text{logarithmic corrections}\}. \tag{12.41}$$

Hence, for $\varepsilon \ll 1$, the measurable entropy is vanishingly small, even though (12.37) gives a high measurement entropy.

The discrepancy arises from the fact that in deriving (12.37), we implicitly assumed that the density of states around $C = \mu_c$ is high; that is, that within each interval of width $\Delta$, there exists at least one state. Expressed more formally, the assumption is $D(\mu_c) > 1/\Delta$. For small $q$, the assumption does not hold. From (12.23) and (12.22) we see that almost all states are concentrated in a small region of width $\mathcal{O}(\sqrt{\varepsilon/n})$ around $C/C_{\max} \approx \varepsilon \ln \varepsilon^{-1}$. When $q$ is made so small as to become of order $\varepsilon$, (12.40) shows that the capacitance interval $C \in (\mu_c - \sigma_c, \mu_c + \sigma_c)$ relevant for the entropy computation lies far outside the high-d.o.s. region. Even though the width $\sigma_c$ can be made large, there are almost no states, and hence no probability mass, around $\mu_c$.

## Taking the Density of States into Account

Eq. (12.37) does not take the d.o.s. into account, but (12.32) does. For $q \ll 1$, the correct expression for the measurement entropy is the smallest of the two:

$$H = \min \{F_1, F_2\}, \tag{12.42}$$

with

$$F_1 = \ln \frac{C_{\mathrm{ref}} \varepsilon_2 \sqrt{2\pi e}}{\Delta \sqrt{mn q^{3/2}}}; \quad F_2 = \tfrac{1}{3} f^3 \sqrt{nq} \left(\ln \frac{m^2}{2\pi nq}\right)^{3/2}. \tag{12.43}$$

Note that $F_1$ is a decreasing function of $q$, $n$, and $m$, whereas $F_2$ is increasing. Clearly, there is an optimum where the measurement entropy reaches its largest value; there the two expressions are equal. The aim is to set that point of equality to a value that is as high as possible.

We briefly comment on the optimization, without going into full detail. First, we observe that, in practice, $m$ and $n$ are almost always coupled. When the particle size is changed, $m$ and $n$ change simultaneously. We write $m = Bn^\gamma$ with $\gamma > 1/2$ and $B$ a constant of order 1. Given this coupling, the measurement entropy (12.42) at fixed geometry ($C_{\mathrm{ref}}$), choice of dielectrics ($\varepsilon_2$ and $\varepsilon_1 \gg \varepsilon_2$) and noise ($\Delta$) is a function of $n$ and $q$. An example is plotted in Fig. 12.6 for $\gamma = 2$, corresponding to a 3-D geometry. Clearly, there is a "ridge" where the entropy is highest, corresponding to $F_1 = F_2$. On this ridge, the entropy varies very slowly. This is due to the fact that $F_1$ depends logarithmically on $n$ and $q$. The largest entropy is obtained at large $n$. Having chosen optimal $n$ and $q$, one has a choice of dielectrics. Note that $\varepsilon_1$ (with $\varepsilon_1 \gg \varepsilon_2$) has completely dropped out of (12.43). $F_1$ is improved by increasing $\varepsilon_2$. Hence, it is advantageous to choose $\varepsilon_2$ as large as possible, provided that the inequality $\varepsilon_1 \gg \varepsilon_2$ still holds.

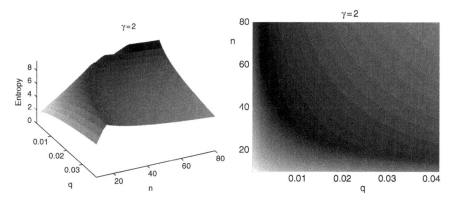

**Fig. 12.6.** The measurement entropy (12.42), with $m = n^2$, as a function of $q$ and $n$, for $C_{\mathrm{ref}} \varepsilon_2 \sqrt{2\pi e}/\Delta = 10^3$. We have set $f = 1$. Dark shades represent high entropy.

# 13

# Entropy Estimation for Optical PUFs Based on Context-Tree Weighting Methods©

Tanya Ignatenko, Frans Willems, Geert-Jan Schrijen, Boris Škorić, and Pim Tuyls

In this chapter we discuss estimation of the secrecy rate of fuzzy sources—more specifically of optical physical unclonable functions (PUFs)—using context-tree weighting (CTW) methods [291]. We show that the entropy of a stationary 2-D source is a limit of a series of conditional entropies [6] and extend this result to the conditional entropy of one 2-D source given another one. Furthermore, we show that the general CTW-method approaches the source entropy also in the 2-D stationary case. Moreover, we generalize Maurer's result [196] to the ergodic case, thus showing that we get realistic estimates of the achievable secrecy rate. Finally, we use these results to estimate the secrecy rate of speckle patterns from optical PUFs.

## 13.1 Generating a Shared Secret Key

Consider a source that generates sequences of random variables from a finite alphabet. A shared secret key can be produced by two terminals if these terminals observe dependent sequences and at least one of the terminals is allowed to transmit a message to the other one. Although the transmitted message is public, it needs not reveal information about the secret key that is generated. This concept was described by Maurer [196] when he realized that the secrecy capacity of a broadcast channel could be significantly enhanced if a public feedback link from the (legitimate) receiver to the transmitter was present. A little later, Ahlswede and Csiszár [4] investigated similar problems and called the situation, in which the terminals observe dependent sequences, the source-type model; see Fig. 13.1. There, an encoder

---

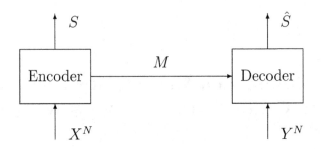

**Fig. 13.1.** Generating a shared secret key. © 2006 IEEE

forms a secret $S$ after observing a sequence $X^N = (X_1, X_2, \ldots, X_N)$ of symbols from the finite alphabet $\mathcal{X}$. The encoder sends a public helper-message $M \in \mathcal{M} = \{1, 2, \ldots, |\mathcal{M}|\}$ to a decoder. The decoder observes the sequence $Y^N = (Y_1, Y_2, \ldots, Y_N)$ of symbols from the finite alphabet $\mathcal{Y}$ and produces an estimate $\hat{S}$ of the secret $S$ using the helper-message $M$. It was assumed in [196] and [4] that the sequence pair $(X^N, Y^N)$ is independent and identically distributed (i.i.d.); that is, $\mathbb{P}[X^N = x^N, Y^N = y^N] = \prod_{n=1}^{N} Q(x_n, y_n)$ for some distribution $\{Q(x, y), x \in \mathcal{X}, y \in \mathcal{Y}\}$.

In the described model, the terminals want to produce as much key information as possible. The probability that the estimated secret $\hat{S}$ is not equal to the secret $S$ should be close to zero and the information that the helper-message reveals about the secret should also be negligible. Finally, we are interested in the number of helper-message bits that are needed. More formally, a secrecy rate $R_s$ is achievable if for all $\varepsilon > 0$, for all large enough $N$, there exist encoders and decoders such that

$$\mathsf{H}(S) \geq N(R_s - \varepsilon),$$

$$\mathbf{I}(S; M) \leq N\varepsilon, \tag{13.1}$$

$$\mathbb{P}[\hat{S} \neq S] \leq \varepsilon.$$

**Theorem 13.1.** *The largest possible achievable secrecy rate $R_s$ is equal to $\mathbf{I}(X; Y)$. Moreover, for all $\varepsilon > 0$, for all large enough $N$ a helper rate*

$$\frac{1}{N} \log_2 |\mathcal{M}| \leq \mathsf{H}(X|Y) + \varepsilon \tag{13.2}$$

*suffices to achieve $R_s = \mathbf{I}(X; Y)$. Both $\mathbf{I}(X; Y)$ and $\mathsf{H}(X|Y)$ are based on the joint distribution $\{Q(x, y), x \in \mathcal{X}, y \in \mathcal{Y}\}$.*

For a detailed proof of Theorem 13.1, see [196] and [4]. Here, we only provide a sketch. The achievability proof relies on random binning of the space $\mathcal{X}^N$ (i.e., partitioning the set of typical $X^N$-sequences into codes for the channel from $X$ to $Y$). There are roughly $2^{N\mathsf{H}(X|Y)}$ such codes. The index of the code containing $x^N$ is sent to the decoder. All of these codes contain approximately $2^{NI(X;Y)}$ codewords. The decoder now uses $y^N$ to recover $x^N$. If we define the secret to be the index of $x^N$ within the code, the code-index reveals practically no information about this index.

## 13.2 Physical Unclonable Functions

Measured responses from PUFs, which were already discussed in Chapters 1 and 12, are a good example of dependent random sequences. A typical PUF-based authentication and key-agreement protocol involves an enrollment measurement of a challenge response pair (CRP) and a verification measurement of the same CRP. (See Chapter 16.) Since these measurements are separated in time, and often performed using different hardware, there is inevitably some measurement noise, caused, for example, by differences in temperature, moisture, and calibration. We identify the enrollment response with the sequence $X^N$ in Fig. 13.1, and the verification response with the sequence $Y^N$.

The Maurer scheme guarantees that the helper data reveal only a negligible amount of information about the extracted key. There is no guarantee, on the other hand, that the information revealed about the PUF response $X^N$ is also small. This may pose a problem that an attacker could mimic or reproduce the PUF based on the information leaked from helper data. However, the unclonability properties of the PUF prevent this attack. Therefore, PUFs are very suitable as a source of common randomness for the Maurer scheme.

In this chapter we concentrate on optical PUFs. This type of PUF consists of a transparent material with randomly distributed scatterers. Different challenges are obtained by shining a laser beam under different angles onto the PUF. These challenges lead to speckle patterns (responses) that are recorded by a camera. We have analyzed data that was acquired with the experimental setup described in Section 15.3.1 and the glass samples of Section 15.3.2. For this setup, the measurement noise is mainly caused by inaccuracies in repositioning the samples. We have investigated five PUFs (labeled "A," "B," "C," "D," and "E"), and for each of these five PUFs, we have considered two challenges (laser angles, labeled "0" and "1"). We mapped each speckle pattern to a 2-D binary image by Gabor filtering and thresholding as proposed by Pappu [221]; see Section 16.5. Each of the 10 challenges resulted in two binary images: an enrollment image **X** and a verification image **Y**. Our aim is to find out how much secret key information can be extracted from the image pairs (**X**,**Y**) and how this matches the results obtained with the algorithm described in Section 16.4.

## 13.3 Entropy of a Two-Dimensional Stationary Process

In order to find out how large the mutual information is between an enrollment image and a verification image for optical PUFs, we consider the 2-D process

$\{X_{v,h} : (v, h) \in \mathbb{Z}^2\}$ (also called random field) and assume that it is stationary (homogeneous); that is,

$$\mathbb{P}[X_{\mathcal{T}} = x_{\mathcal{T}}] = \mathbb{P}[X_{\mathcal{T}+(s_v, s_h)} = x_{\mathcal{T}}], \tag{13.3}$$

for any template $\mathcal{T}$, any shift $(s_v, s_h)$, and any observation $x_{\mathcal{T}}$. A template is a set of coordinate-pairs (i.e., $\mathcal{T} \subset \mathbb{Z}^2$). Moreover, $\mathcal{T}+(s_v, s_h)$ denotes the set of coordinate pairs resulting from a coordinate pair from $\mathcal{T}$, to which the integer shift pair $(s_v, s_h)$ is added. We assume that all symbols take values from the finite alphabet $\mathcal{X}$. If we first define, for positive integers $L$,

$$\mathsf{H}_{(L)}(X) \triangleq \frac{1}{L^2} \mathsf{H} \begin{pmatrix} X_{1,1} & \cdots & X_{1,L} \\ \vdots & \ddots & \vdots \\ X_{L,1} & \cdots & X_{L,L} \end{pmatrix}, \tag{13.4}$$

then the entropy of a 2-D stationary process can be defined[1] as

$$\mathsf{H}_{(\infty)}(X) \triangleq \lim_{L \to \infty} \mathsf{H}_{(L)}(X). \tag{13.5}$$

It follows from the stationarity of the stochastic process $X$, the chain rule for entropies, and the fact that conditioning can only decrease entropy that

$$N\mathsf{H} \begin{pmatrix} X_{1,1} & \cdots & X_{1,N+1} \\ \vdots & \ddots & \vdots \\ X_{M,1} & \cdots & X_{M,N+1} \end{pmatrix} - (N+1)\mathsf{H} \begin{pmatrix} X_{1,1} & \cdots & X_{1,N} \\ \vdots & \ddots & \vdots \\ X_{M,1} & \cdots & X_{M,N} \end{pmatrix}$$

$$= N\mathsf{H} \begin{pmatrix} X_{1,N+1} & X_{1,1} & \cdots & X_{1,N} \\ \vdots & \vdots & \ddots & \vdots \\ X_{M,N+1} & X_{M,1} & \cdots & X_{M,N} \end{pmatrix} - \mathsf{H} \begin{pmatrix} X_{1,1} & \cdots & X_{1,N} \\ \vdots & \ddots & \vdots \\ X_{M,1} & \cdots & X_{M,N} \end{pmatrix}$$

$$\leq 0. \tag{13.6}$$

**Lemma 13.1.** *The limit defined in relation (13.5) exists.*

**Proof.** Using inequality (13.6) for $(M, N) = (L, L)$ and, subsequently, a transposed version of this inequality for $(M, N) = (L, L + 1)$, it follows that $\mathsf{H}_{(L+1)}(X) - \mathsf{H}_{(L)}(X) \leq 0$. Hence, the sequence $\mathsf{H}_{(L)}(X)$ is a non-increasing non-negative sequence in $L$. This concludes the proof.

The definition of entropy in relation (13.5) focuses on block entropies. We will show next that the entropy of a stationary 2-D process can also be expressed as a limit of conditional entropies. To this end, we define the conditional entropy

$$G_{(L)}(X) \triangleq \mathsf{H}(X_{L,L} | X_{1,1}, \ldots, X_{1,2L-1}, \ldots, X_{L,1}, \ldots, X_{L,L-1}). \tag{13.7}$$

A visualization of this definition is presented in Fig. 13.2.

---

[1] In information theory the entropy of a stationary process is usually denoted by $\mathsf{H}_\infty(X)$. However, in cryptography this notation is used for min-entropy. Therefore, to avoid confusion we use the notation $\mathsf{H}_{(\infty)}(X)$.

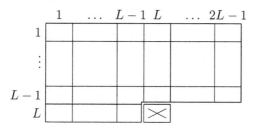

**Fig. 13.2.** The symbol $X_{L,L}$ and the symbols on which it is conditioned in relation (13.7). © 2006 IEEE

**Lemma 13.2.** *The limit*

$$G_{(\infty)}(X) \triangleq \lim_{L \to \infty} G_{(L)}(X) \tag{13.8}$$

*exists.*

**Proof.** From stationarity and the fact that conditioning never increases entropy, it follows that the sequence $G_{(L)}(X)$ is non-increasing in $L$. Since $G_{(L)}(X) \geq 0$, the proof follows.

In order to demonstrate that the limits (13.5) and (13.8) are equal, we first observe (using the chain rule, stationarity, and the fact that conditioning never increases entropy) that

$$\mathsf{H}_{(L)}(X) = \frac{1}{L^2} \sum_{v=1}^{L} \sum_{h=1}^{L} \mathsf{H}(X_{v,h}|X_{1,1}, \ldots, X_{1,L}, \ldots, X_{v,1}, \ldots, X_{v,h-1})$$
$$\geq G_{(L)}(X). \tag{13.9}$$

On the other hand, it follows (using similar arguments) that

$$\mathsf{H}_{(j+2L-2)}(X) \leq \frac{\mathsf{H}(\sqcap) + j(j+L-1)G_{(L)}(X)}{(j+2L-2)^2}, \tag{13.10}$$

where $\mathsf{H}(\sqcap)$ corresponds to all the symbols in the horseshoe region; see Fig. 13.3. These observations yield

$$\mathsf{H}_{(\infty)}(X) = \lim_{j \to \infty} \mathsf{H}_{(j+2L-2)}(X) \leq G_{(L)}(X). \tag{13.11}$$

**Theorem 13.2.** *The limits* $\mathsf{H}_{(\infty)}(X)$ *and* $G_{(\infty)}(X)$ *are equal; that is,*

$$G_{(\infty)}(X) = \mathsf{H}_{(\infty)}(X). \tag{13.12}$$

**Proof.** Follows directly from (13.9) and (13.11).

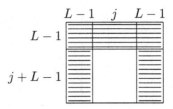

**Fig. 13.3.** Horseshoe region in a square of size $(j + 2L - 2)^2$. © 2006 IEEE

Our arguments are a generalization of the arguments for (1-D) stationary sources that can be found in Gallager [119]. Moreover, they are only slightly different from those given by Anastassiou and Sakrison [6], who first showed that in the 2-D case, the block-entropy limit equals the conditional-entropy limit.

We conclude that the entropy of a 2-D stationary process can be computed by considering the conditional entropy of *a single symbol* given more and more neighboring symbols.

## 13.4 Conditional Entropy of a Two-Dimensional Stationary Process Given a Second One

Next, we consider the 2-D joint process $\{XY_{v,h} : (v, h) \in \mathbb{Z}^2\}$. We assume that it is stationary; that is,

$$\mathbb{P}[XY_{\mathcal{T}} = xy_{\mathcal{T}}] = \mathbb{P}[XY_{\mathcal{T}+(s_v,s_h)} = xy_{\mathcal{T}}], \qquad (13.13)$$

for any template $\mathcal{T}$, any shift $(s_v, s_h)$, and any observation $xy_{\mathcal{T}}$. Again, we assume that the $X$ symbols and $Y$ symbols take values from the finite alphabets $\mathcal{X}$ and $\mathcal{Y}$, respectively.

We may consider the joint entropy $\mathsf{H}_{(\infty)}(XY)$ of the joint process $XY$ and then obviously Theorem 13.2 holds. We can then compute this joint entropy by considering conditional entropies.

It also makes sense to look at the conditional entropy $\mathsf{H}_{(\infty)}(X|Y)$ and to find out whether a theorem similar in style to Theorem 13.2 can be proved for this situation. This turns out to be possible if we define, for positive integers $L$,

$$\mathsf{H}_{(L)}(X|Y) \triangleq \frac{1}{L^2} \mathsf{H} \begin{pmatrix} X_{1,1} & \cdots & X_{1,L} & Y_{1,1} & \cdots & Y_{1,L} \\ \vdots & \ddots & \vdots & \vdots & \ddots & \vdots \\ X_{L,1} & \cdots & X_{L,L} & Y_{L,1} & \cdots & Y_{L,L} \end{pmatrix} \qquad (13.14)$$

and define the conditional entropy of a 2-D joint stationary process $XY$ as

$$\mathsf{H}_{(\infty)}(X|Y) \triangleq \lim_{L \to \infty} \mathsf{H}_{(L)}(X|Y). \qquad (13.15)$$

We first observe that since conditioning never increases entropy, the following inequality holds

$$
\mathsf{H}\begin{pmatrix} X_{1,1} & \cdots & X_{1,L} & Y_{1,1} & \cdots & Y_{1,L+1} \\ \vdots & \ddots & \vdots & \vdots & \ddots & \vdots \\ X_{L,1} & \cdots & X_{L,L} & Y_{L+1,1} & \cdots & Y_{L+1,L+1} \end{pmatrix} \leq \mathsf{H}\begin{pmatrix} X_{1,1} & \cdots & X_{1,L} & Y_{1,1} & \cdots & Y_{1,L} \\ \vdots & \ddots & \vdots & \vdots & \ddots & \vdots \\ X_{L,1} & \cdots & X_{L,L} & Y_{L,1} & \cdots & Y_{L,L} \end{pmatrix}.
$$

$$(13.16)$$

**Lemma 13.3.** *The limit in relation (13.15) exists.*

***Proof.*** The proof that the sequence $\mathsf{H}_{(L)}(X|Y)$ is non-increasing in $L$ follows from arguments similar to the ones used to show that $\mathsf{H}_{(L)}(X)$ is non-increasing (see proof of Lemma 13.1) and from inequality (13.16).

In order to demonstrate that the conditional entropy $\mathsf{H}_{(\infty)}(X|Y)$ can be expressed as a limit of entropies of a *single symbol* conditioned on surrounding $X$ symbols and $Y$ symbols, we define

$$
G_{(L)}(X|Y) \overset{\Delta}{=} \mathsf{H}(X_{L,L}|X_{1,1},\ldots,X_{1,2L-1},\ldots,X_{L,1},\ldots,X_{L,L-1},
$$
$$
\ldots,Y_{1,1},\ldots,Y_{2L-1,2L-1}). \tag{13.17}
$$

For a visualization, we refer to Fig. 13.4.

**Lemma 13.4.** *The limit*

$$
G_{(\infty)}(X|Y) \overset{\Delta}{=} \lim_{L\to\infty} G_{(L)}(X|Y) \tag{13.18}
$$

*exists.*

***Proof.*** It is easy to see that $G_{(L+1)}(X|Y) \leq G_{(L)}(X|Y)$ using arguments as in the proof of Lemma 13.2, from which the proof follows.

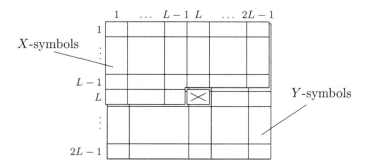

**Fig. 13.4.** The symbol $X_{L,L}$ and its conditioning symbols. Note that the $X$ symbols are drawn on top of a square with the $Y$ symbols.

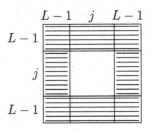

**Fig. 13.5.** Edge region in a square of size $(j + 2L - 2)^2$. © 2006 IEEE

In order to demonstrate that the limits (13.15) and (13.18) are equal, we observe that (according to the same arguments as used for relations (13.9) and (13.10))

$$\mathsf{H}_{(L)}(X|Y) \geq G_{(L)}(X|Y), \tag{13.19}$$

$$\mathsf{H}_{(j+2L-2)}(X|Y) \leq \frac{H(\square) + j^2 G_{(L)}(X|Y)}{(j + 2L - 2)^2}, \tag{13.20}$$

where $H(\square)$ corresponds to the $X$ symbols in the edge region; see Fig. 13.5. Hence, we obtain

$$\mathsf{H}_{(\infty)}(X|Y) = \lim_{j \to \infty} \mathsf{H}_{(j+2L-2)}(X|Y) \leq G_{(L)}(X|Y). \tag{13.21}$$

**Theorem 13.3.** *The limits* $\mathsf{H}_{(\infty)}(X|Y)$ *and* $G_{(\infty)}(X|Y)$ *are equal; that is,*

$$G_{(\infty)}(X|Y) = \mathsf{H}_{(\infty)}(X|Y). \tag{13.22}$$

***Proof.*** The proof follows from relations (13.19) and (13.21).

We conclude that, in the stationary case, also the conditional entropy of one 2-D process $X$ given a second 2-D process $Y$ can be computed by considering the conditional entropy of a single $X$ symbol given more and more "causal" neighboring $X$ symbols, and more and more "non-causal"[2] neighboring $Y$ symbols.

## 13.5 Mutual Information Estimation: Convergence

We estimate the mutual information $\mathbf{I}_{(\infty)}(X;Y)$ either by estimating $\mathsf{H}_{(\infty)}(X)$, $\mathsf{H}_{(\infty)}(Y)$, and $\mathsf{H}_{(\infty)}(XY)$ or by estimating $\mathsf{H}_{(\infty)}(X)$ and $\mathsf{H}_{(\infty)}(X|Y)$ (or, equivalently $\mathsf{H}_{(\infty)}(Y)$ and $\mathsf{H}_{(\infty)}(Y|X)$) using CTW methods. CTW is a

---

[2] "Causal" symbols are past symbols, whereas "non-causal" symbols might be both future and past symbols with respect to a certain symbol.

universal data compression method that achieves optimal redundancy behavior for tree sources. It weights the coding distributions corresponding to all bounded memory tree source models and realizes an efficient coding distribution for unknown models with unknown parameters. This weighted distribution can be used for sequential data compression. In a sequential scheme, the codeword is constructed by processing the source symbols one after the other.

The basic CTW method was proposed [293]. In [294], it was shown how to deal with more general context structures (which is necessary to determine, e.g., $H_\infty(X|Y)$). In [291], it was shown that the CTW method approaches entropy in the 1-D ergodic case. The following theorem applies to the 2-D case.

**Theorem 13.4.** *For joint processes $XY$, the general CTW method achieves entropy $H_{(\infty)}(XY)$, as well as $H_{(\infty)}(X)$ and $H_{(\infty)}(Y)$, and conditional entropies $H_{(\infty)}(X|Y)$ and $H_{(\infty)}(Y|X)$ in the 2-D ergodic case.*

**Proof.** From Theorems 13.2 and 13.3 we conclude that we can focus on conditional entropies of a single symbol (or pair of symbols). These are the entropies that the CTW method achieves when the observed image gets larger and larger and more and more context symbols become relevant. It is important to use the right ordering of the context symbols. Therefore, the symbols for $L = 2$ should be included first, then those for $L = 3$, and so on. The rest of the proof is similar to that in [291].

## 13.6 The Maurer Scheme in the Ergodic Case

Section 13.1 contains the theorem on the amount of secret-key material that can be generated from a pair of correlated sequences in the i.i.d. setting. The coding strategy outlined there is actually Slepian-Wolf coding [256], as was observed by Ahlswede and Csiszár [4]. Cover [67] proved that the Slepian-Wolf result does not only hold for i.i.d. sequences, but it carries over to the ergodic case. Therefore, we can generalize Theorem 13.1 to the ergodic case; see Theorem 13.5. Using the ideas of Cover, one can prove achievability. The converse given by Maurer [196] also applies to the ergodic case.

**Theorem 13.5.** *Theorem 13.1 also holds for the ergodic case if we replace $I(X;Y)$ by $I_{(\infty)}(X;Y) = H_{(\infty)}(X) + H_{(\infty)}(Y) - H_{(\infty)}(XY)$ and $H(X|Y)$ by $H_{(\infty)}(X|Y) = H_{(\infty)}(XY) - H_{(\infty)}(Y)$.*

## 13.7 Context-Tree Weighting Methods

Consider a source that has produced a sequence $\ldots, x_{t-2}, x_{t-1}$ so far. Then at time $t$, this source generates a new symbol $x_t$. The context for this symbol $x_t$ in the basic context-tree method [293] consists of the previous $D$ symbols $x_{t-D}, \ldots, x_{t-2}, x_{t-1}$. For our purposes we need more flexibility in choosing the context symbols, however. This flexibility is provided in [294], where four weighting methods are described. Here, we consider the two simplest classes— class IV and class III. To be more specific, we denote the context symbols for symbol $x_t$ by $z_{t1}, z_{t2}, \ldots, z_{tD}$. Observe that each of these symbols could be any symbol available at both the encoder and decoder while encoding/decoding $x_t$; for example, the basic context-tree method corresponds to the assignment $z_{td} = x_{t-d}$. On the other hand, if there is a "side-information" sequence $y^N$ available, then we could take $z_{td} = y_{t+d-1}$, but also combinations of both past $x$ symbols and past and/or future $y$ symbols are possible.

In a class IV method, it is assumed that the actual probability of the next symbol $x_t$ being 1 is based on the first $d$ context symbols $z_{t1}, z_{t2}, \ldots, z_{td}$, where $d$ depends on the context $z_{t1}, z_{t2}, \ldots, z_{tD}$ that occurred; for example, if the source model corresponds to the tree in Fig.13.6(a) and the context $z_{t1}, z_{t2}, \ldots, z_{tD}$ at time $t$ is $011\epsilon \ldots \epsilon$, the probability $\theta_{011}$ of the next symbol $x_t$ being 1 can be found in the leaf 011. We have denoted a "don't care" context symbol by $\epsilon$ here. The subscript 011 refers to the values 0, 1, and 1 of the context symbols $z_{t1}$, $z_{t2}$, and $z_{t3}$, respectively.

Class III models can also be described using a tree. However, the ordering of the context symbols is not fixed as in class IV. For a source model corresponding to the tree in Fig.13.6(b), when the context $z_{t1}, z_{t2}, \ldots, z_{tD}$ at time $t$ is $\epsilon 001\epsilon \ldots \epsilon$, the probability $\theta_{010}^{243}$ of the next symbol $x_t$ being 1 can be found in leaf 010. Note that the superscript 243 denotes the context ordering; that is, first $z_{t2}$ is used, then $z_{t4}$, and, finally, $z_{t3}$. The subscript 010 now refers to the values 0, 1, and 0 of these context symbols $z_{t2}$, $z_{t4}$, and $z_{t3}$, respectively.

Context-weighting methods are based on splitting up the observations corresponding to the nodes in a data structure. In class IV methods, this splitting is done by first splitting according to the first context symbol, then splitting is done using the second context symbol, and so on; see Fig. 13.6(a). In class

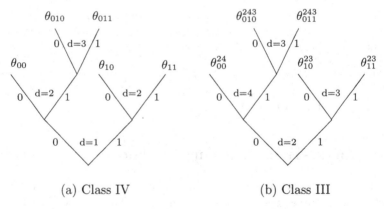

(a) Class IV                    (b) Class III

**Fig. 13.6.** Example of class IV and class III models.

III, each splitting operation can be performed according to all of the context symbols that have not been used in previous splittings; see Fig. 13.6(b).

For both model classes, a CTW encoder (implicitly) specifies the context structure and corresponding parameters to a decoder. This results in an increased codeword length or redundancy. The redundancy based on the parameter specification is called parameter redundancy. Specifying the context structure leads to model redundancy. It will be clear that class III methods are more general than class IV methods. Since they adapt better to the source, the performance of class III methods should therefore be better. Indeed the so-called parameter redundancy is smaller for class III than for class IV, but since class III is richer than class IV, its model redundancy is also larger. It depends on the length of the source sequence which of the two effects will dominate. For small lengths, class IV methods will outperform the class III method. For large lengths, the effect of model redundancy becomes negligible and a class III method gives a smaller codeword length.

## 13.8 Analysis of Speckle Patterns

We use the methods that were described in the previous sections to estimate the mutual information between noisy speckle measurements. From [108] it is known that the two-point intensity correlations in a speckle pattern are translation invariant. Therefore, we may conclude that a speckle pattern can be modeled as a stationary process. Moreover, the process is also ergodic due to the statistical properties of speckle patterns; namely the spatial distribution of intensities is the same as the PUF ensemble distribution of intensities [136]. Therefore, the methods given in the previous sections are applicable.

The secrets are extracted from pre-processed speckle patterns. Pre-processing includes Gabor filtering at 45°, thresholding, and subsampling (see Section 16.5). As $\mathbf{X}$- and $\mathbf{Y}$-sequences we use $64 \times 64$ binary images. An example of a pair $\mathbf{X}, \mathbf{Y}$ is depicted in Fig. 13.7. We observe that the enrollment and verification images differ slightly due to the measurement noise. Moreover, we see that application of a 45° Gabor filter results in diagonal stripes. These stripes are caused by the high Gabor component correlations perpendicular to the direction of the filter [287]. Since the correlation decreases with distance, it is natural to consider positions for context candidates as shown in Fig. 13.8. This template turns out to have a good balance between performance and complexity. We have also considered a larger template. However, using this larger template did not lead to smaller entropy estimates. We can calculate mutual information with two alternative formulas: either by estimating it as $\mathbf{I}_{(\infty)}(X;Y) = \mathsf{H}_{(\infty)}(X) + \mathsf{H}_{(\infty)}(Y) - \mathsf{H}_{(\infty)}(XY)$ or as $\mathbf{I}_{(\infty)}(X;Y) = \mathsf{H}_{(\infty)}(X) - \mathsf{H}_{(\infty)}(X|Y)$. Note that for each of the entropies involved in the formulas, we have to compress an image (or a pair of images) using a CTW method. In what follows we describe in more detail the analysis that we have conducted.

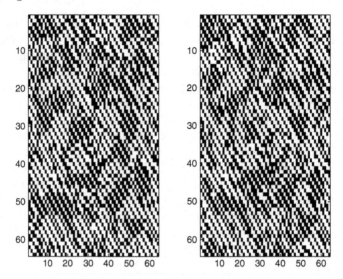

**Fig. 13.7.** Images **X** (left) and **Y** (right) resulting from experiment A0 with Gabor angle $\varphi = 45°$. © 2006 IEEE

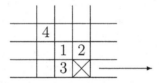

**Fig. 13.8.** Template showing four context symbols and their ordering. Note that the ordering is only important for class IV. The arrow indicates the direction in which the image is processed.

### 13.8.1 Class IV Analysis

1. The basic approach that we have used is based on the template shown in Fig. 13.8. This template contains four context positions. Using the class IV method, we have determined codeword lengths $\lambda(X)$ and $\lambda(Y)$ and the joint codeword length $\lambda(XY)$. Note that $\lambda(XY)$ results from compressing a quaternary image, since both symbols in a $XY$ symbol pair are binary. Using the symmetric mutual information formula, we computed a mutual information estimate for each of the 10 experiments ("A0," "A1," "B0," etc.). Table 13.1(a) lists these estimates in the column labeled "bas." Table 13.2(a) shows the results for the corresponding entropy estimates $\widehat{H}(X)$, $\widehat{H}(Y)$, and $\widehat{H}(XY)$. The mutual information averaged over the 10 experiments turns out to be 0.2911 bit/pixel. Figure 13.9 shows the codeword lengths for experiment A0.

**Table 13.1.** Mutual information estimates

| Exp | bas | sym | sym+lar | sym+con |
|-----|-----|-----|---------|---------|
| (a) Class IV | | | | |
| A0 | 0.2236 | 0.2224 | 0.2231 | 0.2469 |
| A1 | 0.3348 | 0.3393 | 0.3386 | 0.3586 |
| B0 | 0.2782 | 0.2825 | 0.2824 | 0.3075 |
| B1 | 0.2664 | 0.2722 | 0.2731 | 0.2769 |
| C0 | 0.3271 | 0.3408 | 0.3368 | 0.3567 |
| C1 | 0.2735 | 0.2834 | 0.2794 | 0.2919 |
| D0 | 0.3233 | 0.3310 | 0.3293 | 0.3407 |
| D1 | 0.2951 | 0.3078 | 0.3046 | 0.3183 |
| E0 | 0.2699 | 0.2742 | 0.2748 | 0.2869 |
| E1 | 0.3192 | 0.3203 | 0.3193 | 0.3378 |
| Ave. | 0.2911 | 0.2974 | 0.2961 | 0.3122 |
| Std. | 0.0352 | 0.0374 | 0.0365 | 0.0369 |

| | | | | |
|-----|-----|-----|---------|---------|
| (b) Class III | | | | |
| A0 | 0.2288 | 0.2211 | 0.2246 | 0.2522 |
| A1 | 0.3394 | 0.3414 | 0.3416 | 0.3644 |
| B0 | 0.2851 | 0.2899 | 0.2906 | 0.3127 |
| B1 | 0.2666 | 0.2704 | 0.2759 | 0.2837 |
| C0 | 0.3384 | 0.3458 | 0.3403 | 0.3670 |
| C1 | 0.2763 | 0.2816 | 0.2786 | 0.2964 |
| D0 | 0.3252 | 0.3313 | 0.3292 | 0.3447 |
| D1 | 0.2990 | 0.3068 | 0.3043 | 0.3236 |
| E0 | 0.2770 | 0.2778 | 0.2784 | 0.2935 |
| E1 | 0.3285 | 0.3228 | 0.3240 | 0.3463 |
| Ave. | 0.2964 | 0.2989 | 0.2987 | 0.3184 |
| Std. | 0.0363 | 0.0385 | 0.0366 | 0.0376 |

2. The second approach is based on the assumption that the statistics of binarized Gabor-filtered speckle patterns are symmetric; that is, the probability of a binary symbol $x$ given context $c_1, c_2, c_3,$ and $c_4$ is the same as the probability of $1 - x$ given $1 - c_1, 1 - c_2, 1 - c_3,$ and $1 - c_4$, respectively. There are good reasons for this assumption. Although the statistics of the original, unfiltered speckle pattern are not symmetric under dark↔bright reversal (due to the exponential intensity distribution [136]), the binarization of the Gabor coefficients discards most of the asymmetry-related effects.

The symmetry assumption reduces the number of parameters that need to be handled by the CTW method and, therefore, should result in more reliable estimates of the entropy and, consequently, more reliable estimates of the mutual information. From comparison of the column "sym" and column "bas" in Table 13.2(a) we conclude that the symmetry assumption

**Table 13.2.** Entropy estimates

| Exp | $\widehat{H}(X)$ bas | sym | sym+lar | $\widehat{H}(Y)$ bas | sym | sym+lar | $\widehat{H}(XY)$ bas | sym | sym+lar | $\widehat{H}(X|Y)$ sym |
|---|---|---|---|---|---|---|---|---|---|---|
| | | | | | (b) Class IV | | | | | |
| A0 | 0.5194 | 0.5125 | 0.5135 | 0.5241 | 0.5181 | 0.5193 | 0.8198 | 0.8081 | 0.8097 | 0.2656 |
| A1 | 0.5213 | 0.5142 | 0.5154 | 0.5189 | 0.5119 | 0.5126 | 0.7054 | 0.6868 | 0.6895 | 0.1557 |
| B0 | 0.5289 | 0.5216 | 0.5229 | 0.5284 | 0.5217 | 0.5230 | 0.7791 | 0.7609 | 0.7635 | 0.2141 |
| B1 | 0.5188 | 0.5122 | 0.5126 | 0.5219 | 0.5161 | 0.5170 | 0.7743 | 0.7561 | 0.7565 | 0.2353 |
| C0 | 0.5238 | 0.5173 | 0.5166 | 0.5116 | 0.5056 | 0.5041 | 0.7083 | 0.6822 | 0.6839 | 0.1606 |
| C1 | 0.5404 | 0.5339 | 0.5327 | 0.5384 | 0.5321 | 0.5318 | 0.8053 | 0.7826 | 0.7851 | 0.2420 |
| D0 | 0.5305 | 0.5253 | 0.5246 | 0.5273 | 0.5228 | 0.5236 | 0.7345 | 0.7171 | 0.7190 | 0.1846 |
| D1 | 0.5260 | 0.5192 | 0.5188 | 0.5194 | 0.5126 | 0.5117 | 0.7503 | 0.7241 | 0.7259 | 0.2009 |
| E0 | 0.5291 | 0.5223 | 0.5235 | 0.5346 | 0.5285 | 0.5294 | 0.7938 | 0.7767 | 0.7780 | 0.2355 |
| E1 | 0.5492 | 0.5420 | 0.5423 | 0.5296 | 0.5232 | 0.5234 | 0.7596 | 0.7449 | 0.7465 | 0.2042 |
| Ave. | 0.5287 | 0.5221 | 0.5223 | 0.5254 | 0.5193 | 0.5196 | 0.7630 | 0.7439 | 0.7458 | 0.2098 |
| Std. | 0.0096 | 0.0096 | 0.0093 | 0.0079 | 0.0080 | 0.0085 | 0.0390 | 0.0412 | 0.0411 | 0.0358 |
| | | | | | (a) Class III | | | | | |
| A0 | 0.5177 | 0.5113 | 0.5136 | 0.5219 | 0.5167 | 0.5187 | 0.8108 | 0.8068 | 0.8077 | 0.2591 |
| A1 | 0.5196 | 0.5133 | 0.5157 | 0.5163 | 0.5103 | 0.5116 | 0.6965 | 0.6823 | 0.6857 | 0.1488 |
| B0 | 0.5270 | 0.5207 | 0.5234 | 0.5270 | 0.5208 | 0.5234 | 0.7688 | 0.7516 | 0.7562 | 0.2080 |
| B1 | 0.5171 | 0.5114 | 0.5123 | 0.5208 | 0.5156 | 0.5176 | 0.7713 | 0.7566 | 0.7541 | 0.2276 |
| C0 | 0.5223 | 0.5166 | 0.5174 | 0.5100 | 0.5045 | 0.5040 | 0.6939 | 0.6753 | 0.6811 | 0.1496 |
| C1 | 0.5395 | 0.5332 | 0.5331 | 0.5365 | 0.5310 | 0.5312 | 0.7997 | 0.7826 | 0.7857 | 0.2368 |
| D0 | 0.5289 | 0.5244 | 0.5254 | 0.5265 | 0.5223 | 0.5246 | 0.7301 | 0.7155 | 0.7207 | 0.1796 |
| D1 | 0.5245 | 0.5185 | 0.5185 | 0.5183 | 0.5123 | 0.5122 | 0.7438 | 0.7240 | 0.7264 | 0.1948 |
| E0 | 0.5265 | 0.5209 | 0.5232 | 0.5323 | 0.5274 | 0.5291 | 0.7818 | 0.7705 | 0.7738 | 0.2274 |
| E1 | 0.5478 | 0.5416 | 0.5434 | 0.5270 | 0.5219 | 0.5233 | 0.7463 | 0.7407 | 0.7427 | 0.1952 |
| ave | 0.5271 | 0.5212 | 0.5226 | 0.5236 | 0.5183 | 0.5196 | 0.7543 | 0.7406 | 0.7434 | 0.2027 |
| std | 0.0098 | 0.0098 | 0.0096 | 0.0078 | 0.0080 | 0.0085 | 0.0398 | 0.0422 | 0.0410 | 0.0365 |

leads to improved (smaller) entropy estimates for all Gabor images. This implies that the symmetry assumption is reasonable. The corresponding estimates of the mutual information are listed in the column "sym" in Table 13.1(a). From Table 13.1(a) we see that the average of the 10 "sym" estimates is larger than the average found using the basic approach. More specifically, 9 out of 10 estimates are larger than for the basic approach.

3. In the third approach, we have increased the template size from four to six context symbols; see Fig. 13.10. Just as in the previous approach, we assumed symmetry of the statistics. The resulting entropy estimates (column "sym+lar") show that we do not gain from increasing the template size.

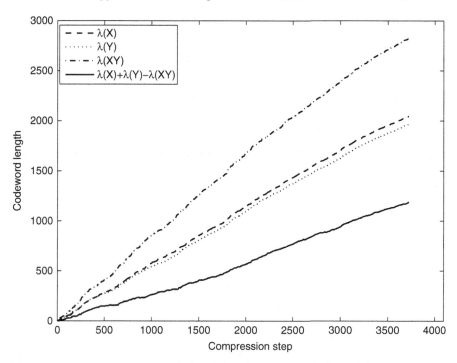

**Fig. 13.9.** Codeword lengths $\lambda(X)$, $\lambda(Y)$, $\lambda(XY)$, and $\lambda(X) + \lambda(Y) - \lambda(XY)$ as a function of the number of processed positions.

|  |  |  |  | 4 |  |  |  | 6 |  |  |  |
|  |  |  |  |  | 1 | 2 | 5 |  |  |  |  |
|  |  |  |  |  |  | 3 | ✕ |  |  |  |  |

**Fig. 13.10.** Template showing increased number of context symbols and their ordering.

4. In the fourth approach, we have determined the mutual information using the conditional formula $\mathbf{I}(X;Y) = \mathsf{H}(X) - \mathsf{H}(X|Y)$. To determine the codeword length $\lambda(X|Y)$, we selected seven context symbols in total from both the **X** and **Y** images. The resulting template is shown in Fig. 13.11. Again, we assumed that the statistics are symmetric. This method leads to higher mutual information estimates than the estimates based on $\mathsf{H}(X) + \mathsf{H}(Y) - \mathsf{H}(XY)$; see the column labeled "sym+con."

## 13.8.2 Class III Analysis

The same analysis was performed using the class III CTW method. We used the same context positions as earlier, but note that the ordering is irrelevant

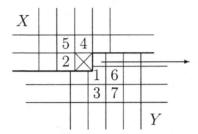

**Fig. 13.11.** Template showing the context symbols and their ordering for computation of $\lambda(X|Y)$. The current position ($\times$) in the **X** image corresponds to position 1 in the **Y** image.

now. Tables 13.2(b) and 13.1(b) describe the results of the class III analysis. Just as in class IV, the estimates based on the symmetry assumption are more reliable than those obtained from the basic approach. Moreover, for class III, a larger template does not improve the estimates and also here the conditional formula leads to the highest mutual information estimates.

From the entropy Table 13.2, we may conclude that the entropy estimates for class III are smaller and, consequently, more reliable than the estimates for class IV. Therefore, we have more confidence in the mutual information estimates obtained from class III weighting methods than from class IV methods. The difference between corresponding estimates is always quite small. These small differences can be explained by noting that the template ordering was optimized to perform well for class IV methods.

*Remark 13.1.* Looking at the entropy estimates in Table 13.2, we notice that for both class IV and class III models, $\widehat{H}(XY) - \widehat{H}(Y) > \widehat{H}(X|Y)$. From this we conclude that the conditional entropy estimate from $\lambda(X|Y)$ is more reliable than the estimate from $\lambda(XY) - \lambda(Y)$. As a consequence, the conditional formula for mutual information does lead to more accurate estimates than the symmetric formula.

## 13.9 Conclusions

We have used CTW methods to estimate the secrecy rate of binarized Gabor-filtered speckle patterns obtained from optical PUFs. Several alternative approaches lead to the conclusion that secrecy rates of 0.31 bit/pixel are possible. This corresponds to 0.7 bit per average speckle area. (The average speckle width is approximately 12 pixels in the unfiltered image; see Section 15.3.1).

Class III gives more reliable and slightly higher estimates of the secrecy rate than class IV, since it is based on a richer model class than class IV. In theory, our methods only converge to the entropy for asymptotically large images if there is no bound on the context size. Note that we have definitively not reached this situation here.

In the present chapter we have focused on estimating the secrecy rate from 45° Gabor images. It is obvious that similar estimates can be found for images that result from 135° Gabor filtering. The 45° and 135° Gabor images are very weakly correlated to each other [287], representing almost independent data, but their statistics are equivalent and, therefore, it is possible to compress both images using the same context tree [150]. The estimates obtained in this way are, in principle, more reliable than estimates based only on 45° Gabor images.

The secrecy rate estimates obtained in this chapter are significantly larger (approximately by a factor of 7) than those obtained with the schemes proposed in Chapter 16. This indicates that there is still much room for improvement in designing secret-key extraction techniques.

Finally, we mention that techniques like the ones that we have applied here can be used to estimate the identification capacity of biometric systems [292]; see also Chapter 4.

# Controlled Physical Random Functions

Blaise Gassend, Marten van Dijk, Dwaine Clarke, and Srinivas Devadas

The cryptographic protocols that we use in everyday life rely on the secure storage of keys in consumer devices. Protecting these keys from invasive attackers, who open a device to steal its key, is a challenging problem. We propose controlled physical random functions[1] (CPUFs) as an alternative to digital key storage, and we describe the core protocols that are needed to use CPUFs.

A PUF is a physical system with an input and an output. The functional relationship between input and output looks like that of a random function. The particular relationship is unique to a specific instance of a PUF; hence, one needs access to a particular PUF instance to evaluate the function it embodies. The cryptographic applications of a PUF are quite limited unless the PUF is combined with an algorithm that limits the ways in which the PUF can be evaluated; this is a CPUF.

A major difficulty in using CPUFs is that one can only know a small set of outputs of the PUF, the unknown outputs being unrelated to the known ones. We present protocols that get around this difficulty and allow a chain of trust to be established between the CPUF manufacturer and a party that wishes to interact securely with the PUF device. We also present some elementary applications such as certified execution.

## 14.1 Introduction

Typically, cryptography is used to secure communication between two parties connected by an untrusted network. In such communication, each party has privately stored key information that allows it to encrypt, decrypt, and authenticate the communication. It is implicitly assumed that each party is capable of securing its private information. This assumption is reasonable

---

[1] The words physical random function and physical unclonable function (PUF) are used interchangeably.

when a party is a military installation, or even a person, but breaks down completely for low-cost consumer devices. Once a secret key is compromised, eavesdropping and impersonation attacks become possible. In a world where portable devices need to authenticate credit card transactions and prevent copyright circumvention, protecting the keys in the devices that surround us is of utmost importance.

To be successful, a key-protection scheme has to protect keys from application programming interface (API) attacks in which the device's API is tricked into releasing trusted information, from non-invasive attacks in which the key is deduced from unintended signals emanating from the device, and from invasive attacks in which the attacker opens the device to find the key. All these types of attack have been demonstrated in real systems [7, 9, 141, 172].

Focusing on the problem of invasive attacks, it is apparent that once a device has been opened, the large difference in state between a 0 and a 1 makes it relatively easy to read out the device's digitally stored secrets. Traditionally, such attacks are avoided by detecting intrusion and erasing the key memory when an intrusion is detected [259]. However, tamper-sensing environments are expensive to make, and as long as a key is being protected, the intrusion sensors need to be powered, further increasing costs.

Since it is the digital nature of the secret-key material that makes it easy to extract invasively, we can try to use information of a continuous nature instead. For example, by measuring a complex physical system and performing suitable processing, a key can be generated [123, 254, 265]. The invasive adversary now has to study a complex physical system, measure it, and simulate it precisely enough to determine the device's key. With careful design, the complex physical system can be fabricated such that an invasive adversary who wants to measure it has to destroy it in the process. Thus, unless the adversary successfully models or clones the physical system, his tampering will be noticed.

These physically obfuscated keys seem to increase the difficulty of an attack, but they still have a single digital point of failure. When the device is in use, the single physically obfuscated master key is present on it in digital form. If an adversary can get that key, he has totally broken the device's security. Going one step farther, we get to PUFs: Instead of being used to generate the same key every time, the complex physical system is parameterizable. For each input to the physical system, a different key is produced. Thus, the complexity of the physical system is exploited to the utmost.

However, by getting rid of the single digital point of failure, we have produced a device that has a family of secrets that are not computationally related to each other. In public-key cryptography, publishing the public key of a device is sufficient to allow anybody to interact securely with that device. With PUFs, if the multiplicity of generated keys is to be used, then there is no direct equivalent to publishing a public key. Our main contribution in this chapter is to show how to build a key management infrastructure that exploits all the key material provided by a PUF. We also present some basic applications like certified execution. Because there is no algorithmic way to tie together all of the keys produced by a given device, the device will have to take an active part in protocols, like certificate verification, that would not usually need any device involvement. This limitation should be offset by a decreased vulnerability to invasive attacks.

### 14.1.1 Physical Random Functions

We now look more closely at what exactly a PUF is. It is a random function (i.e., a function for which knowing some outputs does not help one guess the output for other inputs). A PUF has the additional characteristic that it can only be evaluated with the help of a physical system. In a nutshell, we have the following:

**Definition 14.1.** *A physical random function is a random function that can only be evaluated with the help of a specific physical system. We call the inputs to a physical random function* challenges, *and we call the outputs* responses.

To better understand what a PUF is, we consider a few example implementations:

Digital PUFs are conceptually the simplest kind of PUF. A digital secret key K is embedded in a tamper-proof package along with some logic that computes `Response = RF(K, Challenge)`, where `RF` is some random function. Whenever a `Challenge` is given to the device, it outputs the corresponding `Response`.

Such a device is a PUF. Possessing the device allows one to easily get responses from challenges, but the tamper-proof package prevents attackers from getting K and forging responses. However, it is not a compelling PUF, as it relies on the secrecy of the digital secret K, which is precisely what we would like to avoid by using PUFs.

Optical PUFs were originally proposed by Ravikanth [221, 222]. They are made up of a transparent optical medium containing bubbles. Shining a laser beam through the medium produces a speckle pattern (the response) behind the medium that depends on the exact position and direction of the incoming beam (the challenge). A study has also been made of the information content of an optical PUF [272].
Silicon PUFs have also been considered [123, 125, 126, 175, 181]. In this case, the challenge is an input to the circuit that reconfigures the path that signals follow through the circuit. The response is related to the time it takes for signals to propagate through a complex circuit.

Both optical and silicon PUFs generate responses from physical systems that are difficult to characterize and analyze. They rely on the difficulty of taking a complex physical system, extracting all necessary parameters from it, and simulating it to predict responses. A sufficiently advanced attacker should be able to break the PUF by following this path. However, we expect the difficulty to be greater than the difficulty of extracting a digital secret from a device. Moreover, an attacker who attempts to invade one of these devices to measure its physical parameters is likely to modify it in the process, breaking the PUF. Thus, these PUFs offer some degree of tamper evidence.

Another interesting point about these PUF implementations is that the PUF arises from random manufacturing variations such as bubble position or exact wire delays. Consequently, the PUF is even a mystery for the manufacturer of the PUF. Also, the manufacturer cannot make two identical PUFs even if he wants to. We call these PUFs manufacturer-resistant.

Moreover, these PUF implementations are relatively inexpensive to produce. In particular, silicon PUFs can be realized on standard Complementary Metal-Oxide-Semiconductor (CMOS) technology [289], potentially making them more attractive than Electronically Programmable ROM (EPROM) for identification of integrated circuits. Indeed, circuits with EPROM require extra processing steps, which drive up the cost of a chip.

One difficulty with optical and silicon PUFs is that their output is noisy. Therefore, error correction that does not compromise the security is required to make them noise-free. This problem has been considered elsewhere [180, 265, 279], and we ignore it in the rest of this chapter.

The canonical application for PUFs is to use them as keycards [221]. In this application, a lock is initially introduced to a PUF, and stores a database of challenge response pairs (CRPs) corresponding to that PUF. Later, when the bearer of the PUF wants to open the lock, the lock selects one of the challenges it knows and asks the PUF for the corresponding response. If the response matches the stored response, the lock opens. In this protocol, CRPs can be used only once, so the lock eventually runs out of CRPs. Because the lock cannot get securely introduced to new CRPs without a trusted third party, the keycard application is not very compelling. Nevertheless, it is all that can be done with a PUF until we make it into a CPUF.

### 14.1.2 Controlled Physical Random Functions

**Definition 14.2.** *A controlled physical random function (CPUF) is a PUF that has been bound with an algorithm in such a way that it can only be accessed through a specific API.*

As we will see in Section 14.2.2, the main problem with uncontrolled PUFs is that anybody can query the PUF for the response to any challenge. To engage in cryptography with a PUF device, a user who knows a CRP has to use the fact that only he and the device know the response to the user's challenge. However, to exploit that fact, the user has to tell the device his challenge so that it can get the response. The challenge has to be told in the clear because there is no key yet. Thus, a man in the middle can hear the challenge, get the response from the PUF device, and use it to spoof the PUF device (this attack is detailed in Section 14.2.2).

Clearly, the problem in this attack is that the adversary can freely query the PUF to get the response to the user's challenge. By using a CPUF in which access to the PUF is restricted by a control algorithm, this attack can be prevented. The API through which the PUF is accessed should prevent the man-in-the-middle attack that we have described without imposing unnecessary limitations on applications.

A key contribution of this chapter is the description in Section 14.2 of a simple but very general API for limiting access to a PUF. Some interesting properties of our API are as follows:

- Anybody who knows a CRP that nobody else knows can interact with the CPUF device to obtain an arbitrary number of other CRPs that nobody else knows. Thus, users are not limited to using a small number of digital outputs from the PUF. Moreover, if one of these new CRPs was revealed to an adversary, transactions that use the other CRPs are not compromised. This is analogous to key management schemes that uses session keys derived from a master key.
- Anybody can use a CRP that only he know to establish a shared secret with the PUF device. Having a shared secret with the PUF device enables a wide variety of standard cryptographic primitives to be used.
- The control algorithm is deterministic. Since hardware random number generators are sensitive and prone to attack, being able to avoid them is advantageous.
- The only cryptographic primitive that needs to be built into the control algorithm is a collision-resistant hash function. All other cryptographic primitives can be updated during the lifetime of the CPUF device.

By selecting an appropriate API, a CPUF device can be resistant to protocol attacks. We have already mentioned that for optical and silicon PUFs, taking the PUF apart causes the physical parameters that are being measured to vary, thus destroying the PUF. By embedding the control logic for the PUF within the physical system that makes up the PUF, we make it very difficult to conduct invasive attacks on the control logic. As we illustrated in Fig. 14.1,

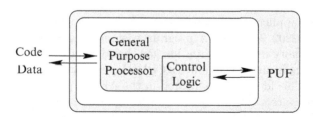

**Fig. 14.1.** We model a PUF device as a general-purpose processing element with possibly restricted access to a PUF. The processing element protects the PUF from protocol attacks, whereas the PUF protects the processing element from invasive attacks.

the PUF and its control logic have complementary roles. The PUF protects the control logic from invasive attacks, whereas the control logic protects the PUF from protocol attacks. This synergy makes a CPUF far more secure than either the PUF or the control logic taken independently.

Based on the above examples, we assume in the remainder of this chapter that PUFs exist, and we focus on designing an API together with protocols that allow a chain of trust to be established between the CPUF manufacturer and a party that wishes to interact securely with the PUF device. This chapter is based on [128], which extends [124], where CPUFs were introduced. Here, we use hashblocks in our API design, which are used in [128] to give more advanced application protocols.

### 14.1.3 Applications

There are many applications for which CPUFs can be used, and we describe a few examples here. Other applications can be imagined by studying the literature on secure coprocessors, in particular [307]. We note that the general applications for which this technology can be used include all of the applications today in which there is a single symmetric key on a chip.

The easiest application is in smartcards, which implement authentication. Current smartcards have hidden digital keys that can be extracted using various attacks [8]. With a unique PUF on the smartcard that can be used to authenticate the chip, a digital key is not required: The smartcard *hardware* is itself the secret key. This key cannot be duplicated, so a person can lose control of a smartcard, retrieve it, and continue using it. With today's cards, the card should be canceled and a new one made because somebody might have cloned the card while it was out of its owner's control.

A bank could use certified execution to authenticate messages from PUF smartcards. This guarantees that the message the bank receives originated from the smartcard. It does not, however, authenticate the bearer of the smartcard. Some other means such as a PIN number or biometrics must be used by the smartcard to determine if its bearer is allowed to use it. If the privacy of the smartcard's message is a requirement, then the message can also be encrypted.

A second application is for computers that implement private storage [5, 56, 178, 179, 202, 264, 267]. A program wishing to store encrypted data in untrusted memory uses an encryption key that depends uniquely on the PUF and its program hash. This requires a CPUF in order to accomplish the unique dependency. This idea is implemented in the AEGIS processor [264, 265].

These computers can be used in grid computation, where the spare computation of thousands of machines on the internet is pooled to solve computationally challenging problems [87, 247]. One issue in grid computation is ensuring that the computation has been correctly carried out by the computers on the grid. This is especially important if people are paid for the computing power they put on the grid, as there is pressure to provide fake results in order to increase revenue.

In [128], it is shown how programs can generate common secret keys that no user or other program can retrieve. This concept has applications in Digital Rights Management and Software Licensing. It can also be used to create shared private memory.

### 14.1.4 Organization

So far we have seen what a CPUF is, without detailing what API should be used to access the PUF. This API is described in Section 14.2, where we present a general-purpose CPUF device, how it is programmed, and how it can access the PUF. Then, in Section 14.3, we solve the problem of CRP management: How does a user who wants to use a CPUF device get a CRP that he trusts for that device? Finally, Section 14.4 shows some basic protocols that can be used by applications that interact with a CPUF device.

## 14.2 CPUF Primitives

In Section 14.1, we saw that a PUF can be used as a keycard. This application was proposed in [221], and it is the only application for a PUF without control. In this section we see why other applications fail and we show how control can be used to make them work.

### 14.2.1 The Execution Environment

Without loss of generality, we model a PUF device as a general-purpose processing element that has access to a PUF (see Fig. 14.1). The device is willing to run any program that is given to it by the outside world. Initially, we consider that the processing element has unrestricted access to the PUF, but, in Section 14.2.2, we will see that some restrictions need to be applied. This model does not imply that all PUF devices must actually be general-purpose computing devices. In practice, one might want to implement only a limited set of functions on the device, and hard-wire them.

We make the assumption that programs running on the PUF device execute in a private and authentic way; that is, their internal data are inaccessible to an attacker, and nobody can cause the program to execute incorrectly. This assumption is not trivial. We can partially justify it by the fact that the CPUF should be designed so that the logic functionality of the device is embedded within the physical system of the PUF, and many kinds of invasive attack will destroy the PUF before giving the adversary access to the logic. In [123], we have additionally considered the "open-once" model in which the adversary can gain access to a single snapshot of internal variables while breaking the PUF.

We now give a brief description of the execution environment that we use. The reader may want to refer back to this description later in the chapter. Programs will be described using a syntax close to C. A few notable changes are as follows:

- We will often be identifying a piece of code by its hash. In the code, we indicate what region the hash should cover by using the `hashblock` keyword. During execution, whenever a hashblock is reached, a hash is computed over its arguments and stored in a special system register `PHashReg` that cannot be directly modified by the program. More precisely, each hashblock has two sets of arguments: variable arguments and code arguments. `PHashReg` is a hash of all the arguments of the hashblock concatenated together, with program blocks in the code section replaced by their hash. We assume that all the hashing is done using a cryptographically strong hash function. Moreover, concatenation is done in a way that ensures that a different sequence of arguments will always produce a different string to hash. Any code arguments to the hashblock that are executable are then executed. When execution leaves the hashblock, the previous value of `PHashReg` is restored (popped off an authentically stored stack). The need for hashblocks will become apparent in Section 14.2.3.

- We declare variables using the keyword `my` as in the Perl language. We do this to avoid worrying about types while still specifying where the variable is declared. Variables declared within a hashblock are automatically cleared on exit from the hashblock. This way, data in variables that are declared in a hashblock cannot be accessed once the block's execution has completed.

An example illustrates the use of `hashblock` and `my`. Note that we have given each hashblock a name (A or B). This name will be used to designate the code and variables of a particular hashblock when explaining how programs work.

```
1  Foo(Bar)
2  {
3      // PHashReg has value inherited from caller.
4      hashblock(Bar)( // A
5      {
6      // PHashReg is Hash(Bar; Hash(code in lines 6 to 14),
       Dummy).
7      my FooBar = Bar / 2;
8      hashblock()( // B
9      {
10         // PHashReg is Hash(; Hash(code in lines 10 to 11)).
```

```
11         my BarFoo = FooBar + 3;
12     });
13     // PHashReg is Hash(Bar; Hash(code in lines 6 to 14),
       Dummy).
14     // The value of BarFoo has been purged from memory.
15     }, Dummy);
16     // PHashReg has value inherited from caller.
17     // The value of FooBar has been purged from memory.
18  }
```

A number of cryptographic primitives will be used in what follows:

- MAC(message, key) produces a Message Authentication Code (MAC) of message with key.
- EncryptAndMAC(message, key) is used to encrypt and MAC message with key.
- PublicEncrypt(message, key) is used to encrypt message with the public-key key.
- Decrypt(message, key) is used to decrypt message that was encrypted with key.
- PHash(HB) is the value of PHashReg in the hashblock denoted by HB. For example, A represents (Bar; Hash(code from lines 6 to 14), Dummy). In this sequence, the comma (,) and the semicolon (;) represent different concatenations so that variable and code arguments can be distinguished. While the code from lines 6 to 14 is executing, PHashReg contains PHash(A).

Of these primitives, only PHash has to be permanently built into the CPUF device, as it participates in the generation of program hashes. All of the other primitives can be updated. The only requirement is that the code of the primitives participates in the generation of program hashes. In an actual implementation PHash would therefore incorporate a hash of the primitives. For the rest of this chapter we ignore this issue and assume that all the primitives are hard-coded.

### 14.2.2 The Man-in-the-Middle Attack

Suppose that Alice wants to perform a computation on a device containing a PUF. She knows a set of CRPs for the PUF and would like to know the result of the computation. Unfortunately, she is communicating with the device over an untrusted channel to which Oscar has access. Oscar would like Alice to accept an incorrect result as coming from the device. This example, as we will see, captures the limitations of uncontrolled PUFs.

Alice attempts the following method:

1. She picks one of her CRPs (Chal, Response) at random.
2. She executes GetAuthenticBroken(Chal) on the PUF device (it is sent in the clear and without authentication).

```
GetAuthenticBroken(Chal)
{
   my Resp = PUF(Chal);
   ... Do some computation, produce Result ...
   return (Result, MAC(Result, Resp));
}
```

3. Alice uses the MAC and Response to check that the data she receives are authentic.

Unfortunately, this protocol does not work, as Oscar can carry out a man-in-the-middle attack:

1. He intercepts the message in which Alice sends GetAuthenticBroken to the PUF and extracts Chal from it.
2. He executes StealResponse(Chal) on the PUF device.

```
StealResponse(Chal)
{
   return PUF(Chal);
}
```

3. Now that he knows the Response, he sends Alice the message MAC(FakeResult, Response).
4. Since the MAC was computed with the correct response, Alice accepts FakeResult as valid.

The problem here is that as soon as Alice releases her challenge, Oscar can simply ask the PUF for the corresponding response and can then impersonate the PUF. As long as the PUF is willing to freely give out the response to challenges, this problem will persist.

### 14.2.3 The GetSecret Primitive

To solve this problem, we will move from a PUF that is wide open to one that is severely restricted. Suppose that we will only allow access to the PUF via a primitive called GetSecret, defined by

$$GetSecret(Chal)=Hash(PHashReg, PUF(Chal)).$$

This primitive is designed so that the CPUF device will not reveal a response to anybody. Instead, it will reveal a combination of the response and the program that is being executed, which cannot be used to recover the response because we assume that Hash is a one-way function.

Alice changes her GetAuthenticBroken program in the following way:

```
GetAuthentic(Chal)
{
  hashblock()( // HB
  {
    my Result;
    hashblock ()(
    {
      ... Do some computation, produce Result ...
    });
    my Secret = GetSecret(Chal);
    return (Result, MAC(Result, Secret));
  });
}
```

Alice computes Secret from Response by computing Hash(PHash(HB), Response), which allows her to check the MAC. Oscar, on the other hand, is now stuck. He has no way of getting Secret. If he sends a program of his own and calls GetSecret, he will get a different secret from the one Alice's program got. Also, GetAuthentic is well written; it does not leak Secret to the outside world (the inner hashblock prevents the computation from producing/revealing Secret). Thus, Alice is now certain when the MAC check passes that she is looking at the result that is computed by the PUF device.

### 14.2.4 The GetCRP Primitive

Unfortunately for Alice, the latest version of the CPUF device is too restrictive. If Alice has a CRP, then she can indeed interact securely with the device, but there is no way for her to get that CRP in the first place, since the device will never reveal a Response.

To solve this problem, we slightly lighten the restrictions that are placed on access to the PUF. For example, we could add a primitive called GetCRP. This primitive would pick a random challenge, compute its response, and return the newly found CRP to the caller. In this way, anybody would have access to an arbitrary number of CRPs, but as long as the space of challenges is large enough, the probability that the same CRP will be given to two different people is extremely small.

### 14.2.5 The GetResponse Primitive

In theory, a secure system could be built from GetCRP. In practice, however, random number generators are often vulnerable to attack. Since the scheme relies heavily on the strength of the random number generator, it would be nice to see if an alternative solution exists that is deterministic.

That solution does indeed exist. We replace `GetCRP` by `GetResponse`, which is defined by

$$\text{GetResponse()=PUF(PHashReg)}. \tag{14.1}$$

This way, anybody can generate a CRP (`PHashReg`,`GetResponse()`), but because of the hash function with which `PHashReg` is computed, nobody can choose to generate a specific CRP. The code of the hashblock contributes to `PHashReg` so that the CRP that is generated is program dependent.

The challenge that is generated in `GetResponse` is equal to `PHashReg`. It depends on the code contained within the hashblock, as well as on the variables that are arguments to the hashblock. Often one of these variables will simply be a nonce, that we call *pre-challenge* because it is used to determine the challenge.

Figure 14.2 summarizes the possible ways of going between pre-challenges, challenges, responses and secrets. In this diagram, moving down is easy. You just have to calculate a few hashes. Moving up is hard because it involves inverting one-way hashes. Going from left to right is easy for the program whose hash is used in the `GetResponse` or `GetSecret` primitives, and hard for all other programs. Going from right to left is hard because the PUF is hard to invert.

The man-in-the-middle attack is prevented by each user having her own list of CRPs, where the challenges can be public, but the responses have to

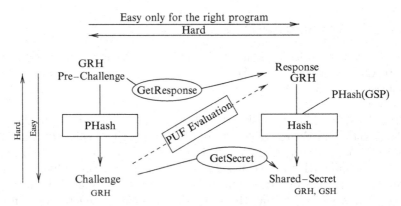

**Fig. 14.2.** This diagram shows the ways of moving among pre-challenges, challenges, responses, and secrets. Rectangles show elementary operations that can be performed. Ellipses represent operations that are made by composing elementary operations. The dotted arrow indicates that because the PUF is controlled, nobody can actually evaluate it directly. GRH and GSH are the hashblocks that call `GetResponse` and `GetSecret`, respectively. If GRH or GSH appears below a value, then that value depends on one of these hashblocks.

be private. From Fig. 14.2, we see that to get his hands on a secret produced by some hashblock GSH, an adversary has three options: he can be told the secret, he can use GetSecret from within GSH or he can hash an appropriate response. If the user does not tell the secret to the adversary and GSH does not leak the secret, then only the third option is possible. So the adversary has to get his hands on the response. There are only two ways for him to do so: he can be told the response, or he can use GetResponse from within the hashblock GRH in which it was created. If the user does not tell the adversary the response and if GRH doesn't leak the response then the adversary is out of options. In Section 14.3, we will see how GRH can be designed to use encryption to get the response to the legitimate user without leaking it to the adversary.

With the two primitives GetSecret and GetResponse that we have introduced, anybody can generate CRPs and use them to generate a secret value that is known only to them and to a program running on the PUF device. This choice of primitives is not unique, but we believe that this combination is particularly satisfying. Indeed, they make no assumptions on what use will be made of the secret value once it is generated. Moreover, in addition to the PUF itself, the only cryptographic primitive that needs to be built into the device is a hash function, for GetSecret and GetResponse to be implemented.

## 14.3 Challenge Response Pair Management

In Section 14.2, we saw that access to the PUF had to be limited in order to prevent man-in-the-middle attacks. We proposed to make the PUF accessible only by the two primitives GetResponse and GetSecret. This places just the right amount of restriction on access to the PUF. The man-in-the-middle attack is thwarted, whereas anybody can get access to a CRP and interact securely with the PUF.

In this section, we go into the details of how a flexible trust infrastructure can be built in this model. It allows a chain of trust to be built from the manufacturer of a CPUF device to the end user, via an arbitrary sequence of certification authorities (which we will call certifiers). First, just after the CPUF device is manufactured, the manufacturer uses Bootstrap in a secure factory environment to get a CRP for the device. The manufacturer can then use Introduction to provide CRPs to certification authorities, who, in turn, can provide them to end users. Anybody who has a CRP can use Renew to generate more CRPs. This is analogous to using keys derived from a master key. An attacker who manages to obtain a small number of CRPs (or derived keys) is unable to completely break the security of the device.

### 14.3.1 Bootstrapping

Bootstrapping is the most straightforward way to obtain a CRP. It is illustrated in Fig. 14.3. No encryption or authentication is built into the protocol,

Fig. 14.3. Model for bootstrapping.

as it is designed for users who are in physical possession of the device and who can therefore directly hold a secure communication with the device. A CPUF device manufacturer would use bootstrapping to get CRPs for devices that have just been produced, so that their origin can later be verified.

1. The user who wishes to get a CRP picks a pre-challenge PreChal at random.
2. The user executes Bootstrap(PreChal) on the CPUF device.

```
Bootstrap(PreChal)
{
   hashblock (PreChal)( // HB
   {
      return GetResponse();
   });
}
```

3. The user gets the challenge of his newly created CRP by calculating PHash(HB), the response is the output of the program.

If an adversary gets to know PreChal, he can replay the bootstrapping program with PreChal as input to obtain the corresponding CRP. Therefore, the user should discard PreChal after use. If PreChal is not known, then the security of the bootstrapping program relies on the one-wayness of the hash function with which PHashReg=PHash(HB) is computed.

### 14.3.2 Renewal

Renewal is a process by which a user who has a CRP for a CPUF can generate more CRPs over an untrusted network. It is illustrated in Fig. 14.4. In this protocol, the user uses his CRP to create a secure channel from the CPUF device to himself, and the CPUF sends the new response over that channel.

1. The user who wishes to generate a new CRP picks a pre-challenge PreChal at random.

Fig. 14.4. Model for renewal.

2. The user executes `Renew(OldChal, PreChal)` on the CPUF device, where `OldChal` is the challenge of the CRP that the user already knows.

```
Renew(OldChal, PreChal)
{
  hashblock (OldChal, PreChal)( // HB
  {
    my NewResponse = GetResponse();
    my Secret = GetSecret(OldChal);
    return EncryptAndMAC(NewResponse, Secret);
  });
}
```

3. The user computes `Hash(PHash(HB), OldResponse)` to calculate `Secret` and uses it to check the MAC and retrieve `NewResponse`. The new challenge is computed by `PHash(HB)`.

Note that `PreChal` is included in the hashblock so that it participates in the generation of `Secret` and therefore in the MAC. Thus, if any tampering occurs with `PreChal`, it will be detected in step 3.

Also, `OldChal` is included in the hashblock so that it participates in the generation of `NewResponse`. Thus, an adversary cannot retrieve `NewResponse` by replaying the renew program with inputs `PreChal` and an old challenge different from `OldChal` for which he knows the corresponding response.

The security of renewal relies on whether the response corresponding to `OldChal` is only known to the user. Note that the use of `PreChal` allows the user to derive multiple new CRPs by using renewal with the same `OldChal`. The corresponding responses are only known to the user if the response to `OldChal` is not compromised.

### 14.3.3 Introduction

Introduction is an operation that allows a user who has a CRP for a CPUF to provide a CRP to another user, assuming that there is a trusted channel between the users (established using public-key cryptography, e.g.), but that communication with the PUF device is untrusted. It is illustrated in Fig. 14.5. This operation could be used, for example, by a user who wants to be sure that he is getting a CRP to a genuine CPUF device.

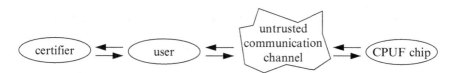

**Fig. 14.5.** Model for introduction.

In a real-world deployment, a chain of trust would be built from the manufacturer to the end user of the CPUF device. The manufacturer would collect CRPs on the production line using bootstrapping and use them to introduce the PUF to various competing certifiers. The end user would then ask a certifier of his choosing to introduce him to the device.

Many variants of introduction are possible depending on how much trust the user is willing to place in the certifier. Here, we present our strongest version, which uses public-key cryptography and protects against passive attacks (i.e., attacks in which the certifier gives the user a valid CRP but keeps a copy of it to eavesdrop on the user). We do not, however, protect against active attacks in which the certifier simply gives the user an incorrect CRP and makes him think that he is talking to a PUF when in fact he is not. This is the minimum amount of trust that the user must place in the certifier in order to make introduction possible.

With this protocol, the user can also get introduced to the same CPUF device by many different certifiers. They would all have to actively attack him in a consistent way for the attack to succeed. In this protocol, the user needs to have a public key PubKey that is used to encrypt the new response. The user would run Introduction multiple times with the same PubKey and PreChal, but a different OldChal for each certifier.

1. The certification authority picks (OldChal,OldResponse) from one of its CRPs and computes Secret as Hash(PHash(HB), OldResponse), where HB is the hashblock in the introduction program given in step 2. The certification authority gives (OldChal,Secret) to the user.
2. The user picks a pre-challenge PreChal at random. Next, the user executes Introduction(OldChal, PubKey, PreChal).

```
Introduction(OldChal, PubKey, PreChal)
{
  hashblock (PubKey, PreChal)( // HB
  {
    my NewResponse = GetResponse();
    my Message = PublicEncrypt(NewResponse, PubKey);
    my Secret' = GetSecret(OldChal);
    return (Message, MAC(Message, Secret'));
  });
}
```

3. The user uses Secret to check the MAC. Notice that Secret equals Secret', since both are computed as Hash(PHash(HB), OldResponse) by the certification authority and introduction program, respectively. The user decrypts Message with his private key to get the response and computes PHash(HB) to get the challenge.

In the protocol, the certification authority does not communicate with the PUF. We prefer for the user to communicate with the PUF because he will often be the one who has a channel open to the PUF.

Since NewResponse is encrypted with PubKey, an adversary cannot directly use it to get NewResponse. Moreover, PubKey is included in the hashblock so that it participates in the generation of NewResponse. Thus, an adversary cannot retrieve NewResponse by replaying the introduction program with his own public key, as changing the public key changes the secret that is produced. Even the certifier, who knows (OldChal, OldResponse), cannot retrieve NewResponse.

There are other ways of doing introduction; for example, a slightly different protocol was used in [123, 124]. In that protocol, the certifier gives OldResponse to the user, who can then compute Secret himself. The user then has to perform a *private renewal* that uses public-key cryptography to prevent passive attacks from the certification authority. In this case, the certifier cannot use the CRP (OldChal, OldResponse) a second time.

## 14.4 Certified Execution

In certified execution, a certificate is produced that guarantees to the user that the program was run without being tampered with on a processor. We discuss how a certificate is produced that can only be verified by the user of the processor. It relies on a shared secret between the user and the processor with the PUF. In [128], it is discussed how a certificate can be produced that can be verified by any third party. We call such a certificate a proof of execution. It relies on the ability to share a secret between different programs.

It is possible to produce a certificate that proves to the user of a specific CPUF that a specific computation was carried out on this CPUF and that the computation produced a given result. The person requesting the computation can then rely on the trustworthiness of the CPUF manufacturer, who can vouch that he produced the CPUF, instead of relying on the owner of the CPUF. We call this *certified execution*. It is essentially the same as GetAuthentic, which was presented in Section 14.2.3 (in fact, Renewal and Introduction are also special cases of certified execution).

1. The user who wishes to run a program with program code Prog on a specific CPUF picks (Challenge, Response) from one of his CRPs for the CPUF.
2. The user executes CertifiedExecution(Challenge, Prog) on the CPUF device.

```
CertifiedExecution(Challenge, Prog)
{
  hashblock (Prog)( // HB
  {
```

```
        my Result;
        hashblock ()(
        {
          Result = RunProg(Prog);
        });
        my Secret = GetSecret(Challenge);
        my Certificate = (Result, MAC(Result, Secret));
        Return Certificate;
      });
    }
```

3. The user computes `Hash(PHash(HB), Response)` to calculate `Secret` and uses it to check the MAC in `Certificate` and to accept the returned `Result` as authentic.

Notice that `Secret` depends on `Prog`. This means that tampering with `Prog` will be detected in step 3 when the user checks the MAC in `Certificate`. Thus, if the returned `Result` is authentic, then it is equal to the output of `Prog`.

In this application, the user is trusting that the CPUF performs the computation correctly. This is easier to ensure if all of the resources used to perform the computation (memory, CPU, etc.) are on the same CPUF device and included in the PUF characterization. In [264, 265], a more sophisticated architecture is discussed in which a chip can securely utilize off-chip resources. It uses ideas from [179] and it uses a memory integrity scheme that can be implemented in a hardware processor [127].

It is also possible for a CPUF to use the capabilities of other networked CPUF devices. In that case, the CPUF has CRPs for each of the other CPUF devices it is using, and it performs computations using protocols similar to the one described in this section.

## 14.5 Conclusion

In this chapter, we have presented CPUFs, which are physical random functions that can only be accessed through a restricted API. CPUFs hold the promise of being a low-cost way to increase the resistance to invasive attacks of devices that participate in cryptographic protocols.

We have presented a particular API in which the CPUF device has a general-purpose processing element that can access a PUF using two primitives called `GetResponse` and `GetSecret`. These primitives use a hash of the program fragment that is being run to identify that program fragment. `GetResponse` allows anybody to get a large number of CRPs, without letting anybody choose a specific CRP that somebody else is already using. `GetSecret` allows the bearer of a CRP to generate a secret value that is known only to himself and his program running on the CPUF device.

Using this API, we have shown how the identity of a CPUF device can be verified by its end user, using a few simple protocols. First, the manufacturer uses `Bootstrap` to get a CRP from the PUF, as it is sitting in the secure environment where it was made. Then the `Renew` and `Introduce` protocols can be used to generate more CRPs and to give a CRP to another person, respectively. `Renew` and `Introduce` leverage the existing CRP to establish a secure channel between the CPUF device and the person interacting with it, relieving the need for the device to be in a secure environment after the initial `Bootstrap`. Using these protocols, the identity of the device can be passed from the device manufacturer to the end users via an arbitrary number of certification authorities.

Finally, we have presented a building block that can be useful in applications. Certified execution allows a user to run a program on a CPUF device and be sure that the output he receives was indeed generated on a specific device. Proof of execution [128] goes one step farther, allowing the user to prove to a third party that a program has been executed on a specific device. In proof of execution, two programs running on the same CPUF device at different times can communicate securely together.

Overall, we feel that CPUFs should allow the potential of physical random functions to be fully exploited. This should provide inexpensive devices with much increased resistance to invasive physical attacks, in a world where cryptography has become pervasive in our cell phones, PDAs, and even credit cards.

# 15

# Experimental Hardware for Coating PUFs and Optical PUFs

Boris Škorić, Geert-Jan Schrijen, Wil Ophey, Rob Wolters, Nynke Verhaegh, and Jan van Geloven

## 15.1 Introduction

In this chapter we discuss the hardware that was used to perform experiments on physical unclonable functions (PUFs). We describe the measurement setups and experimental samples in the case of coating PUFs and optical PUFs. These are two vastly different systems—the former based on integrated circuit (IC) technology and the latter on laser optics.

The aim of this chapter is to provide some technological background to the highly theoretical analyses in Part I, explaining the origin of the raw data used as the source of common randomness for the fuzzy extractors of Chapters 4–6 and the extraction methods of Chapters 13 and 16. This gives the reader a concrete picture of PUFs as objects that really exist, instead of hypothetical physical systems with a number of abstract properties. The examples we give serve as a proof of principle, showing that PUF systems can be built effectively using existing technology and indicating what is involved in building a working PUF system. Even if our setups are not necessarily typical for a commercial product, they give a good of indication of which components and manufacturing steps are needed and how much data processing is to be expected in a real-life PUF application. The handling of the raw data obtained from these PUFs is discussed in Chapter 16.

This chapter differs from the others in listing a large number of hardware details. Although such a list is not easy to read, we feel that the level of detail is justified by the importance of having a good understanding of the experimental data. Coating PUFs are discussed in Section 15.2. We present the required IC processing steps, the capacitor design used in the experiments, the chemical composition of the coating, the method for depositing the coating on wafers, the on-chip measurement circuit, and the layout of the circuit board.

Optical PUFs are discussed in Sections 15.3 and 15.4. First, we describe the experimental setup for measuring speckle patterns of bare samples, consisting of a fairly straightforward combination of laser, sample holder, and camera. We also give details on the used PUF samples. The experimental data of Chapters 13 and 16 were acquired with this setup. We finish by presenting a small integrated device containing a fixed sample, a camera, and a mechanism for selecting multiple challenges. This architecture demonstrates that an optical PUF system can be miniaturized.

## 15.2 Coating PUF Test ICs

A coating PUF is a coating layer on top of an IC, containing a random mixture of particles with different dielectric properties. The IC is equipped with an array of small metal structures, which we refer to as sensors, directly beneath the coating. Each sensor represents a small capacitor; the part of the coating directly above the sensor plays the role of the dielectric layer of the capacitor. Hence, each sensor locally probes the dielectric properties of the coating. A schematic picture is shown in Fig. 15.1. The IC is also equipped with circuitry for selecting a sensor and measuring its capacitance. The manufacture of the coating is an unpredictable mixing process. Consequently, the measured capacitance values are unpredictable.[1] Using challenge response pair (CRP) terminology, we say that the coating is challenged by selecting a specific sensor; the response is the measured capacitance.

The particles have a high dielectric constant and their size is of the same order of magnitude as the sensors, leading to a strong dependence of the measured capacitance values on the precise particle locations. This property makes it difficult to produce a second coating that yields the same capacitance values; that is, the coating is *physically* unclonable. On the other hand, the coating is not *mathematically* unclonable (see Chapter 1 for definitions), since modeling of the system poses no serious problems.

Strictly speaking, the coating does not comply with the definition of a PUF in Chapter 1 due to the relatively small number of CRPs and the feasibility of mathematical cloning. However, characterization of the coating can be made

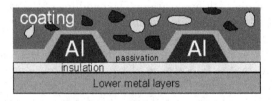

**Fig. 15.1.** Schematic cross-section of coating PUF IC. The upper metal layer contains aluminum (Al) sensor structures that are used to measure the local capacitance of the coating.

---

[1] The probability distribution of measurement outcomes can, of course, be determined from the ensemble properties, but the values of individual capacitances cannot be predicted.

very hard by properly choosing its chemical composition. This makes the coating ideally suited for implementing a physically obfuscated key (POK) [124], a key that is difficult for attackers to extract from the hardware. The application of the IC coating for secure key storage is further explored in Chapter 16. In a slight abuse of terminology, the name PUF is still used for the coating.

The manufacture of coating PUFs is non-trivial, requiring processing technologies from the IC industry. In the following subsections we give a detailed description of the test ICs that were designed [271] and of the processing steps. In Section 15.2.1 we motivate the basic design choices. Sections 15.2.2 to 15.2.6 contain details on the IC process technology, the sensor structures, the passivation layer, the chemistry of the coating, the measurement circuit, and the printed circuit board (PCB). This provides insight into the design principles for coating PUFs, as well as a good understanding of the nature of the raw measurement data used as input in Chapter 16.

### 15.2.1 Design Choices

The main choices are the chemical composition of the coating, the shape and size of the sensors, and the type of circuitry used to measure the capacitances. The choice for the composition of the coating was dictated by a number of practical requirements apart from PUF properties. First, the coating should be easy to deposit onto the IC by a *spray-coating* process and, second, the coating should also serve as a protective barrier that shields the IC from both non-invasive and invasive attacks (see Section 16.2). A mixture of $TiO_2$ and TiN particles in a tough $Al(PO_3)_3$ matrix (aluminum metaphosphate) was identified that satisfies all the requirements. Apart from being resilient to mechanical and chemical attacks, it sticks firmly to the IC, absorbs light from the infrared part of the spectrum to the ultrviolet, and shields off electromagnetic emissions of the IC. The $TiO_2$ particles, which are very small, give an overall high dielectric constant. The TiN particles, which are much larger, give rise to large variations. The coating starts as a viscous liquid that is spray-coated on top of a wafer that contains many ICs. Then the coating is dried and annealed at high temperature.

The form of the sensors was based on two requirements. First, the amount of capacitance per unit area must be large in order to obtain a good signal-to-noise ratio. Second, the electric field lines must substantially penetrate the coating, so that the measured capacitance strongly depends on the local composition of the coating. This led to an interlocked finger design, as shown in Fig. 15.3. The IC has multiple metal layers. The sensors are situated in the upper metal layer. The aluminum parts in Fig. 15.1 are the cross-section view of two of the sensor fingers. The "passivation layer" depicted in the figure serves as a seal to chemically protect the IC. The width of the sensor fingers is of the same order of magnitude as the TiN particles, giving rise to large capacitance variations from sensor to sensor.

The measurements are performed on the IC itself, using a circuit known as a "switched capacitor relaxation oscillator". The choice was motivated by the fact that this provides a tried and tested method to measure small capacitances [266]. A stable current source charges the selected capacitor until a certain threshold voltage is reached. The same current source is used to discharge the capacitor until a second threshold voltage is reached. Then the whole process is repeated from the start. The frequency of the resulting current oscillation is inversely proportional to the capacitance.

After the coating process, the wafers were diced using a wafer saw. Finally, the resulting ICs were mounted in plastic packages such that they could be inserted in the sockets of a PCB. A special PCB was made for demonstration purposes.

### 15.2.2 The IC Process

Our coating PUF IC was made in standard CMOS18 process technology. Figure 15.2 shows a cross-section of a part of a coated IC and its main components. Starting from a silicon wafer, electrically active elements such as transistors, resistors, and capacitors are built onto the silicon. MOS transistors are created by growing a thin $SiO_2$ gate dielectric and defining a polycrystalline silicon gate. Source and drain regions are made by ion implantation and thermal annealing. All of the electrically active parts in the silicon are

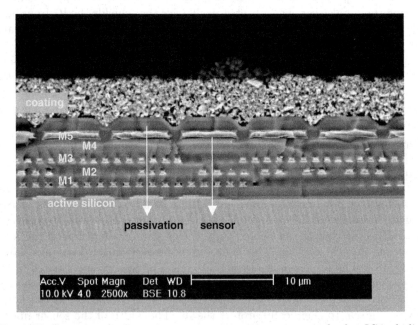

**Fig. 15.2.** Scanning electron microscope cross-section micrograph of an IC including the coating. The metal layers are denoted as M1,. . . ,M5.

now combined into a circuit using up to five levels (M1–M5) of metal wiring. The metal interconnections are made from an aluminum alloy. Metal lines and levels are separated by SiO$_2$ layers. The lower levels (M1, M2) have the highest density, whereas the highest level, in general, has a much lower density, as it carries mainly the input/output and power lines. Therefore, in most IC designs, there is some space left in the upper metal layer to place sensor structures.

On top of the upper metal interconnection layer, the IC structure is covered with a so-called passivation layer [297]. This last dielectric layer covers the whole IC. It consists of a phosphour-silicate-glass (PSG) layer, typically 500–1000 nm thick, and a 500-nm silicon nitride layer. The passivation layer forms a scratch protection that protects the IC against contamination and moisture attack. Electrical connections from the upper metal interconnection to the outside world are accomplished by local openings (bond pads) through the passivation layer.

After deposition of the passivation layer, the silicon wafers with the ICs leave the manufacturing site. Ordinarily, the wafers are then diced and the separate ICs are mounted into packages. In our case, however, we first deposit a coating onto the wafer before dicing (see Section 15.2.4).

### 15.2.3 Sensor Structures

The coating is probed locally by capacitive sensors in the upper metal layer (M5) directly underneath the passivation layer. Specially designed comb structures, made of aluminum, are defined in the upper metal-level interconnection. A top view of a scanning electron microscopy (SEM) micrograph of a sensor is shown in Fig. 15.3. There are three main contributors to the measured capacitance: the coating, the oxide/nitride passivation stack, and the underlying interconnection/oxide structure.

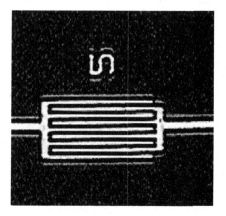

**Fig. 15.3.** Top view of a single comb-shaped sensor structure in the top metal layer of the IC.

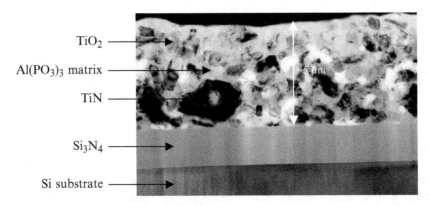

TiO$_2$

Al(PO$_3$)$_3$ matrix

TiN

Si$_3$N$_4$

Si substrate

**Fig. 15.4.** Transmission electron micrograph image of the coating on a Si$_3$N$_4$ layer on a Si substrate.

### 15.2.4 The Coating

The coating consists of a Al(PO$_3$)$_3$ (aluminum metaphosphate) matrix [83] with TiO$_2$ and TiN particles. A transmission electron micrograph of the coating is shown in Fig. 15.4.

The coating is a few micrometers thick. The TiO$_2$ particles are small (average size 300 nm) and the size distribution is narrow. The TiN particles are relatively large and they exhibit a wide size distribution. The largest particles are 1–2 $\mu$m. The Al(PO$_3$)$_3$ matrix has a dielectric constant of 7–8. The TiO$_2$ particles have a dielectric constant in the order of 70–180. The TiN particles are conductive.

The coating is prepared wet-chemically: First an aqueous suspension is made, containing a monoaluminum phosphate (MAP) precursor and the TiO$_2$ and TiN particles. The suspension is homogenized by ball milling. The suspension is deposited by spray-coating followed by a first drying process at 140°C to remove the excess of water. Finally, the coating is annealed at 400°C for 30 minutes to form the stable Al(PO$_3$)$_3$ phase. The spray-coating occurs on the wafer level; that is, complete silicon wafers with finished ICs from an IC manufacturing line are treated with this process.

In order to allow for dicing and assembly of the ICs, the saw lines (for dicing) and the bond pads (for assembly) are kept free of coating. Prior to the spray-coating, these areas are covered with a standard photoresist. Subsequently, the wafer is treated in a fluor-containing plasma to make the photoresist surface extremely hydrophobic. The aqueous spray solution is repelled from the photoresist areas. After the first drying process (140°C), the photoresist is selectively removed from the wafer, leaving defined areas free of coating. The result is shown in Fig. 15.5.

Wafers are thinned by means of a mechanical grinding process, sometimes combined with an etching step to remove any remaining damaged silicon.

**Fig. 15.5.** Part of a coated wafer showing the coated ICs and the clean areas.

After dicing of the thinned wafers, the coated ICs can be assembled for their application (e.g., embedded into a smartcard or mounted into a package).

### 15.2.5 Measurement Circuit

The coating PUF capacitances are measured by means of a switched capacitor relaxation oscillator. High measurement accuracies are reported [177,188,266] for this type of measurement method. Furthermore, this measurement method is commercially available in the form of a capacitor measurement board [257]. Figure 15.6 depicts the architecture of the measurement circuit. It consists of the following:

- An oscillator measurement circuit (including sensor selection), an output divider, and an accurate counter.
- Address registers to track which capacitor is read out and control registers to set the division factor of the output divider).
- Data registers in which the measured values are stored.
- An I$^2$C interface [1] to read out the data registers and to program address and control registers. Via the control registers, a reset of the data registers can be done and a new measurement can be initiated.
- A controller block that controls correct functionality via the status register.

The basic concept of the measurement circuit and the two most important signals "OTA out" and "Comp out" are shown at the top of Fig. 15.6. The oscillator consists of an Operational Transconductance Amplifier (OTA) switched as integrator, a comparator "Comp", a current source $I_{int}$ that feeds the integrator circuit (hence the subscript "int") with a selectable current direction, and a selection for the capacitor that is being addressed. When a capacitor is selected, the output of the integrator starts rising or falling due to the current injected by the source. As soon as the integrator output reaches the reference voltage $V_{ref}$, the comparator switches the capacitor and also the

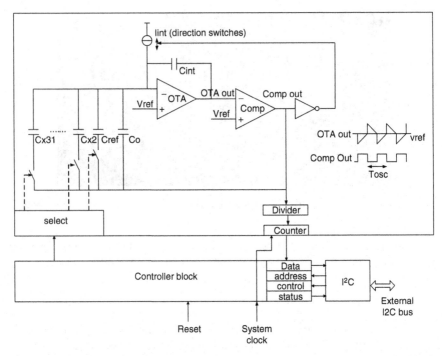

**Fig. 15.6.** Measurement circuit architecture. The coating is situated between the symbolic capacitor plate pairs Cx31··· Cref.

direction of the current source. Since the comparator switches between the supply voltage $V_{dd}$ and ground $(= 0)$, the oscillation period is given by

$$T = 2 \cdot (\text{Cx} + \text{Co}) \cdot V_{dd}/I_{\text{int}} + T_d. \qquad (15.1)$$

Here, Co represents an internal offset capacitance value (as depicted in Fig. 15.6) and Cx denotes one of the selected capacitors that is being measured (either a reference capacitor Cref or one of the capacitors Cx2 to Cx31). $T_d$ stands for the internal delay in the components. We measure the oscillation period by counting the number of system clocks over multiple oscillation cycles that are depicted by the divider (e.g., division $N = 128$). This results in a quantization error $T_{\text{clk}}/(\sqrt{6} \cdot T_{\text{osc}} \cdot N)$ [266].

The capacitors Cx2 to Cx31 and Cref in Fig. 15.6 represent the capacitances of the coated finger structures. Co is a metal capacitor that sets an offset oscillation frequency. Oscillation frequencies are always measured for a triplet (Cref, Co, Cx), and a so-called "three-signal approach" is applied. Effects due to environment, voltage, temperature, and circuit inaccuracies can be eliminated [266] by calculating the factor

$$M = (Tx - To)/(T_{\text{ref}} - To). \qquad (15.2)$$

The stray capacitance can be relatively high due to routing in order to connect the capacitors. A nice feature of the oscillator measurement circuit is that all stray capacitances to power and ground are eliminated in the measurement due to the fixed voltage at the bottom (ideal voltage source) and virtual OTA reference at the top of the capacitance (ideal current source) [266].

### 15.2.6 Printed Circuit Board

Our PCB serves as a demonstration and testing board. Via a USB -I$^2$C bridge, it can be connected to a USB port. This allows for easy transfer of the raw measurement data to a PC, where it is straightforward to try out data processing algorithms. Figure 15.7 shows a photo of the PCB. The PCB consists of the following parts:

- Four sockets with coating PUF ICs. One of these can be selected to be active.
- A power supply. This can be either connected to the main AC power supply via a 6-V DC adapter or to a regulated DC power supply.
- A clock generator and divider, for selection of a clock frequency. It is also possible to connect an external clock (e.g., from a waveform generator).
- An I$^2$C bus and a I$^2$C selection to select one of the four coating PUF ICs. The I$^2$C bus allows interfacing to a PC via an USB-I$^2$C bridge. The selection is software-programmable.
- Power-on reset circuitry that keeps the reset signal to the logic blocks high when the power is switched on and releases the reset signal only after some time. This prevents incorrect behavior at start-up. The reset signal can also be invoked manually by means of a switch.

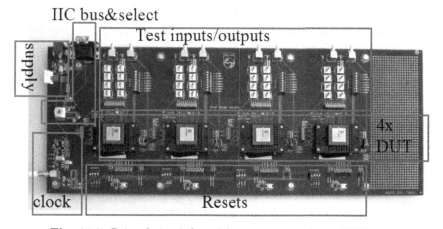

**Fig. 15.7.** Printed circuit board for measuring coating PUF ICs.

- Test inputs and outputs. These enable the monitoring of, for example, the oscillator output and allow testing of the coating PUF ICs. Jumpers are integrated as well, to allow direct external access to each input and output of the coating PUF ICs.

## 15.3 Bare Optical PUFs

Here, we describe the experimental setup used to study bare optical PUFs. The measurement data used in Chapters 13 and 16 were acquired using this setup. Section 15.3.1 gives details on the equipment, which is a straightforward arrangement of a laser, a sample holder, and a camera. Section 15.3.2 gives details on the PUF samples that were tested.

The setup allows for accurate alignment (and realignment) of the laser relative to the sample. Hence, it can be used to study the amount of noise between enrollment measurements and authentication measurements as a function of alignment errors such as shifts and rotations.

### 15.3.1 Measurement Setup

Figure 15.8 shows a schematic overview of the setup for measuring speckle patterns. A laser shines on the PUF, and part of the reflected light is recorded by a camera. Figure 15.9 is a photo of the experimental setup that was used. The laser is a temperature-controlled DFB (Distributed Feedback) laser with wavelength $\lambda = 780$ nm, producing a parallel beam with a diameter $d = 1.0$ mm. The intensity of the beam can be regulated by rotating a polarizer.

The PUF is fastened in a 25 mm circular hole in a metal card the size of a credit card. The metal card is placed in a credit card holder. This allows for accurate repositioning of multiple PUF samples.

The camera is mounted at a fixed location $z = 100$ mm above the card. It is a Charge-Coupled Device (CCD) camera with a pixel pitch of 6.25 μm, taking 1024×768 pixel images with 256 gray levels.

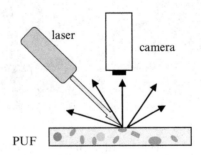

**Fig. 15.8.** Schematic picture of the speckle measurement setup.

**Fig. 15.9.** Photo of the setup.  **Fig. 15.10.** Example of a speckle pattern.

The card holder is linearly adjustable in one direction (left and right in Fig. 15.9, in the plane of the laser and the camera) by means of a motor-driven micrometer. Furthermore, the laser is connected to a motor-driven micrometer as well. This allows one to vary the angle of incidence of the beam while keeping the location of incidence on the PUF constant. The motors and the camera are controlled from a PC.

An example of a speckle pattern recorded with the setup is shown in Fig. 15.10. The typical speckle width at the location of the camera is of the order $\lambda z/d = 78\,\mu$m, corresponding to 12 pixels in the bitmap.

### 15.3.2 PUF Samples

We did experiments with various types of scattering particle in a 0.4 mm thick matrix of acrylic resin. We worked with aluminum particles, mica, and rutile. We determined the memory angle [136] of these samples by studying the correlation between speckle patterns obtained from different angles of incidence. (The memory angle is defined as the angle over which the laser beam must be rotated in order to get a completely decorrelated speckle pattern.) The correlation $C_{BB'}$ between two bitmaps $B$ and $B'$ was computed according to

$$C_{BB'} = \max_{\mathbf{a}} \frac{N^{-1}\sum_{\mathbf{x}} B(\mathbf{x})B'(\mathbf{x}+\mathbf{a}) - [N^{-1}\sum_{\mathbf{x}} B(\mathbf{x})][N^{-1}\sum_{\mathbf{x}} B'(\mathbf{x})]}{\sigma_B \sigma_{B'}}$$

$$\sigma_B^2 := N^{-1}\sum_{\mathbf{x}} B^2(\mathbf{x}) - [N^{-1}\sum_{\mathbf{x}} B(\mathbf{x})]^2. \tag{15.3}$$

We made use of an operational definition of the memory angle as the change in the angle of incidence that causes the correlation to drop below 0.1. With all particle types, we obtained memory angles as low as 6 mrad. By increasing the sample thickness to 1 mm, we were able to reduce the memory angle to less than 2 mrad.

However, we noticed that the mechanical stability of the acrylic resin is not satisfactory: Temperature variations cause deformations of the resin, leading to significant changes of the speckle pattern. Instead, we decided to use glass samples, which are very stable. For practical reasons we did not work with scattering particles embedded in glass, but with 0.4 mm thick glass plates, roughened on one side by grinding and the other side coated with a reflective layer. The combination of scattering from the rough surface and reflections from the coating creates a quasi-3-D PUF structure. We measured a memory angle of approximately 2 mrad.

The results given in Chapters 13 and 16 were obtained with this type of glass sample.

## 15.4 Integrated Optical PUF

Although the setup described in Section 15.3.1 is very useful for doing reasearch, it is too bulky for practical applications. To demonstrate that an optical PUF system can be miniaturized, we built an integrated device containing a laser, a fixed PUF sample, a camera, and a movable lens for applying different challenges. Such a small device could be used as a controlled PUF (see Chapter 14).

A schematic overview is shown in Figs. 15.11 and 15.12, and a photo of the device is shown in Fig. 15.13. The total size of the device is 21.5 mm× 21.5 mm×13.5 mm. The laser is a VCSEL chip of size 0.23 mm×0.28 mm× 0.25 mm; the wavelength is 850 nm. The temperature stability is $\triangle\lambda/\triangle T = 0.06$ nm/K. The current stability is $\triangle\lambda/\triangle I = 0.39$ nm/mA. The laser light

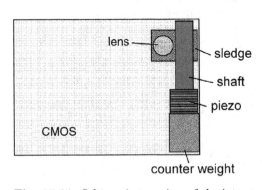

Fig. 15.11. Schematic top view of the integrated optical PUF.

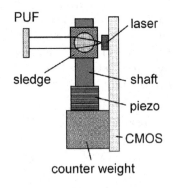

Fig. 15.12. Side view.

**Fig. 15.13.** Photo of the stick-slip motor.

is collimated by a spherical lens, located at 0.3 mm from the laser, and then scatters from the PUF, which has a distance of 5 mm from the lens. The beam width at the location of the PUF is approximately $d = 100 \, \mu$m.

The PUF is a piece of rough glass with a reflective back side, as described in Section 15.3.2. The distance between the PUF and the sensor (perpendicular to the sensor plane) is $z = 6.5$ mm. The camera is a CMOS (Complementary Metal-Oxide-Semiconductor) sensor with area 5 mm×3.75 mm and pixel pitch 6.5 $\mu$m. The typical speckle width on the sensor is of order $\lambda z / d = 55 \, \mu$m, corresponding to 9 pixels.

Multiple PUF challenges are achieved by moving the lens perpendicular to the beam. By doing so, the collimated beam coming out of the lens rotates, changing the angle and location of incidence of the light beam on the PUF. The lens is mounted on a sledge. The sledge is driven by a so-called "stick-slip" motor, which can perform tiny displacements of the order of 0.1 $\mu$m. The sledge can move along a shaft. The sledge is displaced by applying a sawtooth-shaped voltage to a piezo, which pushes the shaft. Each period of this sawtooth results in a tiny displacement, and the direction of the slope of the sawtooth determines the direction in which the sledge is moved. Figure 15.13 shows a photo of this motor mounted on a CMOS sensor. The maximum displacement of the sledge is 0.4 mm, corresponding to a range of 0.6 rad for the angle of incidence. As the memory angle is 2 mrad, the number of different challenges is approximately 300. An example of a speckle pattern obtained with the integrated PUF is shown in Fig. 15.14. The bottom right corner is overexposed because it is located next to the laser. The dark band

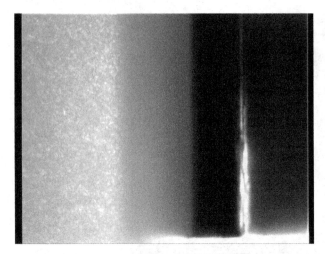

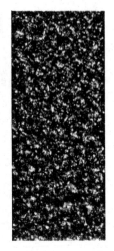

**Fig. 15.14.** Raw image recorded by the CMOS sensor.     **Fig. 15.15.** Part of the image after local logarithmic equalization.

on the right-hand side of the picture is the shadow cast by a barrier next to the laser. Cropping a 240×574 pixel properly exposed part of the bitmap and applying a local logarithmic gray-scale equalization yields the pattern shown in Fig. 15.15.

# Secure Key Storage with PUFs

Pim Tuyls, Geert-Jan Schrijen, Frans Willems, Tanya Ignatenko, and Boris Škorić

## 16.1 Introduction

Nowadays, people carry around devices (cell phones, PDAs, bank passes, etc.) that have a high value. That value is often contained in the data stored in it or lies in the services the device can grant access to (by using secret identification information stored in it). These devices often operate in hostile environments and their protection level is not adequate to deal with that situation. Bank passes and credit cards contain a magnetic stripe where identification information is stored. In the case of bank passes, a PIN is additionally required to withdraw money from an ATM (Automated Teller Machine). At various occasions, it has been shown that by placing a small coil in the reader, the magnetic information stored in the stripe can easily be copied and used to produce a *cloned* card. Together with eavesdropping the PIN (by listening to the keypad or recording it with a camera), an attacker can easily impersonate the legitimate owner of the bank pass by using the cloned card in combination with the eavesdropped PIN.

A higher level of protection is obtained when the magnetic stripe is replaced by an integrated circuit (IC) to store secret or valuable information and to carry out the critical security operations. Using state-of-the-art cryptographic techniques, a very strong solution is guaranteed as long as the IC acts as a black box.

It has, however, been shown that the black-box assumption does not fit real life very well, especially for devices (smart cards, PDAs, mobile phones) that operate in hostile environments, even for ICs. Although the use of an IC makes a device harder to attack, it turns out that there are many successful physical attacks on ICs. These attacks can be divided into three classes: non-invasive physical attacks (e.g., side channel attacks: Simple Power Analysis, Differential Power Analysis, ElectroMagnetic Analysis attacks [9,172]), invasive physical attacks (attacks that modify the physical structure: e.g., focused ion beam, etching, etc.), and fault attacks [29] (attacks that cause faults in the cryptographic operations). The fact that some of those attacks are carried out in a relatively simple way (some without requiring knowledge about implementation details) makes them very dangerous. Often, the attacker can retrieve the whole secret key from the physical attack alone. Sometimes, the attack is combined with a traditional cryptanalytic attack to reveal the whole key. In order to bridge the gap between the black-box model and real life, new models and technological components have to be developed that take into account attackers that have some access to the devices carrying out cryptographic operations. This extended set of cryptographic techniques is what we call *grey-box cryptography*.

In a first and practical approach to deal with this critical gap, the smartcard industry is working on protective measures against invasive attacks, namely protective layers and coatings that are difficult to remove. Removing the layer implies removing part of the IC, which renders the IC unusable. Furthermore, sensors are sometimes built into the IC to check for the presence of the protective layer. If removal is detected, the IC will stop functioning and hence prevent an attacker from learning its secrets. Although such coatings further increase the threshold, it turns out that, in practice, an attacker can often still successfully remove a coating (and possibly fool the sensors) and get access to the IC's interior (e.g., by using a focused ion beam (FIB)). The FIB is used to influence the (yes/no) signal that indicates the presence of the protective coating. A more secure form of protective coatings, which has the potential to protect even against these sophisticated attacks, is the *active coating* that was first introduced in [226] and further investigated in [163].

*Memory encryption* [304] is an important algorithmic component used to protect sensitive information. The encryption protects information from being exposed to an attacker who gets access to the memory. However, it is important to observe that a key is still needed to encrypt and decrypt that information. The problem is then reduced to the secure storage of the secret key of the memory encryption scheme.

Recently, a fundamental theoretical approach [130, 200] was developed to tackle this problem and deal with the current unsatisfactory situation. In [200], a theoretical model dubbed *physically observable cryptography* was proposed and investigated. The concept of *algorithmic tamper-proof security* was introduced in [130] to provide very strong security against physical attacks. Within this last concept, three basic components were identified to achieve this: (1) *read-proof hardware*, (2) *tamper-proof hardware*, and (3) *a self-destruction capability*. Unfortunately, no practical implementations were presented in [130].

### Contributions of This Chapter

In this chapter, we focus on the development of *practical* read-proof hardware against invasive physical attacks. The word "security" has to be understood in this context.

We explain how physical unclonable functions (PUFs) can be used for this goal. In particular, we describe how secure keys are extracted from PUFs in practice. We investigate two important kinds of PUFs: coating PUFs [271] and optical PUFs [221]. Note that we do not provide a solution against side-channel attacks.

We first give some intuition for the use of (optical) PUFs for building read-proof hardware in a very simple situation. Optical PUFs consist of a 3-D physical structure that produces a speckle pattern (response) when irradiated with a laser beam. A slight change in the conditions under which they are challenged produces a completely different response. It was shown in [272] that they support a very large number of challenge response pairs (CRPs). By embedding a PUF into a credit card, the card becomes unclonable and can hence be identified with an extremely high degree of confidence.

Upon reading, the reader checks the authenticity of the card by challenging the structure with a randomly chosen challenge and verifies the obtained response versus a reference response stored in a database. Even if the attacker captures such a card and gains access to it, he cannot make a clone in a reasonable amount of time. This implies that optical PUFs represent a gray-box equivalent of other identifiers such as holograms, which fit more in the black-box model.

As a first example of secure key storage, we present coating PUFs. Coating PUFs are based on on-chip capacitive measurements of random dielectric properties of a protective layer on top of an IC [271]. Their main application is to serve as the secure storage medium on the IC from which the secret keys are extracted at the point in time when they are needed. When the coating is attacked, it is damaged to such an extent that the key can be retrieved only with great effort.

As a more sophisticated and more powerful example, we consider optical PUFs integrated with an IC (introduced in Chapter 15). From a security perspective, the main difference with coating PUFs is that optical PUFs have a much higher number of CRPs and more entropy per response (see Chapters 12 and 13). Experiments show that slight changes in the PUF material (e.g., caused by an attack) create substantially different speckle patterns and hence destroy the key. Additionally, when the response of one challenge is compromised, many other challenges with unpredictable responses remain to extract a key. These properties make optical PUFs well suited to implement a strong version of read-proof hardware.

Read-proof hardware in general, and our construction in particular, can be applied for secure key storage in smartcards, SIM (Subscriber Identity Module) cards, TPMs (trusted platform modules), DRM (digital rights management) systems, and RFID (Radio-Frequency Identification) tags [269].

## 16.2 PUFs for Read-Proof Hardware

In order to protect a long-term key $K$ against physical attacks, we propose the following principles:

- Do not store long-term keys in non-volatile digital memory.
- During cryptographic operations with a long-term key in volatile memory, do not at any time let significant portions of the key reside in the volatile memory.

The motivation for these principles is as follows. Digital storage is susceptible to powerful attacks whose effectiveness is based on the strong distinguishability of physical states representing a "0" or "1" value. Instead, we propose to extract keys from a *tamper-evident* physical structure (possibly integrated with the device) such that the key is only temporarily present in the device (only at the point in time when used). PUFs are a natural candidate for these physical sources. Furthermore, there are powerful attacks that "freeze" volatile (RAM) memory. We assume that such an attack critically damages a PUF, but it still allows the attacker to get information about the key that is present in the RAM at the time of attack. In order to reduce this information, the RAM should not contain a significant part of $K$ at any time. The attack cannot be repeated (since the PUF is effectively destroyed), and, hence, most of the key then remains unknown to the attacker.

### 16.2.1 Attack Model for Read-Proof Hardware

To put the discussion on a more formal footing, we describe in detail the attacks against which the read-proof hardware must be resistant. An attack is considered to be successful if the attacker obtains sufficient information to reconstruct the key $K$. We consider a device containing a long-term storage medium (the physical structure), means for extracting responses from this medium (sensors), a processing unit, separate long-term memory for storing the instructions that run on the processor, and volatile memory in which cryptographic operations are performed with $K$. The attacker is allowed to attack any of these. It is assumed that the method of challenging the physical structure is known to him, as well as the precise challenges used to extract $K$. We consider the following attacks:

1. **Non-invasive inspection of the volatile memory, processor, or sensors.** These methods do not damage any part of the device. Examples are optical imaging and side-channel attacks.
2. **Invasive inspection of the volatile memory, processor, or sensors.** These methods physically modify/damage at least one part of the device. Examples are etching and FIBs.
3. **Detachment of the long-term storage medium.** The attacker detaches the physical structure from the rest of the device without

damaging it. Then he challenges it (using his own measurement device) to obtain $K$ from the measured responses.

4. **Non-invasive physical attack on the long-term storage medium.** The attacker first subjects the physical structure to non-destructive scrutiny (e.g., by microscopy or X-ray imaging). Then he uses the obtained information to get $K$ in one of the following ways:
   (a) He makes a physical clone of the structure and challenges it (using his own measurement device) to obtain $K$ from the measured responses.
   (b) He mathematically models the physical structure. He computes the responses to the appropriate challenges to obtain $K$.

5. **Invasive physical attack on the long-term storage medium.** The attacker first subjects the physical structure to a destructive analysis (e.g., by etching, drilling, or sawing). Then he uses the obtained information to get $K$ in one of the following ways:
   (a) He makes a physical clone of the structure and challenges it (using his own measurement device) to obtain $K$ from the measured responses.
   (b) He mathematically models the physical structure. He computes the responses to the appropriate challenges to obtain $K$.

6. **Code modification.** The attacker modifies the algorithms stored in the device such that $K$ is revealed.

## 16.2.2 Requirements

In order to be resistant against all of the above-mentioned attacks, the hardware has to meet the following requirements:

1. The physical structure must be bound inseparably to the rest of the hardware. Any attempt to separate it should result in significant damage to the structure. (This gives resistance against attack 3.)
2. "Inscrutability": Measurements (both destructive and non-destructive) must not reveal accurate information about the composition of the physical structure. (This protects against the data acquisition phase of attacks 4 and 5.)
3. The physical structure has to be opaque and it has to cover the sensors, the processor, and the volatile memory. (This gives resistance against attack 1.)
4. The structure has to be *unclonable*. This is defined as follows:
   (a) *Physical unclonability.* It should be hard to make a physical copy that has a similar challenge-response behavior as the original structure, even given accurate knowledge of the structure's composition.
   (b) *Mathematical unclonability.* It should be hard to construct a mathematical model that has a non-negligible probability of correctly predicting responses, even given accurate knowledge of the structure's composition.
   (This property protects against the cloning phase of attacks 4 and 5.)

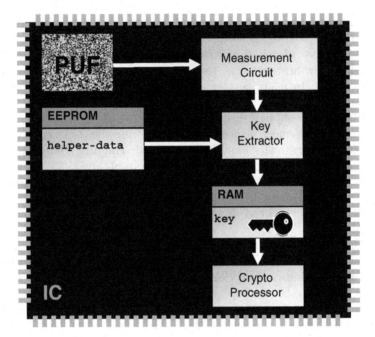

**Fig. 16.1.** Schematic layout of an IC with a PUF for secure key storage.

5. The physical structure has to be tamper-evident. Physical damage should significantly[1] change the challenge-response behavior. (This protects against attack 2 and adds resistance against the data acquisition phase of attack 5.)
6. The hardware must contain tamper-proof memory that can be read but not modified. In this memory, public data are stored (e.g., algorithms and public keys) that are not secret but whose integrity must be guaranteed. (This prevents attack 6.)

Finally, in order to be practically feasible, it must be easy to challenge the structure and measure its response. Preferably, the structure is inexpensive and easy to integrate in a device.

Given the requirements stated above, PUFs form a natural candidate technology as a basis for a secure key storage device. There are two main ways to use them for this purpose.

1. The long-term key $K$ is extracted from one or more PUF responses by means of a helper-data algorithm (fuzzy extractor).
2. The long-term key $K$ is stored in encrypted form, $E_{K_i}(K)$, in some non-secure memory. The short-term keys $K_i$ used for encrypting the long-term key $K$ are extracted from the PUF.

---

[1] This statement is made more precise in Section 16.6.3.

The second option has several advantages: (1) When the PUF has many challenges, the short-term keys are different every time they are generated. This provides protection against side-channel attacks on the PUF readout. (2) Additional protection against side-channel attacks is achieved when the key $K$ is considered as a long-term secret on which several secret keys in later stages are based. These keys are derived by using so-called exposure-resilient functions [52].

A schematic overview of an IC with PUF-based secure key storage is shown in Fig. 16.1.

## 16.3 Cryptographic Preliminaries

We propose to extract a key from physical sources (PUFs) present on an IC. Since measurements on a physical structure are inherently noisy, the responses of such a structure cannot be directly used as a key. An additional problem is that these responses are not uniformly random. In order to guarantee security, the extracted key should have entropy equal to its length.

This implies that we need a helper-data algorithm/fuzzy extractor [91,182] for reconstruction of the keys. A helper-data scheme consists of a pair of algorithms $(G, W)$ and two phases: an *enrollment* and a *reconstruction* phase. We will use the following notation: $x$ denotes the measurement value of a response during the enrollment phase and $y$ denotes the corresponding value during the reconstruction phase. During enrollment, the key $K$ is created for the first time. The helper-data algorithm $W(\cdot, \cdot)$ is used during the enrollment phase and creates the helper data $w$ based on the measurement value $x$ during enrollment and the randomly chosen key $K$. The algorithm $G(\cdot, \cdot)$ is used during the key reconstruction phase for reconstruction of the key $K$ as follows: $K = G(w, y)$. It was proven in [278] that this approach is equivalent to a fuzzy extractor.

As a second primitive, we need a standard digital signature scheme (SS): is $(\text{SK}_g, \text{Sign}, V)$, where $\text{SK}_g$ is the secret-key generation algorithm, Sign is the signing algorithm, and $V$ is the verification algorithm. The enroller runs $\text{SK}_g$ and obtains a secret-public key pair $(sk, pk)$. This is a one-time action. The public key $pk$ is hard-wired in each IC (in tamper-proof memory). With the private key $sk$, the enroller signs the helper data $w$ and $P(K)$ (where $P$ is a one-way function). The signatures $\sigma(w)$ and $\sigma(P(K))$ are then stored in the EEPROM (Electrically Erasable Programmable ROM) of the IC together with the helper data $w$.[2]

---

[2] Instead of storing $\sigma(P(K))$, it is more secure to store $\sigma(P(K), \tilde{x})$, where $\tilde{x}$ is additional unpredictable key material that is obtained from the PUF (if necessary, derived from the response of a second challenge). We have chosen not to include this in the notation for the sake of transparency.

### 16.3.1 Procedure for Generation and Reconstruction

Creation and reconstruction of the key $K$ is done as follows. First, the global statistical properties (noise level, etc.) of the behavior of the physical structure are determined. In particular, the entropy of the output of the physical structure is estimated and the secrecy capacity $\mathbf{I}(X;Y)$ (mutual information) is estimated of the channel describing the noisy observation.[3] This can be done using the methods described in [150]. These parameters determine the choice of the key length $k$ and of an appropriate helper-data algorithm $(G, W)$.

### Enrollment

This phase consists of two steps:

1. Generation of a key $K \in \{0,1\}^k$ and helper data $w$ by $w \leftarrow W(x, K)$.
2. The IC interprets $K$ as a private key and generates the corresponding public key $P(K)$. Then the IC outputs $(w, P(K))$. The enroller signs these data and stores the signatures $\sigma(w)$ and $\sigma(P(K))$ in the IC's EEPROM.[4]

### Reconstruction

The IC performs the following steps:

1. It retrieves $w, \sigma(w)$ from EEPROM and checks the signature $\sigma(w)$ by running $V$ on $w$ and $\sigma(w)$ using the public key $pk$. If the signature is not OK, the IC shuts down permanently. Otherwise, it continues.
2. The IC challenges its physical structure and obtains the measurement value $y$ (note that, typically, $y \neq x$ due to noise).
3. The data $w$ and $y$ are processed by the helper-data algorithm $G$. This yields the key $K' \leftarrow G(w, y)$.
4. The IC computes $P(K')$. Then it runs $V$ on $P(K')$ and $\sigma(P(K))$ using the public key $pk$. If the signature is OK, the IC proceeds and $K$ can be used as a private key. Otherwise, the IC shuts down permanently.

### 16.3.2 The Continuous Case

Helper data and fuzzy extractors have been extensively studied in the discrete case, but only few papers have studied the continuous situation [182]. Since, in reality, PUF responses are often continuous data rather than discrete data, it is worthwhile to spend a few words on techniques for the continuous case.

---

[3] This is a one-time event that is performed during a pre-processing step.
[4] Alternatively, $K$ is used as a symmetric key. The IC outputs $K$ and the enroller stores $\sigma(P(K))$ in the EEPROM. The circuit that outputs $K$ is destroyed after this procedure.

For discrete PUF responses $\mathbf{X} \in \{0,1\}^n$, a fuzzy extractor performs two steps:

- Information reconciliation, which is basically an error-correction step;
- Privacy amplification, which guarantees that the extracted string is uniformly random.

When the PUF response is continuous (i.e., the PUF response $\mathbf{X}$ is a random variable on $\mathbb{R}^n$), the situation is slightly different. Since keys are binary strings, a discretization (quantization) step has to be performed. We identify the following two steps:

- *Fuzzy discretization*: During this step, the continuous variable $\mathbf{X}$ is turned into a binary string $\mathbf{S}$ such that (1) when a noisy version $\mathbf{Y}$ of $\mathbf{X}$ is measured, a string $\mathbf{S}'$ is obtained that lies close to $\mathbf{S}$ according to some distance measure and (2) the string $\mathbf{S}$ is uniformly random distributed.
- A *discrete fuzzy extractor/helper data algorithm* is applied to the (noisy) string $\mathbf{S}$ in order to remove the noise and to guarantee the randomness of the extracted key $K$.

The main difference between the continuous case and the discrete case is the fact that in order to perform the *fuzzy discretization* step, the probability distribution has to be known. It turns out that by performing a sufficient amount of measurements on the PUF, this distribution can be determined in practice. Below, we illustrate how a fuzzy discretization is performed in some concrete cases such as optical and coating PUFs.

## 16.4 Secure Key Storage with Optical PUFs

In this section we describe some techniques for using optical PUFs as a source of large amounts of secret-key material. Details on the physical structure of optical PUFs can be found in Chapter 15.

An optical PUF consists of a physical structure containing many random, uncontrollable components. Typically, one can think of a piece of glass containing randomly distributed light-scattering particles. When irradiated with a laser beam, they produce a speckle pattern (see Fig. 16.2 for an example). This speckle pattern can be considered as the unique fingerprint of the structure. We distinguish between *bare* optical PUFs and *integrated* ones. Bare optical PUFs are simply referred to as optical PUFs and consist of the physical structure only. Integrated optical PUFs consist of a physical structure integrated with the laser and reading device, and all are optionally integrated into an IC. Note that an integrated PUF is not necessarily a controlled PUF (see Chapter 14). As usual with physical systems, the responses are not exactly equal when the system is measured several times, even when challenged under seemingly identical circumstances. This is what we call the robustness or noise problem.

**Robustness**

We briefly describe some noise sources for optical PUFs.

1. **Interdevice variation:** For bare PUFs, the external reader that challenges the PUF and detects the response during the verification phase is typically a different device than the one that was used during the enrollment phase. Alignment and sensitivity differences between readers give rise to noise, unless great pains are taken to enforce very small mechanical and/or electrical tolerances. However, the potential number of readers is enormous, making such a standardization impractical and expensive.
2. **Physical environment:** Even repeated measurements with the same challenging and detection device do not give identical results. Time-dependent external influences like temperature, moisture, vibrations, stray light, stray fields, and so forth can have an impact on the measurements.
3. **Interaction with environment:** The PUF itself is not immutable. It can accidentally get damaged. Another problem is spontaneous degradation. Most materials slowly change over time due to chemical reactions, friction, and repeated thermal deformations. The rate of drifting determines the lifetime of the key material in the PUF.

In order to get a sufficient level of robustness one can use several methods (which are best combined): (a) **physical noise reduction:** reducing the noise at the source; (b) **algorithmic noise correction:** given a certain level of noise, extracting as much robust key material as possible by properly choosing a fuzzy discretizer and fuzzy extractor. In the remainder of this chapter we discuss algorithmic countermeasures. Hardware countermeasures have been described in [287].

## 16.5 Key Extraction from Speckle Patterns

In this section, we present a concrete implementation of a fuzzy discretizer and a fuzzy extractor for speckle patterns.

### 16.5.1 Pre-processing

In order to turn the speckle pattern into a compact binary representation, it is first filtered using a 2-D Gabor transform, which is defined as follows [287]. The basis function $\Gamma(s, \mathbf{k}, \mathbf{x_0}, \mathbf{x})$ is the product of a plane wave with wave vector $\mathbf{k}$ and a Gaussian with width $s$ centered on $\mathbf{x_0}$. Here, $\mathbf{x}$ denotes a location in the speckle image. The Gabor basis functions $\Gamma$ and the Gabor coefficients $G$ are given by

$$G(s, \mathbf{k}, \mathbf{x_0}) = \int d^2x \ \Gamma(s, \mathbf{k}, \mathbf{x_0}, \mathbf{x}) I(\mathbf{x}) \qquad (16.1)$$

$$\Gamma(s, \mathbf{k}, \mathbf{x_0}, \mathbf{x}) = \frac{1}{s\sqrt{2\pi}} \ \sin[\mathbf{k} \cdot (\mathbf{x} - \mathbf{x_0})] \ \exp\left[-\frac{(\mathbf{x} - \mathbf{x_0})^2}{4s^2}\right]. \qquad (16.2)$$

**Fig. 16.2.** Speckle pattern, **Fig. 16.3.** 45° Gabor Co- **Fig. 16.4.** Binarization of
512x512 pixels.                   efficients of Fig. 16.2 after Fig. 16.3.
                                  subsampling, 64x64 pixels.

$I(\mathbf{x})$ denotes the light intensity at location $\mathbf{x}$. We have selected the imaginary part of the transform since it is invariant under spatially constant shifts of $I$. In our experiments, the following parameters have been used for the Gabor transform: A single Gaussian width $s = 18$ pixels; a single length $|\mathbf{k}| = \pi/(8$ pixels); the direction of $\mathbf{k}$ is 45° with respect to the horizontal axis; $\mathbf{x}_0$ are positions in a square grid with a spacing of 8 pixels. This yields a Gabor image as depicted in Fig. 16.3, consisting of 4096 Gabor coefficients.

In order to turn this analog representation into a binary representation, the Gabor coefficients are binarized by quantizing the values into two quantization intervals: Positive values of $G$ are mapped to 1 and negative values to are mapped to 0. The resulting image is depicted in Fig. 16.4.

### 16.5.2 Fuzzy Discretiser: The Concept of Robust Components

Here, we briefly describe the general idea of how to get a noise-robust vector from a speckle pattern. First we introduce some notation. For a vector $\mathbf{V} \in \mathbb{R}^n$ and a set $A \subset \{1,\ldots,n\}$, we denote by $\mathbf{V}_A$ the restriction of $\mathbf{V}$ to its components indexed by the set $A$. Based on the nature of a speckle pattern, we model the Gabor coefficients on the $\mathbf{x}_0$ grid as a real-valued vector $\mathbf{g} \in \mathbb{R}^n$. The binarized coefficients are denoted as a vector $\mathbf{X} \in \{0,1\}^n$. The enrollment measurement is denoted by $\mathbf{X}$ and the later measurements are denoted by $\mathbf{Y}$, which are noisy versions of $\mathbf{X}$.

We introduce the notion of *robust components*. Loosely speaking, a component $i$ of $\mathbf{X}$ is called *robust* if the probability of a bit flip in that component is low. More precisely, we define this as follows:

**Definition 16.1.** *Let* $m, \epsilon > 0$ *and let* $\mathbf{g}^1, \ldots, \mathbf{g}^m \in \mathbb{R}^n$ *be a sequence of vectors. Then, for* $i \in \{1, \ldots, n\}$, *we say that the ith component is* $(\epsilon, m)$*-robust if and only if*

$$\left| \frac{1}{m} \sum_{j=1}^{m} \mathrm{sgn}(g_i^j) \right| \geq 1 - \epsilon.$$

The sequence $\mathbf{g}^1, \ldots, \mathbf{g}^m$ has to be interpreted as a sequence of measurement results (analog Gabor coefficients) performed during enrollment.

The fuzzy discretizer performs two steps. First, robust components are selected from $\mathbf{X}$ and their positions are stored in a first set of helper data $w_1$. Since the components of $\mathbf{X}_{w_1}$ are not uniformly random distributed, a further (random) subselection of components is made in such a way that this subselection *is* uniformly distributed. The positions of the remaining bits are stored in helper data $w_2 \subset w_1$.

Several methods have been developed to determine the robust components. Below, we present two practical schemes. The first scheme (Section 16.5.3) selects the analog Gabor coefficients with the highest absolute value. In the second scheme (Section 16.5.4), the selection is based on an estimate of the probability distribution of the binarized Gabor coefficients.

### 16.5.3 Robust Components: Scheme 1

Robust components are selected using soft-decision information available before binarization. They are selected as the $m$ components $i$ with the largest corresponding absolute Gabor value $|g_i|$ (in our experiments, $m$ was typically 511). It is intuitively clear that this is consistent with Definition 16.1. In Fig. 16.5 the selected robust bits are depicted as black (0) and white (1) pixels, whereas the non-robust bits are gray. The locations of these black and white pixels are stored in helper data $w_1$. By restricting $\mathbf{X}$ to its robust components, we obtain a binary string $\mathbf{S} = \mathbf{X}_{w_1} \in \{0,1\}^m$.

### 16.5.4 Robust Components: Scheme 2

In this scheme, the robust components are selected by predicting the value of a second enrollment image $\mathbf{X}^2$ given the values of neighboring pixels in a first enrollment image $\mathbf{X}^1$. The pixels whose values can be well predicted are defined as the robust ones. A well-known algorithm to construct a probabilistic model that allows to make such predictions is the context-tree weighting (CTW) compression algorithm [293].

Let $\mathbf{X}^1, \mathbf{X}^2 \in \{0,1\}^n$ be two observations of the same (ergodic) source over a noisy channel. Let $A$ be a finite subset of $\{0, \ldots, n-1\}$. We use the CTW

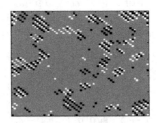

**Fig. 16.5.** Robust bits from large Gabor coefficients. Black = 0, white = 1, gray = non-robust.

algorithm [293] to estimate the model statistics $\mathbb{P}[X_t^2 = 1|\{X_{t-a}^1, a \in A\}]$ for $t \in \{0, \ldots, n-1\}$. Typically, the set $A$ is defined as a number of positions in the neighborhood of the position $t$.

We define $\epsilon$-robust components as those positions $t$ for which, according to the estimated model, $\mathbb{P}[X_t^2 = 1|\{X_{t-a}^1, a \in A\}] \leq \epsilon$ or $\mathbb{P}[X_t^2 = 1|\{X_{t-a}^1, a \in A\}] \geq 1 - \epsilon$, where $\epsilon < 0.5$ is a positive constant. The positions $t$ (in the enrollment image) that satisfy this criterion are stored in helper data $w_1 \subset \{0, \ldots, n-1\}$ and the string $\mathbf{S}$ is defined as $\mathbf{S} = \mathbf{X}_{w_1}^1$.

We apply this method to speckle patterns. During enrollment, we start from four (as an example) pre-processed speckle patterns $\mathbf{X}^1, \ldots, \mathbf{X}^4$. Then the CTW algorithm is used to estimate the model statistics $\mathbb{P}[X_t^2 = 1|\{X_{t-a}^1, a \in A\}]$. In order to get better estimates, based on more data, the CTW statistics are updated two more times. First, it is updated with probabilities $\mathbb{P}[X_t^3 = 1|\{X_{t-a}^1, a \in A\}]$ and then with probabilities $\mathbb{P}[X_t^4 = 1|\{X_{t-a}^1, a \in A\}]$. The set $A$ consists of the local pixel ($t$) itself and the eight surrounding pixels.

This statistical model obtained with this procedure is employed to identify which bits are highly predictable (i.e., robust). An example is shown in Figs. 16.6 and 16.7 for $\epsilon = 0.1$. The locations of the robust pixels are stored as helper data $w_1 \subset \{0, \ldots, n-1\}$, and the string $\mathbf{S}$ is defined as $\mathbf{S} = X_{w_1}^1$.

### 16.5.5 Fuzzy Discretizer: Randomness Extractor

The robust bits $\mathbf{S}$, specified in the set $W_1$, are not uniformly random distributed. In other words, these bits do not have full entropy. Intuitively, this can be seen from the fact that the bits appear in diagonal stripes of equal value in the Gabor transformed images.[5] This is furthermore confirmed by compressing $\mathbf{S}$

**Fig. 16.6.** Binarized Gabor image.    **Fig. 16.7.** Robust pixel locations (black = 0, white = 1). Non-robust pixels are depicted in gray.

---

[5] Note that the direction of the sequences is related to the 45° direction in which the Gabor transform was applied [287].

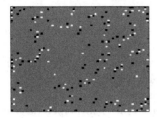

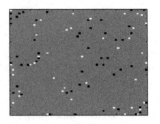

**Fig. 16.8.** Decimated robust bits.     **Fig. 16.9.** Random sub-selection of decimated robust bits.

with the CTW universal source-coding algorithm [150,293], using neighboring pixels from Fig. 16.5 as context. With this method, the $m = 511$ bits can be compressed into 138 bits, a compression ration of 27%. Although this is merely an upper bound for the compression ratio, it clearly shows that the 511 bits certainly do not have full entropy. This is due to the fact that there are still strong correlations between the pixels. In order to remove the correlations in **S**, the following steps are performed during enrollment:

- **S** is *decimated*: For every sequence of correlated bits (i.e., a sequence that forms a stripe), a single bit is randomly chosen. This process is called *decimating*. An example is shown in Fig. 16.8. From the original $m = 511$ robust bits, only 190 are left. (Using the CTW method, it turns out that these 190 bits can be compressed into 179 bits (94%), which shows that the decimated bits still do not have full entropy.)
- From this selection of bits, a further random subselection is made. Figure 16.9 shows an example: Fifty percent of the bits of Fig. 16.8 are randomly selected; only 95 bits are left.
- The resulting string should have entropy equal to its length, given all side information that is available (e.g., helper data and the knowledge that one has about the original measurement data). We verify this randomness property by running the CTW compression algorithm and checking whether the string is properly incompressible. When that is the case, the positions of those remaining bits are stored in the helper dataset $w_2 \subset w_1$. In the example case given above, the string turns out to be incompressible and, hence, the remaining 95 bit positions are stored in dataset $w_2$.

We note that the rate of the above scheme is equal to 2.5%, which is rather low when compared with the secrecy capacity of such a channel that has been reported to be equal to 25% in [150].

### 16.5.6 Discrete Fuzzy Extractor

In order to guarantee that no errors remain in the final key $K$, a discrete fuzzy extractor is applied in the final step to the string $\mathbf{X}_{w_2}$. Since the string $\mathbf{X}_{w_2}$ is uniformly random distributed by construction, this can be done by the so-called *code offset* approach. This technique is described in Chapter 4. The fuzzy extractor yields the final key $K$. It is guaranteed to be close to random and no longer contains noise.

### 16.5.7 Two-Way Use of Helper Data

In all schemes discussed so far, helper data are generated during enrollment and applied at the time of key reconstruction. However, the measuring device is capable of producing helper data also in the verification/key reconstruction phase. Instead of discarding this extra information, one can use it to improve the robustness of the extracted keys. We present an interactive protocol between a reader and a verifier. The robust components obtained from enrolment and verification are combined using an "AND" operation.

- **Enrollment:** The Verifier subjects the PUF to a challenge $C$ and converts the analog response $R$ to a bitstring $\mathbf{X}$. He determines robust components and constructs the helper dataset $w$ of pointers to the robust parts of $\mathbf{X}$. He stores $(\mathrm{ID}_{\mathrm{PUF}}, C, w, \mathbf{X})$.
- **Key reconstruction:** The PUF is inserted into the reader and the reader sends $\mathrm{ID}_{\mathrm{PUF}}$ to the Verifier. The Verifier sends $C$ and $w$. The reader challenges the PUF with $C$ and measures a response $R'$, which it converts into a bitstring $\mathbf{X}'$. It determines the robust components of $X'$ and constructs new helper data $w'$. It sends $w'$ to the Verifier. Both the reader and the Verifier now compute the *combined helper data* $W = w \cap w'$. The Verifier computes $\mathbf{S} = \mathbf{X}_W$, and the reader computes $\mathbf{S}' = \mathbf{X}'_W$. Finally, $\mathbf{S}$ and $\mathbf{S}'$ are used for the construction of a secret key (e.g., using a fuzzy extractor).

An analysis of error probabilities and key lengths was presented in [287]. It was shown there that the bit error probability in $\mathbf{S}$ is drastically improved, compared to the "one-way" case, where only the enrolled helper data are used ($\mathbf{S}_{1\mathrm{way}} = \mathbf{X}_w$; $\mathbf{S}'_{1\mathrm{way}} = \mathbf{X}'_w$). As a consequence, the amount of computational effort spent on the error correction is greatly reduced. Furthermore, it turns out that the extracted keys are longer because fewer redundancy bits are needed. For a reasonable choice of parameters, the improvement in bit error probability in $S'$ can be as small as a factor 5 and as large as 50. The simultaneous improvement in key length varies between 20% and 70%. The difference between the two methods is most pronounced when the measurements are very noisy.

## 16.6 Secure Key Storage with Coating PUFs

In this section we discuss secure storage of keys in ICs using coating PUFs. First, we briefly list the properties of the coating. (See Chapter 15 for more details on the hardware.) Then we give a fuzzy discretization algorithm for obtaining uniformly distributed bitstrings from the capacitance measurements. Finally, we present experimental results, including an analysis of the resistance against FIB attacks.

### 16.6.1 Coating PUF Properties

A coating PUF consists of a coating with random dielectric particles that is deposited on top of the IC. The top metal layer of the IC contains sensors that locally measure the capacitance values of the coating. The chemical composition of the coating gives it a number of favorable properties. (1) The coating is opaque, absorbing light from the infrared part of the spectrum to the ultraviolet. (2) The conductive particles in the coating shield off electromagnetic emissions of the IC. (3) The coating is mechanically tough and very strongly bound to the IC. (4) It is resistant against chemical substances.

Furthermore, inspection of the coating PUF from the outside is difficult. Measuring from the outside gives different capacitance results than from the inside, since the on-chip measurements are very sensitive to the precise locations of the dielectric particles.

The information content of a coating is much lower than that of an optical PUF. The theoretical value is 6.6 bits of entropy per $(120\,\mu m^2)$ sensor (see Chapter 12). In practice (Section 16.6.3), we extract less than 4 bits per sensor. However, this is sufficient entropy for key storage in a controlled PUF.

### 16.6.2 Fuzzy Discretization

In this section we describe the algorithmic part of our architecture for coating PUFs. Since a coating PUF consists of $n$ sensors that measure coating properties independently, we model the responses of a coating PUF as a continuous vector $\mathbf{X} \in \mathbb{R}^n$ of independent identically distributed (i.i.d.) random variables with probability distribution $\rho$. Experiments have shown that the i.i.d. property is well satisfied and that $\rho$ is well approximated by a Gaussian distribution.

We describe the discretisation algorithm for a single component $X \in \mathbb{R}$. The generalization to all components is straightforward. In order to extract a binary string $S \in \{0,1\}^l$ from $X$, the following steps are performed during enrollment:

- Choose an equiprobable partition of $\mathbb{R}$, $\mathcal{A} = \{A_0, \ldots, A_{2^l-1}\}$, such that $\mathbb{P}[X \in A_0] = \mathbb{P}[X \in A_1] = \cdots = \mathbb{P}[X \in A_{2^l-1}] = 1/2^l$. Subdivide this partition into equiprobable "left" and "right" parts: $A_i = A_i^{\text{left}} \cup A_i^{\text{right}}$, with $\mathbb{P}[X \in A_i^{\text{left}}] = \mathbb{P}[X \in A_i^{\text{right}}] = 2^{-l-1}$. (The resulting partition is denoted as $\mathcal{A}_{\text{sub}}$.)
- Give $S$ a value according to the interval $i(x)$ in $\mathcal{A}$ to which $x$ belongs; for example, if $l = 3$ and $x \in A_i$ then $S$ is a 3-bit representation of the integer $i$.

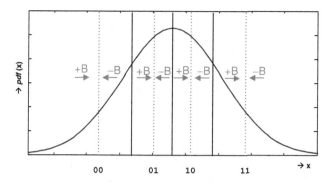

**Fig. 16.10.** The equiprobable partition $\mathcal{A}_{\mathrm{sub}}$ for $l = 2$ and a Gaussian distribution. To each interval $A_i$ (separated by solid lines), a 2-bit code is assigned. The helper data are shown as well.

- Construct helper data $w$ as follows. If $x \in A_i^{\mathrm{left}}$ for some $i$, then set $w = +1$. Otherwise set $w = -1$.
- Create a lookup table (LUT) $B$. The purpose of this LUT is to provide noise resistance during key reconstruction. The LUT contains "step sizes" $B$ for pushing $x$ toward the middle of its interval $A_i$. In the most general case, $B$ is a function of $x$. However, since this could require a large LUT, $B$ can also be defined as a function of the interval index $i$, or, even simpler, $B$ can be a constant.
- Store the partition $\mathcal{A}_{\mathrm{sub}}$, the helper data $w$ and the LUT $B$ in tamper-proof memory.

An example of the partition $\mathcal{A}_{\mathrm{sub}}$ is shown in Fig. 16.10. During key reconstruction, a noisy version $X'$ of $X$ is measured. Then the following steps are performed to extract a bit string $S'$:

- Read $\mathcal{A}_{\mathrm{sub}}$, $w$, and $B$ from tamper-proof memory.
- Compute $q = x' + w \cdot B(x')$.
- Determine the interval index $i' \in \{0, \ldots, 2^l - 1\}$ such that $q \in A_{i'}$.
- Set $S'$ to the $l$-bit encoding of $i'$.

Note that the bitstring $S$ is uniformly distributed by construction. Also note that the partition $\mathcal{A}$, the LUT $B$, and the helper data $w$ are public. However, these reveal no information on $S$, since the probability $\mathbb{P}[X \in A_i | w]$ is equal for all $i$.

Due to the measurement noise, it can happen that $S' \neq S$.[6] The number of bit errors is minimized by using a Gray code. In the step of determining $S$, we set the $l$-bit representation of the interval index $i$ equal to the $i$th codeword of the Gray code (see Fig. 16.11). In this way, a reconstruction error $i' = i \pm 1$ only leads to a single bit flip in $S'$.

---

[6] The error probability $\mathbb{P}[X' + wB(X') \notin A_{i(X)}]$ depends on the choice of $l$ and $B$.

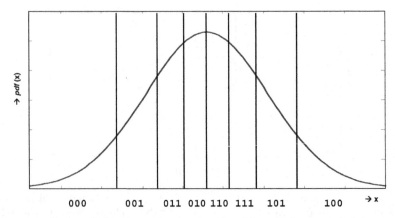

**Fig. 16.11.** Equiprobable discretization into $l = 3$ bits. Robustness is improved by assigning Gray codewords to the intervals.

### 16.6.3 Experimental Results

We have produced a batch of coated ICs as described in Chapter 15. The top metal layer of the IC contains 31 sensor structures. We have measured the capacitances from 90 different ICs.

#### Capacitance Measurements

As explained in Chapter 15, a capacitance measurement at location $i$ yields an integer counter value $C_i$. In order to suppress noise, each measurement is immediately followed by a "blank" measurement in which no capacitor is addressed. This results in a counter value $C_0$. The difference $D_i := C_i - C_0$ is proportional to the RC time of the $i$th capacitor. In order to obtain stochastic variables with zero average, we subtract the average over all sensors ($D_{av} = \sum_{i=1}^{m} D_i$, where $m$ is the number of sensors) from each measurement:

$$f_i = D_i - D_{av}. \tag{16.3}$$

On each IC, one of the 31 sensors is used as a reference sensor (with value $f_{ref}$) for compensating temperature variations. We assume that all enrollment measurements $f_i$ and $f_{ref}$ are done at a controlled temperature $T_0$. The enrolled value $f_{ref}$ is stored along with the helper data.

However, in the key reconstruction phase, the temperature is not under control. Measurements under these conditions are denoted with a prime (i.e., $f_i'$ and $f_{ref}'$). Only the quotient of two such measurements yields a reproducible value. Hence, we define temperature-compensated values $B_i$ as follows:

$$b_i = \frac{f_i'}{f_{ref}'} f_{ref}. \tag{16.4}$$

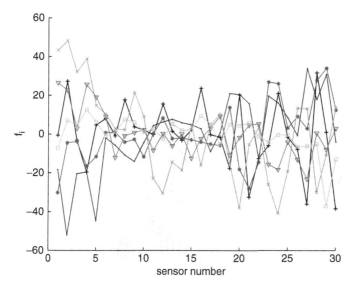

**Fig. 16.12.** Capacitance values $f_i$ at 30 sensors of 6 different ICs.

Figure 16.12 shows the $f_i$ values of 30 sensors, measured at 6 different ICs. Measurements of similar coating and sensor structures with a Hewlett Packard 4192 impedance analyzer show that the average capacitance value is around 0.18 pF (i.e., corresponding to 0 in Fig. 16.12). The capacitance measurements show an average within-class standard deviation of $\sigma_N = 0.95$ and an average between-class standard deviation of $\sigma_f = 18.8$. In our practical setup, we derive 3 bits per sensor, which gives the best robustness results.

### Fingerprints

By way of example, we show key extraction from our experimental data according to the method of Section 16.6.2. First, the distribution $\rho(f_i)$ was estimated empirically by measuring all 30 sensors on 90 ICs. The range of measured $f_i$ values was divided into $L = 2^3 = 8$ intervals and assigned a 3-bit Gray code to each interval. In this way, we derived fingerprints of 90 bits. Histograms of the fractional Hamming distances between the extracted fingerprints for the between-class distribution are shown in Fig. 16.13. The between-class distribution is centered around a fractional Hamming distance of 0.5, which means that the fingerprints derived from two different ICs will, on average, differ in 50% of the bits.

It turns out that bitstrings derived from the same IC (within-class distribution) have at most four bit errors, with an average of approximately one error. Hence, an error-correcting code that corrects 4/90 of all bits is suitable in this case. For example, a (127, 99, 9) BCH code that corrects 4 errors from 127-bit codewords (with 99 information bits) can be used. By setting 37 of

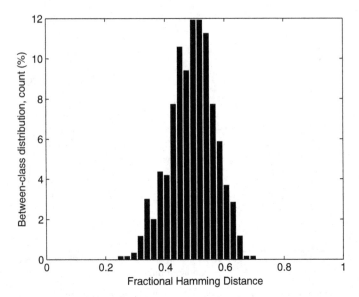

**Fig. 16.13.** Histogram of fractional Hamming distances between fingerprints derived from different ICs (between-class).

the information bits to 0 (code shortening) we effectively achieve a code that corrects 4 out of 90 bits and the remaining key size is $99 - 37 = 62$ bits. This corresponds to an entropy density of the order of 100 bits per square millimeter of the coating.

### Robustness against Temperature Variations

The measured capacitance values $f_i'$ and $f_{\text{ref}}'$ increase with increasing temperature. This is shown in Fig. 16.14. In the key reconstruction phase, dividing the enrolled reference value $f_{\text{ref}}$ by the measured $f_{\text{ref}}'$ gives a temperature compensation factor. The resulting $B_i$ values (16.4) are depicted in Fig. 16.15. Note that the temperature effects are almost completely compensated.

### Attack Detection

Physical attacks in which the coating is damaged are detected from the capacitance measurements. A well-known method for getting access to internal circuit lines of an IC is making a hole through the IC with a FIB. Afterward the hole is filled with metal such that a surface contact is created. This can be used by the attacker for easy access to an internal line.

A FIB was used to create a hole in the coating of an IC by shooting gallium particles on an area of size $10\,\mu\text{m} \times 10\,\mu\text{m}$ above sensor 18 (see Fig. 16.16). The depth of the hole was around $5\,\mu\text{m}$, whereas the coating thickness was around $4.5\,\mu\text{m}$.

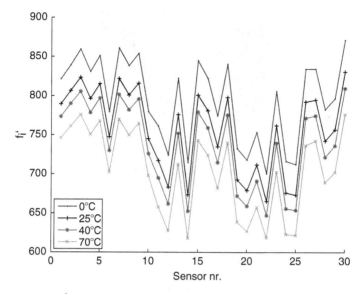

**Fig. 16.14.** $f_i'$ values for IC 2, measured at 0°C, 25°C, 40°C, and 70°C.

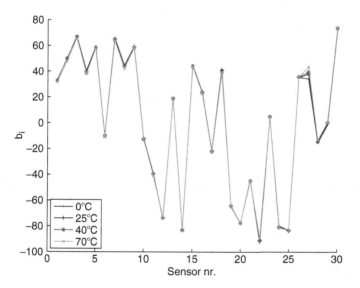

**Fig. 16.15.** $B_i$ values for IC 2, measured at 0°C, 25°C, 40°C, and 70°C.

Figure 16.17 shows the effect of the FIB attack on the measured capacitances $f_i'$. A significant decrease in capacitance is measured at sensor 18, right under the area of impact of the FIB beam. The measurement values at other sensors are also slightly influenced. A cross-sectional scanning electron micrography image of the created hole is depicted in Fig.16.18. Table 16.1 summarizes the direct effect of gallium FIB and argon beam attacks with different hit areas.

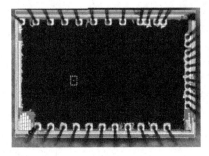

**Fig. 16.16.** Top view of a coating PUF IC in which a hole has been shot with a gallium FIB.

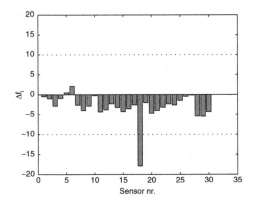

**Fig. 16.17.** Differences in capacitance $f_i'$ before and after the gallium FIB attack.

**Fig. 16.18.** Cross-sectional scanning electron micrography image of a FIB hole above sensor 18 of the IC. The hole has an area of $10\,\mu m \times 10\,\mu m$ and a depth of approximately $4\,\mu m$.

**Table 16.1.** Average change of capacitance measured by the sensor lying under the area of impact of the beam

| Beam type | Hit Area | Depth | $\Delta f$ |
|---|---|---|---|
| Gallium | $100\,\mu m \times 100\,\mu m$ | $1.5\,\mu m$ | $-40$ |
| Gallium | $15\,\mu m \ \times 15\,\mu m$ | $4\,\mu m$ | $-34$ |
| Gallium | $10\,\mu m \ \times 10\,\mu m$ | $5\,\mu m$ | $-15$ |
| Argon | $100\,\mu m \times 100\,\mu m$ | $1.5\,\mu m$ | $-28$ |

## 16.6.4 Security of the Coating

Since the coating is opaque, optically looking into the digital memory is very hard without damaging the coating. Furthermore, since the coating is tough and chemically inert, it is very hard to remove mechanically or chemically. In a more advanced attack, the attacker first uses a FIB to make a hole in the coating and then makes the IC start the key reconstruction phase. During this phase, the attacker uses microprobes to retrieve key bits. Obviously, since he has damaged the coating, the original key will not be reconstructed. Yet, the attacker might still be able to retrieve information about the original key. In Section 16.6.5, the FIB attack is modeled as an additional bit error rate $\epsilon$ on top of the errors $\alpha$ due to measurement noise (where $\epsilon > \alpha$). This effectively leads to a noisy channel with combined error rate $\chi = \alpha(1 - \epsilon) + \epsilon(1 - \alpha)$, as seen by the attacker. The amount of uncertainty he has about the key $K$ can be expressed as a number $N_c$ of "candidate" keys, which turns out to be of the order

$$N_c = \mathcal{O}\left(2^{n[h(\chi) - h(R\alpha)]}\right), \tag{16.5}$$

where $R > 1$ is a constant such that the code corrects error rates up to $R\alpha$, and the function h is defined as $h(p) = -p\log p - (1 - p)\log(1 - p)$. This formula is derived in Section 16.6.5. Based on experimentally measured error rates, we estimate the parameters $\alpha$ and $R\alpha$ by $\alpha = 1/30$ and $R\alpha = 4/90$. The values for $\epsilon$ range from $\epsilon = 8/90$ to $\epsilon = 14/90$. Therefore, we take an average value $\epsilon = 11/90$. In practice, one would like to have a key of length 128 bits for encryption purposes. Given these error rates that would require $n = 174$ (in order to have a mutual information of 128 bits between two noisy strings). Substituting this value of $n$ into (16.5), we obtain $N_c = 2^{51}$.

## 16.6.5 FIB Attack Model

In this subsection we estimate the impact of a FIB attack on the secrecy of the key $K \in \{0,1\}^k$. We model the output of the enrollment phase as a binary string $X \in \{0,1\}^n$. The string $X$ is modeled as a string of $n$ i.i.d. random variables. The measurement results during the key reconstruction phase of an undamaged coating are modeled as random variables $Y \in \{0,1\}^n$. The "noise" between $X$ and $Y$ is modeled as a binary symmetric channel $X \to Y$ with bit flip probability $\alpha$. Hence, this situation allows one to use the technique based on error-correcting codes described at the end of Section 16.3.1. The Error-Correcting Code (ECC) $\mathcal{C}$ is capable of correcting $nR\alpha$ errors, where $R > 1$ is a constant slightly larger than 1. Hence, if the Hamming distance between $Y$ and the codeword $c_K$ is smaller than $nR\alpha$, then $Y$ is successfully decoded to $K$. As we saw in Section 16.6.3, an invasive attack with a FIB damages the coating (which changes its challenge response behavior). We denote the outcome of the measurement after FIB attack by a random variable $Z \in \{0,1\}^n$. The process of damaging the coating is modeled as an adversarial channel $Y \to Z$

with crossover probability $\epsilon > \alpha$. The total error rate $\chi$ (for the attacker) is the result of two independent error-inducing processes, namely noise and damage:

$$\chi = \alpha(1 - \epsilon) + \epsilon(1 - \alpha) = \alpha + \epsilon - 2\alpha\epsilon. \tag{16.6}$$

We assume that the parameters $\alpha$ and $\epsilon$ are known to the attacker. The attack is successful if $Z$ still provides enough information to efficiently compute $K$.

We present an estimate (in the case of large $n$) of the amount of effort needed to obtain $K$ from the knowledge of $Z, \alpha$, and $\epsilon$. The attacker knows that any $n$-bit string within a "sphere" of radius $nR\alpha$ around $c_K$ will decode to $K$. He also knows the probability distribution of the Hamming distance $D$ between $c_K$ and $Z$. It is the binomial distribution

$$\mathbb{P}[D = \beta] = \binom{n}{\beta}\chi^\beta(1 - \chi)^{n-\beta}. \tag{16.7}$$

The attacker knows the average $\langle D \rangle = n\chi$ and the variance $\sigma_D = \sqrt{n\chi(1 - \chi)}$. There is an overwhelming probability (due to the law of large numbers) that $c_K$ lies in a shell of thickness $\sigma_D$ at a distance $\langle D \rangle$ from $Z$. The attacker makes a list of all codewords lying in that shell. With overwhelming probability, one of those codewords will decode to $K$. The number $N_c$ of "candidate" codewords in the shell is given by the volume of the shell times the density of codewords in the space $\{0, 1\}^n$. This number represents the amount of computational effort that the attacker has to expend in an exhaustive attack to find the secret $K$ or, equivalently, the uncertainty that he still has about the key $K$.

The shell volume is of the order $\sigma_D\binom{n}{\langle D \rangle}$. Assuming that the codewords are uniformly distributed, the density of codewords is $2^{k-n}$, where $k$ is the number of information bits of the codewords. Thus, the required attack effort is given by

$$N_c \approx 2^{k-n}\sigma_D\binom{n}{\langle D \rangle} = 2^{k-n}\sqrt{n\chi(1 - \chi)}\binom{n}{n\chi} \approx (2\pi)^{-1/2}2^{nh(\chi)+k-n},$$
$$\tag{16.8}$$

where h is the binary entropy function. Here, we have used Stirling's formula to approximate the binomial. An "optimal" code for correcting $nR\alpha$ errors has message length $k = n - nh(R\alpha)$. For such a code, the complexity of the attack effort is of the order

$$N_c = \mathcal{O}\left(2^{n[h(\chi)-h(R\alpha)]}\right). \tag{16.9}$$

# 17

# Anti-Counterfeiting

Pim Tuyls, Jorge Guajardo, Lejla Batina, and Tim Kerins

## 17.1 Introduction

Counterfeiting of goods is becoming a very huge problem for our society. It not only has a global economic impact, but it also poses a serious threat to our global safety and health. Currently, global economic damage across all industries due to the counterfeiting of goods is estimated at over $600 billion annually [2]. In the United States, seizure of counterfeit goods has tripled in the last 5 years, and in Europe, over 100 million pirated and counterfeit goods were seized in 2004. Fake products cost businesses in the United Kingdom approximately $17 billion [2]. In India, 15% of fast-moving consumer goods and 38% of auto parts are counterfeit. Other industries in which many goods are being counterfeit are the toy industry, content and software, cosmetics, publishing, food and beverages, tobacco, apparel, sports goods, cards, and so forth.

The above-mentioned examples show that counterfeiting may lead to highly reduced income for companies and to a damaged brand. Perhaps more unexpectedly, counterfeiting has some impact on our safety too. In some cases, this is even tragic. Counterfeited spare parts of planes have caused planes to crash [148]. Counterfeiting of medicines poses a real growing threat to our health. Thousands of people die because of taking medicines containing ingredients that are very dangerous or taking medicines that do not contain any active ingredient at all. This kind of problem is very large in Southeast Asia where many fake anti-malaria drugs containing no active ingredient are being distributed. The World Health Organisation (WHO) estimates that counterfeit drugs account for 10% of the world pharmaceutical market, representing currently a value of $32 billion. In developing countries, these numbers are often much higher: In China and Colombia, 40% of drugs are counterfeit; in Vietnam, 33% of the anti-malaria drugs are fake; and in Nigeria, 50% of the drugs are counterfeit. According to the Food and Drug Administration, in the United States there has been a rise of 600% in counterfeit drugs since 1997. In Europe, the rise increased by 45% since 2003.

In order to solve these problems, industries and governments have to take measures that reduce the size of the counterfeit problem drastically. On top of several legislations, procedural measures, and control mechanisms (which are necessary), good technological counter measures are needed in order to have a serious impact. More precisely, technological components are required that allow control mechanisms to verify the authenticity of a product undoubtedly in an economic way. Many technologies have been developed to thwart the counterfeiting problem: holograms, watermarks, security threads, security films, bar codes, taggants, security inks, and so forth. Radio-frequency identification (RFID) is a new technology that is being considered for those purposes. A major advantage of RFID tags is that no line-of-sight communication is required for read out, in contrast to other systems such as bar-code-based systems. This might speed up the authentication procedure drastically.

The RFID tags are low-cost pervasive devices that consist of an antenna connected to a microchip. Because of the presence of this microchip, they are considered as the next-generation bar codes with added functionality. Typically, they are passive, thus obtaining their energy from the electromagnetic field generated by the reader with whom they communicate. The reader is often connected with a back-end system (e.g., a database) where it can store information or from where information can be retrieved. In supply-chain management, they allow for tracking of a product in several stages and locations. Other applications include automated inventory management, automated quality control, access control, payment systems, and general security applications. Currently, the prices range from a few cents (tags with low processing capabilities, limited memory, etc.) up to $2 (tags with added functionality on board).

An emerging application that goes beyond identification is the use of RFID tags for anti-counterfeiting purposes [162]. By locating a RFID tag containing specific product and reference information on a product, one aims to verify the authenticity of the product. Loosely speaking the verification is performed as follows. When a product passes a reader, the reader checks whether the necessary reference information is present on the tag. For this purpose, the tag and the reader run a protocol. If the required information is there and verified to be authentic, the product is declared to be genuine and otherwise not. However, by eavesdropping on the channel between the tag and the reader, recording their communications, and storing this information in a new chip, the attacker can effectively make a clone of the original tag that cannot be distinguished from the original tag by the reader. In order to make tag cloning infeasible, it should not be possible to derive the tag secrets by active, passive, or physical attacks on the tag.[1] By using good cryptographic protocols, active

---

[1] A passive attack is an attack in which the attacker eavesdrops on the communication between the reader and the tag. An active attack is an attack in which the attacker actively participates in such a protocol (e.g., by installing a fake reader). A physical attack is an attack in which an attacker attacks the tag itself using some sophisticated physical tools (photo flash lamps, focused ion beams, etc.).

and passive attacks are thwarted. Recently, a lightweight version of a protocol protecting against non-physical attacks was developed in [162].

We stress, however, that it is rather easy to *physically* clone a tag. This means that an attacker can capture the RFID tag, investigate it, use physical means to read out its memory and its security sensitive data (identification number, reference information, keys, etc.), and produce a new tag with exactly the same data in memory. When this tag is embedded into a product, it is impossible for a reader to distinguish an authentic product from a fake one. In order to protect a RFID tag against this type of cloning attack, one can attempt to prevent reading out its memory by using several protective measures [213, 255]. These measures often increase the price of the tag so much that it becomes unacceptably high for its main application. In order to thwart the physical cloning attacks, we propose to integrate physical unclonable functions (PUFs) with RFID tags. The secret-key material in the tag is extracted from these structures. PUFs have been proposed as a cost-effective means to produce unclonable tokens for identification purposes [222]. They are realized as a physical system such that the function is easy to evaluate but hard to clone.

This chapter discusses the following:

1. The technological components of anti-counterfeiting technology and a general protocol for verifying the authenticity of an item as presented in [269].
2. We describe a solution for anti-counterfeiting based on RFID tags and PUFs [222, 272, 274, 287]. Our solution [269] withstands physical cloning attacks as well as active and passive attacks on the verification protocols. In particular, we present a solution based on PUFs that are inseparably bound to an IC.
3. We present protocols for the off-line situation. The construction for the off-line case is designed in such a way that it inherits its security from the underlying cryptographic algorithms (signature and secure identification scheme) used.
4. We show that the construction that we propose is feasible on a constrained device such as a RFID tag. We give detailed results of our implementation as presented in [10]. In order to minimize the area constraints of a tag, we sacrifice slightly the efficiency of the involved cryptographic algorithms. The obtained performance is still sufficient for our application.

This chapter is organized as follows. In Section 17.2 we give the security model for the anti-counterfeiting situation, identify the required technological components for anti-counterfeiting technology, and detail a general anti-counterfeiting protocol. Furthermore, we explain the advantage of an unclonable RFID tag and introduce briefly the concept of a fragile PUF. In Section 17.3 we describe in detail the hardware configuration of an unclonable RFID tag. Additionally, we specify verification protocols for the on and off-line situation. Finally, in Sections 17.5 and 17.6, we investigate the hardware implementation of the off-line verification protocol in detail.

## 17.2 Model

In order to protect a product against cloning (counterfeiting), a detection mark is embedded into the product (ideally) or its packaging. This detection mark consists of a physical part and a digital part. The mark is put there by a legitimate authority (which is trusted). When the product is in the field, the attacker (counterfeiter) has access to all components of this detection mark; that is, she can read it, remove it from the product and investigate it, challenge/communicate with it, and so forth. Based on the information that she obtains from investigating the legal detection mark, she produces a fake detection mark. The goal of the attacker is to produce a fake detection mark that can only be distinguished from an authentic one with negligible probability.

### 17.2.1 Components of Anti-Counterfeiting Technology

In order to protect a product against counterfeiting, technological means are needed to verify whether the product is authentic or not. In order to make an item unclonable, the following two properties are needed:

1. *Physical protection.* This is obtained by using unclonable physical structures embedded in the product or its package (removal of the structure should lead to its destruction). One or more unique *fingerprints* derived from the physical structure will be printed on the product for the verification of the authenticity of the product. (In an on-line situation, these fingerprints are stored in a database.)
2. *Cryptographic protection* serving two goals. First, cryptography provides techniques (digital signatures) to detect and prevent tampering with data (fingerprints) derived from a physical object. Second, it provides secure identification protocols to identify a product. Those protocols do not leak any necessary identification information to an eavesdropper attacking (actively or passively) the communication channel.

The physical protection layer makes the product physically unclonable. The cryptographic layer allows to check that the physical layer has been applied by a legitimate authority, not by bogus organization. Good candidates for unclonable physical structures, which can be used for physical protection purposes, are so-called PUFs. Examples of PUFs that can be embedded into a package are optical PUFs. We describe optical PUFs very briefly here. PUFs are discussed in more detail in Chapters 12, 13, 15, and 16.

Optical PUFs consist of a piece of glass that contains light-scattering particles. When those structures are irradiated (challenged) by a laser beam, a speckle pattern is generated. This speckle pattern can be seen as the unique fingerprint of the structure. When the angle, wavefront, or position of the laser is slightly changed, a new unpredictable speckle pattern is generated. In order to copy such a structure, a piece of glass has to be constructed with the same configuration of light-scattering particles. No need to explain that this is certainly not an easy task.

## 17.2.2 A General Anti-counterfeiting Protocol

First, we give some intuition for protocols that can be used to check the authenticity of a product based on the two technological components previously described. In order to determine the unique properties of the PUF and use them to generate the reference information, there is first an enrollment phase, which is performed by some *trusted authority*. During this phase the following steps are performed:

1. Several fingerprints are derived from the PUF by challenging it with multiple challenges and recording the responses. These responses are then turned into binary fingerprints (and some auxiliary data are derived for use during the verification phase).
2. For use in off-line situations: These challenges, fingerprints, and auxiliary data are then signed with the secret key $sk$ of the issuer of the product (the issuer is assumed to be trustworthy). For the on-line case: the challenges, fingerprints, and auxiliary data are then stored in a verification database (which we assume to be secure).
3. The signatures, the challenges (corresponding to the fingerprints), and perhaps some auxiliary data (needed to perform processing during the authentication phase) are also printed on the product.

During the verification (or authentication) phase, the authenticity of the product is checked by running the following protocol:

1. The verification device reads the challenges and auxiliary data of the detection mark embedded in the product.
2. The verification device challenges the physical structure with one of the challenges printed on the product. After having measured the responses, it derives the fingerprint from the response based on the auxiliary data.
3. Then, using the fingerprint derived in step 2, the verification device checks the signature to verify that the fingerprint, challenges, and auxiliary data were printed on the product by a legitimate authority. If the signature is not correct, the product is not authentic; otherwise it is.

We briefly analyze the security of this protocol. An attacker who wants to counterfeit the product has to embed a fake physical structure on the product that produces correct fingerprints to the challenges (with correct signatures). Under the assumption that the physical structure is unclonable, she cannot produce a clone of the originally embedded physical structure. More precisely, we assume that given some challenges $c_1, \ldots, c_n$ and corresponding finger-prints $s_1, \ldots, s_n$, she cannot produce a (fake) physical structure that produces the same fingerprints $s_1, \ldots, s_n$ given the original challenges $c_1, \ldots, c_n$. On the other hand, she can produce another structure and create challenges, auxiliary data, and fingerprints $s_1', \ldots, s_n'$ according to the procedures used during enrollment. However, since she does not know the trusted authority's secret key $sk$ and the responses of her fake structure will be different from the authentic $s_i$'s with very high probability, she will not be able to compute the correct signatures on these data. The verification device will detect that the signatures are not correct and reject this as a fake product. We note that, in reality, the number of fingerprints that can be verified during a verification session is very limited by time and space constraints. Clearly, the attacker can easily capture the required fingerprints (by measuring the responses according to the challenges printed on the product). Therefore, in reality the production of a clone requires the fabrication of a physical structure (PUF) producing the same fingerprints for a limited number of challenges. Due to the above-mentioned constraints, a practical implementation is not guaranteed to provide the same security level as the one argued in theory. In the following sections, it will be explained how the use of an unclonable RFID tag can minimize the disparity between theoretical and practical security.

### 17.2.3 RFID-Based Systems

The previously described PUF-based solution for preventing counterfeiting of goods can be improved when active components are used, which are insep-arably linked to a PUF. An example consists of a RFID tag equipped with a microchip that is inseparably bound to a PUF. The precise construction is explained in Section 17.3. Because of the presence of a microchip a more pow-erful cryptographic protocol can be run between the tag and the reader such that no information on the fingerprint of the PUF is revealed. Additionally, by inseparably linking the chip and the PUF, it becomes possible to prevent leakage of the PUF measurement to the outside world. This makes it much harder for an attacker to launch a physical attack on the tag to extract its secret information and produce a clone.

Typical RFID systems consist of the following two components: the *RFID tag* and a *reader*. The reader will perform the verification test to detect whether a tag is authentic or not. The RFID tag consists of an antenna con-nected to a microchip that can store and read data and has possibly some dedicated hardware to perform a small number of computations. Tags obtain their power from the RF-field generated by the reader, which can read and write data from/to the tag. The reader is often linked with some back-end system that can perform computations on the data received from the tags.

In order to use RFID tags for anti-counterfeiting purposes, we proceed as follows. A RFID tag containing reference information is embedded in a prod-uct. The (identification) data stored in the tag's memory are signed with the secret key *sk* of the legitimate issuer. The tag communicates with a reader for verification purposes over a public channel. The ROM or EEPROM (Electrically Erasable Programmable ROM) memory of the tag is accessible to the attacker. The reader has a certified public key *pk* corresponding to the issuer's secret key for verification of the digital signatures.

### 17.2.4 Fragile PUFs

An additional threat might exist, even when the above-explained techniques have been applied. Let us consider therefore the example where the detection mark is embedded in the package (not on the product). Instead of trying to copy the package, the attacker may try to get hold of "old" used packages and "refill" those with his own fake surrogates. This can be prevented by using a *fragile* PUF instead of a normal PUF. A *fragile* PUF is a PUF that is destroyed when the user (or an attacker) opens the package. Furthermore, the same procedure is applied as with usual PUFs (fingerprints and accompanying signatures/helper data are printed on the package or stored in the database). This has two advantages. A fake product cannot enter the supply chain of a company by putting it in old/used packages. This allows legitimate companies to better protect their supply chain. For the enduser on the other hand, the use of a fragile PUF has the advantage that he can verify whether he indeed bought an unused and authentic product or not. This is done by checking the fragile PUF authenticity before it is destroyed.

## 17.3 Unclonable RFID Tags

In order to make unclonable RFID tags, we introduce RFID tags whose microchips are equipped with an integrated PUF, the so-called I-PUF.

**Definition 17.1.** *An integrated physical unclonable function (I-PUF) is a PUF that additionally satisfies the following properties:*

1. *The I-PUF is inseparably bound to a chip. This means that any attempt to remove the PUF from the chip leads to the destruction of the PUF and the chip.*
2. *It is impossible to tamper with the communication (measurement data) between the chip and the PUF.*
3. *The output of the PUF is inaccessible to an attacker.*

In the remainder of the chapter we will refer to I-PUFs as PUFs unless we say something to the contrary. In our construction, the PUF is used as a secure memory (more precisely *read-proof hardware*) for storing secret keys [271]. The secret key *s*, which is usually stored in (protected) ROM or EEPROM, is derived from the PUF at the point in time when it is needed. After the operations with the key are performed, the key is deleted from volatile memory. In order to enable the generation of the secret key $s$ during authentication, helper data $w$ are stored in non-secure memory (ROM or EEPROM). The key $s$ is derived from the response $X$ of the PUF by means of a key extraction algorithm (fuzzy extractor and the helper data $w$ are used in this algorithm). It was shown in, for example, Chapter 5 that the public helper data $w$ reveal only a negligible amount of information on the key $s$. Given our assumption on I-PUFs in Definition 17.1, it follows that the key $s$ is securely stored in the PUF.[2]

### 17.3.1 On-Line Authentication

Although we consider below the situation in which the detection mark is implemented by a RFID tag containing a PUF, many protocols also hold (in a slightly changed form) for the case where the detection mark just consists of a PUF not embedded on a tag. In this case, we assume that every reader is connected with a reference database through an authenticated channel. The reference database contains for each tag ID a list of challenge response pairs (CRPs) $(c_1, x_1), \ldots, (c_n, x_n)$ of its corresponding PUF. We distinguish between two different situations: (1) We assume that there is a *large* number of CRPs available for the PUF (i.e., $n$ is a large number). We refer to this case as *strong PUFs*. If the number of different CRPs $n$ is rather small, we refer to it as a *weak PUF*. More precisely, a strong PUF is a PUF that has so many CRPs such that an attack (performed during a limited amount of time) based on exhaustively measuring CRPs only has a negligible probability of success $O(2^{-n})$ [272].

### Strong PUFs

During the **enrollment phase**, the PUF is challenged by a Certification Authority (CA) with $n$ independent challenges [269], say $c_1, \ldots, c_n$, and the corresponding responses $x_1, \ldots, x_n \in \{0, 1\}^k$ are measured. The data $(c_i, x_i), i = 1, \ldots, n$, are securely stored in the database (and unknown to an attacker). No additional information is stored in the (ROM) memory of the RFID tag. During the **authentication phase**, the following protocol is performed between the tag and the reader:

1. The reader asks the tag for its identification number, ID.
2. The reader gets from the database a random CRP say $(c_i, x_i)$, for this ID.
3. The reader sends the challenge $c_i$ over a public channel to the tag.
4. The tag challenges its PUF according to the challenge $c_i$, measures $y_i$, and sends $y_i$ over the public channel to the reader.
5. The reader verifies whether $d_H(x_i, y_i) \leq \delta$, where $\delta$ is some pre-determined threshold. If this condition is satisfied, the reader considers the tag to be authentic; in the other case, it is decided that this is a counterfeited tag.
6. The database removes the pair $(c_i, x_i)$ from the database.

---

[2] The word *securely* has to be understood here in the sense of read-proof hardware.

*Security.* It is clear that in order to have a secure system, for RFID tags with some reasonable lifetime, a large number of CRPs is needed (e.g., $\sim 10^9$ [272]). Since the various CRPs are independent, a passive attacker has a probability of guessing a response $z_i$ with $d_H(z_i, r_i) \leq \delta$ to a challenge $c_i$ equal to $\sum_{i=0}^{\delta} \binom{k}{i}/2^k \approx 2^{(h(\alpha)-1)k}$ when $\delta = \alpha k$ and $h$ denotes the binary entropy function.[3]

Note that an active attacker will probe the PUF of the tag with a fake reader that sends arbitrarily chosen challenges $c'_1, \ldots, c'_m$ to the tag. When the responses $y_1, \ldots, y_m$ are returned, he records them and uses them to make a model of the PUF and to guess the responses to other remaining CRPs. It was shown in [272] that the number of responses that can be obtained in a limited amount of time is small compared to the total number of challenges (i.e., $m \ll n$) (typically $m = 100$ and $n = 10^9$). Hence, the probability that $c_j \in \{c'_1, c'_2, \ldots, c'_m\}$ for some $j \in_R \{1, \ldots, n\}$ is $\mathcal{O}(m/n)$. This implies that the verifier has to keep its database with CRPs secret. Finally, we note that after some time, the database might run out of CRPs. In [125], protocols have been developed to update a CRP database with new CRPs. Since this can only be done over a secure authenticated channel, it requires that first a secure channel is established between the RFID tag and the reader over which the update protocol is run.

*Complexity.* We note that from a computational point of view, this protocol is very inexpensive for the RFID tag. It only has to measure responses to challenges. This requires only 1000 gates [269]. No cryptographic operations have to be performed. In order to prevent the attack, a message authentication code (MAC) can be used too. Then the PUF and the reader first establish a shared secret (based on a CRP of the PUF) with which the challenges sent by the reader are MACed. Then the tag checks the MAC, and if it does not match, the tag does not respond any further to the reader's queries.

## Weak PUFs

*First Protocol.* During the enrollment phase the PUF is challenged by a CA with $n$ challenges, say $c_1, \ldots, c_n$, and the corresponding responses $x_1, \ldots, x_n$ are measured. Then a secret $s_i \in_R \{0,1\}^k$ for $i = 1, \ldots, n$ is randomly chosen for each response $x_i$. The corresponding helper data $w_1, \ldots, w_n$ are computed by means of the *key extraction* algorithms explained in Chapters 3–5. In the (ROM) memory of the RFID tag, the challenges $c_1, \ldots, c_n$ are stored. In the database of the verifier, the triples $(c_i, w_i, s_i)$ for $i = 1, \ldots, n$ are stored. Let $\text{MAC}_k(\cdot)$ denote a MAC-ing algorithm using key $k$. Then the authentication protocol performs the following steps [269]:

1. The reader contacts the tag that sends its ID.

---

[3] The binary entropy function $h(p)$ is defined as $h(p) = -p \log_2 p - (1-p) \log_2(1-p)$.

2. The reader contacts the database and gets a random challenge response pair for this ID, say $(c_i, s_i)$, together with the helper data $w_i$. It sends the data $(c_i, w_i)$ together with $MAC_{s_i}(w_i)$ to the tag. Additionally, the reader chooses a random nonce $m \in \{0,1\}^t$ and sends it to the tag too.

3. The tag challenges its PUF according to the challenge $c_i$, and measures the response $y_i$. Then it uses the helper data $w_i$ to derive $s'_i = G(y_i, w_i)$. Using $s'_i$ and $w_i$, the tag checks $MAC_{s_i}(w_i)$ using $s'_i$. If the MAC is not OK, the tag stops. Otherwise it proceeds. Note that in this step, we have in fact transformed the key extraction function $G$ into a robust key extraction function $G^*$ in a similar way to the one presented in [42].

4. Finally, the tag MACs the message $m$ and sends $MAC_{s'_i}(m)$ to the reader.

5. The reader checks $MAC_{s'_i}(m)$. If the MAC is OK, it considers the tag as authentic and otherwise not.

The authentication technique in step 2 prevents an active attack by a fake reader. If the challenge-response protocol carried out in steps 3 and 4 uses a secure MAC-ing algorithm, it reveals no information on the used key $s_i$. Finally, notice that this protocol requires only symmetric crypto primitives, which require a few thousand gates.

*Second Protocol.* A more light weight protocol is obtained by applying the $HB^+$ protocol (developed in [162]) to the case of a RFID tag equipped with a PUF. For the sake of completeness, we give the complete protocol here (using the $HB^+$ protocol of [162] as a black box).

1. The reader contacts the tag.

2. The reader contacts the database and gets two random CRPs, say $(c_i, s_i)$ and $(c_j, s_j)$ (with $i \neq j$), together with the corresponding helper data $w_i$ and $w_j$ and sends the data $(c_i, w_i)$ and $(c_j, w_j)$ to the tag.

3. The tag challenges its PUF according to the challenges $c_i$ and $c_j$, and it measures the responses $y_i$ and $y_j$. Then it uses the helper data $w_i$ and $w_j$ to derive the secrets $s'_i = G(y_i, w_i)$ and $s'_j = G(y_j, w_j)$, respectively.

4. The tag starts the $HB^+$ protocol with the reader based on the secrets $s'_i$ and $s'_j$.

5. If the tag passes the authentication protocol, the reader decides that the tag is authentic and otherwise not.

6. The tag removes the secrets $s'_i$ and $s'_j$ from its memory.

Note that the $HB^+$ protocol is just one example and is certainly not required to be used. Any other light weight protocol could also be deployed in this case. Regarding the security of this construction, note that the secrets $s'_i$ and $s'_j$ are only temporarily available in the memory of the tag. When the tag is not working, the secrets are not available on the RFID tag, which makes the tag resistant against reading the secret data from memory. The implementation complexity is minimal, as running the protocol only requires that the tag computes exclusive ORs (XORs), which can be done very efficiently. Notice that a linear-time active attack against the $HB^+$ protocol was presented in [131].

## 17.3.2 Off-Line Authentication

In the off-line situation, the reader is not connected to a verification database. This implies that the reader has to carry out the verification protocol on its own. Thus, in order to provide off-line authentication, we introduce a PUF-certificate-identity-based identification scheme (PUF-Cert-IBI) by following the definition of a certificate-based IBI in [18].

Let $\mathcal{SI} = (K_g, P, V)$ denote a standard identification scheme (SI-scheme), where $K_g$ denotes the key generation algorithm, and $P$ and $V$ denote the interactive protocols run by the prover and verifier, respectively. Let $\mathcal{SS} = (\mathrm{SK}_g, \mathrm{Sign}, V_f)$ be a standard signature scheme (SS-scheme) [89], where $\mathrm{SK}_g$ denotes the key generation algorithm, Sign denotes the signing algorithm and $V_f$ denotes the verification algorithm run by a verifier. We assign to each tag an identity $I$ (this might be the serial number or EPC-code of the tag or the serial number of the product in which it has been embedded). An IBI scheme $(\mathrm{MK}_g, \mathrm{UK}_g, \hat{P}, \hat{V})$ is associated to the PUF, the $\mathcal{SI}$, the $\mathcal{SS}$ scheme, and the identity $I$ as follows. During **enrollment**, the issuer uses $\mathrm{SK}_g$ as the master-key generation algorithm $\mathrm{MK}_g$. This means that the master key $msk$ is used for generating signatures and the corresponding public key $mpk$ for verification of the signatures. The user-key generation algorithm $\mathrm{UK}_g$ consists of the following steps. For each RFID tag, having identity $I$, the issuer then creates a public-secret key pair $(pk, sk)$ using algorithm $K_g$ on input $1^k$. The couple $(pk, sk)$ is the public-secret key pair for the SI-scheme. The issuer runs the following protocol with the tag:

- It requests the tag to challenge its PUF with a challenge $c$ and to measure the response $x(c)$.
- The tag sends $x(c)$ to the issuer.
- Based on the knowledge of $x(c)$ and $sk$, the issuer determines the helper data $w$ such that $sk = G(x, w)$.
- The helper data $w$ are written into the ROM (EEPROM) memory of the tag.

Finally, the issuer creates the following certificate that is also stored in the ROM of the tag Cert $\leftarrow (pk, \mathrm{Sign}(msk, pk\|I))$. The $usk$ is then set to $usk \leftarrow (\mathrm{PUF}, \mathrm{Cert})$. Here, $usk$ denotes the user's secret key corresponding to the user identity $I$. During **authentication**, the tag (in the role of the prover) runs the following steps with a verifier:

- The tag runs the protocol $\hat{P}$ which consists of the following steps:
  - It challenges the PUF with $c$, measures the response $y(c)$, and computes $sk \leftarrow G(y(c), w)$.
  - Initialization of the prover protocol $P$ of the $\mathcal{SI}$-scheme with $sk$.
  - It includes the certificate Cert in the first step of the algorithm $P$.
- The verifier uses $(mpk, I)$ as input for the verification algorithm $\hat{V}$.
- When the verifier receives Cert from the tag, it first verifies Cert by running $V_f(mpk, pk\|I, \mathrm{Sign}(msk, pk\|I))$.

- If the certificate Cert is invalid, the protocol is aborted.
- If Cert is valid, the verifier initializes $V$ with $pk$ and runs it.
- If $V$ returns accept, then the verifier accepts.

The security of our PUF-Cert-IBI scheme follows from Theorem17.1 [269], whose proof is similar to the proof of Theorem 4.2 in [18] and thus is omitted.

**Theorem 17.1.** *Let $\mathcal{SI}$ be an SI-scheme and SS a uf-cma[4] secure SS-scheme. Let PUF-Cert-IBI be the corresponding PUF-Certificate-Identity-based Identification scheme presented above. If the scheme $\mathcal{SI}$ is impersonation-atk secure, then PUF-Cert-IBI is impersonation-atk secure for atk $\in \{pa, aa, ca\}$ (pa: passive attack, aa: active attack, ca: concurrent attack).*

It follows from this theorem that by choosing an appropriate SI-scheme (withstanding a *pa*, *aa* or *ca*), the PUF-Cert-IBI inherits the same property. If only resistance against passive attacks is needed, the Schnorr identification scheme can be used. It is known that this scheme is secure against passive attacks under the discrete logarithm assumption. It is also secure against active attacks under the one-more-discrete-logarithm assumption. An alternative is to use Okamoto's identification scheme [199], which is secure against passive, active, and concurrent attacks under the discrete logarithm assumption.

The security of this construction follows from the following arguments. If the attacker was able to obtain the secret key from the tag, it would imply that she has either broken the digital signature scheme, or broken the secure identification protocol, or broken the fuzzy extractor. Physical security follows from the following facts. First, since the PUF is unclonable, the attacker cannot produce a new physical structure that produces the same key when challenged (note, moreover, he does not know which key to produce). Since the PUF is tamper-evident, this implies that when the PUF is attacked invasively (e.g., with a focused ion beam), the PUF properties are changed to such a degree that it will produce different responses to the same challenges. In other words, the key is destroyed. More details on these physical properties can be found in Chapter 16 and in [271].

### 17.3.3 Storage Requirements:

In order to minimize the size of the ROM memory of the tag, we propose to use elliptic curve (EC)-based secure identification schemes. For the signature algorithm $\mathcal{SS}$, we choose then ECDSA. This makes the size of the signatures no larger than 326 bits (when using the field $\mathbb{F}_{2^{163}}$). The identification protocol investigated in detail is Schnorr's identification protocol. The total storage requirement for the public information $(sP, \text{Cert})$ is about 500 bits.

---

[4] *uf-cma*: existential unforgeability under chosen message attack.

1. **Common Input:** The set of system parameters in this case consists of: $(q, a, b, P, n, h)$. Here, $q$ specifies the finite field, $a$, $b$, define an elliptic curve, $P$ is a point on the curve of order $n$ and $h$ is the cofactor. In the case of tag authentication, most of these parameters are assumed to be fixed.
2. **Prover-Tag Input:** The prover's secret $a$ such that $Z = -a \cdot P$.
3. **Protocol:** The protocol involves exchange of the following messages:

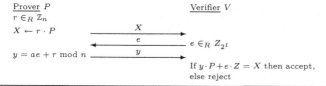

Fig. 17.1. Schnorr's identification protocol.

## 17.4 Secure Identification Protocols

Schnorr's identification protocol is shown in Fig. 17.1. In this case, a tag (prover) proves its identity to a reader (verifier) in a three-pass protocol. As it can be observed from the protocol, the critical operation is the point multiplication. On the other hand, in Okamoto's scheme [216], the tag needs to compute $kP + lQ$ (i.e., a so-called multiple-point multiplication). For the purpose of speeding up this computation, one uses Shamir's trick. The scalars $k$ and $l$ are stored in a two-row matrix. Each row contains the binary representation of one of the scalars. Then all values of the form $iP + jQ$, $0 \leq i, j < 2^w$, are pre-calculated and stored in a table, where $w$ is referred to as the window size. The algorithm to perform this so-called simultaneous point multiplication computes at each of $\lceil t/w \rceil$ steps, $w$ doublings, and one addition from the list of the pre-computed values. Here, $t$ is the bit length of a scalar multiplier. As the parameter $w$ is a variable that allows some trade-off, we chose the smallest window (i.e., $w = 1$) in order to maintain memory utilization as low as possible. In the remainder of the chapter, we describe a processor specifically suited for this operation and to anti-counterfeiting RFID-based applications [10].

## 17.5 ECC Implementations for RFID

In this section we elaborate on our choice of algorithms and we explain our strategy to minimize the area of an EC processor suited to the constrained RFID environment. Our strategy can be summarize as follows: (1) We reduce the total number of intermediate registers for the calculation of point operations, (2) we use small digit sizes in our multiplier designs and investigate the effect of a dedicated squarer in the design's area and performance, and (3) we avoid having to recover the $y$-coordinate of the elliptic curve point in the tag and, in fact, only operate on the $x$-coordinate during the protocol. This, in turn, helps us avoid dealing with finite field inversion operation on the tag.

### 17.5.1 Elliptic Curve Operations

A non-supersingular elliptic curve $E$ over $\mathbb{F}_{2^n}$ is defined as the set of solutions $(x, y) \in \mathbb{F}_{2^n} \times \mathbb{F}_{2^n}$ to the equation $y^2 + xy = x^3 + ax^2 + b$, where $a, b \in \mathbb{F}_{2^n}, b \neq 0$, together with the point at infinity, denoted by $\infty$. The point or scalar multiplication is the basic operation for cryptographic protocols and it is easily performed via repeated group operations. Here, we describe ECC operations at each level by following the top-down approach. For the point multiplication, we chose Montgomery's method [208], which maintains the relationship $P_2 - P_1$ as invariant. We use the variant presented in [156], which provides basic resistance against simple power analysis (SPA) attacks. It uses a representation where computations are performed on the $x$-coordinate only in affine coordinates (or on the $X$- and $Z$-coordinates in projective representation). That fact allows us to save registers, which is one of the main criteria for obtaining a compact solution. For the group operation, we modified the order in which the computation is performed in the point addition and doubling formulas of Lopez and Dahab [184]. The original formulas in [184] require three intermediate registers (two for addition and one for doubling). In our case, we eliminate one intermediate register without adding more steps to the original algorithms. The result of our optimizations are depicted in Algorithm 1. Thus, point addition requires four multiplications, one squaring, and two additions, whereas point doubling requires two multiplications, four squarings, and one addition.

---

**Algorithm 1** EC point addition and doubling: operations that minimize the number of registers

| **Require:** $X_1, Z_1, X_2, Z_2, x_4 = x(P_2 - P_1)$ | **Require:** $b \in \mathbb{F}_{2^n}, X_1, Z_1$ |
|---|---|
| **Ensure:** $X(P_1 + P_2) = X(P_3) = X_3, Z_3$ | **Ensure:** $X(2P_1) = X(P_5) = X_5, Z_5$ |
| 1: $Z_3 \leftarrow X_2 \cdot Z_1$ | $Z_5 \leftarrow X_1{}^2$ |
| 2: $X_3 \leftarrow X_1 \cdot Z_2$ | $T \leftarrow Z_1{}^2$ |
| 3: $T \leftarrow X_3 + Z_3$ | $X_5 \leftarrow T \cdot Z_5$ |
| 4: $X_3 \leftarrow X_3 \cdot Z_3$ | $T \leftarrow T^2$ |
| 5: $Z_3 \leftarrow T^2$ | $T \leftarrow b \cdot T$ |
| 6: $T \leftarrow x_4 \cdot Z_3$ | $Z_5 \leftarrow Z_5{}^2$ |
| 7: $X_3 \leftarrow X_3 + T$ | $Z_5 \leftarrow Z_5 + T$ |

---

### 17.5.2 Field Arithmetic

Fields of characteristic 2 in polynomial basis were chosen, as field arithmetic can be implemented efficiently and relatively inexpensively in hardware. Notice that the emphasis is on minimizing area rather than performance. Addition of two elements $C = A + B \in \mathbb{F}_{2^n}$ is performed via an $n$-bitwise logical XOR operation. The simplest multiplier is based on Horner's scheme for multiplication. In particular, to compute the product $C = A \cdot B \in \mathbb{F}_{2^n} \cong \mathbb{F}_2[x]/f(x)$, where $A = \sum_{i=0}^{n-1} a_i x^i$, $B = \sum_{j=0}^{n-1} b_j x^j$, and $f = x^n + \sum_{i=0}^{s} f_i x^i$, $s < n$, we process one bit of $B$ at the time, thus obtaining $C \equiv A \sum_{j=0}^{n-1} b_j x^j \bmod f$. The multiplication process then requires $n$ iterations. Digit serial multiplication [260] is a generalization of this in which several coefficients of $B$ are processed in parallel. Thus, we trade off area for performance. Algorithm 2 describes how to perform Most Significant Digit multiplication according to [139], which reduces the area of the multiplier with respect to [260] and [10].

---

**Algorithm 2** Most significant digit multiplication in $\mathbb{F}_{2^n}$

---

**Require:** $A = \sum_{i=0}^{n-1} a_i x^i$, where $a_i \in \mathbb{F}_2$, $B = \sum_{j=0}^{d-1} \widehat{b}_j x^{jD}$ where
  $\widehat{b}_j = \sum_{l=0}^{D-1} b_{Dj+l} x^l$, $b_i \in \mathbb{F}_2$, and $d = \lceil \frac{n}{D} \rceil$.
**Ensure:** $C = A \cdot B \bmod f(x)$
1: $C \leftarrow 0$
2: **for** $i = 0$ to $d - 1$ **do**
3:     $C \leftarrow \left( \widehat{b}_{d-1-i} A + C x^D \right) \bmod f$
4: **end for**
5: Return $C$

---

For security reasons, it is typically recommended to use fields $\mathbb{F}_{2^p}$ where $p$ is a prime. Thus, we investigate the cases where $p = 131$ and $p = 139$. However, we also consider EC over a quadratic extension of $\mathbb{F}_{2^p}$. For example, $\mathbb{F}_{2^{134}} \equiv \mathbb{F}_{(2^{67})^2} \equiv \mathbb{F}_{2^{67}}[y]/g(y)$, where $\deg(g) = 2$ and $g$ is an irreducible polynomial over $\mathbb{F}_{2^{67}}$. In this way, we can translate the arithmetic from $\mathbb{F}_{(2^p)^2}$ to $\mathbb{F}_{2^p}$, which results in a reduction in the size of the arithmetic logic unit (ALU) by a factor of 2 approximately. In a composite field $\mathbb{F}_{(2^p)^2}$, each element can be represented as $z = xt + y$, where $x, y \in \mathbb{F}_{2^p}$. No attacks are known against EC defined over this type of field.

### 17.5.3 Recovering the $y$-Coordinate of $Q = k \cdot P$

Traditionally, after computing $Q = k \cdot P$, it is required to transform the result back to affine coordinates and compute the $y$-coordinate of $Q$. Instead we advocate sending both end values at the end of the Montgomery ladder [156] to the verifier so that the verifier himself can recover the $y$-coordinate of $Q$. This would incur in the sending of four finite field elements, corresponding to the projective coordinate representation of $P_1$ and $P_2$. Alternatively, the protocol can be run by only using the $x$-coordinates of all points involved. This was originally observed by Miller in [203]. In either case, the projective coordinates sent to the verifier should be masked with a random value to avoid the attack described in [209]. This requires two extra multiplications at the end of the point multiplication with negligible time overhead.

## 17.5.4 Elliptic Curve Processor Architecture

Our Elliptic Curve Processor (ECP) for RFID is shown in Fig. 17.2. The operational blocks are as follows: a Control Unit(CU), an Arithmetic Logic Unit (ALU), and Memory (RAM and ROM). In ROM the ECC parameters and the constants $x_4$ (the $x$-coordinate of $P_2 - P_1$) and $b$ are stored. RAM memory contains all input and output variables and it therefore communicates with both the ROM and the ALU. The CU controls scalar multiplication and point operations. In the case of composite fields implementations, it also controls the operations in extension fields. In addition, the controller commands the ALU, which performs field multiplication, addition, and squaring. The CU consists of a number of simple state machines and a counter and its area cost is small. The processor memory consists of the equivalent to seven $n$-bit ($n = p$) registers for ordinary fields and nine $n$-bit ($n = 2p$) registers for composite fields. Tables 17.1 and 17.2 summarize the number of cycles required for basic operations and for a whole-point multiplication in an EC over $\mathbb{F}_{2^p}$. The complexity for whole-point multiplication over $\mathbb{F}_{2^{2p}}$ can be obtained directly from Table 17.2 and our previous discussion on composite fields.

The largest contribution in area to the overall design comes from the ALU, illustrated in Fig. 17.3. It consists of two $n$-bit registers $a$ and $c$ and one $n$-bit shift-register $b$ that outputs $D$ bits at the time. In addition, the ALU has circuitry for implementing addition, squaring, and multiplication in $\mathbb{F}_{2^n}$. Load and store operations between the ALU and memory cost a single clock cycle. The ADD block consists of $n$ XOR gates, and the SQR block consists

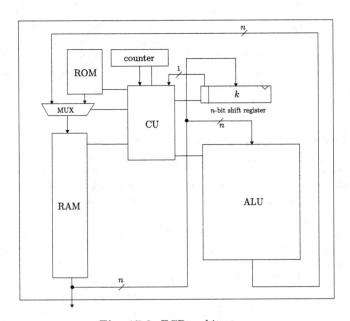

**Fig. 17.2.** ECP architecture.

**Table 17.1.** Cycle count for basic field operations L: load, C: computation, S: store

| $\mathbb{F}_{2^p}$ Operation | L | C | S | Total Cycles |
|---|---|---|---|---|
| Addition | 2 | 1 | 1 | 4 |
| Squaring | 1 | 1 | 1 | 3 |
| Multiplication | 2 | $\lceil\frac{p-1}{D}\rceil$ | 1 | $\lceil\frac{p-1}{D}\rceil + 3$ |

**Table 17.2.** Cycle count for elliptic curve operations over $\mathbb{F}_{2^p}$

| EC Operation | EC operations with a squarer | EC operations without a squarer |
|---|---|---|
| Addition | $4\ MUL + 1\ SQ + 2\ ADD = 4\lceil\frac{p-1}{D}\rceil + 23$ | $5\ MUL + 2\ ADD = 5\lceil\frac{p-1}{D}\rceil + 23$ |
| Doubling | $2\ MUL + 4\ SQ + 1\ ADD = 2\lceil\frac{p-1}{D}\rceil + 22$ | $6\ MUL + 1\ ADD = 6\lceil\frac{p-1}{D}\rceil + 22$ |
| Point mult. | $(n-1)\left(6\lceil\frac{p-1}{D}\rceil + 45\right)$ | $(n-1)\left(11\lceil\frac{p-1}{D}\rceil + 45\right)$ |

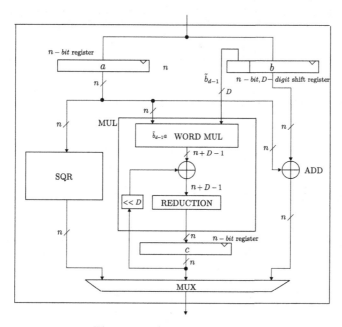

**Fig. 17.3.** ALU architecture.

of at most $3n/2$ XOR gates and computes $\mathbb{F}_{2^n}$ additions and squarings in a single clock cycle once data have been loaded into the ALU. The MUL block implements an iteration of step 3 of Algorithm 2 in a single clock cycle. Multiplication is calculated then in $d = \lceil n/D\rceil$ clock cycles. For composite fields, the field arithmetic translates to the arithmetic in the subfield as follows: (1) Addition in $\mathbb{F}_{(2^p)^2}$ requires two additions in $\mathbb{F}_{2^p}$, (2) multiplication in $\mathbb{F}_{(2^p)^2}$ requires three multiplications and four additions in $\mathbb{F}_{2^p}$, and (3) squaring in $\mathbb{F}_{(2^p)^2}$ requires two squaring and one addition in $\mathbb{F}_{2^p}$.

## 17.6 Results and discussion

In this section, we provide estimates for the latency and the area complexity of Schnorr's protocol. As mentioned earlier, the core part of the protocol is one-point multiplication. The results for various architectures are given in Tables 17.3 and 17.4. We considered solutions with or without the squarer, as it allows also for a trade-off between area and performance. For the case of composite fields, the ALU shrinks in size but some speed-up is then necessary, which we obtain by means of a digit-serial multiplier (instead of a bit-serial one, (i.e., $D = 1$). The performance in each case is calculated by the use of

**Table 17.3.** Implementation results at 175 kHz and assuming a dedicated squarer

| Implementation | | ALU | RAM | Perf. | Area No | AT Factor | AT Factor |
|---|---|---|---|---|---|---|---|
| Digit Size | Field Type | [gates] | [bits] | [s] | RAM [gates] | [wo RAM] | [w RAM] |
| D=1 | $\mathbb{F}_{2^{131}}$ | 6,306 | 917 | 0.61 | 8,582 | 5,260 | 8,632 |
| | $\mathbb{F}_{(2^{67})^2}$ | 3,274 | 1,206 | 1.09 | 6,074 | 6,611 | 14,486 |
| | $\mathbb{F}_{2^{139}}$ | 6,690 | 973 | 0.69 | 9,044 | 6,227 | 10,246 |
| D=2 | $\mathbb{F}_{2^{131}}$ | 6,962 | 917 | 0.32 | 9,233 | 2,984 | 4,762 |
| | $\mathbb{F}_{(2^{67})^2}$ | 3,610 | 1,206 | 0.64 | 6,410 | 4,083 | 8,691 |
| | $\mathbb{F}_{2^{139}}$ | 7,379 | 973 | 0.36 | 9,734 | 3,524 | 5,637 |
| | $\mathbb{F}_{(2^{71})^2}$ | 3,648 | 1,278 | 0.70 | 6,534 | 4,602 | 10,001 |
| D=3 | $\mathbb{F}_{(2^{67})^2}$ | 3,789 | 1,206 | 0.49 | 6,589 | 3,205 | 6,725 |
| | $\mathbb{F}_{(2^{71})^2}$ | 3,833 | 1,278 | 0.54 | 6,719 | 3,660 | 7,837 |
| D=4 | $\mathbb{F}_{(2^{67})^2}$ | 4,103 | 1,206 | 0.42 | 6,903 | 2,886 | 5,911 |
| | $\mathbb{F}_{(2^{71})^2}$ | 4,152 | 1,278 | 0.46 | 7,038 | 3,321 | 6,731 |

**Table 17.4.** Implementation results at 175 kHz and assuming no dedicated squarer

| Implementation | | ALU | RAM | Perf. | Area No | AT Factor | AT Factor |
|---|---|---|---|---|---|---|---|
| Digit Size | Field Type | [gates] | [bits] | [s] | RAM [gates] | [wo RAM] | [w RAM] |
| D=1 | $\mathbb{F}_{2^{131}}$ | 5,679 | 917 | 1.10 | 7,953 | 8,715 | 14,743 |
| | $\mathbb{F}_{(2^{67})^2}$ | 2,953 | 1,206 | 1.88 | 5,708 | 10,746 | 24,368 |
| | $\mathbb{F}_{2^{139}}$ | 6,018 | 973 | 1.23 | 8,380 | 10,329 | 17,525 |
| D=2 | $\mathbb{F}_{2^{131}}$ | 6,335 | 917 | 0.56 | 8,603 | 4,858 | 7,964 |
| | $\mathbb{F}_{(2^{67})^2}$ | 3,289 | 1,206 | 1.05 | 6,044 | 6,376 | 14,009 |
| | $\mathbb{F}_{2^{139}}$ | 6,718 | 973 | 0.63 | 9,079 | 5,757 | 9,458 |
| | $\mathbb{F}_{(2^{71})^2}$ | 3,463 | 1,278 | 1.17 | 6,304 | 7,386 | 16,369 |
| D=3 | $\mathbb{F}_{(2^{67})^2}$ | 3,468 | 1,206 | 0.78 | 6,224 | 4,849 | 10,486 |
| | $\mathbb{F}_{(2^{71})^2}$ | 3,647 | 1,278 | 0.88 | 6,489 | 5,705 | 12,445 |
| D=4 | $\mathbb{F}_{(2^{67})^2}$ | 3,782 | 1,206 | 0.65 | 6,537 | 4,273 | 9,003 |
| | $\mathbb{F}_{(2^{71})^2}$ | 3,967 | 1,278 | 0.72 | 6,808 | 4,899 | 10,416 |

formulas for point operations as in Algorithm 1 and we calculate the total number of cycles for each case assuming the numbers for field arithmetic provided in Section 17.5.4.

The designs were synthesized using a Synopsis Design-analyzer for the frequency of 175 kHz and a 0.25 $\mu$m CMOS library. One of our main reasons for using composite fields was to reduce the ALU's area. This is clearly visible in Tables 17.3 and 17.4. We notice that the ALU varies in size from 2863 to 7379 gates and the smallest one is obtained for the field $\mathbb{F}_{(2^{67})^2}$, without the squarer and with a bit-serial multiplier. However, the performance is the worst for this case, requiring 1.88 seconds for one-point multiplication. The total area without RAM includes the sizes of the ALU, the CU, the counter, and the shift-register. The largest portion of that is occupied by the key register (i.e., 1400 and 1500 gates for fields $\mathbb{F}_{2^{131}}$ and $\mathbb{F}_{2^{139}}$, respectively). The control logic takes between 10% and 15% of a whole design.

In the last two columns, we computed the area-time product for two cases, including RAM and not including RAM. To map the number of bits to be stored to actual gates, we used a factor of 6, which is conservative when using SRAM. If we were to use dedicated embedded RAM, it would be possible to half the area requirement (see, e.g., [154, 210]), at the very least. From Table 17.3 and looking at the AT-product values, we conclude that, in general, it is beneficial to use a digit-serial multiplier and a squarer. However, these options are not the most compact. For compactness, one should choose an implementation without squarer. The total area is expressed without RAM for two reasons. First, it is hard to exactly map it to the corresponding number of gates and, second, most tags have RAM available. Some high-end tags have therefore the possibility to store 1000 bits, which would be enough in some cases presented in Table 17.3.

We compare our results with other related work in Table 17.5. It is hard to compare with other related work, as there are only a few previous ECC implementations suitable for RFIDs. We chose to provide two values: the architecture with the best AT product and best timing and the architecture with the smallest area. We stress here again that we obtain these figures by including very conservative estimates for RAM in the total gate count. In fact, a RAM cell that requires six equivalent gates to be implemented is a register cell. A typical full-custom RAM cell requires somewhere between one and two equivalent gates, thus bringing the total area required for the design under 10,000 gates. Other optimizations involve the shift-register for the key, which is of full length and requires 1500 gates. This can still be improved by loading the key in two or more parts, thus reducing the area significantly.

Regarding Okamoto's scheme, we notice that implementing it requires more storage (e.g., we need two scalar multipliers instead of one), thus increasing the area requirement between 20% and 50%. This is a consequence

**Table 17.5.** Performance and area of different algorithms and implementations

| Source | Algorithm | Finite Field/ Parameter Size | Area [gates] | Technology [$\mu$m] | Op. Frequency [kHz] | Performance [ms] |
|---|---|---|---|---|---|---|
| [129] | NTRU-Encrypt | $N = 167, p = 3,$ q=128 | 3,000 | 0.13 | 500 | 58.45 |
| [106] | AES | block size $= 128$ bits | 3,595 | 0.35 | 100 | 10.2 (1016 cycles) |
| [165] not including RAM | SHA-1 | block size $= 512$ bits | 4,276 | 0.13 | 500 | 0.81 (405 cycles) |
| [107] including RAM | SHA-256 | block size $= 512$ bits | 10,868 | 0.35 | 100 | 11.28 (1128 cycles) |
| this work (smallest area) | EC | $\mathbb{F}_{(2^{67})^2}$ | 12,944 | 0.25 | 175 | 1.88 sec. |
| this work (smallest AT product, fastest) | EC | $\mathbb{F}_{2^{131}}$ | 14,735 | 0.25 | 175 | 320 |
| [129] | EC | $\mathbb{F}_{P100}$ | 18,720 | 0.13 | 500 | 410.5 |
| [300] | EC | $\mathbb{F}_{2^{191}}$ and $\mathbb{F}_{P192}$ | 23,000 | 0.35 | 68,500 | 6.7 |
| [219] | EC | $\mathbb{F}_{P166}$ | 30,333 | 0.13 | 20,000 | 31.9 |

of the cost of RAM, which is significant when compared to the ALU and control logic. In addition, the performance is substantially affected as in the simultaneous multiplication case: The computation of $kP + lQ$ is at least 25% slower than the computation of $kP$.

# References

1. E. S. Academy. I2c (inter-integrated circuit) bus technical overview and frequently asked questions. Available from `http://www.esacademy.com/faq/i2c/`.
2. ADT/Tyco Fire and Security, A. Technology, I. Inc., I. Corporation, S. T. Inc., and Xterprice. RFID and UHF: A prescription for RFID success in the pharmaceutical industry. White paper, Pharmaceutical Online, June 2006. Available at `http://www.pharmaceuticalonline.com/uhf/`.
3. S. Agarwal, V. Chauhan, and A. Trachtenberg. Bandwidth efficient string reconciliation using puzzles. *IEEE Transactions on Parallel and Distributed Systems*, 17(11):1217–1225, 2006.
4. R. Ahlswede and I. Csiszár. Common randomness in information theory and cryptography — part i: Secret sharing. *IEEE Transactions on Information Theory*, 39(4):1121–1132, 1993.
5. T. Alves and D. Felton. Trustzone: Integrated hardware and software security. white paper ARM Ltd., July 2004.
6. D. Anastassiou and D. J. Sakrison. Some results regarding the entropy rate of random fields. *IEEE Transactions on Information Theory*, 28(2):340–343, 1982.
7. R. Anderson and M. Kuhn. Tamper resistance—A cautionary note. In *Proceedings of the Second Usenix Workshop on Electronic Commerce*, pages 1–11, Berkeley, CA, November 1996. Usenix Association.
8. R. J. Anderson. *Security Engineering: A Guide to Building Dependable Distributed Systems*. John Wiley & Sons, Hoboken, NJ, 2001.
9. R. J. Anderson and M. G. Kuhn. Low cost attacks on tamper resistant devices. In B. Christianson, B. Crispo, T. M. A. Lomas, and M. Roe, editors, *Security Protocols Workshop*, Lecture Notes in Computer Science, Vol. 1361, pages 125–136. Springer-Verlag, New York, 1997.
10. L. Batina, J. Guajardo, T. Kerins, N. Mentens, P. Tuyls, and I. Verbauwhede. Public-key cryptography for RFID-tags. In *IEEE Conference on Pervasive Computing and Communications Workshops—PerCom 2007 Workshops*, New York, March 19–23, IEEE Computer Society, New York, 2007.
11. A. M. Bazen and S. H. Gerez. Systematic methods for the computation of the directional fields and singular points of fingerprints. *IEEE Transactions on Pattern Analysis and Machine Intelligence*, 24(7):905–919, 2002.

12. A. M. Bazen and R. N. J. Veldhuis. Detection of cores in fingerprints with improved dimension reduction. In: *4th IEEE Benelux Signal Processing Symposium (SPS-2004), Hilvarenbeek, The Netherlands IEEE Benelux Signal Processing Chapter*, pages 41–44, 2004.

13. A. M. Bazen and R. N. J. Veldhuis. Likelihood-ratio-based biometric verification. *IEEE Transactions on Circuits and Systems for Video Technology*, 14(1):86–94, 2004.

14. D. Beaver. Multiparty protocols tolerating half faulty processors. In Gilles Brassard, editor, *Advances in Cryptology—CRYPTO 1989*, Lecture Notes in Computer Science, Vol. 435, pages 560–572. Springer-Verlag, New York, 1989.

15. D. Beaver. Foundations of secure interactive computing. In Joan Feigenbaum, editor, *Advances in Cryptology—CRYPTO 1991*, Lecture Notes in Computer Science, Vol. 1233, pages 377–391. Springer-Verlag, New York, 1992.

16. D. Beaver. Precomputing oblivious transfer. In Louis C. Guillou and Jean-Jacques Quisquarter, editors, *Advances in Cryptology—EUROCRYPT 1995*, Lecture Notes in Computer Science, Vol. 963, pages 97–109. Springer-Verlag, New York, 1995.

17. M. Bellare, A. Boldyreva, A. Desai, and D. Pointcheval. *Key-privacy in public-key encryption*. Lecture Notes in Computer Science, Vol. 2248, Springer-Verlag, New York, 2001.

18. M. Bellare, C. Namprempre, and G. Neven. Security proofs for identity-based identification and signature schemes. In C. Cachin and J. Camenisch, editors, *Advances in Cryptology—Eurocrypt 2004*, Lecture Notes in Computer Science, Vol. 3027, pages 268–286. Springer-Verlag, New York, 2004.

19. M. Bellare, D. Pointcheval, and P. Rogaway. Authenticated key exchange secure against dictionary attacks. In B. Preneel, editor, *Advances in Cryptology—EUROCRYPT 2000*, Lecture Notes in Computer Science, Vol. 1807, pages 139–155. Springer-Verlag, New York 2000.

20. M. Bellare and P. Rogaway. Entity authentication and key distribution. In D. R. Stinson, editor, *Advances in Cryptology—CRYPTO 1993*, Lecture Notes in Computer Science, Vol. 773, pages 232–249. Springer-Verlag, New York, 1993.

21. M. Bellare and P. Rogaway. Random oracles are practical: a paradigm for designing efficient protocols. In V. Ashby, editor, *1st ACM Conference on Computer and Communications Security*, pages 62–73. ACM Press, New York, 1993.

22. M. Ben-Or, S. Goldwasser, and A. Wigderson. Completeness theorems for non-cryptographic fault-tolerant distributed computation. In R. Cole, editor, *Proceedings 20th Symposium on Theory of Computing (STOC '88)*, pages 1–10, ACM Press, New York, 1988.

23. C. H. Bennett and G. Brassard. Quantum cryptography: Public-key distribution and coin tossing. In *Proceedings of IEEE International Conference on Computers, Systems and Signal Processing*, pages 175–179, 1984.

24. C. H. Bennett, G. Brassard, S. Breidbard, and S. Wiesner. Quantum cryptography, or unforgeable subway tokens. In David Chaum, Ronald L. Rivest, Alan T. Sherman, editors, *Advances in Cryptology—CRYPTO 1982*, pages 267–275, 1982.

25. C. H. Bennett, G. Brassard, C. Crépeau, and U. M. Maurer. Generalized privacy amplification. *IEEE Transactions on Information Theory*, 41(6):1915–1923, 1995.

26. C. H. Bennett, G. Brassard, C. Crépeau, and M.-H. Skubiszewska. Practical quantum oblivious transfer. In J. Feigenbaum, editor, *Advances in Cryptology—CRYPTO 1991*, Lecture Notes in Computer Science, Vol. 576, pages 351–366. Springer-Verlag, New York, 1991.

27. C. H. Bennett, G. Brassard, and J.-M. Robert. Privacy amplification by public discussion. *SIAM Journal on Computing*, 17(2):210–229, 1988.

28. E. Berlekamp, R. McEliece, and H. van Tilborg. On the inherent intractability of certain coding problems. *IEEE Transactions on Information Theory*, 24:384–386, 1978.

29. E. Biham and A. Shamir. Differential fault analysis of secret key cryptosystems. In B. S. J. Kaliski, editor, *Advances in Cryptology—CRYPTO 1997*, Lecture Notes in Computer Science, Vol. 1294, pages 513–525. Springer-Verlag, New York, 1997.

30. M. Blum. Coin flipping by telephone: A protocol for solving impossible problems. In *Proceedings of the 24th IEEE Computer Conference*, pages 133–137, 1982.

31. M. Blum and S. Micali. How to generate cryptographically strong sequences of pseudo-random bits. *SIAM Journal on Computing*, 13(4):850–864, 1984.

32. A. Bodo. Method for producing a digital signature with aid of a biometric feature. German Patent, DE 4243908A1, 1994.

33. R. M. Bolle, J. Connell, S. Pankanti, N. K. Ratha, and A. W. Senior. Biometrics 101. Report RC22481, IBM Research, 2002.

34. R. M. Bolle, J. H. Connell, S. Pankanti, N. K. Ratha, and A. W. Senior. *Guide to Biometrics*. Springer-Verlag, New York, 2003.

35. J. Bolling. A window to your health. *Jacksonville Medicine, Special issue: Retina diseases*, 51(9), September 2000.

36. D. Boneh and X. Boyen. Efficient selective-id secure identity based encryption without random oracles. In C. Cachin and J. Camenisch, editors, *Advances in Cryptology—EUROCRYPT 2004*, Lecture Notes in Computer Science, Vol. 3027, Springer-Verlag, New York, 2004.

37. D. Boneh and M. K. Franklin. Identity-based encryption from the Weil pairing. In J. Kilian, editor, *Advances in Cryptology—CRYPTO 2001*, Lecture Notes in Computer Science, Vol. 2139, pages 213–229. Springer-Verlag, New York, 2001.

38. J. Bos and B. Boer. Detection of disrupters in the DC protocol. In Jean-Jacques Quisquater and Joos Vandewalle, editors, *Advances in Cryptology—EUROCRYPT 1989*, Lecture Notes in Computer Science, Vol. 434, pages 320–327. Springer-Verlag, New York, 1990.

39. T. Boult. Robust distance measures for face recognition supporting revocable biometric tokens. In *Proceedings of the International Conference on Face and Gesture*, pages 560–566, April 2006.

40. K. W. Bowyer, K. Chang, and P. J. Flynn. A survey of approaches and challenges in 3D and multi-modal 3D + 2D face recognition. *Computer Vision and Image Understanding*, 101(1):1–15, 2006.

41. X. Boyen. Reusable cryptographic fuzzy extractors. In V. Atluri, B. Pfitzmann, and P. D. McDaniel, editors, *ACM Conference on Computer and Communications Security*, pages 82–91. ACM Press, New York, 2004.

42. X. Boyen, Y. Dodis, J. Katz, R. Ostrovsky, and A. Smith. Secure remote authentication using biometric data. In R. Cramer, editor, *Advances in Cryptology—Eurocrypt 2005*, Lecture Notes in Computer Science, Vol. 3494, pages 147–163. Springer-Verlag, New York, 2005.

43. J. Bringer, H. Chabanne, and Q. D. Do. A fuzzy sketch with trapdoor. *IEEE Transactions on Information Theory*, 52(5):2266–2269, 2006.

44. A. Broder. On the resemblance and containment of documents. In *Proceedings of Compression and Complexity of Sequences*, 1997.

45. A. Brouwer. Bounds on linear codes. In *Handbook of Coding Theory*, pages 295–461. Elsevier, Amsterdam, 1998.

46. I. Buhan, A. M. Bazen, P. H. Hartel, and R. N. J. Veldhuis. Fuzzy extractors for continuous distributions. In *Proceedings ACM Symposium on Information, Computer and Communications Security (ASIACCS'07)*, 2007.

47. C. J. C. Burges. A tutorial on support vector machines for pattern recognition. *Data Mining and Knowlege Discovery*, 2(2):121–167, 1998.

48. J. M. Butler. *Forensic DNA Typing 2nd ed.* Elsevier Academic, Amsterdam, 2005.

49. C. Cachin. Entropy Measures and Unconditional Security in Cryptography. PhD thesis, No. 12187, ETH Zurich, Switzerland, 1997.

50. R. Canetti. Security and composition of multi-party cryptographic protocols. *Journal of Cryptology*, 13(1):143–202, 2000.

51. R. Canetti. Universally composable security: A new paradigm for cryptographic protocols. In *Proceedings of the 42nd IEEE Symposium on Foundations of Computer Science (FOCS)*, pages 136–145, 2001.

52. R. Canetti, Y. Dodis, S. Halevi, E. Kushilevitz, and A. Sahai. Exposure-resilient functions and all-or-nothing transforms. In B. Preneel, editor, *Advances in Cryptology—EUROCRYPT 2000*, pages 453–469, 2000.

53. R. Canetti, O. Goldreich, and S. Halevi. The random oracle methodology, revisited. In Jeffrey Vitter, editor, *Proceedings of the 30th Annual ACM Symposium on the Theory of Computing (STOC98)*, pages 209–218. ACM Press, New York, 1998.

54. R. Canetti, S. Halevi, and J. Katz. A forward-secure public-key encryption scheme. In *Proceedings of Eurocrypt 2003*. Springer-Verlag, New York, 2003.

55. R. Canetti, S. Halevi, and M. Steiner. Mitigating dictionary attacks on password-protected local storage. In Dwork [98], pages 160–179.

56. A. Carroll, M. Juarez, J. Polk, and T. Leininger. Microsoft "Palladium": A business overview. Technical Report, *Microsoft Content Security Business Unit*, August 2002.

57. J. L. Carter and M. N. Wegman. Universal classes of hash functions. *Journal of Computer and System Sciences*, 18:143–154, 1979.

58. E.-C. Chang and Q. Li. Hiding secret points amidst chaff. In S. Vaudenay, editor, *Advances in Cryptology—EUROCRYPT 2006*, Lecture Notes in Computer Science, Vol. 4004, pages 59–72. Springer-Verlag, New York, 2006.

59. D. Chaum. The dining cryptographers problem: Unconditional sender and recipient untraceability. *Journal of Cryptology*, 1(1):65–75, 1988.

60. D. Chaum, C. Crépeau, and I. Damgård. Multiparty unconditionally secure protocols (extended abstract). In R. Cole, editor, *Proceedings of the 21st Annual ACM Symposium on Theory of Computing (STOC '88)*, pages 11–19. ACM Press, New York, 1988.

61. D. Chaum and S. Roijakkers. Unconditionally-secure digital signatures. In Alfred Menezes and Scott A. Vanstone, editors, *Advances in Cryptology—CRYPTO 1990*, Lecture Notes in Computer Science, Vol. 537, pages 206–214. Springer-Verlag, New York, 1990.

62. B. Chen and G. W. Wornell. Quantization index modulation: A class of provably good methods for digital watermarking and information embedding. *IEEE Transactions on Information Theory*, 47(4):1423–1443, 2001.

63. S. Chikkerur and N. K. Ratha. Impact of singular point detection on fingerprint matching performance. In *Proceedings of the Fourth IEEE Workshop on Automatic Identification Advanced Technologies*, pages 207–212, July 2005.

64. B. Chor and O. Goldreich. Unbiased bits from sources of weak randomness and probabilistic communication complexity. *SIAM Journal on Computing*, 17(2):230–261, 1988.

65. T. Connie, A. Teoh, M. Goh, and D. Ngo. Palmhashing: a novel approach for cancelable biometrics. *Information Processing Letters*, 93(1):1–5, 2005.

66. T. Cover and J. Thomas. *Elements of Information Theory*. Wiley Series in Telecommunication, John Wiley & Sons, New York, 1991.

67. T. M. Cover. A proof of the data compression theorem of Slepain and Wolf for ergodic sources. *IEEE Transactions on Information Theory*, IT-22:226–228, March 1975.

68. R. Cramer, I. Damgård, S. Dziembowski, M. Hirt, and T. Rabin. Efficient multiparty computations secure against an adaptive adversary. In J. Stern, editor, *Advances in Cryptology—EUROCRYPT 1999*, Lecture Notes in Computer Science, Vol. 1592, pages 311–326. Springer-Verlag, New York, 1999.

69. R. Cramer, I. Damgård, and J. Nielsen. Multiparty computation from threshold homomorphic encryption. In Birgit Pfitzmann, editor, *Advances in Cryptology—EUROCRYPT 2001*, Lecture Notes in Computer Science, Vol. 2045, pages 280–300. Springer-Verlag, Berlin, 2001. Full version available from eprint.iacr.org/2000/055, October 27, 2000.

70. C. Crépeau. Efficient cryptographic protocols based on noisy channels. In B. S. J. Kaliski, editor, *Advances in Cryptology—CRYPTO 1997*, Lecture Notes in Computer Science, Vol. 1233, pages 306–317. Springer-Verlag, New York, 1997.

71. C. Crépeau and J. Kilian. Achieving oblivious transfer using weakened security assumptions (extended abstract). In *Proceedings of the 29th Annual IEEE Symposium on Foundations of Computer Science (FOCS '88)*, pages 42–52, 1988.

72. C. Crépeau, K. Morozov, and S. Wolf. Efficient unconditional oblivious transfer from almost any noisy channel. In *Security in Communication Networks (SCN 2004)*, pages 47–59, 2004.

73. I. Csiszár and J. Körner. Broadcast channels with confidential messages. *IEEE Transactions on Information Theory*, 24:339–348, 1978.

74. I. Damgård, S. Fehr, K. Morozov, and L. Salvail. Unfair noisy channels and oblivious transfer. In M. Noar, editor, *Theory of Cryptography Conference—TCC 2004*, Lecture Notes in Computer Science, Vol. 2951, pages 355–373, Springer-Verlag, New York, 2004.

75. I. Damgård, J. Kilian, and L. Salvail. On the (im)possibility of basing oblivious transfer and bit commitment on weakened security assumptions. In M. Wiener, editor, *Advances in Cryptology—CRYPTO 1999*, Lecture Notes in Computer Science, Vol. 1592, pages 56–73, Springer-Verlag, New York, 1999.

76. I. Damgård and J. Nielsen. Universally composable efficient multiparty computation from threshold homomorphic encryption. In D. Boneh, editor, *Advances in Cryptology—CRYPTO 2003*, Lecture Notes in Computer Science, Vol. 2729, pages 247–264, Springer-Verlag, Berlin, 2003.

77. J. Daugman. High confidence visual recognition of persons by a test of statistical independence. *Transactions on Pattern Analysis and Machine Intelligence*, 15(11):1148–1161, 1993.

78. J. Daugman. How iris recognition works. *IEEE Transactions on Circuits and Systems for Video Technology*, 14(1):21–30, 2004.

79. J. Daugman. Probing the uniqueness and randomness of iriscodes: Results from 200 billion iris pair comparisons. *Proceedings of the IEEE*, 94(11):1927–1935, 2006.

80. G. Davida, Y. Frankel, B. Matt, and R. Peralta. On the relation of error correction and cryptography to an offline biometric based identification scheme. In *Proceedings of WCC99, Workshop on Coding and Cryptography*, 1999.

81. G. I. Davida, Y. Frankel, and B. J. Matt. On enabling secure application through off-line biometric identification. In *IEEE 1998 Symposium on Research in Security and Privacy*, pages 148–157, 1998.

82. J. F. de Boer. Optical Fluctuations on the Transmission and Reflection of Mesoscopic Systems.PhD thesis, University of Twente, The Netherlands, 1995.

83. P. E. de Jongh, P. van Tilborg, and H. J. Wongergem. Wet-chemical formation of aluminophosphates. *Journal of Sol-Gel Science and Technology*, 31:241–244, August 2004.

84. Website of the Department of Homeland Security. Available from http://www.dhs.gov/xtrvlsec/programs/content_multi_image_0006.shtm.

85. W. Diffie and M. E. Hellman. New directions in cryptography. *IEEE Transactions on Information Theory*, 22:644–654, 1976.

86. Y. Z. Ding. Error correction in the bounded storage model. In J. Kilian, editor, *Theory of Cryptography Conference (TCC 2005)*, Lecture Notes in Computer Science, Vol. 3378, pages 578–599. Springer-Verlag, New York, 2005.

87. http://distributed.net/.

88. Y. Dodis, J. Katz, L. Reyzin, and A. Smith. Robust fuzzy extractors and authenticated key agreement from close secrets. In Dwork [98], pages 232–250.

89. Y. Dodis, J. Katz, S. Xu, and M. Yung. Strong Key-Insulated Signature Schemes. In Y. Desmedt, editor, *Public Key Cryptography—PKC 2003*, Lecture Notes in Computer Science, Vol. 2567, pages 130–144. Springer-Verlag, New York, 2003.

90. Y. Dodis, R. Ostrovsky, L. Reyzin, and A. Smith. Fuzzy extractors: How to generate strong keys from biometrics and other noisy data. Technical Report 2003/235, Cryptology ePrint archive, 2006. Previous version appeared as [91].

91. Y. Dodis, M. Reyzin, and A. Smith. Fuzzy extractors: How to generate strong keys from biometrics and other noisy data. In C. Cachin and J. Camenisch, editors, *Advances in Cryptology—Eurocrypt 2004*, Lecture Notes in Computer Science, Vol. 3027, pages 523–540. Springer-Verlag, New York, 2004.

92. Y. Dodis and A. Smith. Correcting errors without leaking partial information. In Gabow and Fagin [117], pages 654–663.

93. Y. Dodis and A. Smith. Entropic security and the encryption of high entropy messages. In *Theory of Cryptography Conference—TCC 2005*, Lecture Notes in Computer Science, pages 556–577. Springer-Verlag, New York, 2005.

94. Y. Dodis and J. Spencer. On the (non)universality of the one-time pad. In *Foundations Of Computer Science (FOCS 2002)*, pages 376–385. IEEE Computer Society, New York, 2002.

95. D. Dolev, C. Dwork, and M. Naor. Nonmalleable cryptography. *SIAM Journal on Computing*, 30(2):391–437, 2000.

96. D. Dolev and H. R. Strong. Polynomial algorithms for multiple processor agreement. In *Proceedings of the 21st Annual ACM Symposium on Theory of Computing (STOC '82)*, pages 401–407, 1982.

97. W. Du and M. Atallah. Secure multi-party computation problems and their applications: A review and open problems. In *Proceedigs of the New Security Paradigms Workshop 2001*, pages 13–22. ACM Press, New York, 2001.

98. C. Dwork, editor. *Advances in Cryptology - CRYPTO 2006, 26th Annual International Cryptology Conference, Santa Barbara, California, USA, August 20-24, 2006, Proceedings*, Lecture Notes in Computer Science, Vol. 4117. Springer-Verlag, New York, 2006.

99. C. Dwork. Differential privacy. In M. Bugliesi, B. Preneel, V. Sassone, and I. Wegener, editors, *International Colloquium on Automata, Languages and Programming (ICALP (2))*, Lecture Notes in Computer Science, Vol. 4052, pages 1–12. Springer-Verlag, New York, 2006.

100. A. K. Ekert. Quantum cryptography based on Bell's theorem. *Physical Review Letters*, 67:661, 1991.

101. T. ElGamal. A public-key cryptosystem and a signature scheme based on discrete logarithms. *IEEE Transactions on Information Theory*, IT-31(4):469–472, 1985.

102. Website of the European Union. Available from `http://europa.eu/index_en.htm`.

103. S. Even, O. Goldreich, and A. Lempel. A randomized protocol for signing contracts. *Commun. ACM*, 28(6):637–647, 1985.

104. H. Faulds. On the skin-furrows of the hand. *Nature*, 22:605, 1880.

105. J. Feigenbaum, Y. Ishai, T. Malkin, K. Nissim, M. Strauss, and R. Wright. Secure multiparty computation of approximations. In Fernando Orejas, Paul G. Spirakis and Jan van Leeuwen, editors, *28th International Colloquium on Automata, Languages and Programming—ICALP '01*, Lecture Notes in Computer Science, Vol. 2076, pages 927–938. Springer-Verlag, New York, 2001.

106. M. Feldhofer, S. Dominikus, and J. Wolkerstorfer. Strong authentication for RFID systems using the AES algorithm. In M. Joye and J. J. Quisquater, editors, *Cryptographic Hardware and Embedded Systems—CHES 2004*, Lecture Notes in Computer Science, Vol. 3156, pages 357–370. Springer-Verlag, New York, 2004.

107. M. Feldhofer and C. Rechberger. A case against currently used hash functions in RFID protocols. Printed handout of Workshop on RFID Security—RFIDSec 06, pages 109–122. ECRYPT Network of Excellence, July 2006. Available from `http://events.iaik.tugraz.at/RFIDSec06/Program/index.htm`.

108. S. Feng, C. Kane, P. A. Lee, and A. D. Stone. Correlations and fluctuations of coherent wave transmission through disordered media. *Physical Review Letters*, 61(7):834–837, 1988.

109. M. Fitzi, N. Gisin, and U. Maurer. Quantum solution to the Byzantine agreement problem. *Physical Review Letters*, 87(21):7901-1–7901-4, 2001.

110. M. Fitzi, N. Gisin, U. Maurer, and O. von Rotz. Unconditional Byzantine agreement and multi-party computation secure against dishonest minorities from scratch. In L. Knudsen, editor, *Advances in Cryptology—EUROCRYPT 2002*, Lecture Notes in Computer Science, Vol. 2332, pages 482–501. Springer-Verlag, New York, 2002.

111. M. Fitzi, S. Wolf, and J. Wullschleger. Pseudo-signatures, broadcast, and multi-party computation from correlated randomness. In M. Franklin, editor, *Advances in Cryptology—CRYPTO 2004*, Lecture Notes in Computer Science, Vol. 3152, pages 562–578. Springer-Verlag, New York, 2004.

112. M. Franklin and S. Haber. Joint encryption and message-efficient secure computation. *Journal of Cryptology*, 9(4):217–232, 1996.

113. M. Freedman, K. Nissim, and B. Pinkas. Efficient private matching and set intersection. In C. Cachin and J. Camenisch, editors, *Advances in Cryptology—EUROCRYPT 2004*, Lecture Notes in Computer Science, Vol. 3027, pages 1–19. Springer-Verlag, Berlin, 2004.

114. N. Frykholm and A. Juels. Error-tolerant password recovery. In P. Samarati, editor, *8th ACM Computer and Communication Security Conference*, pages 1–9. ACM Press, New York, 2001.

115. K. Fukunaga. *Introduction to Statistical Pattern Recognition 2nd ed.* Academic Press, New York, 1990.

116. D. Gabor. Light and information. In E. Wolf, editor, *Progress in Optics*, Philips Research Book Series, Vol. I. North-Holland, Amsterdam, 1961.

117. H. N. Gabow and R. Fagin, editors. *Proceedings of the 37th Annual ACM Symposium on Theory of Computing, Baltimore, MD, USA, May 22–24, 2005*. ACM Press, New York, 2005.

118. P. Gacs and J. Körner. Common information is far less than mutual information. *Problems Control and Information Theory*, 2:149–162, 1973.

119. R. G. Gallager. *Information Theory and Reliable Communcation*. John Wiley & Sons, New York, 1968.

120. F. Galton. Personal identification and description. *Nature*, 38:173–177, 1888.

121. J. Garay, B. Schoenmakers, and J. Villegas. Practical and secure solutions for integer comparison. In Tatsuaki Okamoto and Xiaoyun Wang, editors, *Public Key Cryptography—PKC 2007*, Lecture Notes in Computer Science, Vol. 4450, pages 330–342. Springer-Verlag, Berlin, 2007.

122. S. Garfinkel. *Database Nation: The Death of Privacy in the 21st Century*.: O'Reilly & Associates, Cambridge, MA, 2000.

123. B. Gassend. Physical Random Functions. Master's thesis, Massachusetts Institute of Technology, 2003.

124. B. Gassend, D. E. Clarke, M. van Dijk, and S. Devadas. Controlled physical random functions. In *Annual Computer Security Applications Conference (ACSAC 2002)*, pages 149–160. IEEE Computer Society, New York, 2002.

125. B. Gassend, D. E. Clarke, M. van Dijk, and S. Devadas. Silicon physical unknown functions. In V. Atluri, editor, *ACM Conference on Computer and Communications Security—CCS 2002*, pages 148–160. ACM Press, New York, 2002.

126. B. Gassend, D. Lim, D. Clarke, M. van Dijk, and S. Devadas. Identification and authentication of integrated circuits. *Concurrency and Computation: Practice and Experience*, 16(11):1077–1098, 2004.

127. B. Gassend, G. E. Suh, D. Clarke, M. van Dijk, and S. Devadas. Caches and Merkle Trees for Efficient Memory Integrity Verification. In *Proceedings of*

*Ninth International Symposium on High Performance Computer Architecture*, IEEE Press, New York, 2003.

128. B. Gassend, M. van Dijk, D. Clarke, E. Torlak, P. Tuyls, and S. Devadas. Controlled physical random functions and applications. Accepted for publication in *ACM Transactions on Information and System Security*, 10(4), November 2007.

129. G. Gaubatz, J.-P. Kaps, E. Öztürk, and B. Sunar. State of the art in ultra-low power public key cryptography for wireless sensor networks. In *IEEE Conference on Pervasive Computing and Communications Workshops (Per-Com 2005 Workshops)*, pages 146–150. IEEE Computer Society, New York, 2005.

130. R. Gennaro, A. Lysyanskaya, T. Malkin, S. Micali, and T. Rabin. Algorithmic tamper-proof (ATP) security: Theoretical foundations for security against hardware tampering. In Naor [211], pages 258–277.

131. H. Gilbert, M. Robshaw, and H. Sibert. An active attack against HB+: A provably secure lightweight authentication protocol. IACR ePrintArchive 2005/237, 2005.

132. A. Goh and D. N. C. Ling. Computation of cryptographic keys from face biometrics. In A. Lioy and D. Mazzocchi, editors, *Communications and Multimedia Security*, Lecture Notes in Computer Science, Vol. 2828, pages 1–13. Springer-Verlag, New York, 2003.

133. O. Goldreich, S. Micali, and A. Wigderson. How to play any mental game. In Alfred V. Aho, editor, *Proceedings of the 21st Annual ACM Symposium on Theory of Computing (STOC '87)*, pages 218–229. ACM Press, New York, 1987.

134. S. Goldwasser and S. Micali. Probabilistic encryption. *Journal of Computer and System Sciences*, 28(2):270–299, 1984.

135. S. Goldwasser, S. Micali, and C. Rackoff. The knowledge complexity of interactive proof systems. *SIAM Journal on Computing*, 18(1):186–208, 1989.

136. J. W. Goodman. Statistical properties of laser spackle patterns. In J. C. Dainty, editor, *Laser Spackle and Related Phenomena*, 2nd ed. Springer-Verlag, New York, 1984.

137. V. Goyal, O. Pandey, B. R. Waters, and A. Sahai. Attribute-based encryption for fine-grained access control of encrypted data. In *Proceedings of ACM Conference on Computer and Communications Security*, 2006.

138. D. J. Griffiths. *Introduction to Electrodynamics*. Prentice-Hall, Englewood Cliffs, NJ, 1981.

139. J. Guajardo, T. Kerins, and P. Tuyls. Finite field multipliers for area constrained environments. Preprint, 2006.

140. J. Guajardo, S. Kumar, Geert-Jan, and P. Tuyls. FPGA intrinsic PUFs and their use for IP protection (submitted). In *Workshop on Cryptographic Hardware and Embedded Systems (CHES 2007)*, 2007.

141. P. Gutman. Secure deletion of data from magnetic and solid-state memory. In *Sixth USENIX Security Symposium Proceedings*, pages 77–89, Usenix Association, Berkeley, 1996.

142. F. Hao, R. Anderson, and J. Daugman. Combining crypto with biometrics effectively. *IEEE Transactions on Computers*, 55(9):1081–1088, 2006.

143. K. Harmon and L. Reyzin. An implementation of syndrome encoding and decoding for binary BCH codes, secure sketches and fuzzy extractors. Available from `http://www.cs.bu.edu/~reyzin/code/fuzzy.html`.

144. E. R. Henry. *Classification and Uses of Finger Prints*. Routledge, London, 1901.

145. W. Herschel. Skin-furrows of the hand. *Nature*, 25:76, 1880.

146. C. J. Hill. Risk of masquerade arising from the storage of biometrics. thesis, Australian National University, 2001. Available from `http://chris.fornax.net/download/thesis/thesis.pdf`.

147. T. Holenstein and R. Renner. On the randomness of independent experiments. Available from `http://arxiv.org/cs.IT/0608007`, 2006.

148. D. M. Hopkins, L. T. Kontnik, and M. T. Turnage. *Counterfeiting Exposed: Protecting Your Brand and Customers*. John Wiley & Sons, New York, 2003.

149. Website International Civil Aviation Organisation. Available from `http://www.icao.int/`.

150. T. Ignatenko, G. J. Schrijen, B. Škorić, P. Tuyls, and F. M. J. Willems. Estimating the secrecy rate of physical uncloneable functions with the context-tree weighting method. In *Proceedings of the IEEE International Symposium on Information Theory 2006*, pages 499–503, Seattle, WA, July 2006.

151. H. Imai, J. Müller-Quade, A. Nascimento, and A. Winter. Rates for bit commitment and coin tossing from noisy correlation. In *Proceedings of the IEEE International Symposium on Information Theory (ISIT '04)*, 2004.

152. R. Impagliazzo, L. A. Levin, and M. Luby. Pseudo-random generation from one-way functions. In D. S. Johnson, editor, *Proceedings of the 21st Annual ACM Symposium on Theory of Computing (STOC '89)*, pages 12–24. ACM Press, New York, 1989.

153. P. Indyk and D. Woodruff. Polylogarithmic private approximations and efficient matching. In Shai Halevi and Tal Rabin, editors, *Proceedings of the 3rd Theory of Cryptography Conference (TCC 2006)*, Lecture Notes in Computer Science, Vol. 3876, pages 245–264. Springer-Verlag, Berlin, 2006.

154. K. Itoh. Low-voltage embedded RAMs in the nanometer era. In *IEEE International Conference on Integrated Circuits and Technology—ICICT 2005*, pages 235–242. IEEE Computer Society, New York, 2005.

155. A. T. B. Jin, D. N. C. Ling, and A. Goh. Biohashing: two factor authentication featuring fingerprint data and tokenised random number. *Pattern Recognition*, 37(11):2245–2255, 2004.

156. M. Joye. Elliptic curves and side-channel analysis. *ST Journal of System Research*, 4(1):17–21, 2003.

157. A. Juels. Fuzzy commitment. DIMACS Workshop on Cryptography. Available from `http://dimacs.rutgers.edu/Workshops/Practice/slides/juels.ppt`, October 2004.

158. A. Juels and M. Jakobsson. Mix and match: Secure function evaluation via ciphertexts. In T. Okamoto, editor, *Advances in Cryptology—ASIACRYPT 2000*, Lecture Notes in Computer Science, vol. 1976, pages 162–177. Springer-Verlag, Berlin, 2000.

159. A. Juels and M. Sudan. A fuzzy vault scheme. In A. Lapidoth and E. Teletar, editors, *In Proceedings of IEEE Internation Symposium on Information Theory*, page 408. IEEE Press, Lausanne, Switzerland, 2002.

160. A. Juels and M. Sudan. A fuzzy vault scheme. *Designs, Codes, and Cryptography*, 38(2):237–257, 2006.

161. A. Juels and M. Wattenberg. A fuzzy commitment scheme. In G. Tsudik, editor, *Sixth ACM Conference on Computer and Communications Security*, pages 28–36. ACM Press, New York, 1999.

162. A. Juels and S. A. Weis. Authenticating pervasive devices with human protocols. In V. Shoup, editor, *Advances in Cryptology—CRYPTO 2005*, Lecture Notes in Computer Science, Vol. 3621, pages 293–308. Springer-Verlag, New York, 2005.

163. G.-A. Kamendje and R. Posch. Intrusion aware CMOS random pattern generator for cryptographic applications. In Peter Rössler and Andreas Dörderlein, editors, *Proceedings of Austrochip 2001*, Vienna, Austria, 12 October 2001.

164. T. Kanade, A. K. Jain, and N. K. Ratha, editors. *Audio- and Video-Based Biometric Person Authentication, 5th International Conference, AVBPA 2005, Hilton Rye Town, NY, USA, July 20–22, 2005, Proceedings*, Lecture Notes in Computer Science. Vol. 3546.Springer-Verlag, New York, 2005.

165. J.-P. Kaps and B. Sunar. Energy comparison of AES and SHA-1 for Ubiquitous Computing. In X. Zhou, O. Sokolsky, L. Yan, E.-S. Jung, Z. Shao, Y. Mu, D. C. Lee, D. Kim, Y.-S. Jeong, and C.-Z. Xu, editors, *Emerging Directions in Embedded and Ubiquitous Computing, EUC 2006 Workshops: NCUS, SecUbiq, USN, TRUST, ESO, and MSA*, Lecture Notes in Computer Science, Vol. 4097, pages 372–381. Springer-Verlag, New York, 2006.

166. J. Katz, R. Ostrovsky, and M. Yung. Efficient password-authenticated key exchange using human-memorable passwords. In B. Pfitzmann, editor, *Advances in Cryptology—EUROCRYPT 2001*, Lecture Notes in Computer Science, Vol. 2045, pages 475–494. Springer-Verlag, New York, 2001.

167. R. L. Kay. Protecting mobility. *IDC White paper*. Available from http://www.synaptics.com/support/Protecting_Mobility.pdf, 2005.

168. F. Kerschbaum, M. Atallah, D. M'Raïhi, and J. Rice. Private fingerprint verification without local storage. In David Zhang and Anil K. Jain, editors, *Proceedings of the first International Conference on Biometric Authentication*, Lecture Notes in Computer Science, Vol. 3072, pages 387–394. Springer-Verlag, Berlin, 2004.

169. T. A. M. Kevenaar, G. J. Schrijen, A. H. M. Akkermans, M. Damstra, P. Tuyls, and M. van der Veen. Robust and secure biometric-some application examples. In *Proceedings of the Information Security Solution Europe Conference*, pages 196–203. Vieweg, 2006.

170. T. A. M. Kevenaar, G. J. Schrijen, M. van der Veen, A. H. M. Akkermans, and F. Zuo. Face recognition with renewable and privacy preserving binary templates. In Vijayakumar Bhagavatula and Venu Govindaraju (chairs), *IEEE Workshop on Automatic Identification Advanced Technologies (AutoID 2005)*, pages 21–26. IEEE Computer Society, New York, 2005.

171. J. Kilian. Founding cryptography on oblivious transfer. In R. Cole, editor, *Proceedings of the 20th Annual ACM Symposium on Theory of Computing (STOC '88)*, pages 20–31. ACM Press, New York, 1988.

172. P. Kocher, J. Jaffe, and B. Jun. Differential power analysis. In M. Wiener, editor, *Advances in Cryptology—CRYPTO 1999*, Lecture Notes in Computer Science, Vol. 1666, pages 388–397. Springer-Verlag, New York, 1999.

173. L. Lamport. Constructing digital signatures from a one-way function. Technical Report SRI-CSL-98, SRI International Computer Science Laboratory, 1979.

174. L. Lamport, R. Shostak, and M. Pease. The byzantine generals problem. *ACM Transactions on Programming and Language Systems*, 4(3):382–401, 1982.

175. J.-W. Lee, D. Lim, B. Gassend, G. E. Suh, M. van Dijk, and S. Devadas. A technique to build a secret key in integrated circuits with identification

and authentication applications. In *Proceedings of the IEEE VLSI Circuits Symposium*, IEEE Press, New York, 2004.

176. Q. Li, Y. Sutcu, and N. Memon. Secure sketch for biometric templates. In X. Lai and K. Chen, editors, *Advances in Cryptology—ASIACRYPT 2006*, Lecture Notes in Computer Science, Vol. 4284, pages 99–113. Springer-Verlag, New York, 2006.

177. X. Li and G. C. M. Meijer. An accurate interface for capacitive sensors. *IEEE Transactions on Instrumentation and Measurement*, 51(5):935–939, 2002.

178. D. Lie. Architectural support for copy and tamper-resistant software. PhD thesis, Stanford University, 2003.

179. D. Lie, C. Thekkath, M. Mitchell, P. Lincoln, D. Boneh, J. Mitchell, and M. Horowitz. Architectural support for copy and tamper resistant software. In *Proceedings of the 9th Int'l Conference on Architectural Support for Programming Languages and Operating Systems (ASPLOS-IX)*, pages 168–177, November 2000.

180. D. Lim. Extracting secret keys from integrated circuits. Master's thesis, Massachusetts Institute of Technology, 2004.

181. D. Lim, J. W. Lee, B. Gassend, G. E. Suh, M. van Dijk and S. Devadas. Extracting Secret Keys From Integrated Circuits. *IEEE Transactions on Very Large Scale Integration (VLSI) Systems*, 13(10):1200–1205, October 2005.

182. J.-P. M. G. Linnartz and P. Tuyls. New shielding functions to enhance privacy and prevent misuse of biometric templates. In J. Kittler and M. Nixon, editors, *Conference on Audio and Video Based Person Authentication*, Lecture Notes in Computer Science, Vol. 2688, pages 238–250. Springer-Verlag, New York, 2003.

183. R. J. Lipton. A new approach to information theory. In P. Enjalbert, E. W. Mayr, and K. W. Wagner, editors, *STACS*, Lecture Notes in Computer Science, Vol. 775, pages 699–708. Springer-Verlag, New York, 1994.

184. J. López and R. Dahab. Fast multiplication on elliptic curves over $GF(2^m)$. In Ç. K. Koç and C. Paar, editors, *Cryptographic Hardware and Embedded Systems—CHES*, Lecture Notes in Computer Science, Vol. 1717, pages 316–327. Springer-Verlag, New York, 1999.

185. D. Maio, D. Maltoni, R. Cappelli, J. L. Wayman, and A. K. Jain. FVC2000: Fingerprint verification competition. *IEEE Transactions on Pattern Analysis and Machine Intelligence*, 24(3):402–412, 2002.

186. D. Maltoni, D. Maio, A. K. Jain, and S. Prabhakar. *Handbook of Fingerprint Recognition*. Springer-Verlag, New-York, 2003.

187. T. Mansfield, G. Kelly, D. Chandler, and J. Kane. Biometric product testing, final report. Technical report, Centre for Mathematics and Scientific Computing, CESG contract X92A/4009309, 2001.

188. K. Martin. A voltage-controlled switched-capacitor relaxation oscillator. *IEEE Journal of Solid-State Circuits*, 16(4):412–414, 1981.

189. T. Matsumoto, H. Matsumoto, K. Yamada, and S. Hoshino. Impact of artificial "gummy" fingers on fingerprint systems. In R. L. van Renesse, editor, *Optical Security and Counterfeit Deterrence Techniques IV*, SPIE Vol. 4677, pages 275–289. SPIE, Bellingham, WA, 2002.

190. U. Maurer. Conditionally-perfect secrecy and a provably-secure randomized cipher. *Journal of Cryptology*, 5:53–66, 1992.

191. U. Maurer. Information-theoretically secure secret-key agreement by NOT authenticated public discussion. In Walter Fumy, editor, *Advances in Cryptology—EUROCRYPT 1997*, Lecture Notes in Computer Science, Vol. 49, pages 209–225. Springer-Verlag, New York, 1997.

192. U. Maurer. Indistinguishability of random systems. In L. Knudsen, editor, *Advances in Cryptology—EUROCRYPT 2002*, Lecture Notes in Computer Science, Vol. 2332, pages 110–132. Springer-Verlag, New York, 2002.

193. U. Maurer and S. Wolf. Privacy amplification secure against active adversaries. In B. S. J. Kaliski, editor, *Advances in Cryptology—CRYPTO 1997*, Lecture Notes in Computer Science, Vol. 1294, pages 307–321. Springer-Verlag, New York, 1997.

194. U. Maurer and S. Wolf. Information-theoretic key agreement: From weak to strong secrecy for free. In B. Preneel, editor, *Advances in Cryptology—EUROCRYPT 2000*, Lecture Notes in Computer Science, Vol. 1807, pages 351–368. Springer-Verlag, New York, 2000.

195. U. M. Maurer. Conditionally-perfect secrecy and a provably-secure randomized cipher. *Journal of Cryptology*, 5(1):53–66, 1992.

196. U. M. Maurer. Secret key agreement by public discussion from common information. *IEEE Transactions on Information Theory*, 39(3):733–742, 1993.

197. N. Mavrogiannopoulos. Fine-tuned implementation of an efficient secure profile matching protocol. Master's thesis, TU Eindhoven, The Netherlands, 2006.

198. R. McEliece. A public-key cryptosystem based on algebraic coding theory. Technical Report DSN progress report 42–44, Jet Propulsion Laboratory, Pasadena, CA, 1978.

199. A. J. Menezes, P. C. van Oorschot, and S. A. Vanstone. *Handbook of Applied Cryptography*. CRC Press, Boca Raton, FL, 1996.

200. S. Micali and L. Reyzin. Physically observable cryptography (extended abstract). In Naor [211], pages 278–296.

201. S. Micali and P. Rogaway. Secure computation (abstract). In Louis C. Guillou, Jean-Jacques Quisquarter and Joan Feigenbaum, editors, *Advances in Cryptology—CRYPTO 1991*, Lecture Notes in Computer Science, Vol. 576, pages 392–404. Springer-Verlag, New York, 1992.

202. Microsoft. Next-generation secure computing base. Available from http://www.microsoft.com/resources/ngscb/defaul.mspx.

203. V. S. Miller. Use of elliptic curves in cryptography. In H. C. Williams, editor, *Advances in Cryptology—CRYPTO 1985*, Lecture Notes in Computer Science, Vol. 218, pages 417–426. Springer-Verlag, New York, 1986.

204. Y. Minsky, A. Trachtenberg, and R. Zippel. Set reconciliation with nearly optimal communication complexity. *IEEE Transactions on Information Theory*, 49(9):2213–2218, 2003.

205. F. Monrose, M. Reiter, and S. Wetzel. Password hardening based on keystroke dynamics. In G. Tsudik, editor, *ACM Conference on Computer and Communications Security*, pages 73–82. ACM Press, New York, 1999.

206. F. Monrose, M. K. Reiter, Q. Li, D. P. Lopresti, and C. Shih. Toward speech-generated cryptographic keys on resource-constrained devices. In D. Boneh, editor, *USENIX Security Symposium*, pages 283–296. Usenix Associates, Berkeley, CA, 2002.

207. F. Monrose, M. K. Reiter, Q. Li, and S. Wetzel. Cryptographic key generation from voice. In *Proceedings of the IEEE Conference on Security and Privacy*, 2001.

326     References

208. P. Montgomery. Speeding the Pollard and elliptic curve methods of factorization. *Mathematics of Computation*, 48:243–264, 1987.
209. D. Naccache, N. P. Smart, and J. Stern. Projective coordinates leak. In C. Cachin and J. Camenisch, editors, *Advances in Cryptology—EUROCRYPT 2004*, Lecture Notes in Computer Science, Vol. 3027, pages 257–267. Springer-Verlag, New York, 2004.
210. Y. Nakagome, M. Horiguchi, T. Kawahara, and K. Itoh. Review and future prospects of low-voltage RAM circuits. *IBM Journal of Research and Development*, 47(5/6):525–552, 2003.
211. M. Naor, editor. *Theory of Cryptography, First Theory of Cryptography Conference, TCC 2004, Cambridge, MA, USA, February 19-21, 2004, Proceedings*, Lecture Notes in Computer Science, Vol. 2951. Springer-Verlag, New York, 2004.
212. A. Nascimento and A. Winter. On the oblivious transfer capacity of noisy correlations. In *Proceedings of the IEEE International Symposium on Information Theory (ISIT '06)*, 2006.
213. M. Neve, E. Peeters, D. Samyde, and J.-J. Quisquater. Memories: A Survey of their secure uses in smart cards. In *2nd International IEEE Security In Storage Workshop (IEEE SISW 2003)*, pages 62–72. Washington DC, USA, 2003.
214. N. Nisan and A. Ta-Shma. Extracting randomness: A survey and new constructions. *Journal of Computer and System Sciences*, 58(1):148–173, 1999.
215. N. Nisan and D. Zuckerman. Randomness is linear in space. *Journal of Computer and System Sciences*, 52(1):43–52, 1996.
216. T. Okamoto. Provably secure and practical identification schemes and corresponding signature schemes. In E. F. Brickell, editor, *Advances in Cryptology—CRYPTO 1992*, Lecture Notes in Computer Science, Vol. 740, pages 31–53. Springer-Verlag, New York, 1992.
217. R. Ostrovsky and Y. Rabani. Low distortion embeddings for edit distance. In Gabow and Fagin [117], pages 218–224.
218. J. A. O'Sullivan and N. A. Schmid. Large deviations performance analysis for biometrics recognition. In *Proceedings of the 40th Allerton Conference*, 2002.
219. E. Özturk, B. Sunar, and E. Savaş. Low-Power Elliptic Curve Cryptography Using Scaled Modular Arithmetic. In M. Joye and J. J. Quisquater, editors, *Cryptographic Hardware in Embedded Systems—CHES 2004*, Lecture Notes in Computer Science, Vol. 3156, pages 92–106. Springer-Verlag, New York, 2004.
220. P. Paillier. Public-key cryptosystems based on composite degree residuosity classes. In *Advances in Cryptology—EUROCRYPT 1999*, Lecture Notes in Computer Science, Vol. 1592, pages 223–238. Springer-Verlag, Berlin, 1999.
221. R. Pappu. *Physical One-Way Functions*. PhD thesis, MIT, 2001.
222. R. Pappu, B. Recht, J. Taylor, and N. Gershenfeld. Physical one-way functions. *Science*, 297:2026–2030, 2002.
223. L. Penrose. Dermatoglyphic topology. *Nature*, 205:545–546, 1965.
224. B. Pfitzmann and M. Waidner. Information-theoretic pseudosignatures and Byzantine agreement for $t >= n/3$. Technical Report RZ 2882 (#90830), IBM Research, 1996.
225. B. Pfitzmann and M. Waidner. Composition and integrity preservation of secure reactive systems. In *7th ACM Conference on Computer and Communications Security*, pages 245–254. ACM Press, New York, 2000.
226. R. Posch. Protecting devices by active coating. *Journal of Universal Computer Science*, 4(7):652–668, 1998.

227. Website of Privium. Available from `http://www.schiphol.nl/privium`.

228. M. O. Rabin. How to exchange secrets by oblivious transfer. Technical Report TR-81, Harvard Aiken Computation Laboratory, 1981.

229. T. Rabin and M. Ben-Or. Verifiable secret sharing and multiparty protocols with honest majority. In D. S. Johnson, editor, *Proceedings of the 21st Annual ACM Symposium on Theory of Computing (STOC '89)*, pages 73–85. ACM Press, New York, 1989.

230. J. Radhakrishnan and A. Ta-Shma. Bounds for dispersers, extractors, and depth-two superconcentrators. *SIAM Journal on Discrete Mathematics*, 13(1):2–24, 2000.

231. N. K. Ratha, J. H. Connell, and R. M. Bolle. Enhancing security and privacy in biometrics-based authentication systems. *IBM Systems Journal*, 40(3):614–634, 2001.

232. R. Renner. Security of quantum key distribution. PhD thesis, Swiss Federal Institute of Technology (ETH), Zurich, 2005. Available from `http://arxiv.org/abs/quant-ph/0512258`.

233. R. Renner and S. Wolf. New bounds in secret-key agreement: The gap between formation and secrecy extraction. In E. Biham, editor, *Advances in Cryptology—EUROCRYPT 2003*, Lecture Notes in Computer Science, Vol. 2656, pages 562–577. Springer-Verlag, New York, 2003.

234. R. Renner and S. Wolf. Unconditional authenticity and privacy from an arbitrarily weak secret. In D. Boneh, editor, *Advances in Cryptology—CRYPTO 2003*, Lecture Notes in Computer Science, pages 78–95. Springer-Verlag, New York, 2003.

235. R. Renner and S. Wolf. The exact price for unconditionally secure asymmetric cryptography. In C. Cachin and J. Camenisch, editors, *Advances in Cryptology—EUROCRYPT 2004*, Lecture Notes in Computer Science, pages 109–125. Springer-Verlag, New York, 2004.

236. R. Renner and S. Wolf. Smooth Rényi entropy and applications. In *Proceedings of 2004 IEEE International Symposium on Information Theory*, page 233. IEEE Press, New York, 2004.

237. R. Renner and S. Wolf. Simple and tight bounds for information reconciliation and privacy amplification. In B. Roy, editor, *Advances in Cryptology—ASIACRYPT 2005*, Lecture Notes in Computer Science, Vol. 3788, pages 199–216. Springer-Verlag, New York, 2005.

238. R. Rivest, A. Shamir, and L. Adleman. A method for obtaining digital signatures and public-key cryptosystems. *Communications of the ACM*, 21:120–126, 1978.

239. R. L. Rivest. Unconditionally secure commitment and oblivious transfer schemes using private channels and a trusted initializer. Unpublished, 1999.

240. A. A. Ross, K. Nandakumar, and A. K. Jain. *Handbook of Multibiometrics*. Springer-Verlag, New York, 2006.

241. S. Ross. *A First Course in Probability* 6th ed. Prentice-Hall, Englenood Cliffs, NJ, 2001.

242. A. Sahai and B. Waters. Fuzzy identity-based encryption. In *Advances in Cryptology—EUROCRYPT 2005*, pages 457–473, 2005.

243. M. Savvides, B. V. K. V. Kumar, and P. K. Khosla. Cancelable biometric filters for face recognition. In *International Conference on Pattern Recognition (ICPR (3))*, pages 922–925, 2004.

244. B. Schneier. The uses and abuses of biometrics. *Communications of the ACM*, 42(8):136, 1999.

245. B. Schoenmakers and P. Tuyls. Practical two-party computation based on the conditional gate. In P. J. Lee, editor, *Advances in Cryptology—ASIACRYPT 2004*, Lecture Notes in Computer Science, Vol. 3329, pages 119–136. Springer-Verlag, Berlin, 2004.

246. B. Schoenmakers and P. Tuyls. Private profile matching. In Philips Research Book Series, Vol. 7, *Intelligent Algorithms in Ambient and Biomedical Computing*, W. Verhaegh and E. Aarts and J. Korst, editors, pages 259–272. Springer-Verlag, New York, 2006. Preliminary version in Proceedings 2nd Philips Symposium on Intelligent Algorithms-SOIA'04 (2004) pages 149–160.

247. SETI@Home. Available from `http://setiathome.ssl.berkeley.edu/`.

248. R. Shaltiel. Recent developments in explicit constructions of extractors. *Bulletin of the EATCS (European Association for Theoretical Computer Science)*, 77:67–95, 2002.

249. A. Shamir. How to share a secret. *Communications of the Association for Computing Machinery*, 22(11):612–613, 1979.

250. A. Shamir. Identity-based cryptosystems and signature schemes. In G. R. Blakley and David Chaum, editors, *Advances in Cryptology—CRYPTO 1984*, pages 47–53. Springer-Verlag, New York, 1985.

251. C. E. Shannon. A mathematical theory of communication. *Bell System Technical Journal*, 27:379–423 and 623–656, 1948.

252. C. E. Shannon. Communication theory of secrecy systems. *Bell System Technical Journal*, 28(4), 656–715, 1949.

253. G. J. Simmons. Identification of data, devices, documents and individuals. In *Proceedings 25th Annual IEEE International Carnahan Conference on Security Technology*, pages 197–218, 1991.

254. B. Skoric, P. Tuyls, and W. Ophey. Robust key extraction from physical unclonable functions. In J. Ionnidis, A. Keromytis, and M. Yung, editors, *Proceedings of the Applied Cryptography and Network Security Conference 2005*, Lecture Notes in Computer Science, Vol. 3531, pages 407–422. Springer-Verlag, New-York, 2005.

255. S. P. Skorobogatov and R. J. Anderson. Optical fault induction attacks. In Burton S. Kaliski Jr., Çetin Kaya Koç, and Christof Paar, editors, *Cryptographic Hardware and Embedded Systems—CHES 2002*, Lecture Notes in Computer Science, Vol. 2523, pages 2–12. Springer-Verlag, New York, 2002. Available from `http://www.informatik.uni-trier.de/~ley/db/conf/ches/ches2002.html`

256. D. Slepian and J. K. Wolf. Noiseless coding of correlated information sources. *IEEE Transactions on Information Theory*, 19:471–480, 1973.

257. Smartec. Universal transducer interface evaluation board, specifications v3.0. Available from `http://www.smartec.nl/pdf/Dsuti.pdf`.

258. A. Smith. Scrambling aversarial errors using few random bits. In H. Gabow, editor, *SIAM-ACM Symposium on Discrete Algorithms (SODA)*, 2007.

259. S. W. Smith and S. H. Weingart. Building a high-performance, programmable secure coprocessor. *Computer Networks* (Special Issue on Computer Network Security), 31(8):831–860, 1999.

260. L. Song and K. Parhi. Low energy digit-serial/parallell finite field multipliers. *Kluwer Journal of VLSI Signal Processing Systems*, 19(2):149–166, 1998.

261. C. Soutar, D. Roberge, A. Stoianov, R. Gilroy, and B. V. K. V. Kumar. Biometric encryption using image processing. In R. L. V. Renesse, editor, *Optical Security and Counterfeit Deterrence Techniques II*, SPIE Vol. 3314, pages 178–188. SPIE. Bellingham, WA, 1998.

262. D. R. Stinson. Universal hash families and the leftover hash lemma, and applications to cryptography and computing. *Journal of Combinatorial Mathematics and Combinatorial Computing*, 42:3–31, 2002.

263. R. Strait, P. Pearson, and S. Sengupta. Method and system for normalizing biometric variations to authenticate users from a public database and that ensures individual biometric data privacy, U.S patent No. 6,038,315, 2000.

264. G. E. Suh, D. Clarke, B. Gassend, M. van Dijk, and S. Devadas. AEGIS: Architecture for tamper-evident and tamper-resistant processing. In Utpal Banerjee, Kyle Gallivan and Antonio González, editors, *Proceedings of the 17$^{th}$ International Conference on Supercomputing (MIT-CSAIL-CSG-Memo-474 is an updated version)*, ACM Press, New York, 2003.

265. G. E. Suh, C. W. O'Donnell, I. Sachdev, and S. Devadas. Design and implementation of the AEGIS single-chip secure processor using physical random functions. In *Proceedings of the 32$^{nd}$ Annual International Symposium on Computer Architecture (MIT-CSAIL-CSG-Memo-483 is an updated version available at http://csg.csail.mit.edu/pubs/memos/ Memo-483/Memo-483.pdf)*, ACM Press, New York, 2005.

266. F. N. Toth, G. C. Meijer, and H. M. M. Kerkvliet. A very accurate measurement system for multielectrode capacitive sensors. *IEEE Transactions on Instrumentation and Measurement*, 45(2):531–535, 1996.

267. Trusted Computing Group. TCG specification architecture overview revision 1.2. Available from http://www.trustedcomputinggroup.com/home, 2004.

268. P. Tuyls, A. H. M. Akkermans, T. A. M. Kevenaar, G. J. Schrijen, A. M. Bazen, and R. N. J. Veldhuis. Practical biometric authentication with template protection. In Kanade et al. [164], pages 436–446.

269. P. Tuyls and L. Batina. RFID-tags for anti-counterfeiting. In D. Pointcheval, editor, *Topics in Cryptology—CT-RSA 2006*, Lecture Notes in Computer Science, pages 115–131. Springer-Verlag, New York, 2006.

270. P. Tuyls and J. Goseling. Capacity and examples of template protecting biometric authentication systems. In D. Maltoni and A. Jain, editors, *Biometric Authentication Workshop*, Lecture Notes in Computer Science, Vol. 3087, pages 158–170. Springer-Verlag, New York, 2004.

271. P. Tuyls, G. Schrijen, B. Skoric, J. van Geloven, R. Verhaegh, and R. Wolters. Read-proof hardware from protective coatings. In L. Goubin and M. Matsui, editors, *Cryptographic Hardware and Embedded Systems—CHES 2006*, Lecture Notes in Computer Science, Vol. 4249, pages 369–383. Springer-Verlag, New York, 2006.

272. P. Tuyls, B. Skoric, S. Stallinga, A. Akkermans, and W. Ophey. Information theoretical security analysis of physical unclonable functions. In A. Patrick and M. Yung, editors, *Financial Cryptography and Data Security—FC 2005*, Lecture Notes in Computer Science, Vol. 3570, pages 141–155. Springer-Verlag, New York, 2005.

273. P. Tuyls, E. Verbitskiy, T. Ignatenko, D. Schobben, and A. H. M. Akkermans. Privacy-protected biometric templates: Acoustic ear identification. In A. K. Jain and N. K. Ratha, editors, *Biometric Technology for Human Identification*. SPIE, Vol. 5404, pages 176–182. SPIE, Bellingham, WA, 2004.

274. P. Tuyls and B. Škorić. Secret key generation from classical physics. In S. Mukherjee, E. Aarts, R. Roovers, F. Widdershoven, and M. Ouwerkerk, editors, *AmIware: Hardware Technology Drivers of Ambient Intelligence*, Philips Research Book Series, pages 421–447. Kluwer, Academic, Amsterdam, 2005.

275. U. Uludag, S. Pankanti, and A. K. Jain. Fuzzy vault for fingerprints. In Kanade et al. [164], pages 310–319.

276. U. Uludag, S. Pankanti, S. Prabhakar, and A. K. Jain. Biometric cryptosystems: Issues and challenges. *Proceedings of the IEEE*, 92(6):948–960, 2004.

277. T. van der Putte and J. Keuning. Biometrical fingerprint recognition: Don't get your fingers burned. In Domingo-Ferrer, Josep; Chan, David; Watson, Anthony (Eds.), Proceedings *IFIP TC8/WG8.8 Fourth Working Conference on Smart Card Research and Advanced Applications*, IFIP International Federation for Information Processing, Vol. 52, Springer-Verlag, 2000 pages 289–303.

278. M. van Dijk. Robustness, reliability and security of biometric key distillation in the information theoretical setting. In *Proceedings of the 26th Benelux Symposium on Information Theory*, Brussels, 2005.

279. M. van Dijk, D. Lim, and S. Devadas. Reliable secret sharing with physical random functions. MIT CSAIL Computation Structures Group, Technical Memo 475, 2004.

280. M. van Dijk and P. Tuyls. Robustness, reliability and security of biometric key distillation in the information theoretic setting. In N. Cerf and J. Cardinal, editors, *Benelux Symposium on Information Theory*, Proceedings of the WIC, Vol. 26, Working Community for Information and Communication Theory, Delft, The Netherlands, New York, 2005.

281. J. van Lint. *Introduction to Coding Theory*. Springer-Verlag, New York, 1992.

282. V. Vapnik. *The Nature of Statistical Learning Theory*. Springer-Verlag, New York, 1995.

283. E. Verbitskiy, P. Tuyls, D. Denteneer, and J.-P. Linnartz. Reliable biometric authentication with privacy protection. In *Proceedings 24th Benelux Symposium on Information Theory*, 2003.

284. G. S. Vernam. Cipher printing telegraph systems for secret wire and radio telegraphic communications. *Journal of the American Institute of Electrical Engineering*, 55:109–115, 1926.

285. L. von Ahn, M. Blum, N. J. Hopper, and J. Langford. CAPTCHA: Using hard AI problems for security. In E. Biham, editor, *Advances in Cryptology— EUROCRYPT 2003*, Lecture Notes in Computer Science, Vol. 2656, pages 294–311. Springer-Verlag, New York, 2003.

286. B. Škorić, S. Maubach, T. Kevenaar, and P. Tuyls. Information-theoretic analysis of capacitive physical unclonable functions. *Journal of Applied Physics*, 100:024902, 2006.

287. B. Škorić, P. Tuyls, and W. Ophey. Robust key extraction from physical uncloneable functions. In J. Ioannidis, A. D. Keromytis, and M. Yung, editors, *Proceedings of the ACNS*, Lecture Notes in Computer Science, Vol. 3531, pages 407–422. Springer-Verlag, New York, 2005.

288. K. Weissman. Biometrics history. Available from http://www.biometrics.gov/docs/biohistory.pdf, 2006.

289. N. Weste and K. Eshraghian. *Principles of CMOS VLSI Design: A Systems Perspective*. Addison-Wesley, Boston, 1985.

290. S. Wiesner. Conjugate coding. *SIGACT News (Special Interest Group on Algorithms and Computation Theory)*, 15(1):78–88, 1983.

291. F. M. J. Willems. The context-tree weighting method: Extensions. *IEEE Transactions on Information Theory*, 44(2):792–798, 1998.

292. F. M. J. Willems, A. A. C. M. Kalker, J. Goseling, and J.-P. M. G. Linnartz. On the capacity of a biometrical identification system. In *IEEE International Symposium on Information Theory (ISIT 2003)*, page 82, Yokohama, Japan, June 2003.

293. F. M. J. Willems, Y. M. Shtarkov, and T. J. Tjalkens. The context-tree weighting method: Basic properties. *IEEE Transactions on Information Theory*, 41(3):653–664, 1995.

294. F. M. J. Willems, Y. M. Shtarkov, and T. J. Tjalkens. Context weighting for general finite context sources. *IEEE Transactions on Information Theory*, 42:1514–1520, 1996.

295. A. Williams. Hong Kongs mandatory citizen card expedites travel, secures financial transactions. *ContactlessNews*, December 2006.

296. A. Winter, A. C. A. Nascimento, and H. Imai. Commitment capacity of discrete memoryless channels. In *IMA International Conference*, pages 35–51, 2003.

297. S. Wolf and R. N. Tauber. *Silicon Processing for the VLSI Era*, 2nd ed. Lattice Press, Sunset Beach CA 90742 USA, 2000.

298. S. Wolf and J. Wullschleger. Zero-error information and applications in cryptography. In *Proceedings of 2004 IEEE Information Theory Workshop (ITW 2004)*, 2004.

299. S. Wolf and J. Wullschleger. New monotones and lower bounds in unconditional two-party computation. In *Advances in Cryptology—CRYPTO 2005*, Lecture Notes in Computer Science, Vol. 3621, pages 467–477. Springer-Verlag, 2005.

300. J. Wolkerstorfer. Scaling ECC Hardware to a Minimum. In V. Shoup, editor, ECRYPT workshop—Cryptographic Advances in Secure Hardware—CRASH 2005, September 6–7 2005. Invited talk.

301. J. Wullschleger. Oblivious-transfer amplification. In M. Naor, editor, *Advances in Cryptology—EUROCRYPT 2007*, Lecture Notes in Computer Science. Springer-Verlag, New York, 2007.

302. A. D. Wyner. Recent results in Shannon theory. *IEEE Transactions on Information Theory*, IT-20(1):2–10, 1974.

303. A. D. Wyner. The wire-tap channel. *Bell System Technical Journal*, 54:1355–1387, 1975.

304. J. Yang, L. Gao, and Y. Zhang. Improving memory encryption performance in secure processors. *IEEE Transactions on Computers*, 54(5):630–640, 2005.

305. A. C. Yao. Protocols for secure computations. In *Proceedings of the 23rd Annual IEEE Symposium on Foundations of Computer Science (FOCS '82)*, pages 160–164, 1982.

306. D. Yao, N. Fazio, Y. Dodis, and A. Lysyanskaya. ID-based encryption for complex hierarchies with applications to forward security and broadcast encryption. In *ACM Conference on Computer and Communications Security—CCS 2004*, 2004.

307. B. S. Yee. Using secure coprocessors. PhD thesis, Carnegie Mellon University, 1994.

308. R. W. Yeung. A new outlook on Shannon's information measures. *IEEE Transactions on Information Theory*, 37:466–474, 1991.

309. W. Zhang, Y.-J. Chang, and T. Chen. Optimal thresholding for key generation based on biometrics. In *International Conference on Image Processing (ICIP 2004)*, Vol. 5, pages 3451–3454, 2004.

# Index